S0-DVG-012

CONSUMER GUIDE®

NEW
CAR
PRICE GUIDE

CONTENTS

INTRODUCTION

The 1997 edition of the *New Car Price Guide* contains the latest prices and specifications for more than 150 passenger cars, minivans, and sport-utility vehicles that are available in the U.S., including some early 1998 models. To save space, similar vehicles have been combined into a single entry with one specifications chart, such as the Ford Taurus and Mercury Sable. There are separate price lists for each model, except for the Dodge and Plymouth Neon, which are sold at identical prices.

In most cases, the editors were able to provide dealer invoice prices and our estimated fair price. In some cases, only the suggested retail prices were available. In all cases, the prices are subject to change by the manufacturers.

The dealer invoice prices are what the dealer pays the manufacturer for the car, including its factory- or port-installed options. The dealer's cost of preparing a car for delivery to the consumer is included in the invoice price of all domestic cars. On some imported vehicles, this cost may not be included in the dealer invoice.

The fair prices listed in this book are estimates based on national market conditions for each model. Since market conditions can vary greatly in different parts of the country, the fair prices should only be used as a guide. If possible, it's best to price the same car at three or more dealers to get a better idea of the fair price in your area.

Fair prices aren't listed for some models because of insufficient information about market conditions for that particular vehicle.

Cash rebates and dealer incentives are not included

because they change so frequently.

While we have done all we can to see that the prices in this issue are accurate, car companies are free to change their prices at any time.

Many dealers tell our readers that the prices we publish are incorrect so they can eliminate dealer-invoice price from consideration. Once they accomplish that, then they're back in the driver's seat on price negotiations. If a dealer claims our prices are incorrect or the information in this book doesn't match what you see in showrooms, contact us and we'll do our best to help.

The address is listed on the next page.

Destination Charges

The destination charge—the cost of shipping the car to the dealer—is not included in the base price of most cars. This charge must be added to the total price of the car and optional equipment. Dealers do not receive a discount on the destination charge. If the manufacturer's price sticker lists a $500 destination charge, that is what the dealer paid—and you will, too.

On the other hand, the destination charges listed in our price charts (and on the manufacturer's price sticker) are the only *legitimate* shipping charges. Don't let a dealer trick you into paying a bogus charge.

Advertising Fees and Taxes

Advertising fees are not included in the price lists because they vary greatly in different parts of the country and not all dealers try to charge their customers for advertising. We think it's unfair for consumers to reimburse dealers for their advertising expenses, so we strongly suggest you argue against paying such a fee. It's their cost of doing business, not yours.

Two federal taxes affect car prices. First, a gas-guzzler tax is levied on cars that average less than 22.5

mpg in combined city/highway mileage based on EPA estimates. Some manufacturers include the gas-guzzler tax in the base prices; others list it separately. Guzzler taxes range from $1000 to more than $3000, so they can have a substantial impact on the purchase price.

Second, an eight percent "luxury tax" is levied on cars selling for more than $36,000. The tax applies only to the amount over $36,000, so a car that sells for $40,000 will be taxed $320 and one that sells for $50,000 will be taxed $1120. The tax applies to the *transaction* or sale price of the vehicle, not the suggested retail price. In addition, the tax is figured on the full purchase price before any trade-in value is deducted.

The editors invite your questions and comments. Address them to:

Consumer Guide®
7373 N. Cicero Ave.
Lincolnwood, IL 60646

Key to Specifications

Specifications are supplied by the manufacturers. **Body styles: notchback** = coupe or sedan with a separate trunk; **hatchback** = coupe or sedan with a rear liftgate. **Wheelbase** = distance between the front and rear wheels. **Curb weight** = weight of base models, not including optional equipment. **Engines: ohv** = overhead valve; **ohc** = overhead camshaft; **dohc** = dual overhead camshafts; **I** = inline cylinders; **V** = cylinders in V configuration; **flat** = horizontally opposed cylinders; **rpm** = revolutions per minute. **OD** = overdrive transmission. **NA** = not available.

ACURA CL

Acura 2.2CL

Specifications

	2-door notchback
Wheelbase, in.	106.9
Overall length, in.	190.0
Overall width, in.	70.1
Overall height, in.	54.7
Curb weight, lbs.	3009
Cargo vol., cu. ft.	12.0
Fuel capacity, gals.	17.1
Seating capacity	5

Engines

	ohc I-4	ohc V-6
Size, liter/ cu. in.	2.2/132	3.0/183
Horsepower @ rpm	145 @ 5500	200 @ 5500
Torque (lbs./ft.) @ rpm	147 @ 4500	195 @ 4700
EPA city/highway mpg		
5-speed OD manual	25/31	
4-speed OD automatic	23/29	20/28

Built in East Liberty, Ohio.

PRICES

Acura CL	Retail Price	Dealer Invoice	Fair Price
2.2CL 2-door notchback, 5-speed	$22110	$19647	—
2.2CL 2-door notchback, automatic	22910	20358	—
2.2CL 2-door notchback w/Premium Pkg., 5-speed	23160	20580	—

	Retail Price	Dealer Invoice	Fair Price
2.2CL 2-door notchback w/Premium Pkg., automatic	$23960	$21291	—
3.0CL 2-door notchback, automatic	25110	22313	—
3.0CL 2-door notchback w/Premium Pkg., automatic	26460	23512	—
Destination charge	435	435	.435

Fair price not available at time of publication.

Standard Equipment:

2.2CL: 2.2-liter 4-cylinder engine, 4-speed automatic transmission or 5-speed manual transmission, anti-lock 4-wheel disc brakes, driver- and passenger-side air bags, cruise control, variable-assist power steering, automatic climate control, moquette front bucket seats, rear trunk pass-through, 6-way power driver seat w/manual lumbar adjustment, center storage armrest, rear center armrest, cupholders, digital clock, tilt steering wheel, rear defogger, leather-wrapped steering wheel, passenger seatback pocket, 6-speaker AM/FM/CD player, remote keyless entry, security system, power windows and door locks, power mirrors, power moonroof, integrated antenna, illuminated visor mirrors, variable intermittent wipers, remote decklid and fuel-door release, door pockets, courtesy and map lights, front and rear stabilizer bars, front mud guards, 205/55VR16 tires, alloy wheels. **3.0CL** adds: 3.0-liter V-6 engine, 4-speed automatic transmission, 8-way power driver seat, Bose sound system, heated outside mirrors. **2.2CL w/Premium Pkg.** adds to 2.2CL: leather upholstery, seatback pocket. **3.0CL w/Premium Pkg.** adds to 3.0CL: leather upholstery, heated front seats, seatback pocket.

Options are available as dealer-installed accessories.

ACURA INTEGRA

Specifications	2-door hatchback	4-door notchback
Wheelbase, in.	101.2	103.1
Overall length, in.	172.4	178.1
Overall width, in.	67.3	67.3
Overall height, in.	52.6	53.9
Curb weight, lbs.	2529	2628
Cargo vol., cu. ft.	13.3	11.0
Fuel capacity, gals.	13.2	13.2
Seating capacity	4	5

Prices are accurate at time of publication; subject to manufacturer's change.

Acura Integra LS 2-door

Engines

	dohc I-4	dohc I-4
Size, liters/cu. in.	1.8/112	1.8/109
Horsepower @ rpm	142 @ 6300	170 @ 7600
Torque (lbs./ft.) @ rpm	127 @ 5200	128 @ 6200

EPA city/highway mpg

5-speed OD manual	25/31	25/31
4-speed OD automatic	24/31	

Built in Japan.

PRICES

Acura Integra	Retail Price	Dealer Invoice	Fair Price
RS 3-door hatchback, 5-speed	$16100	$14144	—
RS 3-door hatchback, automatic	16900	14847	—
LS 2-door hatchback, 5-speed	18850	16560	—
LS 2-door hatchback, automatic	19650	17263	—
GS 2-door hatchback, 5-speed	20600	18097	—
GS 2-door hatchback, automatic	21400	18800	—
GS-R 2-door hatchback, 5-speed	21100	18536	—
GS-R 2-door hatchback w/leather, 5-speed	21900	19239	—
LS 4-door notchback, 5-speed	19650	17263	—
LS 4-door notchback, automatic	20450	17965	—
GS 4-door notchback, 5-speed	21150	18581	—
GS 4-door notchback, automatic	21950	19283	—
GS-R 4-door notchback, 5-speed	21400	18800	—
GS-R 4-door notchback w/leather, 5-speed	22200	19503	—
Destination charge	435	435	435

Fair price not available at time of publication.

Standard Equipment:

RS: 1.8-liter DOHC 4-cylinder engine, 5-speed manual or 4-speed automatic transmission, 4-wheel disc brakes, driver- and passenger-side air bags, variable-assist power steering, cloth reclining front bucket seats w/driver-side lumbar adjustment, 50/50 split folding rear seat, center console w/armrest, tilt steering column, power windows and mirrors, tachometer, coolant temperature gauge, AM/FM/CD player w/six speakers, power antenna, tinted glass, remote fuel-door and decklid/hatch releases, rear defogger, rear wiper/washer, intermittent wipers, fog lamps, cargo cover, 195/60HR14 tires, wheel covers. **LS** adds: anti-lock brakes, air conditioning, cruise control, 50/50 split folding rear seat (hatchback), one-piece folding rear seat (notchback), power moonroof, power door locks, rear wiper/washer (hatchback), map lights (hatchback), cargo cover (hatchback), Michelin 195/60HR14 tires. **GS** adds: leather upholstery, rear spoiler (hatchback), wood-pattern console trim (notchback), color-keyed bodyside moldings, 195/55VR15 tires, alloy wheels. **GS-R** adds to LS: 1.8-liter DOHC VTEC engine, map lights, rear spoiler (hatchback), 195/55VR15 tires, alloy wheels.

Options are available as dealer-installed accessories.

ACURA RL

Acura 3.5RL

Specifications

	4-door notchback
Wheelbase, in.	114.6
Overall length, in.	195.1
Overall width, in.	71.3
Overall height, in.	56.6
Curb weight, lbs.	3660
Cargo vol., cu. ft.	14.0
Fuel capacity, gals.	18.0

Prices are accurate at time of publication; subject to manufacturer's change.

	4-door notchback
Seating capacity	5

Engines

	ohc V-6
Size, liters/cu. in.	3.5/212
Horsepower @ rpm	210 @ 5200
Torque (lbs./ft.) @ rpm	224 @ 2800
EPA city/highway mpg	
4-speed OD automatic	19/25

Built in Japan.

PRICES

Acura RL	Retail Price	Dealer Invoice	Fair Price
3.5 RL 4-door notchback	$41000	$35190	—
Destination charge	435	435	435

Fair price not available at time of publication.

Standard Equipment:

3.5-liter V-6 engine, 4-speed automatic transmission, front and rear automatic air conditioning, anti-lock 4-wheel disc brakes, driver- and passenger-side air bags, variable-assist power steering, cruise control, leather upholstery, power front seats w/memory, driver-seat lumbar support, rear-seat trunk pass-through, center console, rear armrest, cupholders, tilt/telescopic steering wheel w/memory, power moonroof, power windows and door locks, remote keyless entry, power mirrors w/memory, tinted glass, leather-wrapped steering wheel and shifter, 8-speaker AM/FM/cassette player w/anti-theft, digital clock, integrated antenna, maintenance interval reminder, rear defogger, remote fuel-door and decklid releases, speed-sensitive intermittent wipers, illuminated visor mirrors, theft-deterrent system, map lights, rear reading lights, interior air filter, fog lamps, mud guards, 215/60R16 tires, alloy wheels.

Optional Equipment:

Premium Pkg.	3000	2575	—
Traction Control System, heated front seats, heated outside mirrors, Acura/Bose sound system w/6-disc CD changer, burled walnut interior trim.			
Navigation System	2000	1717	—
Requires Premium Pkg.			

ACURA TL

Acura 3.2TL

Specifications

	4-door notchback
Wheelbase, in.	111.8
Overall length, in.	191.5
Overall width, in.	70.3
Overall height, in.	55.3
Curb weight, lbs.	3252
Cargo vol., cu. ft.	14.1
Fuel capacity, gals.	17.2
Seating capacity	5

Engines

	ohc I-5	ohc V-6
Size, liters/cu. in.	2.5/152	3.2/196
Horsepower @ rpm	176 @ 6300	200 @ 5300
Torque (lbs./ft.) @ rpm	170 @ 3900	210 @ 4500

EPA city/highway mpg

4-speed OD automatic	20/25	19/24

Built in Japan.

PRICES

Acura TL	Retail Price	Dealer Invoice	Fair Price
2.5TL 4-door notchback	$28450	$24993	—
2.5TL 4-door notchback w/Premium Pkg.	30500	26794	—
3.2TL 4-door notchback	32950	28947	—
3.2TL 4-door notchback w/Premium Pkg.	35500	31187	—

Prices are accurate at time of publication; subject to manufacturer's change.

	Retail Price	Dealer Invoice	Fair Price
Destination charge	$435	$435	$435

Fair price not available at time of publication.

Standard Equipment:

2.5: 2.5-liter 5-cylinder engine, 4-speed automatic transmission, driver- and passenger-side air bags, anti-lock 4-wheel disc brakes, variable-assist power steering, automatic climate control, cruise control, cloth reclining front bucket seats, 8-way power driver seat w/lumbar adjuster, front console with armrest, rear armrest, tilt steering column, leather-wrapped steering wheel, tinted glass, power windows and door locks, power mirrors, AM/FM/cassette/CD player, rear defogger, variable intermittent wipers, theft-deterrent system, map lights, visor mirrors, fog lights, 205/60HR15 tires, alloy wheels. **Premium Pkg.** adds: leather upholstery, power moonroof. **3.2** adds: 3.2-liter V-6 engine, power passenger seat, remote keyless entry, 205/65VR15 tires. **Premium Pkg.** adds: traction control, heated front seats, heated mirrors.

Options are available as dealer-installed accessories.

AUDI A4

Audi A4 1.8T

Specifications

	4-door notchback
Wheelbase, in..	103.0
Overall length, in.	178.0
Overall width, in..	68.2

	4-door notchback
Overall height, in.	55.8
Curb weight, lbs.	2877
Cargo vol., cu. ft.	13.7
Fuel capacity, gals.	16.4
Seating capacity	5

Engines

	Turbocharged dohc I-4	ohc V-6
Size, liters/cu. in.	1.8/107	2.8/169
Horsepower @ rpm	150 @ 5700	172 @ 5500
Torque (lbs./ft.) @ rpm	155 @ 1750	184 @ 3000
EPA city/highway mpg		
5-speed OD manual	20/29	19/27
5-speed OD automatic	21/30	18/28

Built in Germany.

PRICES

Audi A4	Retail Price	Dealer Invoice	Fair Price
1.8T 4-door notchback	$22990	$20246	—
2.8 4-door notchback	27430	24109	—
Destination charge	500	500	500

Fair price not available at time of publication.

Standard Equipment:

1.8T: 1.8-liter turbocharged 4-cylinder engine, 5-speed manual transmission, anti-lock 4-wheel disc brakes, automatic air conditioning, power steering, driver- and passenger-side air bags, Electronic Differential Lock, reclining front seats with height adjustment, 60/40 split folding rear seat, velour or leatherette upholstery, front storage console w/cupholders, folding rear storage armrest, tilt/telescope steering wheel, cruise control, leather-wrapped shifter and boot, tachometer, trip odometer, coolant-temperature and oil-temperature gauges, voltmeter, service interval indicator, analog clock, 8-speaker AM/FM/cassette, integrated antenna, power windows and door locks, heated power outside mirrors, tinted glass, rear defogger, remote decklid and fuel-door releases, intermittent wipers, illuminated visor mirrors, interior air filter, front and rear reading lights, anti-theft alarm, headlight washers, front and rear fog lights, 195/65R15 tires, alloy wheels. **2.8** adds: 2.8-liter V-6 engine, 8-way power driver seat w/lumbar adjustment, adjustable front armrest, outside temperature indicator, interior wood trim, floormats, 205/55HR16 tires.

Prices are accurate at time of publication; subject to manufacturer's change.

Optional Equipment:

	Retail Price	Dealer Invoice	Fair Price
5-speed automatic transmission	$975	$925	—
Quattro all-wheel-drive system	1600	1600	1600
All-Weather Package, 1.8T	700	609	—
2.8	630	548	—

Includes outside-temperature indicator (1.8T), temperature gauge, heated driver-side door locks, heated front seats, heated windshield washer nozzles, ski sack.

	Retail Price	Dealer Invoice	Fair Price
Sport Pkg., 1.8T	1000	870	—

Sport front seats, leather-wrapped sport steering wheel, Jacquard satin cloth upholstery, 205/55HR16 tires.

	Retail Price	Dealer Invoice	Fair Price
Audi/Bose 8-speaker sound system	660	574	—
Leather upholstery	1320	1148	—
Leather-wrapped sport steering wheel, 2.8 .	160	139	—
Trip computer	250	218	—
Power sunroof and remote keyless entry	1190	1035	—
Pearlescent metallic paint	570	496	—
Cool Shades paint	460	400	—
Metallic/mica paint, 1.8T	460	400	—
2.8	NC	NC	NC

AUDI A6

Audi A6 4-door

Specifications	4-door notchback	4-door wagon
Wheelbase, in.	105.8	105.8
Overall length, in.	192.6	192.6
Overall width, in.	70.2	70.2
Overall height, in.	56.3	57.7
Curb weight, lbs.	3428	3582

	4-door notchback	4-door wagon
Cargo vol., cu. ft.	16.8	65.5
Fuel capacity, gals.	21.2	21.1
Seating capacity	5	7

Engines

	ohc V-6
Size, liters/cu. in.	2.8/169
Horsepower @ rpm	172 @ 5500
Torque (lbs./ft.) @ rpm	184 @ 3000

EPA city/highway mpg
4-speed OD automatic	19/25

Built in Germany.

PRICES

Audi A6	Retail Price	Dealer Invoice	Fair Price
A6 4-door notchback	$32600	$28684	—
A6 4-door wagon	34400	30250	—
Destination charge	500	500	500

Fair price not available at time of publication.

Standard Equipment:

A6: 2.8-liter V-6 engine, 4-speed automatic transmission, anti-lock 4-wheel disc brakes, Electronic Differential Lock, driver- and passenger-side air bags, automatic air conditioning, speed-sensitive power steering, cruise control, Jacquard satin cloth upholstery, reclining front bucket seats with height and lumbar adjustments, 8-way power driver seat, center storage console with cupholders, adjustable front storage armrest, rear folding armrest, tilt/telescoping steering column, outside-temperature indicator, tachometer, oil-temperature and coolant-temperature gauge, trip odometer, analog clock, service-interval indicator, Active Auto Check System, power windows and door locks, remote fuel-door and decklid release, heated power mirrors, AM/FM/cassette, integrated antenna, tinted glass, leather-wrapped steering wheel, reading lights, illuminated visor mirrors, anti-theft alarm, rear defogger, rear heat ducts, intermittent wipers, front and rear fog lights, ski sack, floormats, walnut interior trim, 195/65R15 tires, alloy wheels. **Wagon** adds: 60/40 split folding rear seat, 2-place rear seat, roof-mounted antenna, rear wiper/washer, remote tailgate release, retractable rear window sunshade, roof rack, cargo-area cover and net.

Prices are accurate at time of publication; subject to manufacturer's change.

Optional Equipment:

	Retail Price	Dealer Invoice	Fair Price
Quattro all-wheel-drive system	$1600	$1600	$1600
Quattro Value Pkg.	2490	2360	—
Quattro all-wheel-drive system, power sunroof, 205/55R16 tires.			
Comfort and Convenience Pkg.	860	748	—
Power front passenger seat, memory driver seat and outside mirrors, remote keyless entry.			
All-Weather Pkg.	520	452	—
Heated front seats, heated windshield washer nozzles, heated front door locks, headlight washers.			
Power sunroof	1000	870	—
Leather upholstery	1550	1349	—
Audi/Bose audio system	660	574	—
Pearlescent metallic paint	570	496	—

BMW Z3

BMW Z3

Specifications

	2-door conv.
Wheelbase, in.	96.3
Overall length, in.	158.5
Overall width, in.	66.6
Overall height, in.	50.7
Curb weight, lbs.	2690
Cargo vol., cu. ft.	5.0
Fuel capacity, gals.	13.5
Seating capacity...	2

Engines

	dohc I-4	dohc I-6
Size, liters/cu. in.	1.9/116	2.8/170

	dohc I-4	dohc I-6
Horsepower @ rpm	138 @ 6000	189 @ 5300
Torque (lbs./ft.) @ rpm	133 @ 4300	203 @ 3950
EPA city/highway mpg		
5-speed manual	23/31	19/27
4-speed OD automatic	23/31	18/25

Built in Spartanburg, S.C.

PRICES

BMW Z3	Retail Price	Dealer Invoice	Fair Price
1.9 2-door convertible	$29425	$25915	—
2.8 2-door convertible	35900	31455	—
Destination charge	570	570	570

Fair price not available at time of publication.

Standard Equipment:

1.9: 1.9-liter 4-cylinder engine, 5-speed manual transmission, All-Season Traction, air conditioning, driver- and passenger-side air bags, variable-assist power steering, anti-lock 4-wheel disc brakes, limited slip differential, cruise control, leatherette upholstery, 4-way power driver seat, 2-way power passenger seat, center storage console, cupholders, 6-speaker AM/FM/cassette with weather band and amplifier, digital clock, power windows, power mirrors, tachometer, trip odometer, coolant-temperature gauge, leather-wrapped steering wheel, shifter, and hand brake, tinted glass, intermittent wipers, fog lights, tool kit, 225/50ZR16 tires, alloy wheels. **2.8:** 2.8-liter DOHC 6-cylinder engine, leather upholstery, wood interior trim, flared rear fenders, front spoiler.

Optional Equipment:

4-speed automatic transmission	975	925	—
Leather upholstery, 1.9	1150	945	—
Includes 4-way passenger seat and leather door trim panels.			
Extended leather upholstery, 2.8	1200	990	—
Includes color keyed leather steering wheel, instrument cluster hood, console sides, door upper ledges & pulls.			
Heated seats	500	410	—
Includes dual heated mirrors, heated windshield washer jets.			
Hi-Fi subwoofer	200	165	—
Sport alloy wheels, 2.8	1125	935	—
Includes 225/45R17 front tires, 245/40R17 rear tires.			

Prices are accurate at time of publication; subject to manufacturer's change.

BMW

	Retail Price	Dealer Invoice	Fair Price
Chrome trim	$150	$125	—
Onboard computer	300	250	—
Special paint	475	390	—
Metallic paint	475	390	—

BMW 3-SERIES

BMW 328i

Specifications	2-door hatchback	2-door notchback	4-door notchback	2-door conv.
Wheelbase, in.	106.3	106.3	106.3	106.3
Overall length, in.	165.7	174.5	174.5	174.5
Overall width, in.	66.9	67.3	66.9	67.3
Overall height, in.	54.8	53.8	54.8	53.1
Curb weight, lbs.	2745	2976	2976	3131
Cargo vol., cu. ft.	15.0	9.2	10.3	8.9
Fuel capacity, gals.	13.7	16.4	16.4	16.4
Seating capacity	5	5	5	4

Engines	dohc I-4	dohc I-6	dohc I-6
Size, liters/cu. in.	1.9/116	2.8/170	3.2/192
Horsepower @ rpm	138 @ 6000	190 @ 5300	240 @ 6000
Torque (lbs./ft.) @ rpm	133 @ 4300	206 @ 3950	225 @ 3800
EPA city/highway mpg			
5-speed manual	23/31	20/29	20/28
4-speed OD automatic	22/31	19/26	
5-speed OD automatic			19/28

Built in Germany.

PRICES

BMW 3-Series	Retail Price	Dealer Invoice	Fair Price
318ti 2-door hatchback	$21390	$19215	—
318i 4-door notchback	25950	22755	—
318is 2-door notchback	28270	24855	—
318i 2-door convertible	33150	28760	—
328i 4-door notchback	32900	28835	—
328i 2-door convertible	41390	36260	—
328is 2-door notchback	32990	28910	—
M3 4-door notchback	39380	34500	—
M3 2-door notchback	39380	34150	—
Destination charge	570	570	570

Fair price not available at time of publication.

Standard Equipment:

318 models: 1.9-liter DOHC 4-cylinder engine, 5-speed manual transmission, variable-assist power steering, anti-lock 4-wheel disc brakes, driver- and passenger-side air bags, air conditioning (318ti), automatic dual climate control (318i, 318is), All Season Traction, cruise control (318i, 318is), cloth upholstery (318ti), leatherette upholstery (318i, 318is), 6-way manual reclining bucket seats with height/tilt adjustments, split folding rear seat (318ti, 318is), rear storage armrest w/rear cupholders (318i convertible), cupholders, leather-wrapped steering wheel and shifter (318is, 318i convertible), front seatback storage nets, power windows and door locks, heated power mirrors, heated windshield washer jets (318ti), manual folding top (318i convertible), 10-speaker AM/FM/cassette, diversity antenna (318i 4-door, 318is), tachometer, trip odometer, digital clock, fuel-economy indicator (318i, 318is), outside temperature indicator (318i, 318is), speed-sensitive intermittent wipers, rear defogger, Service Interval Indicator, map lights (318i, 318is), rear reading lights (318ti, 318i 4-door, 318is), fog lights (318is, 318i convertible), tool kit, cargo-area storage box, 185/65TR15 tires and wheel covers (318ti, 318i 4-door), 205/60HR15 tires and alloy wheels (318is, 318i convertible), full-size spare tire (318i, 318is). **328 models** add to 318i 4-door, 318is, and 318i convertible: 2.8-liter DOHC 6-cylinder engine, Active Check Control system, front reading lights, rear reading lights (328i 4-door, M3 4-door), 8-way power front seats, front center armrest, leather-wrapped steering wheel, shifter, and hand brake, fully automatic power folding top (318i convertible), fog lights, 205/60HR15 tires, alloy wheels. **M3** adds to 328: 3.2-liter DOHC 6-cylinder engine, upgraded brakes, limited-slip differential, sport suspension, leather upholstery, 8-way manual sport seats (4-door), 12-way manual sport seats (2-door), split folding rear seat (2-door), 225/45ZR17 front tires, 245/40ZR17 rear tires, M double-spoke alloy

BMW

wheels. M3 deletes 8-way power front seats, front center armrest, and cruise control.

Optional Equipment:

	Retail Price	Dealer Invoice	Fair Price
4-speed automatic transmission	$975	$925	$887
NA on M3.			
5-speed automatic transmission,			
M3 4-door	1200	1140	1092
Cruise control, 318ti, M3	475	390	432
Rollover Protection System, convertible	1450	1190	1320
Restraint System, Side Impact Air Bag	320	385	—
NA 318ti, 318i, convertible or 318is			
Sport suspension, 318i 4-door, 318is	350	290	319
318i 4-door requires 205/60R15 tires and alloy wheels.			
Active Pkg., 318ti	1350	1150	1229
Cruise control, leather-wrapped steering wheel, remote keyless entry, anti-theft alarm, onboard computer, 205/60HR15 tires, alloy wheels, metallic paint. NA with Sports Pkg.			
318ti Sports Pkg., 318ti	2940	2500	2675
Sport suspension, cloth/leather upholstery, sport seats, leather-wrapped steering wheel, fog lights, M-Technic bumpers and rocker panels, 225/50VR16 tires, alloy wheels. NA with Active Pkg.			
328 Sports Pkg, 328i 4-door, 328is	2125	1750	1934
328i convertible	1775	1465	1615
Sport suspension (328i 4-door, 328is), leather upholstery, 8-way power sport seats, 225/50ZR16 tires, double-spoke alloy wheels.			
Luxury Pkg., M3	3300	2960	3003
Cruise control, onboard computer, 8-way power sports seats, wood interior trim, front center armrest, leather door trim, front spoiler, M-Contour II cast alloy wheels. NA with forged alloy wheels.			
Cloth upholstery, 318i, 318is	NC	NC	NC
Leather upholstery, 318, 328	1450	1190	1320
318ti and 318i 4-door include leather-wrapped steering wheel and shifter. 4-doors include rear storage armrest with cupholders when not ordered with split folding rear seat. 328 includes wood interior trim (NA with 328 Sports Pkg.) and onboard computer. NA 318ti Sports Pkg.			
Suede upholstery, M3 2-door	NC	NC	NC
Heated front seats	500	410	455
Includes heated driver-side door lock and windshield-washer jets. NA 318ti.			
Split folding rear seat, 318i 4-door,			
328i 4-door, M3 4-door	300	245	273
NA w/ski sack.			
Harmon Kardon audio system	675	555	614
NA on 318ti or convertibles.			

	Retail Price	Dealer Invoice	Fair Price
Ski sack, 318i 4-door, 328i 4-door	$300	$245	$273
NA with folding rear seat.			
Fog lights, 318i 4-door	260	215	237
Onboard computer, 318ti	300	250	273
328, M3	500	415	455
Metallic paint, 318, 328	475	390	432
M3	NC	NC	NC
Hardtop, convertible	2295	1885	2088
Power sunroof	950	780	865
NA convertible.			
Rear spoiler, M3	650	535	592
Alloy wheels, 318i 4-door	850	700	774
Forged alloy wheels, M3	1450	1190	1320
NA with Luxury Pkg.			

BMW 5-SERIES

BMW 540i

Specifications

	4-door notchback
Wheelbase, in.	111.4
Overall length, in.	188.0
Overall width, in.	70.9
Overall height, in.	56.5
Curb weight, lbs.	3450
Cargo vol., cu. ft.	11.0
Fuel capacity, gals.	18.5
Seating capacity	5

Engines

	dohc I-6	dohc V-8
Size, liters/cu. in.	2.8/170	4.4/268

Prices are accurate at time of publication; subject to manufacturer's change.

BMW

	dohc I-6	dohc V-8
Horsepower @ rpm	190 @ 5300	282 @ 5700
Torque (lbs./ft.) @ rpm	207 @ 3950	310 @ 3900
EPA city/highway mpg		
5-speed OD manual	20/29	
6-speed manual		15/24
4-speed OD automatic	19/26	
5-speed OD automatic		18/24

Built in Germany.

PRICES

BMW 5-Series	Retail Price	Dealer Invoice	Fair Price
528i 4-door notchback	$38900	$34490	—
540i 4-door notchback, 6-speed manual transmission	52350	45840	—
540i 4-door notchback, 5-speed automatic transmission	49900	43700	—
Destination charge	570	570	570
Gas Guzzler Tax, 540i w/6-speed	1300	1300	1300

Fair price not available at time of publication.

Standard Equipment:

528i: 2.8-liter DOHC 6-cylinder engine, 5-speed manual transmission, All Season Traction, variable-assist power steering, anti-lock 4-wheel disc brakes, front and side driver- and passenger-side air bags, cruise control, air conditioning with dual climate controls, automatic filtered ventilation, 10-way power front seats (with power head restraints and memory driver's seat, steering wheel, and outside mirrors), leatherette upholstery, rear center storage armrest, cupholders, 10-speaker anti-theft AM/FM stereo cassette, diversity antenna, power tilt/telescopic steering wheel, leather-wrapped steering wheel with audio, cruise control, and telephone controls, shift knob, and hand brake, power windows and locks, heated power mirrors, power sunroof, tachometer, trip odometer, outside temperature display, onboard computer, security system, map lights, intermittent wipers, remote decklid release, rear defogger, seatback and door storage, front and rear reading lights, Service Interval Indicator, Active Check Control system, fuel economy indicator, illuminated visor mirrors, filtered ventilation, tool kit, 225/60HR15 tires, alloy wheels. **540i** deletes Active Check Control system and adds: 4.4-liter DOHC V-8 engine, 5-speed automatic transmission, 14-way power front seats (with power head restraints, 4-way power lumbar support, and memory driver's seat, steering wheel, and outside mirrors), leather upholstery, burl walnut interior trim, power moonroof, automatic day/night rearview mirror, remote keyless entry, upgraded onboard computer, metallic paint, 225/55HR16 tires. **540i 6-speed** adds: 6-speed manual transmission, sport suspension, 14-way power front seats (with power head restraints, 4-way power lumbar support, and memory driver's seat, steering wheel, and outside mirrors) or manually adjustable sports seats, 235/45WR17 tires, cross-spoke alloy wheels.

Optional Equipment:	Retail Price	Dealer Invoice	Fair Price
4-speed automatic transmission, 528i	$975	$925	—
Premium Pkg., 528i	3450	2520	—
Leather upholstery, wood interior trim, metallic paint, cross-spoke alloy wheels.			
Power moonroof, 528i	1050	865	—
Navigation system, 528i	2990	2990	2990
540i	2800	2800	2800
Comfort 16-way power front seats	1200	965	—
Includes power lumbar support. Requires Premium Pkg.			
Power lumbar support	400	325	—
Split folding rear seat	575	470	—
Includes ski sack. Requires Premium Pkg.			
14-speaker audio system with upgraded amplifier	1500	1240	—
Heated front seats	500	410	—
Heated front seats and steering wheel	650	535	—
Power rear and manual rear side sunshades	575	470	—
Metallic paint, 528i	475	390	—
540i	NC	NC	NC

BMW 7-SERIES

Specifications	4-door notchback	4-door notchback
Wheelbase, in.	115.4	120.9
Overall length, in.	196.2	201.7
Overall width, in.	73.3	73.3
Overall height, in.	56.5	56.1
Curb weight, lbs.	4255	4288
Cargo vol., cu. ft.	13.0	13.0
Fuel capacity, gals.	22.5	22.5
Seating capacity	5	5

Prices are accurate at time of publication; subject to manufacturer's change.

BMW

BMW 750iL

Engines

	dohc V-8	ohc V-12
Size, liters/cu. in.	4.4/268	5.4/328
Horsepower @ rpm	282 @	322 @
	5700	5000
Torque (lbs./ft.) @ rpm	310 @	361 @
	3900	3900

EPA city/highway mpg

5-speed OD automatic	17/24	15/20

Built in Germany.

PRICES

BMW 7-Series	Retail Price	Dealer Invoice	Fair Price
740i 4-door notchback	$60850	$53920	—
740iL 4-door notchback	64800	56730	—
750iL 4-door notchback	93700	82005	—
Destination charge	570	570	570
Gas Guzzler Tax, 750iL	1700	1700	1700

Fair price not available at time of publication.

Standard Equipment:

740i: 4.4-liter DOHC V-8 engine, 5-speed automatic transmission w/Adaptive Transmission Control, anti-lock 4-wheel disc brakes, variable-assist power steering, front and side driver- and passenger-side air bags, automatic climate control system with dual controls, All Season Traction, 14-way power front seats with driver-side memory system, 4-way lumbar support adjustment, power tilt/telescopic steering wheel with memory, leather upholstery, walnut interior trim, door and seatback pockets, power windows and door locks, heated power mirrors with 3-position memory, remote keyless entry, anti-theft system, remote decklid release, variable intermittent wipers, heated windshield-washer jets, heated driver-side door lock, cruise control, rear head rests, front and rear storage armrests, automatic day/night rearview mirror, front and rear reading lamps, tinted glass, lighted visor mirrors, tachometer, trip odometer, Service Interval Indicator, Active Check Control system, onboard computer, rear defogger, interior air filtration system, power moonroof, fog lamps, 10-speaker AM/FM/cassette with diversity antenna and steering wheel controls, cargo net, tool kit, 235/60HR16 tires, cast alloy wheels, full-size spare tire. **740iL** adds: 16-way power Comfort Seats. **750iL** adds: 5.4-liter V-12 engine, ASC+T traction control with Dynamic Stability Control, Electronic Damping Control, heated seats, power rear seats with power lumbar adjustment, power rear headrests, self-leveling rear suspension, ventilated rear disc brakes, heated steering wheel, cellular telephone, break-resistant security glass, 14-speaker premium sound system w/CD and digital sound processor, 6-disc CD changer, power rear sunshade, parking distance control, Xenon headlamps, headlight washers, ski sack, forged alloy wheels.

Optional Equipment:	Retail Price	Dealer Invoice	Fair Price
Self-leveling rear suspension, 740iL	$1100	$915	—
Electronic Damping Control, 740	2000	1660	—
Cold Weather Pkg., 740	825	685	—
Heated steering wheel, headlight washers, ski sack.			
Heated front seats, 740	500	410	—
16-way power Comfort Seats, 740i	1200	965	—
Includes 2-way power upper backrest adjustment, power lumbar support.			
Navigation system	2800	2800	2800
14-speaker premium sound system, 740	2100	1745	—
Includes CD player and digital sound processor.			
Parking distance control, 740iL	900	750	—
Power rear sunshade, 740iL	740	615	—
Metallic paint	NC	NC	NC

BUICK CENTURY

Specifications	4-door notchback
Wheelbase, in.	109.0
Overall length, in.	194.5
Overall width, in.	72.7
Overall height, in.	57.0
Curb weight, lbs.	3348
Cargo vol., cu. ft.	16.7

Prices are accurate at time of publication; subject to manufacturer's change.

BUICK

Buick Century

	4-door notchback
Fuel capacity, gals.	17.0
Seating capacity	6

Engines

	ohv V-6
Size, liters/cu. in.	3.1/191
Horsepower @ rpm	160 @ 5200
Torque (lbs./ft.) @ rpm	185 @ 4000

EPA city/highway mpg

4-speed OD automatic	20/29

Built in Canada.

PRICES

Buick Century	Retail Price	Dealer Invoice	Fair Price
Custom 4-door notchback	$17845	$16685	—
Limited 4-door notchback	19220	17586	—
Destination charge	550	550	550

Fair price not available at time of publication.

Standard Equipment:

Custom: 3.1-liter V-6 engine, 4-speed automatic transmission, anti-lock brakes, driver- and passenger-side air bags, power steering, air conditioning, cloth reclining 55/45 front bench seat, front storage armrest w/cupholders, rear armrest w/cupholders, automatic power door locks, power windows, tilt steering wheel, dual remote mirrors, tinted glass, solar-control windshield and rear window, coolant-temperature gauge, trip odometer, AM/FM radio, digital clock, rear defogger, Pass-Key theft-deterrent system, interior-air filter, remote

keyless entry, variable intermittent wipers, visor mirrors, rear heat ducts, daytime running lamps, 205/70R15 tires, wheel covers.
Limited adds: variable-assist power steering, dual automatic climate control, heated power mirrors, illuminated visor mirrors, retained accessory power, rear courtesy/reading lights, floormats, striping.

Optional Equipment:

	Retail Price	Dealer Invoice	Fair Price
Pkg. SB, Custom	$330	$283	—

Cruise control, cargo net, map lights on inside rearview mirror, floormats.

	Retail Price	Dealer Invoice	Fair Price
Pkg. SC, Custom	830	714	—

Pkg SB plus 6-way power driver seat, cassette player.

Pkg. SE, Limited	525	452	—

Cruise control, rear storage armrest with cupholders, cassette player, map lights on inside rearview mirror, cargo net.

Pkg. SF, Limited	1620	1393	—

Pkg. SE plus dual automatic climate control, 6-way power driver and passenger seats, upgraded cassette player with automatic tone control and anti-theft feature, Concert Sound II speakers, steering-wheel radio controls, integrated antenna, automatic day/night inside mirror.

Dual automatic climate control, Custom w/Pkg. SC	45	39	—
Leather upholstery, Limited	550	473	—

Includes leather-wrapped steering wheel.

6-way power driver seat	305	262	—
Integrated child seat, Custom	100	86	—
Cruise control	225	194	—
Power glass sunroof	695	598	—

Custom requires Pkg. SC, automatic day/night inside mirror, and illuminated visor mirrors. Limited requires Pkg. SF.

Automatic day/night inside mirror	80	69	—

Custom requires Pkg. SC and illuminated visor mirrors. LImited requires Pkg. SE.

Heated power mirrors, Custom	98	84	—

Requires option pkg.

Illuminated visor mirrors, Custom w/Pkg. SC	137	118	—
Rear storage armrest with cupholders, Limited	45	39	—
Cassette player	195	168	—
Upgraded cassette player, Custom w/Pkg. SB, Limited	220	189	—
Custom w/Pkg. SC, Limited w/Pkg. SE ...	25	22	—

Includes automatic tone control and anti-theft feature. Requires Concert Sound II speakers.

	Retail Price	Dealer Invoice	Fair Price
CD player, Custom w/Pkg. SB, Limited	$320	$275	—
Custom w/Pkg. SC, Limited w/Pkg. SE ...	125	108	—
Limited w/Pkg. SF	100	86	—
Includes automatic tone control and anti-theft feature. Requires Concert Sound II speakers.			
CD/cassette player,			
Custom w/Pkg. SB, Limited	420	361	—
Custom w/Pkg. SC, Limited w/Pkg. SE ...	225	194	—
Limited w/Pkg. SF	200	172	—
Includes automatic tone control and anti-theft feature. Requires Concert Sound II speakers.			
Concert Sound II speakers	70	60	—
Custom requires option pkg.			
Integrated antenna	40	34	—
Requires option pkg.			
Steering-wheel radio controls	125	108	—
Requires upgraded cassette player, CD player, or cassette/CD player. Requires cruise control. Custom requires option pkg.			
Trunk-mounted CD changer prep pkg.	50	43	—
Requires upgraded cassette player, CD player, or cassette/CD player. Custom requires option pkg.			
Striping, Custom	45	39	—
Cargo net	30	26	—
Engine-block heater	18	15	—
Alloy wheels	325	280	—

BUICK LeSABRE/ OLDSMOBILE EIGHTY EIGHT

Specifications

	4-door notchback
Wheelbase, in.	110.8
Overall length, in.	200.4
Overall width, in.	74.1
Overall height, in.	55.7
Curb weight, lbs.	3455
Cargo vol., cu. ft.	18.0
Fuel capacity, gals.	18.0
Seating capacity	6

Buick LeSabre

Engines

	ohv V-6	Supercharged ohv V-6
Size, liters/cu. in.	3.8/231	3.8/231
Horsepower @ rpm	205 @ 5200	240 @ 5200
Torque (lbs./ft.) @ rpm	230 @ 4000	280 @ 3200
EPA city/highway mpg		
4-speed OD automatic	19/29	18/27

Built in Flint and Orion, Mich.

PRICES

Buick LeSabre	Retail Price	Dealer Invoice	Fair Price
Custom 4-door notchback	$22015	$20144	$20644
Limited 4-door notchback	25565	23392	23892
Destination charge	605	605	605

Standard Equipment:

Custom: 3.8-liter V-6 engine, 4-speed automatic transmission, anti-lock brakes, driver- and passenger-side air bags, power steering, air conditioning, 55/45 cloth seats, front storage armrest with cupholders, manual front seatback recliners, power door locks, power windows, AM/FM radio with clock, tilt steering wheel, intermittent wipers, Pass-Key theft-deterrent system, color-keyed left remote and right manual mirrors, solar-control tinted glass, rear defogger, instrument panel courtesy lights, trip odometer, visor mirrors, Twilight Sentinel headlamp control, daytime running lights, 205/70R15 all-season tires, wheel covers. **Limited** adds: front and rear automatic climate control with front dual temperature controls, cruise control, remote keyless entry, memory door locks, remote decklid release, 6-way power seats, voltmeter, tachometer, oil-pres-

BUICK

sure and coolant-temperature gauges, cassette player, Concert Sound II speakers, power mirrors, automatic day/night mirror, rear armrest, lighted visor mirrors, front- and rear-door courtesy lights, front and rear reading lights, striping, floormats, trunk net, 205/70R15 all-season whitewall tires, and alloy wheels.

Optional Equipment:

	Retail Price	Dealer Invoice	Fair Price
Traction control system, Custom w/Pkg. SE, Limited	$175	$151	$158
Luxury Pkg. SD, Custom	941	809	847

Includes cruise control, cassette player, cargo net, floormats, striping, 205/70R15 all-season whitewall tires, alloy wheels.

Prestige Pkg. SE, Custom	1918	1649	1726

Pkg. SD plus 6-way power driver's seat, memory door locks, remote keyless entry, voltmeter, tachometer, oil-pressure and coolant-temperature gauges, power mirrors, Lighting Pkg., remote decklid release, Concert Sound II speakers, door-edge guards.

Prestige Pkg. SE, Limited	609	524	548

Includes automatic level control, automatic day/night left outside rearview mirror, theft-deterrent system, cassette player with automatic tone control, steering-wheel radio controls, cornering lamps.

Gran Touring Pkg., Custom w/Pkg. SE, Limited	512	440	461
Limited w/Pkg. SE	337	290	303

Includes variable-assist power steering, Gran Touring Suspension, 3:06 axle ratio, automatic level control, leather-wrapped steering wheel, 215/60R16 touring tires, alloy wheels. Requires traction control.

Cruise control, Custom	225	194	203
Leather upholstery, Custom	995	856	896
Limited	550	473	495

Custom requires option pkg. Custom with Pkg. SD requires power mirrors, 6-way power driver's seat, remote keyless entry, memory door locks, remote decklid release.

Automatic level control, Custom w/Pkg. SE, Limited	175	151	158
6-way power driver's seat, Custom	305	262	275

Requires power mirrors and cruise control. With Pkg. SD, requires power mirrors, remote keyless entry, memory door locks, remote decklid release.

6-way power passenger seat, Custom w/Pkg. SE	305	262	275
Power mirrors, Custom	78	67	70

Requires 6-way power driver's seat and cruise control. With Pkg. SD, requires 6-way power driver's seat, remote keyless entry, memory door locks, and remote decklid release.

	Retail Price	Dealer Invoice	Fair Price
Lighting Pkg., Custom w/Pkg. SD	$116	$100	$104
Map lights, illuminated visor mirrors			
Remote decklid release,			
Custom w/Pkg. SD	60	52	54
Requires remote keyless entry, 6-way power driver's seat, power mirrors, and memory door locks.			
Remote keyless entry, Custom w/Pkg. SD ..	135	116	122
Requires remote decklid release, 6-way power driver's seat, power mirrors, and memory door locks.			
Memory door locks, Custom w/Pkg. SD	25	22	23
Requires remote decklid release, remote keyless entry, 6-way power driver's seat, and power mirrors.			
UN6 audio system, Custom	195	168	176
Includes cassette player with clock.			
UL0 audio system, Custom w/Pkg. SE,			
Limited	150	129	135
Includes cassette player with clock, automatic tone control, and steering-wheel radio controls.			
UN0 audio system, Custom w/Pkg. SE,			
Limited	250	215	225
Limited w/Pkg. SE	100	86	90
Includes CD player with clock, automatic tone control, and steering-wheel radio controls.			
UP0 audio system, Custom w/Pkg. SE,			
Limited	350	301	315
Limited w/Pkg. SE	200	172	180
UN0 audio system plus cassette player.			
Theft-deterrent system, Limited	159	137	143
Cornering lamps, Limited	60	50	54
Floormats, Custom	45	39	41
Engine block heater	18	15	16
Alloy wheels, Custom	325	280	293
Locking wire wheel covers,			
Custom w/option pkg., Limited	NC	NC	NC
NA with Gran Touring Pkg.			
205/70R15 whitewall tires,			
Custom	76	65	71
NA with Gran Touring Pkg.			
205/70R15 tires, Custom w/option pkg.,			
Limited (credit)	(76)	(65)	(65)
NA with Gran Touring Pkg.			
205/70R15 self-sealing whitewall tires,			
Custom	226	194	203
Custom w/option pkg., Limited	150	129	135

Prices are accurate at time of publication; subject to manufacturer's change.

BUICK

Oldsmobile Eighty Eight

	Retail Price	Dealer Invoice	Fair Price
4-door notchback	$22595	$20674	—
LS 4-door notchback	23895	21864	—
LSS 4-door notchback	27795	25432	—
Regency 4-door notchback	28095	25707	—
Destination charge	605	605	605

Fair price not available at time of publication.

Standard Equipment:

3.8-liter V-6 engine, 4-speed automatic transmission, driver- and passenger-side air bags, anti-lock brakes, power steering, air conditioning, cruise control, 55/45 cloth front seat with reclining seatback, storage armrest w/cupholders, 8-way power driver seat, tilt steering wheel, power windows, left remote and right manual outside mirrors, tinted glass with solar-control windshield and rear window, rear defogger, AM/FM/cassette player w/6-speaker sound system and digital clock, power antenna, auxiliary power outlet, Pass-Key theft-deterrent system, remote decklid release, power door locks, coolant-temperature gauge, trip odometer, courtesy/reading lights, visor mirrors, intermittent wipers, Twilight Sentinel headlight control, daytime running lamps, floormats, tool kit, 205/70R15 tires, bolt-on wheel covers. **LS** adds: traction control system, front bucket seats, remote keyless entry, programmable door locks, power mirrors, illuminated visor mirrors, 215/65R15 touring tires, alloy wheels. **LSS** adds: dual-zone air conditioning with inside/outside temperature indicator, variable-assist power steering, automatic load-leveling touring suspension, leather upholstery, manual lumbar support, 8-way power passenger seat, floor console, overhead storage console, rear seat w/trunk pass-through, rear-seat storage armrest, tachometer, leather-wrapped steering wheel radio and air conditioning controls, cassette/CD player, automatic day/night rearview and driver-side outside mirror, illuminated entry/exit, fog lamps, cargo net, 225/60R16 tires. **Regency** adds to base: traction control system, dual-zone air conditioner with inside/outside temperature indicator, automatic load-leveling touring suspension, leather upholstery, 6-way power front seats with power recliners and lumbar-support adjusters, front and rear storage armrests w/cupholders, overhead storage console w/reading lamps, power mirrors, automatic day/night inside mirror w/compass, driver-seat and outside-mirror memory controls, automatic day/night and heated driver-side outside mirror, AM/FM/cassette/CD player, leather-wrapped steering wheel radio and air conditioning controls, remote keyless entry, illuminated visor mirrors, illuminated entry/exit system, cargo net, 205/70R15 whitewall tires, alloy wheels.

Optional Equipment:

	Retail Price	Dealer Invoice	Fair Price
Supercharged 3.8-liter V-6 engine, LSS	$1022	$909	—
8-way power passenger seat, LS	350	312	—
Split bench seat, LS	NC	NC	NC
Includes 205/70R15 tires.			
Power sunroof, LSS, Regency	995	886	—
Cloth seat trim, Regency	NC	NC	NC
Leather upholstery, LS	515	458	—
Cassette/CD player, LS	200	178	—
Alloy wheels, base.......................................	330	294	—
LS	150	134	—
LS includes 225/60R16 tires.			
Chrome wheels, LSS	600	534	—
Engine block heater	18	16	—

BUICK PARK AVENUE

Buick Park Avenue Ultra

Specifications

	4-door notchback
Wheelbase, in.	113.8
Overall length, in.	206.8
Overall width, in.	74.7
Overall height, in.	57.4
Curb weight, lbs.	3788
Cargo vol., cu. ft.	19.1
Fuel capacity, gals.	18.0
Seating capacity	6

Engines

	ohv V-6	Supercharged ohv V-6
Size, liters/cu. in.	3.8/231	3.8/231

Prices are accurate at time of publication; subject to manufacturer's change.

BUICK

Engines

	ohv V-6	Supercharged ohv V-6
Horsepower @ rpm	205 @ 5200	240 @ 5200
Torque (lbs./ft.) @ rpm	230 @ 4000	280 @ 3600
EPA city/highway mpg		
4-speed OD automatic	19/28	18/27

Built in Lake Orion, Mich.

PRICES

Buick Park Avenue	Retail Price	Dealer Invoice	Fair Price
Base 4-door notchback	$29995	$27145	$27745
Ultra 4-door notchback	34995	31670	32270
Destination charge	665	665	665

Standard Equipment:

Base: 3.8-liter V-6 engine, 4-speed automatic transmission, anti-lock 4-wheel disc brakes, driver- and passenger-side air bags, automatic level-control suspension, automatic climate control with dual temperature controls, rear-seat climate controls, cruise control, 10-way power 55/45 cloth front seat, front storage armrest with cupholders, rear armrest with cupholders, rear head restraints, power windows with passenger lockout, power mirrors, power door locks, remote keyless entry with perimeter lighting and alarm, overhead console, rear defogger, tilt steering wheel, tachometer, trip odometer, coolant-temperature gauge, AM/FM/cassette player, Concert Sound II speakers, rear-window antenna, solar-control tinted glass, Pass-Key theft-deterrent system with starter interrupt, remote deck-lid and fuel-door releases, front and rear reading and courtesy lights, illuminated visor mirrors, intermittent wipers, Twilight Sentinel headlamp control, daytime running lights, cornering lamps, cargo net, floormats, 225/60R16 tires, alloy wheels. **Ultra** adds: supercharged 3.8-liter V-6 engine, traction-control system, variable-assist power steering, leather upholstery, memory driver seat, Seating Pkg. (power lumbar adjustment, heated front seats, front and rear articulating headrests), rear-seat storage armrest with cupholders, rear-seat pass-through, leather-wrapped steering wheel, air filtration system, cellular phone readiness pkg., power door locks, moisture-sensing windshield wipers, driver information center (tire- and oil-pressure warning; volt, oil-life, and oil-level monitors; low-washer-fluid, low-coolant, and door-ajar indicators; and trip computer), automatic day/night rearview mirror, driver-side automatic day/night mirror, heated memory mirrors, CD player with automatic tone control and steering-wheel controls, Concert Sound III speakers, rear illuminated vanity mirrors, wood door trim, 4-note horn.

Optional Equipment:

	Retail Price	Dealer Invoice	Fair Price
SE Prestige Pkg., base	$890	$765	$792

Memory driver-seat and mirrors, heated mirrors, automatic day/night driver-side mirror, automatic day/night rearview mirror, programmable universal transmitter, UL0 audio system (AM/FM/cassette player with clock, seek and scan, automatic tone control, and steering-wheel radio controls), moisture-sensing windshield wipers, driver information center (tire- and oil-pressure warning; volt, oil-life, and oil-level monitors; low-washer-fluid, low-coolant, and door-ajar indicators; and trip computer).

UL0 audio system, base	150	129	134

Includes AM/FM/cassette player with clock, seek and scan, automatic tone control, and steering-wheel radio controls.

UN0 audio system, base	250	215	223
base w/Pkg. SE	100	86	89

Includes AM/FM/CD player with clock, seek and scan, automatic tone control, and steering-wheel radio controls.

UP0 audio system, base	350	301	312
base w/SE Pkg.	200	172	178
Ultra	100	86	89

UN0 audio system plus cassette player.

Trunk-mounted CD changer, Ultra	595	512	530
Concert Sound III speakers, base w/SE Pkg. ..	250	215	223
Automatic day/night rearview mirror w/compass	70	60	62

Base requires SE Pkg.

Electric sliding sunroof	995	856	886

NA with SE Prestige Pkg. on base.

Seating Pkg., base	380	327	338

Power lumbar adjustment, heated front seats, and front articulating headrests.

Convenience Console/Five Person Leather Seating Pkg.	185	159	165

Bucket seats, console with writing surface and accommodations for phone and fax, cupholders, and auxiliary power outlets. Requires leather upholstery and cellular phone readiness pkg.

Gran Touring Pkg., base w/SE Pkg.	240	206	214
Ultra	105	90	93

Includes Gran Touring suspension, aluminum wheels, and 225/60R16 touring tires. Base w/option pkg. also includes 3.05 axle ratio and leather-wrapped steering wheel. Base also includes variable-assist power steering. Requires automatic day/night mirror. Base also requires traction control.

Prices are accurate at time of publication; subject to manufacturer's change.

BUICK

	Retail Price	Dealer Invoice	Fair Price
Traction-control system, base w/SE Pkg.	$175	$151	$156
Eye Cue head-up display	275	237	245
Requires cellular phone readiness pkg. Base requires SE Pkg.			
Cellular phone readiness pkg., base	75	65	67
Base requires optional radio.			
Air filtration system, base w/SE Pkg.	50	43	45
Leather upholstery, base	600	516	534
Rear-seat pass-through, base	50	43	45
Rear storage armrest, base	50	43	45
Requires leather upholstery.			
Four-note horn, base w/SE Pkg.	28	24	25
Engine-block heater	18	15	16
225/60R16 whitewall tires, base	85	73	76
NA with Gran Touring Pkg.			
225/60R16 self-sealing whitewall tires	150	129	134
NA with Gran Touring Pkg.			
16-inch chrome-plated alloy wheels	695	598	619

BUICK REGAL

Buick Regal GS

Specifications

	4-door notchback
Wheelbase, in.	109.0
Overall length, in.	196.2
Overall width, in.	72.7
Overall height, in.	56.6
Curb weight, lbs.	3473
Cargo vol., cu. ft.	16.7
Fuel capacity, gals.	17.0
Seating capacity	5

Engines

	ohv V-6	Supercharged ohv V-6
Size, liters/cu. in.	3.8/231	3.8/231
Horsepower @ rpm	195 @ 5200	240 @ 5200
Torque @ rpm	220 @ 4000	280 @ 3600

EPA city/highway mpg
4-speed OD automatic	19/30	18/28

Built in Canada.

PRICES

Buick Regal	Retail Price	Dealer Invoice	Fair Price
LS 4-door notchback	$20545	—	—
GS 4-door notchback	22945	—	—
Destination charge	550	550	550

Dealer invoice and fair price not available at time of publication.

Standard Equipment:

LS: 3.8-liter V-6 engine, 4-speed automatic transmission, driver- and passenger-side air bags, anti-lock 4-wheel disc brakes, traction control, magnetic variable assist power steering, air conditioning, dual climate control, air filtration system, cruise control, cloth reclining front bucket seats, front console w/dual cupholders and auxiliary power outlet, rear armrest w/dual cupholders, remote keyless entry, programmable automatic power door locks, lockout protection, power windows w/driver's express down feature, leather-wrapped tilt steering wheel, oil-life monitor, trip odometer, tachometer, low-fuel reminder tone, temperature gauge, warning lights for door ajar and trunk ajar, solar-control tinted glass, intermittent wipers, Pass-Key theft-deterrent system, color-keyed heated power mirrors, rear defogger, rear seat pass-through, courtesy/map lights on inside rearview mirror, visor vanity mirrors, daytime running lamps with Twilight Sentinel, integral fog lamps, AM/FM/cassette player with clock, retained accessory power, 215/70R15 tires, wheel covers. **GS** adds: supercharged 3.8-liter V-6 engine, heavy-duty 4-speed automatic transmission with driver selectable shift control, Gran Touring suspension, bright exhaust outlets, traction control, leather seats, front and rear floormats, rear courtesy and reading lamps,automatic radio tone control, Concert Sound II speakers, dual illuminated visor vanity mirrors, Driver Information Center, tire pressure monitor, 225/60R16 touring tires, alloy wheels.

Prices are accurate at time of publication; subject to manufacturer's change.

Optional Equipment:

	Retail Price	Dealer Invoice	Fair Price
Luxury Pkg. SB, LS	$547	$470	—

Includes front and rear floormats, reading/ map lights, dual visor vanity mirrors, 6-way power driver's seat, trunk convenience net.

Prestige Pkg. SC, LS....................................	887	763	—

Luxury package plus rear window antenna, electrochromatic inside rearview mirror, steering wheel mounted radio controls, automatic radio tone control, Concert Sound II speakers.

Luxury Pkg. SE, GS	365	314	—

Includes inside rearview mirror with reading/map lights, 6-way power driver's seat, trunk convenience net.

Prestige Pkg. SF, GS....................................	1060	912	—

Luxury package plus dual climate control, electrochromatic inside rearview mirror, steering wheel mounted radio controls, rear window antenna, 6-way power passenger's seat.

Gran Touring package, LS w/Pkg. SB,SC....	127	109	—

Consists of grand touring suspension and 225/60R16 blackwall tires. Requires 16 -inch wheels.

Cellular phone prewire package..................	75	64	—
Driver information center, LS w/Pkg. SC......	75	64	—
Rear window antenna, LS w/Pkg. SB	40	34	—
Steering wheel mounted radio controls........	125	107	—
CD player prep package	50	43	—
ULO audio system, LS	25	21	—

Includes automatic tone control. Requires Concert Sound II speakers.

UPO audio system, LS w/Pkg. SA, SB	225	193	—
w/Pkg. SC..	200	172	—

CD/cassette player. Requires Concert Sound II speakers.

Concert Sound II speakers, LS	70	60	—
Power glass sunroof....................................	695	598	—

Requires electrochromatic rearview mirror.

Leather bucket seats, LS.............................	550	473	—
Heated front seats	225	193	—

Requires leather seats.

6-way power driver's seat............................	305	262	—
6-way power passenger's seat, LS	305	262	—
Integral rear child safety seat	100	86	—
Trunk convenience net	30	26	—
Front floormats	25	21	—
Rear floormats	20	17	—
Electrchromatic rearview mirror....................	80	69	—
16 inch aluminum wheels.............................	375	322	—
15 inch aluminum wheels.............................	325	279	—
16 inch chrome aluminum wheels.................	1025	881	—

BUICK RIVIERA

Buick Riviera

Specifications

	2-door notchback
Wheelbase, in.	113.8
Overall length, in.	207.2
Overall width, in.	75.0
Overall height, in.	55.2
Curb weight, lbs.	3690
Cargo vol., cu. ft.	17.4
Fuel capacity, gals.	20.0
Seating capacity	6

Engines

	ohv V-6	Supercharged ohv V-6
Size, liters/cu. in.	3.8/231	3.8/231
Horsepower @ rpm	205 @ 5200	240 @ 5200
Torque (lbs./ft.) @ rpm	230 @ 4000	280 @ 3200

EPA city/highway mpg

4-speed OD automatic	19/28	18/27

Built in Orion, Mich.

PRICES

Buick Riviera	Retail Price	Dealer Invoice	Fair Price
2-door notchback	$30110	$27250	$28050
Destination charge	665	665	665

Standard Equipment:

3.8-liter V-6 engine, 4-speed automatic transmission, anti-lock 4-

Prices are accurate at time of publication; subject to manufacturer's change.

wheel disc brakes, driver- and passenger-side air bags, variable-assist power steering, automatic air conditioning with dual climate controls, rear-seat heating vents, automatic level control suspension, cruise control, cloth 6-way power 55/45 split bench front seat, front storage armrest with cupholders, rear-seat armrest, power windows and mirrors, automatic power door locks, remote keyless entry system (w/perimeter lighting, security feedback, and instant alarm), Pass-Key theft-deterrent system, tachometer, coolant-temperature gauge, trip odometer, illuminated passenger-side visor mirror, remote fuel door and decklid releases, solar-control tinted glass, AM/FM/cassette/CD player with clock, Concert Sound II speakers, power antenna, intermittent wipers, rear defogger, tilt leather-wrapped steering wheel, front and rear reading and courtesy lights, Twilight Sentinel headlamp control, daytime running lights, cargo net, 225/60R16 all-season tires, alloy wheels.

Optional Equipment:	Retail Price	Dealer Invoice	Fair Price
3.8-liter supercharged V-6 engine $1195	$1028	$1099
Includes 225/60R16 touring tires and special alloy wheels.			
SE Prestige Pkg. 1065	916	980
Traction-control system, driver-seat power lumbar adjustment, automatic day/night rearview and driver-side mirrors, steering-wheel-mounted radio controls, driver-side lighted visor mirror, theft-deterrent system, remote universal transmitter, cornering lamps, and striping.			
Power sunroof with sunshade 995	856	915
Memory/heated driver's seat w/memory outside mirrors 310	267	285
Power leather front bucket seats with console 750	645	690
Leather 55/45 split bench seats 600	516	552
Automatic day/night rearview mirror w/compass, w/SE Pkg. 70	60	64
Bright white diamond paint 395	340	363
Chrome wheels 695	598	639
Requires supercharged engine.			
Engine block heater 18	15	17

CADILLAC CATERA

Specifications	4-door notchback
Wheelbase, in.	113.8
Wheelbase, in.	107.4
Overall length, in.	194.0

Cadillac Catera

	4-door notchback
Overall width, in.	70.3
Overall height, in.	57.4
Curb weight, lbs.	3770
Cargo vol., cu. ft.	16.6
Fuel capacity, gals.	18.0
Seating capacity	5

Engines

	dohc V-6
Size, liters/cu. in.	3.0/181
Horsepower @ rpm	200 @ 6000
Torque (lbs./ft.) @ rpm	192 @ 3600

EPA city/highway mpg

4-speed OD automatic	18/25

Built in Germany.

PRICES

Cadillac Catera	Retail Price	Dealer Invoice	Fair Price
4-door notchback	$29995	$28645	—
Destination charge	640	640	640

Fair price not available at time of publication.

Standard Equipment:

3.0-liter DOHC V-6 engine, 4-speed automatic transmission, anti-lock 4-wheel disc brakes, dual-zone automatic climate control w/outside temperature indicator, driver- and passenger-side air bags, variable-assist steering, traction control, cloth front bucket seats, 8-way power driver seat with power recliner, passenger-seat power height adjuster, split folding rear bench seat, front articulating and rear headrests, front console w/storage armrest and cupholders, rear armrests, power windows, automatic power door locks, remote keyless entry system, heated power mirrors, cruise control, AM/FM/cassette with eight speakers, integrated rear window antenna, steering-wheel radio controls, tinted glass, wood interior trim, intermittent wipers, leather-wrapped tilt steering wheel, Driver Information Center, analog instrument cluster, tachometer, coolant-temperature and oil-pressure gauge, voltmeter, trip odometer, remote fuel-door and decklid release, rear defogger, anti-theft system, automatic day/night inside mirror, illuminated visor mirrors, front and rear reading lights, illuminated entry, automatic parking-brake release, dual exhaust, Twilight Sentinel headlamp control, wiper-activated headlights, cornering lamps, daytime running lamps, fog lights, trunk mat and cargo net, floormats, 225/55HR16 tires, alloy wheels, full-size spare.

Optional Equipment:

	Retail Price	Dealer Invoice	Fair Price
Comfort Convenience Pkg.	$3000	$1875	—
Leather upholstery, 8-way power front passenger seat, memory seats and mirrors, theft-deterrent system.			
Heated front and rear seats	400	340	—
Power sunroof	995	846	—
Universal garage-door opener	107	91	—
8-speaker Bose sound system	723	615	—
5-spoke alloy wheels	355	156	—
5-spoke chrome wheels	1195	523	—

CADILLAC DE VILLE

Cadillac De Ville

Specifications

	4-door notchback
Wheelbase, in.	113.8

	4-door notchback
Overall length, in.	209.7
Overall width, in.	76.6
Overall height, in.	56.3
Curb weight, lbs.	4009
Cargo vol., cu. ft.	20.0
Fuel capacity, gals.	20.0
Seating capacity	6

Engines

	dohc V-8	dohc V-8
Size, liters/cu. in.	4.6/279	4.6/279
Horsepower @ rpm	275 @ 5600	300 @ 6000
Torque (lbs./ft.) @ rpm	300 @ 4000	295 @ 4400
EPA city/highway mpg		
4-speed OD automatic	17/26	17/26

Built in Hamtramck, Mich.

PRICES

Cadillac De Ville	Retail Price	Dealer Invoice	Fair Price
De Ville 4-door notchback	$36995	$33850	$34650
De Ville d'Elegance 4-door notchback	39995	36595	37395
De Ville Concours 4-door notchback	41995	38425	39225
Destination charge	665	665	665

Standard Equipment:

De Ville: 4.6-liter DOHC V-8 engine (275 horsepower), 4-speed automatic transmission, anti-lock 4-wheel disc brakes, dual-zone automatic climate control w/outside temperature indicator, front and side driver- and passenger-side air bags, Magnasteer variable-assist steering, traction control, automatic level-control suspension, cloth 8-way power front seats with power recliners, front storage armrest w/cupholders, front articulating and rear headrests, overhead storage compartment, power windows, programmable power locks w/valet lockout, remote keyless entry system, illuminated entry, heated power mirrors, cruise control, AM/FM/cassette with six speakers, power antenna, steering-wheel radio and climate controls, power decklid pulldown, tinted glass, wood interior trim, driver-side visor storage, intermittent wipers, Driver Information Center, trip odometer, tilt steering wheel, leather-wrapped steering wheel, power decklid release and pulldown, remote fuel-door release, rear defogger, Pass-Key II anti-theft system, automatic day/night inside rear-view mirror, automatic day/night driver-side

CADILLAC

mirror, illuminated front visor mirrors, front and rear reading lights, Integrated Chassis Control System, automatic parking-brake release, Twilight Sentinel headlamp control, wiper-activated headlights, cornering lamps, daytime running lamps, striping, trunk mat and cargo net, floormats, 225/60R16 all-season whitewall tires, alloy wheels. **De Ville d'Elegance** adds: leather upholstery, power lumbar adjustment, Memory Pkg. (memory seats, outside mirrors, climate control, and radio presets), Zebrano wood trim, Active Audio System with cassette and 11 speakers, automatic windshield wipers, rear illuminated visor mirrors, gold trim/badging, chrome wheels. **De Ville Concours** deletes front storage armrest, gold trim/badging and striping and adds: 4.6-liter DOHC V-8 engine (300 horsepower), continuously variable Road-Sensing Suspension, Stabilitrak, front bucket seats, front floor console, rear storage armrest w/cupholders, analog instrument cluster, tachometer, coolant-temperature gauge, dual exhaust, fog lights, 225/60HR16 blackwall tires.

Optional Equipment:

	Retail Price	Dealer Invoice	Fair Price
Comfort Convenience Pkg., De Ville	$642	$546	$571
Memory Pkg. (memory seats, outside mirrors, climate control, and radio presets), power lumbar adjustment.			
Safety/Security Pkg.	502	427	447
Electronic compass, universal garage-door opener, theft-deterrent system.			
OnStar System	895	761	—
Global Positioning System, voice-activated cellular telephone with steering-wheel radio controls.			
Leather upholstery,			
De Ville	785	667	699
Heated front seats	225	191	200
Power sunroof	1550	1318	1380
Active Audio Sound System,			
De Ville	274	233	244
Includes AM/FM/cassette with 11 speakers.			
Active Audio Sound System, De Ville,			
De Ville d'Elegance and Concours	869	739	773
Includes AM/FM/cassette/CD with 12-disc CD changer and 11 speakers.			
Active Audio Sound System, De Ville,			
De Ville d'Elegance and Concours	1064	904	947
Includes AM/FM/cassette/CD with 12-disc CD changer, digital signal processing, and 11 speakers.			
Chrome wheels	1195	523	1064
3000-lb. Trailer Towing Pkg.	110	94	98
White diamond or			
pearl red paint	500	425	445

CADILLAC ELDORADO

Cadillac Eldorado

Specifications

	2-door notchback
Wheelbase, in.	108.0
Overall length, in.	200.2
Overall width, in.	75.5
Overall height, in.	54.0
Curb weight, lbs.	3821
Cargo vol., cu. ft.	15.3
Fuel capacity, gals.	20.0
Seating capacity	5

Engines

	dohc V-8	dohc V-8
Size, liters/cu. in.	4.6/279	4.6/279
Horsepower @ rpm	275 @ 5600	300 @ 6000
Torque (lbs./ft.) @ rpm	300 @ 4000	295 @ 4400
EPA city/highway mpg		
4-speed OD automatic	17/26	17/26

Built in Hamtramck, Mich.

PRICES

Cadillac Eldorado	Retail Price	Dealer Invoice	Fair Price
2-door notchback	$37995	$34765	$35565
Touring Coupe 2-door notchback	41395	37876	38676
Destination charge	665	665	665

Standard Equipment:

4.6-liter DOHC V-8 engine (275 horsepower), 4-speed automatic

Prices are accurate at time of publication; subject to manufacturer's change.

CADILLAC

transmission, anti-lock 4-wheel disc brakes, driver- and passenger-side air bags, Magnasteer variable-assist steering, Integrated Chassis Control System, automatic level control, traction control, automatic climate control, cruise control, cloth 8-way power front bucket seats, center console with armrest and storage bins, overhead storage compartment, power windows, automatic power locks, remote keyless entry system, heated power mirrors, rear defogger, solar-control tinted glass, automatic day/night rearview mirror, AM/FM/cassette player with six speakers, power antenna, remote fuel-door and decklid release, power decklid pull-down, trip odometer, Driver Information Center, Zebrano wood trim, driver-side visor storage flap, intermittent wipers, leather-wrapped steering wheel with controls for radio and climate system, tilt steering wheel, valet lockout, Pass-Key II theft-deterrent system, automatic parking-brake release, dual exhaust, Twilight Sentinel headlamp control, daytime running lamps, wiper-activated headlights, fog lamps, cornering lamps, illuminated entry, reading lights, illuminated visor mirrors, floormats, trunk mat and cargo net, 225/60R16 tires, alloy wheels. **Touring Coupe** adds: high-output 4.6-liter DOHC V-8 engine (300 horsepower), continuously-variable Road-Sensing Suspension, Stabilitrak, leather upholstery, Memory Pkg. (memory seats, outside mirrors, climate control, and radio presets), power lumbar adjusters, rear-seat storage armrest with cupholders, analog instrument cluster, tachometer, coolant-temperature gauge, automatic windshield wiper system, automatic day/night driver-side mirror, theft-deterrent system, 225/60HR16 tires.

Optional Equipment:

	Retail Price	Dealer Invoice	Fair Price
Sport Pkg., base	$1223	$1040	$1088
Leather upholstery, power lumbar adjusters, Sport Interior (analog instrument cluster, floor console with leather-wrapped shift knob).			
Comfort/Convenience Pkg., base	437	371	389
Memory Pkg. (memory seats, outside mirrors, climate control, and radio presets), automatic day/night driver-side mirror.			
Safety/Security Pkg., base	502	427	447
Electronic compass, universal garage-door opener, theft-deterrent system.			
OnStar System	895	761	—
Global Positioning System, voice-activated cellular telephone with steering-wheel radio controls.			
Power sunroof	1550	1318	1380
Heated front seats	225	191	200
Bose sound system	723	615	643
Includes AM/FM/cassette player with four Bose amplified speakers.			
Bose sound system	1318	1120	1173
Includes AM/FM/cassette/CD player with 12-disc changer and four Bose amplified speakers.			

	Retail Price	Dealer Invoice	Fair Price
Bose sound system	$1513	$1286	$1347

Includes AM/FM/cassette/CD player with 12-disc changer, digital signal processing, and four Bose amplified speakers.

	Retail Price	Dealer Invoice	Fair Price
Electronic compass, Touring Coupe	100	85	89
Universal garage-door opener, Touring Coupe	107	91	95
White diamond or red pearl paint	500	425	445
Striping, base	75	64	67
225/60R16 whitewall tires, base	76	65	68
225/60ZR16 tires, Touring Coupe	250	213	223
Chrome wheels	1195	523	1064

CADILLAC SEVILLE

Cadillac Seville SLS

Specifications

	4-door notchback
Wheelbase, in.	111.0
Overall length, in.	204.1
Overall width, in.	74.2
Overall height, in.	54.5
Curb weight, lbs.	3900
Cargo vol., cu. ft.	14.4
Fuel capacity, gals.	20.0
Seating capacity	5

Engines

	dohc V-8	dohc V-8
Size, liters/cu. in.	4.6/279	4.6/279
Horsepower @ rpm	275 @ 5600	300 @ 6000
Torque (lbs./ft.) @ rpm.....................	300 @ 4000	295 @ 4400

CADILLAC

EPA city/highway mpg

	dohc V-8	dohc V-8
4-speed OD automatic......................................	17/26	17/26

Built in Hamtramck, Mich.

PRICES

Cadillac Seville	Retail Price	Dealer Invoice	Fair Price
SLS 4-door notchback	$39995	$36595	$37395
STS 4-door notchback	44995	41170	41970
Destination charge	665	665	665

Standard Equipment:

SLS: 4.6-liter DOHC V-8 engine (275 horsepower), 4-speed automatic transmission, anti-lock 4-wheel disc brakes, driver- and passenger-side air bags, dual-zone automatic climate control with outside temperature display, MAGNASTEER variable-assist steering, continuously variable Road-Sensing Suspension, traction control, automatic level control, cloth 8-way power front seats with articulating headrests and power recliners, center storage console with armrest, overhead console, driver-side visor storage flap, Zebrano wood trim, power windows, programmable power door locks, valet lockout, cruise control, heated power mirrors, automatic day/night rearview mirror, AM/FM/cassette with six speakers, power antenna, remote fuel-door and decklid releases, power decklid pull-down, Driver Information Center, Pass-Key II theft-deterrent system, remote keyless entry, leather-wrapped tilt steering wheel with controls for radio and climate system, intermittent wipers, wiper-activated headlights, rear defogger, solar-control tinted glass, floormats, decklid liner, trunk mat and cargo net, Twilight Sentinel headlamp control, cornering lamps, daytime running lamps, reading lights, lighted visor mirrors, illuminated entry, trip odometer, automatic parking-brake release, 225/60R16 tires, alloy wheels. **STS** adds: 4.6-liter V-8 DOHC engine (300 horsepower), Stabilitrak, leather upholstery, Memory Pkg. (memory seats, outside mirrors, climate control, and radio presets), rear-seat center storage armrest, power lumbar adjustment, automatic windshield wipers, analog instruments with tachometer, full console, driver-side automatic day/night outside mirror, theft-deterrent system, fog lamps, 225/60HR16 tires.

Optional Equipment:

Sport Pkg., SLS	1223	1040	1088

Leather upholstery, power lumbar adjustment, Sport Interior (analog instruments and floor console with leather-wrapped shift knob).

	Retail Price	Dealer Invoice	Fair Price
Comfort/Convenience Pkg., SLS	$437	$371	$389
Memory Pkg. (memory seats, outside mirrors, climate control, and radio presets), automatic day/night driver-side mirror.			
Safety/Security Pkg., SLS	502	427	447
Electronic compass, universal garage-door opener, theft-deterrent system.			
OnStar System	895	761	—
Global Positioning System, voice-activated cellular telephone with steering-wheel radio controls.			
Power sunroof	1550	1318	1380
Heated front seats	225	191	200
Electronic compass, STS	100	85	89
Bose Sound System	723	615	643
Includes AM/FM/cassette with four Bose amplified speakers.			
Bose Sound System	1318	1120	1173
Includes AM/FM/cassette/CD player with 12-disc CD changer and four Bose amplified speakers.			
Bose Sound System	1513	1286	1347
Includes AM/FM/cassette/CD player with 12-disc CD changer, digital signal processing, and four Bose amplified speakers.			
Universal garage-door opener, STS	107	91	95
White diamond or red pearl paint	500	425	445
Striping, SLS	75	64	67
Chrome wheels	1195	523	1064
225/60ZR16 tires, STS	250	213	223

CHEVROLET BLAZER/ GMC JIMMY/ OLDSMOBILE BRAVADA

Specifications	2-door wagon	4-door wagon
Wheelbase, in.	100.5	107.0
Overall length, in.	174.7	181.2
Overall width, in.	67.8	67.8
Overall height, in.	66.9	66.9
Curb weight, lbs.	3874	4046
Cargo vol., cu. ft.	66.9	74.1
Fuel capacity, gals................................	19.0	18.0
Seating capacity...................................	4	6

Prices are accurate at time of publication; subject to manufacturer's change.

Chevrolet Blazer 4-door

Engines

ohv V-6

Size, liters/cu. in.	4.3/262
Horsepower @ rpm	190 @ 4400
Torque (lbs./ft.) @ rpm	250 @ 2800

EPA city/highway mpg

5-speed OD manual	17/22
4-speed OD automatic	16/21

Built in Moraine, Ohio, and Linden, N.J.

PRICES

Chevrolet Blazer	Retail Price	Dealer Invoice	Fair Price
2-door wagon, 2WD	$20516	$18567	$19716
2-door wagon, 4WD	22116	20015	21316
4-door wagon, 2WD	22041	19947	21241
4-door wagon, 4WD	24116	21825	23316
Destination charge	515	515	515

Standard Equipment:

2WD: 4.3-liter V-6 engine, 4-speed automatic transmission, anti-lock brakes, driver-side air bag, power steering, air conditioning, cloth front bucket seats with manual lumbar adjustment and console (2-door), cloth 60/40 split front bench seat with storage armrest (4-door), solar-control tinted glass, trip odometer, coolant-temperature and oil-pressure gauges, voltmeter, AM/FM radio, digital clock, dual outside mirrors, cupholders, intermittent wipers, floormats, cargo-area tiedown hooks, daytime running lights, bright grille, 5-lead trailer wiring harness, smooth suspension, 205/75R15 all-season tires. **4WD** adds: Insta-Trac part-time 4WD, split folding rear bench seat (4-door), tow hooks.

Optional Equipment:

	Retail Price	Dealer Invoice	Fair Price
5-speed manual transmission, 2-door (credit) ..	($890)	($765)	($765)

Requires tachometer.

	Retail Price	Dealer Invoice	Fair Price
Locking differential	252	217	239
Electronic-shift transfer case, 4WD	123	106	117

Requires automatic transmission when ordered with standard or optional bucket seats.

All-wheel drive, 4-door 4WD w/Group 1SE .	265	228	252

Includes 4-wheel disc brakes. Deletes electronic-shift transfer case. Requires premium suspension (included in Group 1SE). NA with Shield Pkg.

ZQ3 convenience group	395	340	375

Cruise control, tilt steering wheel.

ZQ6 convenience group, 2-door	535	460	508
4-door	710	611	675

Power windows, door locks, and mirrors.

Rear-window convenience pkg.	322	277	306

Rear defogger, remote tailgate release, rear wiper/washer.

Preferred Equipment Group 1SB, 2WD	418	359	397
2-door 4WD	541	465	514
4-door 4WD	66	57	63

Electronic-shift transfer case (4WD w/std. automatic transmission), ZQ3 convenience group (tilt steering wheel, cruise control), split folding rear bench seat, cassette player, luggage rack.

Preferred Equipment Group 1SC,

2-door 2WD	1696	1459	1611
4-door 2WD	2306	1983	2191
2-door 4WD	1819	1564	1728
4-door 4WD	1954	1680	1856

Group 1SB plus ZQ6 convenience group (power windows, door locks, and mirrors), LS Decor Group (upgraded cloth upholstery, deep-tinted rear glass, rear window wiper/washer, additional cupholders [4-door], leather-wrapped steering wheel, remote tailgate release, rear defogger, map light, covered power outlets, rear compartment shade [4-door], bodyside molding [4-door], composite headlights [4-door], argent alloy wheels [2WD], cast alloy wheels [4WD]), touring suspension (2-door), premium suspension (4-door), 235/70R15 tires.

Preferred Equipment Group 1SD,

2-door 2WD	2218	1907	2107
4-door 2WD	2989	2571	2840
2-door 4WD	2341	2013	2224
4-door 4WD	2637	2268	2505

Group 1SC plus bucket seats with console, 6-way power driver seat, overhead console, remote keyless entry.

CHEVROLET

	Retail Price	Dealer Invoice	Fair Price
Preferred Equipment Group 1SE,			
4-door 2WD	$4561	$3922	$4333
4-door 4WD	4094	3521	3889

Group 1SD plus LT Decor Group (LS Decor Group plus leather bucket seats with power lumbar support and 4-way adjustable headrest, Homelink universal garage-door opener (includes trip computer, compass, outside-temperature indicator), front bumper rub strip, color-keyed grille, wheel-lip moldings), cassette player with equalizer and six speakers, air dam with fog lamps (2WD), color-keyed grille, tachometer.

	Retail Price	Dealer Invoice	Fair Price
Split folding rear seat	475	409	451
Bucket seats with console,			
4-door w/Group 1SC	161	138	153
6-way power driver seat, w/Group 1SC	240	206	228

Requires remote keyless entry.

	Retail Price	Dealer Invoice	Fair Price
Power sunroof	695	598	660

Requires overhead console.

	Retail Price	Dealer Invoice	Fair Price
Homelink universal garage-door opener	130	112	124

Includes trip computer, compass, outside-temperature indicator. Requires overhead console.

	Retail Price	Dealer Invoice	Fair Price
Remote keyless entry system	135	116	128

Requires Group 1SC and 6-way power driver seat.

	Retail Price	Dealer Invoice	Fair Price
Cold Climate Pkg.	89	77	85

Includes heavy-duty battery, engine block heater.

	Retail Price	Dealer Invoice	Fair Price
Overhead console	147	126	140

NA with bench seat. Requires power sunroof when ordered without a Preferred Equipment Group or with Group 1SB.

	Retail Price	Dealer Invoice	Fair Price
Luggage rack	126	108	120
Air dam with fog lamps, 2WD	115	99	109

Requires Group 1SC or 1SD.

	Retail Price	Dealer Invoice	Fair Price
Tachometer	59	51	56
Radio delete (credit)	(226)	(194)	(194)

NA with Preferred Equipment Groups.

	Retail Price	Dealer Invoice	Fair Price
Cassette player	122	105	116
Cassette player with equalizer and			
six speakers	327	281	311
with Group 1SB, 1SC, or 1SD	205	176	195
CD player, with Group 1SC or 1SD	329	283	313
with Group 1SE	124	107	118
Shield Pkg., 4WD	126	108	120

Includes transfer case and front differential skid plates, fuel tank and steering linkage shields. NA with all-wheel drive.

	Retail Price	Dealer Invoice	Fair Price
Smooth suspension (credit)	(275)	(237)	(237)

Requires Group 1SC, 1SD, or 1SE.

	Retail Price	Dealer Invoice	Fair Price
ZR2 Wide-Stance Sport Performance Pkg., 2-door 4WD	$1850	$1591	$1758
Heavy-duty wide-stance chassis, heavy-duty suspension, Shield Pkg., LS trim, fender flares, 31×10.5R15 tires, full-size spare tire. Requires Group 1SC, 1SD, or 1SE. NA w/Trailering Special Equipment.			
Touring suspension	197	169	187
w/Group 1SC, 1SD, or 1SE	NC	NC	NC
Includes gas shock absorbers.			
Off-road suspension, 2-door 4WD	610	525	580
2-door 4WD with Group 1SC or 1SD	221	190	210
Includes gas shock absorbers, uprated torsion bar, jounce stabilizer bar, full-size spare tire, 235/75R15 on/off road white-outline-letter tires.			
Premium suspension, 4-door	197	169	187
4-door w/Group 1SC, 1SD, or 1SE	NC	NC	NC
Includes gas shock absorbers.			
Trailering Special Equipment	210	181	200
Includes platform hitch, heavy-duty flasher. 2WD models require automatic transmission.			
Rear liftgate, 4-door	NC	NC	NC
Requires ZQ6 convenience group and rear-window convenience pkg. when ordered without a Preferred Equipment Group or with Group 1SB.			
Heavy-duty battery	56	48	53
Custom 2-tone paint, 4-door	197	169	187
Requires LS Decor Group or LT Decor Group.			
Exterior spare-tire carrier, 2-door 4WD	214	184	203
Includes full-size spare tire and cover.			
Rear compartment shade, 2-door 4WD with LS Decor Group	69	59	66
Requires exterior spare-tire carrier.			
Argent alloy wheels, 2WD	248	213	236
Cast alloy wheels, 4WD	280	241	266
205/75R15 all-season white-letter tires	121	104	115
235/70R15 all-season tires	192	165	182
235/70R15 all-season white-outline-letter tires	325	280	304
w/Group 1SC, 1SD, or 1SE	133	114	126
235/75R15 on/off road white-outline-letter tires, 4WD	335	288	318
4WD w/Preferred Equipment Group	143	123	136
Requires off-road or touring suspension. Includes exterior spare-tire carrier.			

GMC Jimmy	Retail Price	Dealer Invoice	Fair Price
2-door wagon, 2WD	$20639	$18678	$19839
2-door wagon, 4WD	22487	20351	21687
4-door wagon, 2WD	22164	20058	21364
4-door wagon, 4WD	24487	22161	23687
Destination charge	515	515	515

Standard Equipment:

2-door: 4.3-liter V-6 engine, 4-speed automatic transmission, anti-lock brakes, driver-side air bag, air conditioning, power steering, reclining cloth front bucket seats with lumbar adjusters, storage console with cupholders, tinted glass, coolant-temperature and oil-pressure gauges, tachometer, voltmeter, trip odometer, AM/FM radio, digital clock, dual outside manual mirrors, illuminated entry, intermittent wipers, passenger-side visor mirror, rear tailgate, floormats, 205/75R15 tires, trailering harness, wheel trim rings. **4-door** deletes console with storage and cupholders and adds: cloth 60/40 front bench seat with storage armrest, folding rear 3-passenger bench seat. **4WD models** have part-time 4WD with electronic transfer case, front tow hooks.

Optional Equipment:

5-speed manual transmission (credit), 2-door	(890)	(765)	(765)
Roof rack	126	108	120
All-wheel drive, 4-door 4WD	265	228	252

Includes 4-wheel disc brakes. Requires SLT Pkg. 7, Luxury Ride Suspension Pkg. NA w/Shield Pkg.

Optional axle ratio	NC	NC	NC
Locking differential	252	217	239
Manual transfer case, 4WD (credit)	(123)	(106)	(106)

4-door requires 60/40 front bench seat. 2-door requires 5-speed manual transmission.

SL Pkg. 2, 2-door	1342	1154	1275

Base plus cassette player, power windows and door locks, power mirrors, cruise control, tilt steering wheel, split folding rear 3-passenger bench seat, Euro-Ride Suspension Pkg., roof rack, 235/70R15 tires.

SLS Pkg. 3, 2-door	1973	1697	1874

SL Pkg. 2 contents plus SLS Sport Decor Pkg. (auxiliary power outlets, leather-wrapped steering wheel, illuminated visor mirrors, power remote tailgate release, rear defogger, intermittent rear wiper/washer, striping, deep-tinted tailgate glass, cloth door-trim panels, reading lamps, cargo net, alloy wheels).

	Retail Price	Dealer Invoice	Fair Price
SL Pkg. 5, 4-door 2WD	$1517	$1305	$1441
4-door 4WD	1042	896	990

Base plus cassette player, power windows and door locks, power mirrors, cruise control, tilt steering wheel, Luxury Ride Suspension Pkg., roof rack, 235/70R15 tires.

SLS Pkg. 6, 4-door 2WD	2398	2062	2278
4-door 4WD	1923	1654	1827

SL Pkg. 5 plus SLS Sport Decor Pkg. (front reclining cloth bucket seats w/manual lumbar support adjusters, leather-wrapped steering wheel, illuminated visor mirrors, rear liftgate, power remote liftgate release, rear defogger, intermittent rear wiper/washer, console w/storage and cupholders, striping, deep-tinted liftgate glass, cloth door-trim panels, reading lamps, cargo cover, cargo net, alloy wheels).

SLE Pkg. 6, 4-door 2WD	2700	2322	2565
4-door 4WD	2225	1914	2114

SL Pkg. 5 contents plus SLE Comfort Decor Pkg. (front reclining cloth bucket seats with manual lumbar support adjusters, cloth door-trim panels, console with storage and cupholders, reading lamps, dual auxiliary power outlets, leather-wrapped steering wheel, illuminated visor mirrors, rear liftgate, power remote liftgate release, rear defogger, intermittent rear wiper/washer, lower body moldings, deep-tinted rear glass, cargo cover, cargo net, alloy wheels).

SLT Pkg. 7, 4-door 2WD	4350	3741	4133
4-door 4WD	3875	3333	3681

SL Pkg. 5 contents plus SLT Touring Decor Pkg. (leather front bucket seats with power lumbar support adjusters, 6-way power driver seat, leather upholstery, console with storage and cupholders, overhead console with reading lamps, outside-temperature gauge and compass, remote keyless entry system, dual auxiliary power outlets, leather-wrapped steering wheel, illuminated visor mirrors, rear liftgate, power remote liftgate release, rear defogger, intermittent rear wiper/washer, simulated leather door-trim panels, lower body moldings, deep-tinted liftgate glass, cargo cover, cargo net, alloy wheels), cassette player with equalizer. 4WD deletes split folding rear 3-passenger bench seat.

Power glass sunroof	695	598	660

Requires overhead console.

Rear liftgate, base 4-door,			
4-door w/SL Pkg.	NC	NC	NC

Replaces rear tailgate. Requires Convenience Pkg. ZQ6.

Rear tailgate	NC	NC	NC

Replaces rear liftgate in Pkg. SLS, SLE, or SLT.

Split folding rear seat, 2-door	475	409	451
Rear seat delete, SL	NC	NC	NC

Prices are accurate at time of publication; subject to manufacturer's change.

CHEVROLET

	Retail Price	Dealer Invoice	Fair Price
Cloth 60/40 front bench seat with storage armrest, 4-door (credit)	($161)	($138)	($138)

NA with SLT Pkg. 7. NA with 2-door 2WD when ordered with heavy-duty trailering equipment.

6-way power driver seat and remote keyless entry, SLS, SLE	375	323	356
Overhead console	147	126	140

Includes reading lights, outside-temperature gauge, compass. Requires SLS or SLE Pkgs., bucket seats.

Heavy-duty battery	56	48	53
Cold Climate Pkg.	89	77	85

Heavy-duty battery, engine-block heater.

Convenience Pkg. ZQ3	395	340	375

Cruise control, tilt steering wheel.

Convenience Pkg. ZM8	322	277	306

Power remote tailgate/liftgate release, rear defogger, rear wiper/washer.

Convenience Pkg. ZQ6, 2-door	535	460	508
4-door	710	611	675

Power windows, mirrors, and door locks.

Air deflector with fog lamps, 2WD	115	99	109

Requires option pkg.

Cassette player	122	105	116
Cassette player with equalizer	327	281	311
SLS, SLE	205	176	195
CD player, SLS, SLE, SLT	329	283	313
Radio delete, SL (credit)	(226)	(194)	(194)
Homelink universal garage-door opener and trip computer	130	112	124

Requires overhead console.

Shield Pkg., 4WD	126	108	120

Front differential skid plates, transfer-case, steering-linkage and fuel-tank shields.

Smooth Ride Suspension Pkg., 4-door with option pkg.	114	98	108

Gas shock absorbers, front and rear stabilizer bars. Requires 205/75R15 tires.

Luxury Ride Suspension Pkg., 4-door	197	169	187

Gas shock absorbers, urethane jounce bumpers, front and rear stabilizer bars. Requires 235/75R15 tires.

Solid Smooth Ride Suspension Pkg., 2-door with Pkg. 2 or 3	114	98	108

Gas shock absorbers, urethane jounce bumpers, front and rear stabilizer bars, upgraded rear springs. Requires 205/75R15 tires.

	Retail Price	Dealer Invoice	Fair Price
Euro-Ride Suspension Pkg.	$197	$169	$187

Gas shock absorbers, front and rear stabilizer bars, heavy-duty springs. Requires 235/70R15 tires.

Off-road Suspension Pkg., 2-door 4WD	220	189	209

Gas shock absorbers, urethane jounce bumpers, front and rear stabilizer bars, upgraded torsion bars. Requires 235/75R15 on/off-road white-letter tires.

Heavy-duty trailering equipment	210	181	200

Weight distributing hitch platform, 8-lead wiring harness, heavy-duty flasher. NA with 4-door 2WD when ordered with 60/40 front bench seat.

Two-tone paint, 4-door	172	148	162

Requires SLE or SLT Pkgs. NA with Gold Edition.

205/75R15 all-season white-letter tires	121	104	115
235/70R15 all-season tires	192	165	182
235/70R15 all-season white-letter tires	325	280	309
235/75R15 on/off-road white-letter tires,			
2-door 4WD	335	288	318
4-door 4WD	390	335	371

2-door includes full-size spare tire. 2-door requires exterior spare-tire carrier. Requires Euro-Ride or Off-Road Suspension Pkg.

Exterior spare-tire carrier, 2-door 4WD	214	184	203

Includes full-size spare tire.

Alloy wheels, 2WD	248	213	236
4WD	280	241	266
Cargo cover, 2-door 4WD with			
SLS Pkg.	69	59	66

Requires exterior spare-tire carrier.

Oldsmobile Bravada	Retail Price	Dealer Invoice	Fair Price
4-door wagon	$30385	$27498	—
Destination charge	515	515	515

Fair price not available at time of publication.

Standard Equipment:

4.3-liter V-6 engine, 4-speed automatic transmission, 4-wheel drive, anti-lock 4-wheel disc brakes, driver-side air bag, air conditioning, power steering, cruise control, leather upholstery, front reclining bucket seats with power lumbar adjustment, 6-way power driver's seat, split folding rear bench seat, center console with storage armrest and cupholders, overhead storage console (trip computer, compass, reading lamps, outside temperature gauge, and universal garage-door opener), AM/FM/cassette with equalizer, power antenna, digital clock, tilt steering wheel, power windows, rear defogger, tachometer, oil-pressure and coolant-temperature gauges, voltmeter, trip odometer, power mirrors, tinted windows, illuminated visor mirrors, remote keyless entry, intermittent wipers, auxiliary power outlets, front tow hooks, 5-wire trailer-towing electrical harness, luggage rack, fog lamps, daytime running lamps, floormats, cargo net and cover, striping, 235/70R15 all-season tires, alloy wheels.

Optional Equipment:	Retail Price	Dealer Invoice	Fair Price
Cloth upholstery	NC	NC	NC
Power sunroof	$695	$598	—
CD player	124	107	—
Includes six speakers.			
Towing Pkg.	210	181	—
Heavy-duty suspension and hazard lights, 7-wire electrical harness, platform hitch, engine-oil cooler.			
Gold Pkg.	50	43	—
Gold badging, gold wheel trim, beige striping.			
White-letter tires	133	114	—
Engine block heater	33	28	—

CHEVROLET CAMARO/ PONTIAC FIREBIRD

Chevrolet Camaro convertible RS

Specifications	2-door hatchback	2-door convertible
Wheelbase, in.	101.1	101.1
Overall length, in.	193.2	193.2
Overall width, in.	74.1	74.1
Overall height, in.	51.3	52.0
Curb weight, lbs.	3307	3455

	2-door hatchback	2-door convertible
Cargo vol., cu. ft.	33.7	7.6
Fuel capacity, gals.	15.5	15.5
Seating capacity	4	4

Engines

	ohv V-6	ohv V-8	ohv V-8
Size, liters/cu. in.	3.8/231	5.7/350	5.7/350
Horsepower @ rpm	200 @ 5200	285 @ 5200	305 @ 5500
Torque (lbs./ft.) @ rpm	225 @ 4000	325 @ 2400	325 @ 2400
EPA city/highway mpg			
5-speed OD manual	19/30		
6-speed OD manual		16/27	16/27
4-speed OD automatic	19/29	17/25	17/25

Built in Canada.

PRICES

Chevrolet Camaro	Retail Price	Dealer Invoice	Fair Price
2-door hatchback	$16215	$14837	$15337
2-door convertible	21770	19920	20770
RS 2-door hatchback	17970	16443	17243
RS 2-door convertible	23170	21201	22170
Z28 2-door hatchback	20115	18405	19115
Z28 2-door convertible	25520	23351	24520
Destination charge	525	525	525

Standard Equipment:

3.8-liter V-6 engine, 5-speed manual transmission, anti-lock brakes, air conditioning, driver- and passenger-side air bags, power steering, cloth reclining front bucket seats with 4-way adjustable driver seat, center storage console with cupholders and auxiliary power outlet, folding rear seatback, solar-control tinted glass, left remote and right manual sport mirrors, tilt steering wheel, intermittent wipers, AM/FM/cassette, digital clock, day/night rearview mirror with dual reading lights, Pass-Key theft-deterrent system, tachometer, voltmeter, oil-pressure and coolant-temperature gauges, trip odometer, low-oil-level indicator, visor mirrors, daytime running lamps, rear spoiler, front floormats, 215/60R16 all-season tires, wheel covers. **RS** adds: RS ground effects, 235/55R16 tires, alloy wheels. **Z28** adds: 5.7-liter V-8 engine, 6-speed manual transmission, 4-wheel disc brakes, limited-slip differential, performance ride and handling

Prices are accurate at time of publication; subject to manufacturer's change.

suspension, 2-way adjustable driver seat (hatchback), black roof and mirrors, low-coolant indicator system, alloy wheels. **Convertibles** add: rear defogger, power folding top, 3-piece hard boot with storage bag, color-keyed mirrors (Z28), 4-way adjustable driver seat (Z28).

Optional Equipment:

	Retail Price	Dealer Invoice	Fair Price
4-speed automatic transmission	$815	$701	$774
Hurst 6-speed manual shifter, Z28	349	289	321

Includes leather-wrapped shift knob. Requires SS Pkg.

Traction control, Z28	450	387	414

Requires Preferred Equipment Group.

Torsen torque-sensing limited slip differential,

Z28	999	829	919

Includes Performance Lubricants Pkg., aluminum rear-axle cover. Requires SS Pkg.

Removable roof panels, hatchbacks	995	856	945

Includes locks, storage provisions, and sun shade. NA Performance Pkg.

Base Preferred Equipment Group 1,

base hatchback	345	297	307
RS hatchback	565	486	503
Z28 hatchback	600	516	534
convertible	565	486	503

Power door locks (RS, Z28, convertible), cruise control, 4-way adjustable driver seat (Z28), remote hatch/decklid release, fog lights.

Base Preferred Equipment Group 2,

base hatchback	1231	1059	1133
RS hatchback	1231	1059	1133
Z28 hatchback	1266	1089	1127
convertible	1231	1059	1133

Group 1 plus power windows with driver-side express down, power door locks (base hatchback) and mirrors, remote keyless entry, leather-wrapped steering wheel, shifter, and brake handle, theft-deterrent alarm.

Performance Pkg., base, RS	400	344	368

Limited-slip differential, 4-wheel disc brakes, sport steering ratio, dual outlet exhaust, 3.42 rear axle ratio (with automatic transmission). Requires Preferred Equipment Group. Base requires 235/55R16 tires, alloy wheels.

Performance Pkg., Z28 hatchback	1175	1011	1081

Special Handling Suspension System (includes larger stabilizer bars, stiffer adjustable shock absorbers and bushings). Requires performance axle ratio (when ordered with automatic transmission), 245/50ZR16 tires. NA with Preferred Equipment Groups.

	Retail Price	Dealer Invoice	Fair Price
SS Pkg., Z28	$3999	$3439	$3679

Upgraded suspension (hatchback), forced air induction system, synthetic engine oil, rear spoiler, hood scoop, alloy wheels, 275/40ZR17 tires (hatchback). NA w/traction control. Convertible requires 245/50ZR16 tires. Requires performance axle ratio when ordered with automatic transmission.

Performance Lubricants Pkg., Z28	79	68	73

Synthetic engine oil filter and rear axle filter, semi-synthetic power steering fluid. Requires SS Pkg.

30th Anniversary Edition, Z28	575	495	546

White monochromatic exterior with orange striping, 30th Anniversary front floormats and headrests, white 5-spoke alloy wheels. Requires Preferred Group 2, 6-way power driver seat, and 245/50ZR16 tires.

Suspension Pkg., Z28 hatchback	999	829	919

Bilstein shocks, progressive-rate springs. Requires SS Pkg.

6-way power driver seat	270	232	248

Z28 hatchback requires option group. NA Performance Pkg.

Leather bucket seats	499	429	459

Includes 4-way adjustable driver seat. Z28 hatchback requires option group.

Performance axle ratio, Z28	300	258	285

Requires 4-speed automatic transmission and 245/50ZR16 tires.

Performance exhaust system, Z28	499	414	474

Requires SS Pkg.

Rear defogger, hatchbacks	170	146	156
Power door locks, base hatchback	220	189	202

Requires Preferred Group 1.

Remote keyless entry	225	194	214

Includes theft-deterrent alarm. Requires Preferred Group 1. Hatchback requires power door locks.

Color-keyed roof and mirrors, base with removable roof panels	NC	NC	NC
AM/FM/cassette with automatic tone control	215	185	198
AM/FM/CD with automatic tone control	315	271	290
12-disc CD changer	595	512	565

Requires AM/FM/cassette with automatic tone control.

Color-keyed bodyside moldings	60	52	55
Front floormats, Z28	99	82	91

Requires SS Pkg.

Rear floormats	15	13	14
Car cover, Z28	159	132	146

Requires SS Pkg.

Prices are accurate at time of publication; subject to manufacturer's change.

	Retail Price	Dealer Invoice	Fair Price
Engine-block heater	$20	$17	$19
235/55R16 tires, base	132	114	121
Requires alloy wheels.			
245/50ZR16 performance tires, Z28	225	194	207
245/50ZR16 all-season performance tires, Z28	225	194	207
Alloy wheels, base	275	237	253
Requires 235/55R16 tires.			
Chrome wheels, RS	775	667	736
Z28	500	430	460

Pontiac Firebird	Retail Price	Dealer Invoice	Fair Price
2-door hatchback	$17174	15714	—
2-door convertible	23084	21122	—
Formula 2-door hatchback	20724	18962	—
Formula 2-door convertible	26524	24269	—
Trans Am 2-door hatchback	22884	20939	—
Trans Am 2-door convertible	28444	26026	—
Destination charge	525	525	525

Fair price not available at time of publication.

Standard Equipment:

Base: 3.8-liter V-6 engine, 5-speed manual transmission, anti-lock brakes, air conditioning, power steering, driver- and passenger-side air bags, cloth reclining front bucket seats, folding rear bench seat, tilt steering wheel, center console (storage, auxiliary power outlet, and cup holder), 4-speaker AM/FM/cassette player with equalizer, intermittent wipers, tinted glass, left remote and right manual mirrors, coolant-temperature and oil-pressure gauges, tachometer, voltmeter, trip odometer, Pass-Key II theft-deterrent system, dual reading lamps, visor mirrors, remote hatch release, floormats, daytime running lamps, front air dam, decklid spoiler, 215/60R16 touring tires, alloy wheels. **Convertible** adds: cruise control, power door locks, power windows, power mirrors, power top with glass rear window and defogger, 6-speaker sound system, rear decklid release. **Formula** adds to base hatchback: 5.7-liter V-8 engine, 4-speed automatic transmission, anti-lock 4-wheel disc brakes, air conditioning, performance suspension, 235/55R16 touring tires. **Formula convertible** includes Formula and base convertible standard equipment. **Trans Am** adds to Formula hatchback: cruise control, 4-way adjustable driver seat, leather-wrapped steering wheel, shift knob, and parking brake handle, power windows, power mirrors, power door locks, rear defogger, decklid spoiler, fog lights. **Trans Am convertible** adds to Trans Am and base convertible: power antenna, steering-wheel radio controls, remote keyless entry system, 245/50ZR16 all-weather performance tires.

Optional Equipment:

	Retail Price	Dealer Invoice	Fair Price
4-speed automatic transmission, base	$815	$725	$750
6-speed manual transmission, Formula, Trans Am	NC	NC	NC

NA on Formula 2-door with group 1SB.

Traction control, Formula, Trans Am	450	401	414

Requires 235/55R16 touring tires or 245/50ZR16 all-weather performance tires.

Option Group 1SB, base and Formula hatchbacks	1121	998	1031

Cruise control, power mirrors, power windows, power door locks, 4-speaker CD player with equalizer, rear defogger.

Option Group 1SB, base and Formula convertibles	435	387	400

Remote keyless entry, power antenna, steering-wheel with radio controls, leather-wrapped steering wheel and shifter.

3800 Performance Pkg., base	550	490	506

Limited-slip differential, 4-wheel disc brakes, faster-ratio steering gear, dual exhaust outlets, 3.42 rear axle ratio (with automatic transmission), 235/55R16 touring tires.

Sport Appearance Pkg., base	1449	1290	1333

Sport Appearance, fog lights, dual exhaust outlets. Requires 235/55R16 touring tires.

1LE Performance Pkg., Formula hatchback	1175	1046	1081

Requires 6-speed manual transmission and Ram Air Performance and Handling Pkg. Rear defogger is the only available option with this pkg.

Ram Air Performance and Handling Pkg., Formula and Trans Am hatchbacks	3345	2977	3077

Ram Air induction system, upgraded suspension, dual bright exhaust outlets, 275/40ZR17 tires, high-polished alloy wheels.

Ram Air Performance Pkg., Formula and Trans Am convertibles	2995	2666	2755

Ram Air induction system, dual exhaust outlets, 245/50ZR16 high-performance tires, chromed alloy wheels.

Rear performance axle, Formula, Trans Am	225	200	207

Includes 3.23 axle ratio. Requires 4-speed automatic transmission and 245/50ZR16 or 275/40ZR17 tires (in Ram Air Performance and Handling Pkg.).

CHEVROLET

	Retail Price	Dealer Invoice	Fair Price
Cruise control, base and Formula hatchbacks	$235	$209	$216
Rear defogger, base and Formula hatchbacks	180	160	166
Removable locking hatch roof, hatchbacks .	995	886	915
Includes sunshades, lock, and stowage.			
Content theft alarm	90	80	83
Requires remote keyless entry system.			
Power mirrors, base and Formula hatchbacks	96	85	88
Requires power door locks and windows.			
Power door locks, base and Formula hatchbacks	220	196	202
Power windows, base and Formula hatchbacks	290	258	267
Requires power door locks and mirrors.			
CD player with equalizer	100	89	92
Cassette player with equalizer and amplifier, hatchbacks	230	205	212
Includes 10-speaker sound system. Base and Formula require power door locks and windows.			
CD player with equalizer and amplifier, hatchbacks	330	294	304
Includes 10-speaker sound system. Base and Formula require power door locks and windows.			
Trunk-mounted 12-disc CD changer	595	530	547
NA with CD players.			
Power antenna	85	76	78
Steering-wheel radio controls, base, Formula	200	178	184
Trans Am hatchback	125	111	115
Includes leather-wrapped steering wheel and shifter.			
Leather articulating bucket seats, base and Formula hatchbacks, convertibles	804	716	740
Trans Am hatchback	829	738	763
Base and Formula require Group 1SB. Hatchbacks require cassette or CD player with equalizer and amplifier.			
6-way power driver seat	270	240	248
Remote keyless entry system	150	134	138
Base and Formula require power windows, power door locks, and mirrors.			
235/55R16 touring tires, base	132	117	121

	Retail Price	Dealer Invoice	Fair Price
245/50ZR16 high-performance tires, Formula, Trans Am .... *NA with traction control.*	$245	$218	$225
245/50ZR16 all-weather performance tires, Formula, Trans Am hatchback	245	218	225
Chromed alloy wheels	595	530	547

CHEVROLET CAVALIER/ PONTIAC SUNFIRE

Chevrolet Cavalier LS 4-door

Specifications

	2-door notchback	2-door conv.	4-door notchback
Wheelbase, in.	104.1	104.1	104.1
Overall length, in.	180.3	180.3	180.3
Overall width, in.	67.4	67.4	67.4
Overall height, in.	53.2	53.9	54.8
Curb weight, lbs.	2617	2838	2676
Cargo vol., cu. ft.	13.2	13.2	13.2
Fuel capacity, gals.	15.2	15.2	15.2
Seating capacity	5	4	5

Engines

	ohv I-4	dohc I-4
Size, liters/cu. in.	2.2/132	2.4/146
Horsepower @ rpm	120 @ 5200	150 @ 5600
Torque (lbs./ft.) @ rpm..	130 @ 4000	150 @ 4400

EPA city/highway mpg

5-speed OD manual	25/37	23/33

Prices are accurate at time of publication; subject to manufacturer's change.

CHEVROLET

	ohv I-4	dohc I-4
3-speed automatic	24/31	
4-speed OD automatic	25/34	22/32

Built in Lordstown, Ohio, and Lansing, Mich.

PRICES

Chevrolet Cavalier	Retail Price	Dealer Invoice	Fair Price
2-door notchback	$10980	$10376	—
4-door notchback	11180	10565	—
RS 2-door notchback	12225	11308	—
LS 4-door notchback	13380	12377	—
LS 2-door convertible	17935	16590	—
Z24 2-door notchback	14465	13235	—
Destination charge	500	500	500

Fair price not available at time of publication.

Standard Equipment:

Base: 2.2-liter 4-cylinder engine, 5-speed manual transmission, anti-lock brakes, driver- and passenger-side air bags, power steering, tinted glass, cloth/vinyl reclining front bucket seats, folding rear seat, storage console with armrest, left remote and right manual mirrors, theft-deterrent system, intermittent wipers, daytime running lights, 195/70R14 tires, wheel covers. **RS** adds: easy-entry front passenger seat, tachometer, trip odometer, AM/FM radio, visor mirrors, variable intermittent wipers, remote decklid release, color-keyed fascias and bodyside moldings, front mud guards, rear decklid spoiler, floormats, trunk net, 195/65R15 tires. **LS** adds to base: 4-speed automatic transmission, traction control, air conditioning, cloth upholstery, tachometer, trip odometer, AM/FM radio, visor mirrors, digital clock, easy-entry front passenger seat (convertible), front reading lamps, power top (convertible), intermittent wipers, remote decklid release, color-keyed fascias and bodyside moldings, rear decklid spoiler (convertible), front mud guards (notchback), floormats, trunk net, 195/65R15 tires. **Z24** deletes 4-speed automatic transmission, traction control, and mud guards and adds to LS notchback: 2.4-liter DOHC 4-cylinder engine, 5-speed manual transmission, sport suspension, easy-entry front passenger seat, tilt steering wheel, cassette player, rear decklid spoiler, fog lights, 205/55R16 tires, alloy wheels.

Optional Equipment:

2.4-liter DOHC 4-cylinder engine, LS	395	352	—
3-speed automatic transmission, base, RS	550	490	—

	Retail Price	Dealer Invoice	Fair Price
4-speed automatic transmission, base, RS, Z24	$795	$708	—
Includes traction control.			
5-speed manual transmission, convertible (credit)	(795)	(708)	(708)
Air conditioning, base, RS	795	708	—
Preferred Equipment Group 1, base 2-door	240	214	—
base 4-door	223	198	—
Remote decklid release, intermittent wipers, visor mirrors, charcoal bodyside moldings, trunk net, front mud guards, floormats. 2-door adds easy-entry front passenger seat.			
Preferred Equipment Group 2, base 2-door	696	619	—
base 4-door	593	528	—
Group 1 plus cruise control, tilt steering wheel, power mirrors (2-door).			
Preferred Equipment Group 3, base 2-door	1295	1153	—
Group 2 plus power windows and door locks, remote keyless entry. Deletes charcoal bodyside moldings. Requires Exterior Appearance Pkg.			
Preferred Equipment Group 1, RS	456	406	—
Cruise control, tilt steering wheel, power mirrors.			
Preferred Equipment Group 2, RS	1055	939	—
Group 2 plus power windows and door locks, remote keyless entry.			
Preferred Equipment Group 1, LS	435	387	—
Tilt steering wheel, intermittent wipers, cruise control.			
Preferred Equipment Group 2, LS 4-door	1225	1090	—
convertible	1120	997	—
Group 1 plus power mirrors, power windows and door locks, remote keyless entry.			
Preferred Equipment Group 1, Z24	290	258	—
Intermittent wipers, cruise control.			
Preferred Equipment Group 2, Z24	975	868	—
Group 1 plus power mirrors, power windows and door locks, remote keyless entry.			
Exterior Appearance Pkg., base	255	227	—
Color-keyed fascias and bodyside molding, 195/65R15 tires, 15-inch wheel covers. Requires Preferred Equipment Group.			
Vinyl bucket seats, convertible	50	45	—
Includes adjustable lumbar support.			
Rear defogger	170	151	—
Power sunroof, base 2-door, RS, Z24	670	596	—
Includes mirror-mounted front map light. Requires Preferred Equipment Group.			

Prices are accurate at time of publication; subject to manufacturer's change.

CHEVROLET

	Retail Price	Dealer Invoice	Fair Price
Power door locks, 2-doors	$210	$187	—
4-doors	250	223	—
AM/FM radio, base	332	295	—
AM/FM/cassette, base	497	442	—
RS, LS	165	147	—
AM/FM/cassette with automatic tone control,			
base	552	491	—
RS, LS	220	196	—
Z24	55	49	—
AM/FM CD player with automatic tone			
control, base	652	580	—
RS, LS	320	285	—
Z24	155	138	—
Alloy wheels, RS, LS	295	263	—

Pontiac Sunfire	Retail Price	Dealer Invoice	Fair Price
SE 2-door notchback	$12059	$11155	—
SE 4-door notchback	12199	11284	—
SE 2-door convertible	18899	17482	—
GT 2-door notchback	13719	12690	—
Destination charge	500	500	500

Fair price not available at time of publication.

Standard Equipment:

SE: 2.2-liter 4-cylinder engine, 5-speed manual transmission, driver- and passenger-side air bags, anti-lock brakes, power steering, cloth reclining front bucket seats, center console with storage armrest, folding rear seat w/headrests, tinted glass, AM/FM radio, tachometer, coolant-temperature and oil-pressure gauges, trip odometer, left remote and right remote outside mirrors, visor mirrors, PASSLock theft-deterrent system, daytime running lamps, floormats, 195/70R14 tires, bolt-on wheel covers. **Convertible** adds: 4-speed automatic transmission, air conditioning, power top, traction control, cruise control, tilt steering wheel, rear defogger, intermittent wipers, Convenience Pkg. (overhead storage console, remote decklid release, assist handles, trunk net, reading lights), decklid spoiler, 195/65R15 tires. **GT** adds to SE 2-door: 2.4-liter DOHC 4-cylinder engine, tilt steering wheel, decklid spoiler, 205/55R16 tires, alloy wheels.

Optional Equipment:

4-speed automatic transmission	810	721	—
Includes traction control.			

CHEVROLET

	Retail Price	Dealer Invoice	Fair Price
2.4-liter DOHC 4-cylinder engine, SE	$450	$401	—
4-door requires 4-speed automatic transmission. NA with 3-speed automatic transmission.			
3-speed automatic transmission, SE notchbacks	550	490	—
NA with 2.4-liter DOHC 4-cylinder engine.			
5-speed manual transmission, convertible (credit)	(810)	(721)	(721)
Requires 2.4-liter DOHC 4-cylinder engine.			
Air conditioning, notchbacks	830	739	—
Option Group 1SB, SE notchbacks	1355	1206	—
Air conditioning, cassette player, tilt steering wheel, rear defogger.			
Option Group 1SC, SE notchbacks	1735	1544	—
Group 1SB plus cruise control, intermittent wipers, Convenience Pkg.			
Option Group 1SD, SE, 2-door	2745	2443	—
4-door	2050	2537	—
Group 1SC plus CD player with equalizer, steering-wheel radio controls, remote keyless entry system, power mirrors, windows, and door locks.			
Option Group 1SB, convertible	765	681	—
Power mirrors and door locks, CD player with equalizer, steering-wheel radio controls.			
Option Group 1SC, convertible	1205	1072	—
Group 1SB plus remote keyless entry system, power windows.			
Option Group 1SB, GT	1845	1642	—
Air conditioning, cruise control, CD player with equalizer, steering-wheel radio controls, intermittent wipers, rear defogger, Convenience Pkg.			
Option Group 1SC, GT	2570	2287	—
Group 1SB plus remote keyless entry system, power windows, mirrors, and door locks.			
Convenience Pkg., SE notchbacks	80	71	—
with power sunroof	41	36	—
Overhead storage console, remote decklid release, assist handles, trunk net, reading lights. Requires Group 1SB. Deletes remote decklid release when ordered with remote keyless entry system. Deletes overhead console when ordered with power sunroof.			
Sport Interior Pkg.	180	160	—
Vinyl or cloth trim; seat side bolsters; seatback map pockets; leather-wrapped steering wheel, parking brake handle, and shifter; driver-seat lumbar-support adjuster. SE notchbacks require option group.			

CHEVROLET

	Retail Price	Dealer Invoice	Fair Price
Cruise control, SE notchbacks, GT	$235	$209	—
SE notchbacks require option group 1SB.			
Rear defogger, SE notchbacks, GT	180	160	—
Power door locks, SE notchbacks, GT:			
2-doors	220	196	—
4-door	260	231	—
SE requires option group.			
Power windows, SE notchbacks, GT:			
2-doors	290	258	—
4-door	355	316	—
Requires option group, remote keyless entry system, power door locks. SE 2-door notchback requires Group 1SC.			
Power mirrors, SE			
notchbacks, GT	90	80	—
Requires option group and power door locks.			
Remote keyless entry system, SE notchbacks			
w/group 1SB or 1SC, GT w/group 1SB ...	150	134	—
Requires power door locks.			
Cassette player	195	174	—
Not available with option groups.			
Cassette player with equalizer	230	205	—
SE notchback w/group 1SB or 1SC............	35	31	—
SE notchback w/group 1SD, convertible			
or GT w/group 1SB or 1SC (credit)	(100)	(89)	(89)
CD player with equalizer	330	294	—
SE notchbacks w/group 1SB or 1SC	135	120	—
Steering wheel radio controls,			
SE notchbacks w/Group 1SC	125	111	—
Decklid spoiler,			
SE 2-door notchback	125	111	—
Tilt steering wheel,			
SE notchbacks	150	134	—
Power sunroof, SE 2-door notchback with			
Group 1SB, GT	595	530	—
SE 2-door notchback with Group 1SC or			
1SD, GT with option group	556	495	—
Replaces overhead console when ordered with Convenience Pkg.			
Smoker's Pkg.	15	13	—
Lighter and ashtray.			
195/65R15 touring tires,			
SE notchbacks	131	117	—
Alloy wheels, SE	280	249	—
Requires 195/65R15 tires.			
Engine block heater	20	18	—

CONSUMER GUIDE®

CHEVROLET CORVETTE

Chevrolet Corvette

Specifications

	2-door hatchback
Wheelbase, in.	104.5
Overall length, in.	179.7
Overall width, in.	73.6
Overall height, in.	47.7
Curb weight, lbs.	3218
Cargo vol., cu. ft.	25.0
Fuel capacity, gals.	19.1
Seating capacity	2

Engines

	ohv V-8
Size, liters/cu. in.	5.7/350
Horsepower @ rpm	345 @ 5600
Torque @ rpm	350 @ 4400

EPA city/highway mpg

6-speed OD manual	18/28
4-speed OD automatic	17/25

Built in Bowling Green, Ky.

PRICES

Chevrolet Corvette	Retail Price	Dealer Invoice	Fair Price
2-door hatchback	$37495	$32808	—
Destination charge	565	565	565

Fair price not available at time of publication.

Prices are accurate at time of publication; subject to manufacturer's change.

Standard Equipment:

5.7-liter V-8 engine, 4-speed automatic transmission, heavy duty anti-lock 4-wheel disc brakes, driver- and passenger-side air bags, Magnasteer variable-assist power steering, Acceleration Slip Regulation traction control, limited-slip differential, daytime running lights, low-tire pressure warning system, oil-level indicator, cupholder, Pass-Key theft-deterrent system, remote keyless entry with remote hatch release, air conditioning, analog gauges, digital driver information center in 4 languages, AM/FM/cassette, cruise control, rear defogger, reclining leather bucket seats, power driver's seat, center console, auxiliary power outlet, leather-wrapped tilt steering wheel, solar-control tinted glass, heated power mirrors, power windows with driver and passenger express down, power door locks, intermittent wipers, body-color removable roof panel, day/night rearview mirror with reading lights, fog lamps, Goodyear Eagle GS-C extended mobility tires (245/45ZR17 front, 275/40ZR18 rear), alloy wheels.

Optional Equipment:	Retail Price	Dealer Invoice	Fair Price
6-speed manual transmission	$815	$701	—
Air conditioning with dual zone controls	365	314	—
Performance axle ratio	100	86	—
Selective Real Time Damping Suspension	1695	1458	—
Dual roof option	950	817	—
Transparent roof panel	650	559	—
Luggage shade and parcel net	50	43	—
Perforated leather sport seats	625	538	—
6-way power passenger seat	305	262	—
Memory package	150	129	—
Includes settings for driver's seat, exterior mirrors, radio presets and climate control.			
Performance Handling Package	350	301	—
AM/FM/CD player	100	86	—
12-disc CD changer	600	516	—
Color-keyed bodyside moldings	75	65	—
Fog lamps	69	59	—
Floormats	25	22	—

CHEVROLET LUMINA/ MONTE CARLO

Specifications	2-door notchback	4-door notchback
Wheelbase, in.	107.5	107.5
Overall length, in.	200.7	200.9

Chevrolet Lumina LTZ

	2-door notchback	4-door notchback
Overall width, in.	72.5	72.5
Overall height, in.	53.8	55.2
Curb weight, lbs.	3243	3625
Cargo vol., cu. ft.	15.5	15.5
Fuel capacity, gals.	16.6	16.6
Seating capacity	6	6

Engines

	ohv V-6	dohc V-6
Size, liters/cu. in.	3.1/191	3.4/207
Horsepower @ rpm	160 @ 5200	215 @ 5200
Torque (lbs./ft.) @ rpm	185 @ 4000	220 @ 4400

EPA city/highway mpg

4-speed OD automatic	20/29	17/26

Built in Canada.

PRICES

Chevrolet Lumina/Monte Carlo	Retail Price	Dealer Invoice	Fair Price
Lumina 4-door notchback	$16945	$15335	$16445
Lumina LS 4-door notchback	19145	17326	18645
Lumina LTZ 4-door notchback	19445	17792	18945
Monte Carlo LS 2-door notchback	17445	15788	16945
Monte Carlo Z34 2-door notchback	19945	18050	19445
Destination charge	550	550	550

Standard Equipment:

Lumina: 3.1-liter V-6 engine, 4-speed automatic transmission, driver- and passenger-side air bags, power steering, air conditioning,

CHEVROLET

60/40 cloth reclining front seat with center armrest and 4-way manual driver seat, seatback storage pocket, cupholder, tilt steering wheel, AM/FM radio with digital clock, power door locks, visor mirrors, reading lights, Pass-Key theft-deterrent system, trip odometer, tinted glass, left remote and right manual mirrors, intermittent wipers, daytime running lamps, color-keyed grille, bodyside moldings, wheel covers, 205/70R15 touring tires. **Lumina LS** adds: anti-lock brakes, cruise control, power windows, custom cloth upholstery, tachometer, cassette player with automatic tone control, power mirrors, illuminated passenger-side visor mirror, trunk net, QNX 225/60R16 touring tires, alloy wheels. **Lumina LTZ** deletes cruise control and adds: rear spoiler, color-keyed outside mirrors, sport alloy wheels. **Monte Carlo LS** adds to base Lumina: anti-lock brakes, power windows, custom cloth upholstery, split fold-down rear seat, tachometer, cassette player with automatic tone control, illuminated passenger-side visor mirror, chrome grille, floormats, deluxe wheel covers. **Monte Carlo Z34** adds to Monte Carlo LS: 3.4-liter DOHC V-6 engine, 4-wheel disc brakes, custom cloth front bucket seats with center console, power mirrors, cruise control, leather-wrapped steering wheel, steering-wheel radio controls, power decklid release, remote keyless entry, trunk net, alloy wheels, QNX 225/60R16 touring tires.

Optional Equipment:

	Retail Price	Dealer Invoice	Fair Price
3.4-liter DOHC V-6 engine, Lumina LTZ	$1095	$975	$1046
Includes 4-wheel disc brakes. Requires bucket seats, Group 1, QVG 225/60R16 tires.			
Anti-lock brakes, base Lumina	575	512	546
Preferred Equipment Group 1, base Lumina	758	675	720
Power windows and mirrors, cruise control, power decklid release, trunk net, floormats.			
Preferred Equipment Group 1, Lumina LS ..	590	525	561
Remote keyless entry, dual heater/air conditioner controls, rear defogger, power decklid release, floormats.			
Preferred Equipment Group 1, Lumina LTZ	986	878	942
Remote keyless entry, cruise control, dual heater/air conditioner controls, rear defogger, steering-wheel radio controls, power decklid release, floormats.			
Preferred Equipment Group 1, Monte Carlo LS	415	369	394
Cruise control, dual heater/air conditioner controls, power decklid release, trunk net.			
Dual heater/air conditioner controls	100	89	95
NA base Lumina or Lumina LTZ.			
Rear defogger	170	151	162

	Retail Price	Dealer Invoice	Fair Price
Remote keyless entry,			
base Lumina, Monte Carlo LS	$220	$196	$209
Requires Group 1.			
Cassette player, base Lumina	232	206	220
Includes automatic tone control.			
CD player, base Lumina	325	289	309
Lumina LS and LTZ, Monte Carlo	93	83	88
Includes automatic tone control.			
Steering-wheel-mounted radio controls,			
Monte Carlo LS	171	152	162
Power driver seat	305	271	290
Integrated child safety seat, Lumina	195	174	185
Base requires custom cloth 60/40 seat.			
Custom cloth front bucket seats w/center			
console, Lumina LTZ	NC	NC	NC
Monte Carlo LS	150	134	143
Custom cloth 60/40 seat,			
base Lumina	150	134	143
Leather 60/40 seat,			
Lumina LS and LTZ	645	574	613
Leather front bucket seats, Lumina LTZ	695	619	664
Monte Carlo LS	695	619	660
Monte Carlo Z34	645	574	613
Power sunroof	700	623	665
Includes illuminated passenger-side mirror. NA base Lumina.			
Cruise control, base Lumina, Lumina LTZ,			
Monte Carlo LS	225	200	214
Front floormats, Lumina	20	18	19
Rear floormats, Lumina	20	18	19
Chrome wheel covers, base Lumina	100	89	95
Alloy wheels, base Lumina,			
Monte Carlo LS	300	267	285
Requires QNX 225/60R16 touring tires.			
White alloy wheels, Lumina LTZ,			
Monte Carlo	NC	NC	NC
Requires white paint. Monte Carlo LS requires QNX 225/60R16			
touring tires.			
QVG 225/60R16 tires,			
Lumina LTZ	15	13	14
Requires 3.4-liter engine.			
QNX 225/60R16 touring tires,			
base Lumina, Monte Carlo LS	175	156	166
Requires alloy wheels.			
Engine block heater	20	18	19

Prices are accurate at time of publication; subject to manufacturer's change.

CHEVROLET MALIBU/ OLDSMOBILE CUTLASS

Chevrolet Malibu

Specifications

	4-door notchback
Wheelbase, in.	107.0
Overall length, in.	190.4
Overall width, in.	69.4
Overall height, in.	56.4
Curb weight, lbs.	NA
Cargo vol., cu. ft.	16.4
Fuel capacity, gals.	15.0
Seating capacity	5

Engines

	dohc I-4	ohv V-6
Size, liters/cu. in.	2.4/146	3.1/191
Horsepower @ rpm	150 @ 5600	155 @ 5200
Torque (lbs./ft.) @ rpm	155 @ 4400	185 @ 4000
EPA city/highway mpg		
4-speed OD automatic	22/32	20/29

Built in Oklahoma City, Okla., and Wilmington, Del.

PRICES

Chevrolet Malibu	Retail Price	Dealer Invoice	Fair Price
Base 4-door notchback	$15470	14155	—
LS 4-door notchback	18190	16643	—
Destination charge	525	525	525

Fair price not available at time of publication.

Standard Equipment:

Base: 2.4-liter 4-cylinder engine, 4-speed automatic transmission, anti-lock brakes, air conditioning, power steering, driver- and passenger-side air bags, cloth upholstery, reclining front bucket seats, storage console w/armrest, cupholder, tilt steering wheel, dual outside mirrors w/driver-side remote, tachometer, coolant-temperature gauge, trip odometer, tinted glass, AM/FM radio, digital clock, intermittent wipers, visor mirrors, remote decklid release, Passlock II theft-deterrent system, auxiliary power outlet, daytime running lights, rear heat ducts, 215/60R15 tires, bolt-on wheel covers. **LS** adds: 3.1-liter V-6 engine, cruise control, custom cloth upholstery, power driver seat, split folding rear seat, power windows and door locks, power outside mirrors, cassette player, remote keyless entry, rear defogger, illuminated passenger-side visor mirror, dual reading lamps, passenger assist handles, floormats, cargo net, fog lamps, alloy wheels.

Optional Equipment:	Retail Price	Dealer Invoice	Fair Price
3.1-liter V-6 engine, base	$395	$356	—
Preferred Equipment Group 1, base	676	608	—
Power windows and door locks, power outside mirrors.			
Preferred Equipment Group 2, base	1059	953	—
Group 1 plus cruise control, remote keyless entry, dual reading lamps.			
Custom cloth upholstery, base	210	189	—
Includes split folding rear seat, cargo net. Requires Preferred Equipment Group.			
Power driver seat, base	305	262	—
Cassette player, base	220	198	—
CD player, base	320	288	—
LS	100	90	—
Cassette/CD player, base	420	378	—
LS	200	180	—
Remote keyless entry, base	135	122	—
Requires Preferred Equipment Group.			
Rear defogger, base	170	153	—
Floormats, base	30	27	—
Mud guards	50	45	—
Base requires Preferred Equipment Group.			
Alloy wheels, base	295	266	—
Requires Preferred Equipment Group.			
Engine-block heater	20	18	—

Prices are accurate at time of publication; subject to manufacturer's change.

Oldsmobile Cutlass	Retail Price	Dealer Invoice	Fair Price
Base 4-door notchback	$17325	$15852	—
GLS 4-door notchback	19225	17591	—
Destination charge	525	525	525

Fair price not available at time of publication.

Standard Equipment:

Base: 3.1-liter V-6 engine, 4-speed automatic transmission, anti-lock brakes, driver- and passenger-side air bags, air conditioning, cruise control, cloth upholstery, reclining front bucket seats, split folding rear seat w/trunk pass-through, storage console w/armrest, front and rear cupholders, tilt steering column, power door locks, dual outside mirrors w/driver-side remote, tachometer, coolant-temperature gauge, trip odometer, tinted glass, AM/FM radio, digital clock, rear defogger, PassLock II theft-deterrent system, remote decklid release, visor mirrors, auxiliary power outlets, map/reading lights, intermittent wipers, automatic headlamps, daytime running lights, fog lamps, floormats, 215/60R15 tires, bolt-on wheel covers.
GLS adds: leather upholstery, 6-way power driver seat, power windows, power mirrors, cassette player, remote keyless entry, illuminated passenger-side visor mirrors, passenger-assist handles, cargo net, alloy wheels.

Optional Equipment:

Convenience Pkg., base	625	556	—
Power windows and mirrors, remote keyless entry, cargo net.			
6-way power driver seat, base	305	271	—
Cloth upholstery, GLS	NC	NC	NC
Sunroof, GLS	595	530	—
Cassette player, base	220	196	—
Cassette/CD player, base	420	374	—
GLS	200	178	—
Remote keyless entry, base	125	111	—
Alloy wheels, base	315	280	—
Engine-block heater	18	16	—

CHEVROLET VENTURE/ OLDSMOBILE SILHOUETTE/ PONTIAC TRANS SPORT

Chevrolet Venture Extended 4-door

Specifications

	3-door van	3-door van
Wheelbase, in.	112.0	120.0
Overall length, in.	186.9	200.9
Overall width, in.	72.0	72.0
Overall height, in.	67.4	68.1
Curb weight, lbs.	3671	3792
Cargo vol., cu. ft.	126.6	148.3
Fuel capacity, gals.	20.0	25.0
Seating capacity	7	7

Engines

	ohv V-6
Size, liters/cu. in.	3.4/207
Horsepower @ rpm	180 @ 5200
Torque (lbs./ft.) @ rpm	205 @ 4000

EPA city/highway mpg

4-speed OD automatic	18/25

Built in Doraville, Ga.

Prices are accurate at time of publication; subject to manufacturer's change.

CHEVROLET

PRICES

Chevrolet Venture	Retail Price	Dealer Invoice	Fair Price
SWB 3-door van	$19925	18032	—
Extended 3-door van	21090	19086	—
LS SWB 4-door van	21869	19791	—
LS Extended 4-door van	22699	20542	—
Destination charge	570	570	570

SWB denotes short wheelbase. Fair price not available at time of publication.

Standard Equipment:

SWB 3-door: 3.4-liter V-6 engine, 4-speed automatic transmission, anti-lock brakes, driver- and passenger-side air bags, front air conditioning, power steering, 7-passenger seating (front bucket seats, center and rear solid bench seats), center storage console, overhead consolette, front and rear cupholders, tilt steering column, interior air filter, tinted glass, Sungate solar-coated windshield with integrated antenna, intermittent wipers, intermittent rear wiper/washer, AM/FM radio, digital clock, power door locks, power mirrors, visor mirrors, seatback tray, front and rear auxiliary power outlets, daytime running lamps, dual horn, floormats, cargo net, 205/70R15 tires, wheel covers. **Extended 3-door** adds: center and rear split folding bench seats, 215/70R15 tires. **LS SWB 4-door** adds: driver-side sliding door, LS trim (driver-side lumbar support, adjustable headrests, upgraded interior trim and upholstery), power windows, cassette player with automatic tone control, remote keyless entry, cruise control, interior roof-rail lighting, additional sound insulation, liftgate cargo net, 205/70R15 tires. **LS Extended 4-door** adds: 215/70R15 tires.

Optional Equipment:

Preferred Equipment Group 1, 3-door	225	204	—
Cruise control.			
Preferred Equipment Group 1, 4-door	895	810	—
6-way power driver seat, deep-tinted glass, rear defogger, roof rack, 215/70R15 touring tires.			
Preferred Equipment Group 2,			
SWB 3-door	970	878	—
extended 3-door	635	575	—
Group 1 plus power windows, remote keyless entry, center and rear split folding bench seats (SWB).			
Preferred Equipment Group 3,			
SWB 3-door	1344	1216	—

	Retail Price	Dealer Invoice	Fair Price
extended 3-door	$1009	$913	—

Group 2 plus LS trim (driver-side lumbar support, adjustable headrests, upgraded interior trim and upholstery, additional sound insulation, interior roof-rail lighting, liftgate cargo net), cassette player with automatic tone control.

Preferred Equipment Group 4,

extended 3-door	1729	1565	—

Group 3 plus 6-way power driver seat, deep-tinted glass, rear defogger, 215/70R15 touring tires.

Rear air conditioning, extended	450	407	—

Requires deep-tinted glass and rear defogger. 3-door requires a preferred equipment group.

Touring suspension, SWB 3-door,

LS SWB 4-door	218	197	—
extended 3-door w/Group 3, 4-door	215	195	—

extended 3-door w/Group 4,

4-door w/Group 1	180	163	—

Load-leveling suspension, 215/70R15 tires (SWB), 215/70R15 touring tires (extended). 3-door requires Group 3 and 4.

Traction control	175	158	—

3-door requires Group 3 or 4.

Power passenger-side sliding door,

extended	350	317	—

3-door requires Group 2, 3, or 4.

6-way power driver seat	270	244	—

3-door requires Group 3.

Center and rear split folding bench seats,

SWB 3-door w/Group 1	335	303	—
Rear bucket seats	115	104	—

3-door requires Group 3 or 4.

Integrated child seat	125	113	—
Dual integrated child seats	225	204	—

Upgraded interior trim and upholstery,

3-door	NC	NC	NC
Rear defogger	170	154	—
Engine-block heater	20	18	—
Deep-tinted glass	245	222	—

Includes blackout center pillar w/most exterior colors. Requires rear defogger.

Cassette player, 3-door	165	149	—

NA with Group 3 or 4.

CD player	100	91	—

Includes automatic tone control, coaxial speakers, anti-theft feature. 3-door requires Group 3 or 4.

Prices are accurate at time of publication; subject to manufacturer's change.

CHEVROLET

	Retail Price	Dealer Invoice	Fair Price
Cassette/CD player	$200	$181	—
Includes automatic tone control, coaxial speakers, anti-theft feature. 3-door requires Group 3 or 4.			
Rear-seat audio controls	110	100	—
Includes headphone jacks. 3-door requires Group 3 or 4.			
Safety and security system, SWB 3-door,			
LS SWB 4-door	60	54	—
extended 3-door w/Group 3, 4-door	245	222	—
extended 3-door w/Group 4,			
4-door w/Group 1	210	190	—
Theft-deterrent system. Extended 3-door and 4-door also include self-sealing tires. Extended 3-door w/Group 3 and 4-door without Preferred Equipment Group include 215/70R15 touring tires.			
Trailering Pkg., SWB 3-door, LS SWB 4-door	368	333	—
extended 3-door w/Group 3, 4-door	365	330	—
extended 3-door w/Group 4,			
4-door w/Group 1	330	299	—
Includes heavy-duty engine and transmission-oil cooling, touring suspension. 3-door requires Group 3 or 4.			
Roof rack	175	158	—
3-door requires a preferred equipment group.			
215/70R15 tires, SWB 3-door,			
LS SWB 4-door	38	34	—
215/70R15 touring tires, extended	35	32	—
3-door requires preferred equipment group.			
Self-sealing tires, extended	150	136	—
Requires 215/70R15 touring tires. 3-door requires Group 3 or 4.			
Alloy wheels	275	249	—

Oldsmobile Silhouette

	Retail Price	Dealer Invoice	Fair Price
3-door van, SWB	$21675	$19616	—
3-door van, extended	22505	20367	—
GL 3-door van, extended	24025	21743	—
GL 4-door van, extended	24575	22240	—
GLS 3-door van, extended	25685	23245	—
GLS 4-door van, extended	26235	23743	—
Destination charge	570	570	570

Fair price not available at time of publication. SWB denotes standard wheelbase.

Standard Equipment:

3.4-liter V-6 engine, 4-speed automatic transmission, anti-lock brakes, driver- and passenger-side air bags, power steering, front air conditioning, cruise control, reclining front bucket seats w/lumbar adjustment and folding armrest, 4-way adjustable driver seat, second-row 60/40 split folding bench seat, third-row 50/50 split folding bench seat, front storage console, overhead console w/map lights, front and rear cupholders, power windows and door locks, power mirrors, tilt steering wheel, tachometer, coolant-temperature gauge, trip odometer, digital clock, AM/FM/cassette, integrated antenna, under-passenger-seat storage drawer, solar control windshield, intermittent wipers, rear wiper/washer, remote keyless entry, theft-deterrent system, rear defogger, visor mirrors, interior air filter daytime running lights, rear reading lights, fog lamps, front and rear auxiliary power outlets, roof rack, floormats, 205/70R15 tires (SWB), 215/70R15 (extended), wheel covers. **GL** adds: power sliding passenger-side door, 6-way power driver seat, overhead storage console (includes compass, outside temperature indicator, driver information center), deep-tinted glass, cargo net. **GLS** adds: touring suspension w/automatic load leveling, traction control, rear air conditioning and heater, second-row captain's chairs, steering-wheel radio controls, rear-seat radio controls, illuminated visor mirrors, 215/70R15 touring tires, alloy wheels. **4-door models** add: power sliding driver-side door.

Optional Equipment:

	Retail Price	Dealer Invoice	Fair Price
Traction control, GL	$175	$151	—
Power moonroof, GL 3-door, GLS 3-door ...	695	598	—
GL requires Rear Convenience Pkg.			
Touring suspension, GL	270	232	—
Includes automatic load leveling., 215/70R15 touring tires.			
Towing Pkg., base, GL	355	305	—
GLS	85	73	—
Includes touring suspension, automatic load leveling, engine- and transmission-oil coolers, 5-lead wiring harness, 215/70R15 touring tires.			
Rear Convenience Pkg., GL	525	452	—
Rear air conditioning and heater, rear-seat radio controls.			
Leather upholstery, GLS	870	748	—
Includes leather-wrapped steering wheel.			
Integrated child seat, GL	125	108	—
Dual integrated child seats, GL	225	194	—
Deep-tinted glass, base	245	211	—
CD player, GL, GLS	100	86	—
Includes automatic tone control.			
Cassette/CD player, GL, GLS	200	172	—
Includes automatic tone control.			
Alloy wheels, GL	285	245	—

Prices are accurate at time of publication; subject to manufacturer's change.

Pontiac Trans Sport

	Retail Price	Dealer Invoice	Fair Price
SWB 3-door van	$20479	$18534	—
Extended wheelbase 3-door van	21439	19402	—
Extended wheelbase 4-door van	23369	21149	—
Destination charge	570	570	570

Fair price not available at time of publication. SWB denotes standard wheelbase.

Standard Equipment:

3.4-liter V-6 engine, 4-speed automatic transmission, anti-lock brakes, driver- and passenger-side side air bags, power steering, front air conditioning, cloth upholstery, 7-passenger seating (front reclining bucket seats w/manual lumbar adjustment, second- and third-row bench seats), front storage console, cupholders, tilt steering wheel, tinted glass with solar-control windshield, power mirrors, tachometer, coolant-temperature gauge, voltmeter, trip odometer, AM/FM radio, integrated antenna, under-passenger-seat storage, interior air filter, visor mirrors, intermittent wipers, rear wiper/washer, front and rear auxiliary power outlets, Lamp Group (includes front map lights, rear reading lights, cargo-area lights, underhood light), automatic headlights, daytime running lights, fog lamps, floormats, 205/70R15 tires, wheel covers. **Extended** adds: rear split reclining bench seats, 215/70R15 tires. **4-door** adds: sliding driver-side door, cruise control, deep-tinted glass, power windows, power rear quarter windows, remote keyless entry, rear defogger, perimeter lighting, cargo net.

Optional Equipment:

Rear air conditioning, extended	460	409	—
Extended w/Montana Pkg. or automatic level control	450	401	—
Includes saddle-bag storage.			
Rear heater, extended	177	158	—
Extended w/Montana Pkg., automatic level control, or rear air conditioning	167	149	—
Automatic level control	180	160	—
Includes saddlebag storage, 215/70R15 touring tires.			
Traction control	175	156	—
Requires automatic level control.			
Option Pkg. 1SB, 3-door	460	409	—
Cruise control, cassette player, cargo net.			
Option Pkg. 1SC, 3-door	1410	1255	—
Group 1SB plus power windows, power rear-quarter windows, deep-tinted glass, remote keyless entry, rear defogger, perimeter lighting.			

	Retail Price	Dealer Invoice	Fair Price
Option Pkg. 1SD, SWB	$2451	$2181	—
Extended 3-door	2116	1883	—

Group 1SC plus power driver seat, rear split reclining bench seats (SWB), overhead console (storage, outside-temperature indicator, compass), illuminated visor mirrors, roof rack.

Option Pkg. 1SD, Extended 4-door	706	628	—

Power driver seat, overhead console (storage, outside-temperature indicator, compass), illuminated visor mirrors, roof rack.

Montana Pkg., SWB	1537	1368	—
SWB w/Pkg. 1SD	1027	914	—
Extended	1164	1036	—
Extended w/Pkg. 1SD	989	880	—

Traction control, automatic level control, rear split reclining bench seats (SWB), unique exterior appearance, saddle-bag storage, roof rack, self-sealing 215/70R15 outline-white-letter tires, alloy wheels.

Safety and Security Pkg.	210	187	—
ordered w/Montana Pkg. or			
215/70R15 self-sealing touring tires	60	53	—

Theft-deterrent system, remote keyless entry, 215/70R15 self-sealing touring tires.

Power sliding side door, Extended 3-door	400	356	—
Extended 3-door w/Pkg. 1SC or 1SD,			
Extended 4-door	350	312	—

3-door includes power rear-quarter windows. 3-door requires remote keyless entry.

Power sunroof, extended 3-door	695	619	—
Extended 3-door w/Pkg. 1SD	520	463	—

Requires rear air conditioning, power sliding side door.

Power driver seat	270	240	—
Power front seats	305	271	—

Requires rear modular bucket seats, second-row captain's chairs w/split reclining third-row bench seat, or 8-passenger seating.

Rear split reclining bench seats, SWB	335	298	—
Rear modular bucket seats, SWB	450	401	—
SWB w/Pkg. 1SD or Montana Pkg.	115	102	—
Extended	115	102	—
Second-row captain's chairs w/split reclining			
third-row bench seat, SWB	600	534	—
SWB w/Pkg. 1SD or Montana Pkg.	265	236	—
Extended	265	236	—
8-passenger seating, SWB	600	534	—
SWB w/Pkg. 1SD or Montana Pkg.	265	236	—
Extended	265	236	—

Prices are accurate at time of publication; subject to manufacturer's change.

CHEVROLET

	Retail Price	Dealer Invoice	Fair Price
Leather upholstery	$1055	$939	—
Includes leather-wrapped steering wheel w/radio controls. Requires power driver seat.			
Integral child seat	125	111	112
NA w/captain's chairs.			
Two integral child seats	225	200	202
NA w/captain's chairs.			
Power windows, 3-door	275	245	246
Cassette player, 3-door	195	174	—
Cassette player w/equalizer	335	298	—
ordered w/leather upholstery	150	134	—
Includes rear-seat audio controls and earphone jacks, leather-wrapped steering wheel w/radio controls, extended-range coaxial speakers.			
CD player	100	89	—
CD player w/equalizer	435	387	—
ordered w/leather upholstery	250	223	—
Includes rear-seat audio controls and earphone jacks, leather-wrapped steering wheel w/radio controls, extended-range coaxial speakers.			
Cassette/CD player w/equalizer	535	476	—
ordered w/leather upholstery	350	312	—
Includes rear-seat audio controls and earphone jacks, leather-wrapped steering wheel w/radio controls, extended-range coaxial speakers.			
Extended-range coaxial speakers	50	45	—
Leather-wrapped steering wheel w/radio controls	185	165	—
Deep-tinted glass, 3-door	245	218	—
Rear defogger, 3-door	180	160	—
Remote keyless entry, 3-door	150	134	—
Trailer provisions	150	134	—
Trailer wiring harness, heavy-duty cooling, heavy-duty flasher. Requires automatic level control, 215/70R15 touring tires.			
Roof rack	175	156	—
2-tone paint	125	111	—
NA w/Montana Pkg.			
215/70R15 touring tires, SWB	73	65	—
Extended	35	31	—
215/70R15 self-sealing touring tires	150	134	—
Alloy wheels	259	231	—
Requires 215/70R15 touring tires.			
Engine-block heater	20	18	

CHRYSLER LHS

Chrysler LHS

Specifications

	4-door notchback
Wheelbase, in.	113.0
Overall length, in.	207.4
Overall width, in.	74.5
Overall height, in.	55.9
Curb weight, lbs.	3619
Cargo vol., cu. ft.	17.9
Fuel capacity, gals.	18.0
Seating capacity	6

Engines

	ohc V-6
Size, liters/cu. in.	3.5/215
Horsepower @ rpm	214 @ 5850
Torque (lbs./ft.) @ rpm	221 @ 3100

EPA city/highway mpg

4-speed OD automatic	17/26

Built in Canada.

PRICES

Chrysler LHS	Retail Price	Dealer Invoice	Fair Price
LHS 4-door notchback	$30255	$27702	$28502
Destination charge	595	595	595

Standard Equipment:

3.5-liter V-6 engine, 4-speed automatic transmission, anti-lock 4-

Prices are accurate at time of publication; subject to manufacturer's change.

wheel disc brakes, driver- and passenger-side air bags, variable-assist power steering, automatic climate control, touring suspension, traction control, leather upholstery, power front bucket seats with power recliners, center storage console with cupholders and rear ducts, tilt steering wheel, leather-wrapped steering wheel and shifter, cruise control, power windows and locks, heated power mirrors, automatic day/night rearview mirror, rear defogger, mini overhead console with compass and outside temperature readout, trip computer, solar-control tinted glass, tachometer, trip odometer, coolant-temperature gauge, AM/FM/cassette system with equalizer and 11 Infinity speakers, integrated antenna, speed-sensitive intermittent wipers, power decklid release, automatic headlights, universal garage-door opener, remote keyless entry, security alarm, illuminated visor mirrors, reading lights, floormats, trunk cargo net, fog lamps, 225/60R16 touring tires, full-size spare tire, alloy wheels.

Optional Equipment:

	Retail Price	Dealer Invoice	Fair Price
Power moonroof	$795	$708	$755
Front 50/50 split bench seat	NC	NC	NC
Cassette/CD system	300	267	285
Includes equalizer and 11 Infinity speakers.			
Metallic paint	200	178	190
Engine block heater	20	18	19

CHRYSLER SEBRING/ DODGE AVENGER

Chrysler Sebring LX

Specifications

	2-door notchback	2-door conv.
Wheelbase, in.	103.7	106.0
Overall length, in.	191.0	193.0
Overall width, in.	69.7	70.1

	2-door notchback	2-door conv.
Overall height, in.	53.3	54.8
Curb weight, lbs.	2959	3350
Cargo vol., cu. ft.	13.1	11.3
Fuel capacity, gals.	16.9	15.8
Seating capacity	5	4

Engines

	dohc I-4	dohc I-4	ohc V-6	ohc V-6
Size, liters/cu. in.	2.0/122	2.4/148	2.5/152	2.5/152
Horsepower @ rpm	140 @ 6000	150 @ 5200	163 @ 5500	168 @ 5800
Torque (lbs./ft.) @ rpm	130 @ 4800	167 @ 4000	170 @ 4400	170 @ 4350

EPA city/highway mpg

5-speed OD manual	22/31			
4-speed OD automatic	21/30	20/28	20/27	18/27

Built in Normal, Ill., and Mexico.

PRICES

Chrysler Sebring	Retail Price	Dealer Invoice	Fair Price
LX 2-door notchback	$16540	$15231	$15731
LXi 2-door notchback	21120	19307	19807
Destination charge	535	535	535

Standard Equipment:

LX: 2.0-liter DOHC 4-cylinder engine, 5-speed manual transmission, driver- and passenger-side air bags, anti-lock brakes, variable-assist power steering, air conditioning, cloth front bucket seats, console with storage armrest and cupholders, split folding rear seat, rear headrests, tinted glass, rear defogger, tilt steering column, AM/FM/cassette player, trip odometer, oil-pressure and coolant-temperature gauges, tachometer, variable intermittent wipers, remote fuel-door and decklid releases, remote outside mirrors, visor mirrors, map lights, color-keyed front and rear fascias, fog lights, floormats, 195/70R14 tires, wheel covers. **LXi** adds: 2.5-liter SOHC V-6 engine, 4-speed automatic transmission, anti-lock 4-wheel disc brakes, power windows and door locks, heated power mirrors, upgraded cloth upholstery and driver-seat lumbar support, leather-wrapped steering wheel, AM/FM/cassette/CD player, cruise control, remote keyless entry system w/security alarm, automatic day/night rear view mirror, illuminated visor mirrors, Homelink universal garage-door opener, trunk net, 215/50HR17 tires, alloy wheels.

Prices are accurate at time of publication; subject to manufacturer's change.

Optional Equipment:

	Retail Price	Dealer Invoice	Fair Price
2.5-liter SOHC V-6 engine, LX	$830	$739	$764

Includes anti-lock 4-wheel disc brakes, upgraded suspension, dual exhaust outlets, 205/55HR16 tires. Requires 4-speed automatic transmission.

4-speed automatic transmission, LX	695	619	639
Pkg. 21H/22H/24H, LX	771	686	709

Cruise control, power windows, door locks, and mirrors, illuminated visor mirrors, trunk net. Pkg. 22H requires 4-speed automatic transmission. Pkg. 24H requires 2.5-liter V-6 engine and 4-speed automatic transmission.

Pkg. 24K, LXi	626	557	576

Power driver seat, leather upholstery.

Anti-lock brakes, LX	599	533	551
Power driver seat	203	181	187

LX requires Pkg. 21H/22H/24H.

Power sunroof	640	570	589

LX requires Pkg. 21H/22H/24H.

CD/cassette player, LX w/Pkg. 21H/22H/24H	435	387	400
CD/cassette player with eight Infinity speakers and equalizer, LX w/Pkg. 21H/22H/24H	750	676	690
LXi	326	290	300
Automatic day/night rearview mirror, LX w/Pkg. 21H/22H/24H	86	77	79
Remote keyless entry w/security alarm, LX w/Pkg. 21H/22H/24H	287	255	264
16-inch Wheel Group, LX	490	436	451
LX w/2.5-liter engine	333	296	306

Alloy wheels, 205/55HR16 tires.

Chrysler Sebring Convertible	Retail Price	Dealer Invoice	Fair Price
JX 2-door notchback	$20150	$18504	—
JXi 2-door notchback	24760	22606	—
Destination charge	535	535	535

Fair price not available at time of publication.

Standard Equipment:

JX: 2.4-liter DOHC 4-cylinder engine, 4-speed automatic transmission, driver- and passenger-side air bags, variable-assist power steering, air conditioning, vinyl convertible top with glass rear window, front bucket seats, vinyl upholstery, console with storage armrest, tinted glass, power windows, rear defogger, tilt steering column,

AM/FM radio, digital clock, trip odometer, oil-pressure and coolant-temperature gauges, tachometer, variable intermittent wipers, dual remote mirrors, map lights, 205/65R15 tires, wheel covers. **JXi** adds: anti-lock brakes, touring suspension, cruise control, Firm Feel power steering, cloth convertible top with glass rear window, leather/vinyl upholstery, 6-way power front seats, programmable power door locks, heated power mirrors, leather-wrapped shifter and steering wheel, trip computer, cassette player with eight Infinity speakers, power antenna, remote keyless entry, illuminated visor mirrors, alarm system, remote decklid release, fog lamps, floormats, 215/55HR16 touring tires, alloy wheels.

Optional Equipment:

	Retail Price	Dealer Invoice	Fair Price
2.5-liter SOHC V-6 engine, JX	$1365	$1215	—
JXi	800	712	—
Includes anti-lock brakes, bright exhaust outlets. Requires option pkg.			
Anti-lock brakes, JX	565	503	—
Pkg. 24B/26B, JX	1585	1411	—
6-way power driver seat, cruise control, Power Convenience Group, cassette player and CD changer control, remote keyless entry, headlamps-off delay, remote decklid release, illuminated visor mirrors, additional trunk trim, floormats. Pkg. 26B requires 2.5-liter V-6 engine.			
Pkg. 26C, JX	1780	1584	—
Pkg. 24B/26B plus Autostick 4-speed automatic transmission. Requires 2.5-liter V-6 engine.			
Pkg. 26E, JXi	195	174	—
Autostick 4-speed automatic transmission.			
Cruise control, JX	240	214	—
Premium cloth upholstery, JX	95	85	—
JXi (credit)	(250)	(223)	(223)
Luxury Convenience Group	175	156	—
Universal garage-door opener, automatic day/night rearview mirror. JX requires option pkg.			
Power Convenience Group, JX	360	320	—
Programmable power door locks, heated power mirrors.			
Security Group, JX	150	134	—
Alarm system, programmable power door locks. Requires Pkg. 24B/26B.			
Cassette player, JX	275	245	—
Cassette player w/amplifier and eight Infinity speakers, JX	440	392	—
Includes amplifier, power antenna. Requires Pkg. 24B/26B.			
CD player, JX	445	396	—
JX w/Pkg. 24B/26B	170	151	—
Includes graphic equalizer.			

Prices are accurate at time of publication; subject to manufacturer's change.

CHRYSLER

	Retail Price	Dealer Invoice	Fair Price
CD/cassette player w/amplifier and eight Infinity speakers	$780	$694	—
JXi	340	303	—
Includes amplifier, power antenna. JX requires Pkg. 24B/26B.			
6-disc CD changer	500	445	—
JX requires cassette player. NA with CD/cassette player.			
16-inch Touring Group, JX	495	441	—
Firm Feel power steering, touring suspension, 215/55R16 touring tires, alloy wheels.			
Candy-apple-red metallic paint	200	178	—

Dodge Avenger	Retail Price	Dealer Invoice	Fair Price
2-door notchback	$14620	$13462	$13962
ES 2-door notchback	17590	16105	16716
Destination charge	535	535	535

Standard Equipment:

Base: 2.0-liter DOHC 4-cylinder engine, 5-speed manual transmission, driver- and passenger-side air bags, variable-assist power steering, cloth reclining front bucket seats, console with storage armrest and cupholders, split folding rear seat, rear headrests, tinted glass, rear defogger, tilt steering column, AM/FM radio, trip odometer, oil-pressure and coolant-temperature gauges, tachometer, intermittent wipers, dual remote mirrors, map lights, visor mirrors, 195/70HR14 tires, wheel covers. **ES** adds: anti-lock 4-wheel disc brakes, air conditioning, upgraded cloth upholstery and driver-seat lumbar support, cruise control, handling suspension, cassette player, decklid spoiler, fog lights, floormats, cargo nets and hooks, 205/55HR16 tires, alloy wheels.

Optional Equipment:

2.5-liter OHC V-6 engine, base w/Pkg. 24V	830	739	764
ES	715	636	658
Includes anti-lock 4-wheel disc brakes, upgraded suspension, dual exhaust outlets, 205/55HR16 tires. Requires 4-speed automatic transmission.			
4-speed automatic transmission	695	619	639
Pkg. 21B/22B, base	1308	1164	1203
Air conditioning, cruise control, cassette player, floormats. Pkg. 22B requires 4-speed automatic transmission.			
Pkg. 21C/22C, base	1844	1641	1696
Pkg. 21B/22B plus power windows and door locks, power mirrors, trunk net. Pkg. 22C requires 4-speed automatic transmission.			

	Retail Price	Dealer Invoice	Fair Price
Pkg. 24V, base	$2177	$1938	$2003

Pkg. 21C/22C plus 16-inch Wheel Group (alloy wheels, 205/55HR16 tires). Requires 2.5-liter engine and 4-speed automatic transmission.

Pkg. 21E/24E, ES	536	477	493

Power windows and door locks, power mirrors, illuminated visor mirrors. Pkg. 24E requires 2.5-liter engine and 4-speed automatic transmission.

Pkg. 21F/24F, ES	1569	1396	1443

Pkg. 24E plus cassette/CD player, power driver seat, security alarm, universal garage-door opener, remote keyless entry. Pkg. 21F requires 2.5-liter engine and 4-speed automatic transmission.

Anti-lock brakes, base	599	533	551
Air conditioning, base w/option pkg.	788	701	725
Leather upholstery, ES	423	376	389

Requires option pkg. and power driver seat.

Power driver seat, base w/Pkg. 21C/22C or Pkg. 24V, ES w/Pkg. 21E/24E	203	181	187
CD/cassette player, base w/option pkg., ES w/Pkg. 21E/24E	435	387	400
CD/cassette player with eight Infinity speakers and equalizer, ES w/Pkg. 21E/24E	760	676	699
ES w/Pkg. 21F/24F	326	290	300
Power sunroof	640	570	589

Requires option pkg.

Security alarm, base w/Pkg. 21C/22C or Pkg. 24V, ES w/Pkg. 21E/24E	287	255	264

Includes remote keyless entry.

16-inch Wheel Group, base w/option pkg. ..	490	436	451

Alloy wheels, 205/55HR16 tires.

DODGE CARAVAN/ CHRYSLER TOWN & COUNTRY/ PLYMOUTH VOYAGER

Specifications	3-door van	3-door van
Wheelbase, in.	113.3	119.3

Prices are accurate at time of publication; subject to manufacturer's change.

Dodge Grand Caravan SE Sport

	3-door van	3-door van
Overall length, in.	186.3	199.6
Overall width, in.	76.8	76.8
Overall height, in.	68.5	68.5
Curb weight, lbs.	3544	3711
Cargo vol., cu. ft.	142.9	168.5
Fuel capacity, gals.	20.0	20.0
Seating capacity	7	7

Engines

	dohc I-4	ohc V-6	ohv V-6	ohv V-6
Size, liters/cu. in.	2.4/148	3.0/181	3.3/202	3.8/231
Horsepower @ rpm	150 @ 5200	150 @ 5200	158 @ 4850	166 @ 4300
Torque (lbs./ft.) @ rpm	167 @ 4000	176 @ 4000	203 @ 3250	227 @ 3100

EPA city/highway mpg

3-speed automatic	20/25	19/24		
4-speed OD automatic	18/25		18/24	17/24

Built in St. Louis, Mo., and Canada.

PRICES

Dodge Caravan	Retail Price	Dealer Invoice	Fair Price
Base 3-door van, SWB	$17235	$15687	—
Base Grand 3-door van	18580	16910	—
SE 3-door van, SWB	19925	18054	—
Grand SE 3-door van	20755	18824	—
Grand SE 4-door van, AWD	25475	22978	—
LE 4-door van, SWB	25215	22709	—
Grand LE 4-door van	25905	23356	—

	Retail Price	Dealer Invoice	Fair Price
Grand LE 4-door van, AWD	$29070	$26142	—
ES 4-door van, SWB	25805	23228	—
Grand ES 4-door van	26495	23876	—
Grand ES 4-door van, AWD	29600	26608	—
Destination charge	580	580	580

Fair price not available at time of publication. SWB denotes short wheelbase. AWD denotes all-wheel drive.

Standard Equipment:

Base: 2.4-liter DOHC 4-cylinder engine, 3-speed automatic transmission, driver- and passenger-side air bags, power steering, cloth reclining front bucket seats, 3-passenger rear bench seat (SWB), 2-passenger middle bench seat (Grand), folding 3-passenger rear bench seat (Grand), cupholders, tinted glass, variable intermittent wipers, variable intermittent rear wiper/washer, coolant-temperature gauge, trip odometer, AM/FM radio, digital clock, front map/reading lights, dual outside mirrors, visor mirrors, front and rear auxiliary power outlets, 205/75R14 tires, wheel covers. **SE** adds: 4-speed automatic transmission, anti-lock brakes, cruise control, tilt steering column, passenger-side underseat storage drawer, heated power mirrors, tachometer, cassette player, 215/65R15 tires. **LE** and **ES** add: 3.3-liter V-6 engine, air conditioning, upgraded cloth upholstery, sliding driver-side door, computer with compass, temperature, and travel displays, overhead storage console, CD/cassette storage, power windows and door locks, power windows, oil-pressure gauge, voltmeter, windshield wiper de-icer, rear defogger, ignition-switch light, illuminated visor mirrors, remote keyless entry w/headlight-off delay and illuminated entry, deluxe sound insulation, floormats, striping. **AWD models** add: 3.8-liter V-6 engine, load-leveling suspension, sliding driver-side door (SE), power door locks (SE).

Optional Equipment:

Anti-lock brakes, base	565	480	—
4-speed automatic transmission, base	250	213	—
3.0-liter V-6 engine, base, 2WD SE	770	655	—

Requires 3-speed automatic transmission. Base requires option pkg. Not available with base or SE in California, New York, and Massachusetts.

3.3-liter V-6 engine, base, 2WD SE	970	825	—

Requires 4-speed automatic transmission. Base requires Pkg. 28T. SE requires option pkg. 28B, 28C, 28D, or 28E. Available only in California, New York, and Massachusetts when ordered with base.

Prices are accurate at time of publication; subject to manufacturer's change.

	Retail Price	Dealer Invoice	Fair Price
3.8-liter V-6 engine, 2WD LE, 2WD ES	$325	$276	—

Requires option pkg.

3-speed automatic transmission (credit), 2WD SE	(250)	(213)	(213)

Requires 3.0-liter engine. NA with SE Sport Pkgs. Deletes tachometer.

Pkg. 22T/24T/28T,

SWB base	390	332	—
2WD base Grand	40	34	—

Air conditioning, 7-passenger seating (SWB), passenger-side underseat storage drawer, dual horns, rear-floor sound insulation. Pkg. 24T requires 3.0-liter V-6 engine. Pkg. 28T requires 3.3-liter V-6 engine.

Pkg. 23B/24B/28B, 2WD SWB SE,

2WD Grand SE	505	429	—

Air conditioning, Deluxe 7-passenger Seating Group (includes middle- and rear-seat recliners and headrests), rear defogger. Pkg. 24B requires 3.0-liter V-6 engine. Pkg. 28B requires 3.3-liter V-6 engine.

Pkg. 28C (Sport), 2WD SE	1665	1415	—

Pkg. 23B/24B/28B plus Sport decor group (touring suspension, leather-wrapped steering wheel, Sport decals, sunscreen/solar glass, windshield wiper de-icer, body-color door handles, fascias, luggage rack, and bodyside moldings, fog lights, sparkle-silver alloy wheels, 215/65R16 touring tires). Requires 3.3-liter V-6 engine.

Pkg. 24D/28D/29D, SE	1240	1054	—

Pkg. 23B/28B plus power windows and door locks, power rear quarter vent windows, illuminated visor mirrors, Light Group (interior courtesy lights, illuminated ignition), additional sound insulation, floormats. Pkg. 24D requires 3.0-liter V-6 engine. Pkg. 28D requires 3.3-liter V-6 engine. Pkg. 29D requires AWD.

Pkg. 28E (Sport), 2WD SE	2400	2040	—

Pkg 24D/28D plus Sport decor group (touring suspension, leather-wrapped steering wheel, Sport decals, sunscreen/solar glass, windshield wiper de-icer, body-color door handles, fascias, luggage rack, and bodyside moldings, fog lights, sparkle-silver alloy wheels, 215/65R16 touring tires). Requires 3.3-liter V-6 engine and sliding driver-side door.

Pkg. 28K/29K, LE	430	366	—

Air conditioning with dual controls, 8-way power driver seat, solar-control glass, 10-speaker cassette player. Pkg. 29K requires 3.8-liter V-6 engine.

Pkg. 28M/29M, 2WD ES	750	638	—

	Retail Price	Dealer Invoice	Fair Price
AWD ES	$665	$430	—

Pkg. 28K/29K plus traction control (2WD), ES Decor Group (Touring Handling Group [rear sway bar, touring handling suspension upgraded front struts and rear shocks, 215/65R16 tires], color-keyed fascias, bodyside moldings, and lower bodyside appliqués, leather-wrapped steering wheel, striping, fog lights, sparkle-gold alloy wheels), automatic day/night mirror, passenger assist strap. Pkg. 29M requires 3.8-liter V-6 engine.

7-passenger seating, SWB base	350	298	—

2-passenger middle bench seat, 3-passenger rear bench seat.

7-passenger seating w/integrated child seat, base	285	242	—

2-passenger reclining middle bench seat with headrest and integrated child seats, 3-passenger rear bench seat. Requires option pkg.

Deluxe 7-passenger seating w/integrated child seats, SE, LE, ES	225	191	—

Premium cloth 2-passenger reclining middle bench seat with headrests and integrated child seats, 3-passenger reclining rear bench seat. Requires option pkg.

Deluxe 7-passenger seating w/quad bucket seats, SE, LE, ES	625	531	—

Premium cloth reclining middle bucket seats, 3-passenger reclining rear bench seat with headrests. SE requires Pkg. 24D/28D/29D or 28E, and sliding driver-side door. LE requires option pkg.

Air conditioning, base, 2WD SE	860	731	—
Rear heater/air conditioning, Grand LE	470	400	—
Grand ES	405	344	—

Requires option pkg.

Rear heater/air conditioning w/overhead console,			
2WD Grand SE w/Pkg. 24B/28B	1130	961	—
2WD Grand SE w/Pkg. 28C	615	523	—
Grand SE w/Pkg. 24D/28D/29D	1020	867	—
2WD Grand SE w/Pkg. 28E	505	429	—
Sunscreen/solar glass, base, SE	450	383	—

Includes windshield wiper de-icer. Requires option pkg.

Convenience/Security Group 1, base	435	370	—

Cruise control, tilt steering column, power mirrors. Requires option pkg.

Convenience/Security Group 2, base	750	638	—

Group 1 plus power door locks. Requires option pkg.

Convenience/Security Group 2, 2WD SE ...	315	268	—

Power door locks. Requires option pkg.

DODGE

	Retail Price	Dealer Invoice	Fair Price
Convenience/Security Group 3, 2WD SE ...	$685	$582	—
Power door locks, power windows and rear quarter vent windows. Requires option pkg.			
Convenience/Security Group 4, SE..............	235	200	—
Remote keyless entry, illuminated entry, headlamp-off delay. Requires Pkg. 24D/28D/29D or 28E.			
Convenience/Security Group 5, SE	385	327	—
Convenience/Security Group 4 plus security alarm. Requires Pkg. 24D/28D/29D or 28E.			
Convenience/Security Group 5, Grand LE, Grand ES	150	128	—
Security alarm. Requires option pkg.			
Loading & Towing Group 1	110	94	—
Full-size spare tire. Requires option pkg.			
Loading & Towing Group 2, 2WD SE, LE ...	180	153	—
2WD LE with Wheel/Handling Group 2, 2WD ES	145	123	—
Full-size spare tire, heavy load/firm ride suspension. Requires option pkg. NA with Pkg. 28C or 28E.			
Loading & Towing Group 3, Grand SE w/Pkg. 28D/29D and rear heater/air conditioning w/overhead console	380	323	—
Grand SE w/Pkg. 28D/29D or 28E, LE	445	378	—
Grand LE w/Pkg. 28K/29K and rear heater/air conditioning	380	323	—
2WD LE with Wheel/Handling Group 2 ...	410	349	—
ES	345	293	—
Group 2 plus Heavy Duty Trailer Tow Group (heavy-duty battery alternator, brakes, and radiator, heavy-duty transmission-oil cooler, trailer wiring harness).			
Wheel/Handling Group 2, 2WD LE	470	400	—
Touring Handling Group (rear sway bar, touring handling suspension upgraded front struts and rear shocks, 215/65R16 tires), sparkle-silver alloy wheels. Requires option pkg.			
Load-leveling suspension, 2WD Grand SE w/Pkg. 24D/28D or 28E, 2WD LE, 2WD ES	290	247	—
Requires option pkg.			
Traction control, 2WD LE	175	149	—
Sliding driver-side door, base, 2WD SE	595	506	—
Requires option pkg.			
Rear defogger, base	195	166	—
base w/Convenience/Security Group 1 or 2, 2WD SE	230	196	—
Includes windshield wiper de-icer.			

	Retail Price	Dealer Invoice	Fair Price
Leather bucket seats, LE, ES	$890	$757	—
Requires option pkg. and deluxe 7-passenger seating w/quad bucket seats.			
Cassette player, base	180	153	—
Requires option pkg.			
10-speaker cassette player with equalizer, SE w/Pkg. 24D/28D/29D or 28E	325	276	—
10-speaker CD player with equalizer, SE w/Pkg. 24D/28D/29D or 28E	720	612	—
LE, ES	395	336	—
LE and ES require option pkg.			
Luggage rack	175	149	—
Requires option pkg.			
Candy-apple-red metallic paint, 2WD SE w/Pkg. 28C or 28E, LE, ES	200	170	—
White-pearl paint, ES	200	170	—
Engine block heater	35	30	—
Smoker's Group	20	17	—
Cigarette lighter, ashtrays.			
Alloy wheels, Grand SE w/Pkg. 23B/24B/28B or 24D/28D/29D	415	353	—
LE w/Pkg. 28K/29K	410	349	—

Chrysler Town & Country	Retail Price	Dealer Invoice	Fair Price
LX 4-door van, FWD	$26895	$24403	—
LX 4-door van, AWD	29885	27034	—
SX 4-door van, short wheelbase, FWD	26680	24213	—
LXi 4-door van, FWD	31565	28512	—
LXi 4-door van, AWD	33940	30602	—
Destination charge	580	580	580

Fair price not available at time of publication. AWD denotes all-wheel drive. FWD denotes front-wheel drive.

Standard Equipment:

LX: 3.3-liter V-6 engine (FWD), 3.8-liter V-6 engine (AWD), 4-speed automatic transmission, driver- and passenger-side air bags, anti-lock brakes, power steering, air conditioning with dual controls, traction control (FWD), dual sliding side doors, cruise control, seven passenger seating (cloth reclining front bucket seats, reclining and folding middle bucket seats, rear-seat recliner and headrests), passenger-side underseat storage drawer, tinted glass, tilt steering column, leather-wrapped steering wheel, overhead console with compass and trip computer, AM/FM/cassette, digital clock, tachometer, coolant-temperature gauge, trip odometer, power windows and door locks, remote keyless entry, heated power mirrors, variable intermittent wipers, variable intermittent rear wiper/washer, windshield wiper de-icer, rear defogger, reading lights, fog lights, front and rear auxiliary power outlets, illuminated visor mirrors, floormats, 215/65R15 tires (FWD), 215/70R15 tires (AWD), wheel covers. **SX** adds: 3.3-liter V-6 engine, striping, 215/65R16 tires, alloy wheels. **LXi** adds: 3.8-liter V-6 engine, rear air conditioning, load-leveling suspension, sunscreen/solar tinted windshield, rear privacy glass, 8-way power front bucket seats with driver-side memory, leather upholstery, CD player with 10-speaker Infinity sound system and equalizer, automatic day/night mirror, outside memory mirrors, security alarm, rear reading lights, roof rack, 215/70R16 tires (AWD), full-size spare tire.

Optional Equipment:

	Retail Price	Dealer Invoice	Fair Price
3.8-liter V-6 engine, LX, SX	$325	$276	—
Requires option pkg.			
Pkg. 28R/29R LX, Pkg. 28H/29H SX	385	327	—
Sunscreen/solar glass, 10-speaker Infinity sound system, equalizer, 8-way power driver seat. Pkg. 29R and 29H require 3.8-liter V-6 engine.			
Integrated child seats	NC	NC	NC
Reclining and folding middle bench seat with two integrated child seats replaces middle bucket seats. LX and SX require option pkg. NA with leather upholstery on LX and SX.			
Rear air conditioning and heater, LX	405	344	—
Requires option pkg.			
Loading and Towing Group I, LX, SX	110	94	—
Full-size spare. Requires option pkg.			
Loading and Towing Group II, LX, SX	180	153	—
ordered with Touring Handling Group	145	123	—
Includes Heavy Load/Firm Ride Suspension and full-size spare. Requires option pkg. NA with AWD.			
Loading & Towing Group III, LX, SX	380	323	—
ordered with Touring Handling Group	345	293	—
Trailer Tow Group, Heavy Load/Firm Ride Suspension, and full-size spare. Requires option pkg.			
Trailer Tow Group, LXi	270	230	—
Heavy-duty battery, brakes, suspension, and radiator; heavy-duty transmission oil cooler; trailer wiring harness.			
Touring Handling Group, LX	470	400	—
SX	60	51	—
Touring suspension, upgraded front struts and rear shock absorbers, rear stabilizer bar, alloy wheels (LX), 215/65R16 tires (LX). Requires option pkg. NA with AWD.			

	Retail Price	Dealer Invoice	Fair Price
Load-leveling suspension, LX, SX	$290	$247	—
Requires option pkg. NA with AWD.			
Leather bucket seats, LX, SX	890	757	—
NA with integrated child seats.			
Cassette/CD player with ten Infinity speakers and equalizer, LX, SX	395	336	—
Requires option pkg.			
Security alarm, LX, SX	150	128	—
Requires option pkg.			
Roof rack, LX, SX	175	149	—
Requires option pkg.			
Metallic paint	200	170	—
Engine block heater	35	30	—
Smoker's Group	20	17	—
Cigarette lighter, ashtrays.			
Alloy wheels, LX with option pkg.	410	349	—

Plymouth Voyager	Retail Price	Dealer Invoice	Fair Price
Base 3-door van, SWB	$17235	$15687	—
Base Grand 3-door van	18580	16910	—
SE 3-door van, SWB	19925	18054	—
Grand SE 3-door van	20755	18824	—
Destination charge	580	580	580

Fair price not available at time of publication. SWB denotes short wheelbase.

Standard Equipment:

Base: 2.4-liter DOHC 4-cylinder engine, 3-speed automatic transmission, driver- and passenger-side air bags, power steering, tinted glass, cloth reclining front bucket seats, 3-passenger rear bench seat (SWB), folding 2-passenger middle bench seat (Grand), folding 3-passenger rear bench seat (Grand), AM/FM radio, digital clock, trip odometer, dual exterior mirrors, variable intermittent wipers, variable intermittent rear wiper/washer, visor mirrors, auxiliary power outlet, 205/75R14 tires, wheel covers. **SE** adds: 4-speed automatic transmission, anti-lock brakes, cruise control, tilt steering column, folding 2-passenger middle bench seat with armrest (SWB), deluxe cloth upholstery, cassette player, tachometer, heated power mirrors, storage drawer below passenger seat, dual horns, additional sound insulation, cargo net, 215/65R15 tires.

Optional Equipment:

Anti-lock brakes, base	565	480	—

Prices are accurate at time of publication; subject to manufacturer's change.

DODGE

	Retail Price	Dealer Invoice	Fair Price
3.0-liter V-6 engine	$770	$655	—

NA with 4-speed automatic transmission. Base requires option pkg. NA SE Pkgs. 28C, 28E, 28L, or 28N.

3.3-liter V-6 engine	970	825	—

Requires 4-speed automatic transmission (std. on SE) and option pkg.

4-speed automatic transmission, base	250	213	—

Requires 3.3-liter V-6 engine and option pkg.

3-speed automatic transmission (credit), SE	(250)	(213)	(213)

Requires 3.0-liter V-6 engine. NA SE Pkgs. 28C, 28E, 28L, or 28N.

Pkg. 22T/24T/28T, base SWB	390	332	—
base Grand	40	34	—

Air conditioning, CYE 7-passenger Seating Group (folding 2-passenger middle bench seat, folding 3-passenger rear bench seat) (SWB), rear sound insulation, storage drawer below passenger seat, dual horns. Pkg. 24T requires 3.0-liter V-6 engine. Pkg. 28T requires 3.3-liter V-6 engine.

Pkg. 23B/24B/28B, SE	505	429	—

Air conditioning, CYN 7-passenger Deluxe Seating Group (reclining/folding 2-passenger middle bench seat and 3-passenger rear bench seat with adjustable headrests), rear defogger. Pkg. 24B requires 3.0-liter V-6 engine. Pkg. 28B requires 3.3-liter V-6 engine.

Pkg. 28C (Rallye), SE	1340	1139	—

Pkg. 23B/24B/28B plus Rallye Decor Group (solar-control glass, Rallye decals, striping, body-color grille and door handles, roof rack, alloy wheels). Requires 3.3-liter V-6 engine.

Pkg. 24D/28D, SE	1240	1054	—

Pkg. 23B/24B/28B plus power windows and door locks, Light Group (courtesy lights, illuminated ignition w/time delay), illuminated visor mirrors, added sound insulation, floormats. Pkg. 24D requires 3.0-liter engine. Pkg. 28D requires 3.3-liter V-6 engine.

Pkg. 28E (Rallye), SE	2075	1763	—

Pkg. 24D/28D plus Rallye Decor Group. Requires 3.3-liter V-6 engine.

Pkg. 28L, SE	3080	2618	—

Pkg. 24D/28D plus CYS Deluxe 7-passenger Seating Group (reclining/folding middle bucket seats, and rear 3-passenger bench seat with adjustable headrests), premium cloth upholstery, 8-way power driver seat, sliding driver-side door, overhead console w/trip computer, intermediate map/courtesy lights. Requires 3.3-liter V-6 engine.

	Retail Price	Dealer Invoice	Fair Price
Pkg. 28N (Rallye), SE	$3915	$3327	—

Pkg. 28L plus Rallye Decor Group. Requires 3.3-liter V-6 engine.

CYE 7-passenger Seating Group,
| base SWB .... | 350 | 298 | — |

Folding 2-passenger middle bench seat, folding 3-passenger rear bench seat.

| CYK 7-passenger Seating Group, base ...... | 285 | 242 | — |

Reclining/folding 2-passenger middle bench seat with two integrated child seats and adjustable headrests, folding 3-passenger rear bench seat. Requires option pkg.

| CYR Deluxe 7-passenger Seating Group, SE . | 225 | 191 | — |

CYN Deluxe 7-passenger Seating Group with two integrated child seats in middle bench. Requires option pkg. (NA with Pkg. 28L or 28N).

CYS Deluxe 7-passenger Seating Group,
| SE .... | 625 | 531 | — |

Reclining/folding middle bucket seats and rear 3-passenger bench seat with adjustable headrests. Requires Pkg. 24D/28D or 28E. Requires sliding driver-side door.

| Climate Group 1 .... | 860 | 731 | — |

Air conditioning.

| Climate Group 2 .... | 450 | 383 | — |

Solar-control glass, windshield wiper de-icer. Requires option pkg. Included with Rallye Decor Group.

Climate Group 3,
Grand SE w/Pkg. 23B/24B/28B	1130	961	—
Grand SE w/Pkg. 28C	680	578	—
Grand SE w/Pkg. 24D/28D	1020	867	—
Grand SE w/Pkg. 28E	570	485	—
Grand SE w/Pkg. 28L	940	799	—
Grand SE w/Pkg. 28N	490	417	—

Rear heater and air conditioning, overhead console. Requires optional engine.

| Convenience/Security Group 1, base .... | 435 | 370 | — |

Cruise control, tilt steering, power mirrors. Requires option pkg.

| Convenience/Security Group 2, base .... | 750 | 638 | — |
| SE .... | 315 | 268 | — |

Group 1 plus power locks. Requires option pkg.

| Convenience/Security Group 3, SE .... | 685 | 582 | — |

Group 1 plus power windows and rear quarter vent windows. Requires option pkg.

| Convenience/Security Group 4, SE .... | 235 | 200 | — |

Remote keyless entry, illuminated entry, headlight-off delay. Requires Pkg. 24D/28D, 28E, 28L, or 28N.

DODGE

	Retail Price	Dealer Invoice	Fair Price
Convenience/Security			
Group 5, SE	$385	$327	—
Group 3 plus security alarm. Requires Pkg. 24D/28D, 28E, 28L, or 28N.			
Loading & Towing Group 1	110	94	—
Full-size spare tire. Requires option pkg.			
Loading & Towing Group 2, SE	180	153	—
Group 1 plus heavy load/firm ride suspension. Requires option pkg.			
Loading & Towing Group 3,			
Grand SE	445	378	—
ordered w/Climate Group III	380	323	—
Group 2 plus Heavy Duty Trailer Tow Group (heavy-duty battery alternator, brakes, and radiator, heavy-duty transmission-oil cooler, trailer wiring harness). Requires Pkg. 28D, 28E, 28L, or 28N. Requires 3.3-liter V-6 engine.			
Load-leveling suspension,			
Grand SE	290	247	—
Requires Pkg. 24D/28D, 28E, 28L, or 28N.			
Rear defogger,			
base w/o Convenience/			
Security Group	195	166	—
base w/Convenience/			
Security Group,			
SE	230	196	—
Includes windshield wiper de-icer.			
Sliding driver-side door	595	506	—
Requires option pkg.			
AM/FM/cassette, base	180	153	—
Requires option pkg.			
10-speaker cassette			
player w/equalizer,			
SE	325	276	—
Requires Pkg. 24D/28D, 28E, 28L, or 28N.			
10-speaker cassette/CD			
w/equalizer, SE	720	612	—
Requires Pkg. 24D/28D, 28E, 28L, or 28N.			
Roof rack	175	149	—
Requires option pkg.			
Engine-block heater	35	30	—
Smoker's Group	20	17	—
Cigarette lighter, ashtrays.			
Alloy wheels, Grand SE	415	353	—
Requires Pkg. 23B/24B/28B, 24D/28D, or 28L.			

CONSUMER GUIDE®

DODGE INTREPID/ CHRYSLER CONCORDE/ EAGLE VISION

Dodge Intrepid

Specifications

	4-door notchback
Wheelbase, in.	113.0
Overall length, in.	201.8
Overall width, in.	74.4
Overall height, in.	56.3
Curb weight, lbs.	3411
Cargo vol., cu. ft.	16.7
Fuel capacity, gals.	18.0
Seating capacity	6

Engines

	ohv V-6	ohc V-6
Size, liters/cu. in.	3.3/202	3.5/215
Horsepower @ rpm	161 @ 5300	214 @ 5850
Torque (lbs./ft.) @ rpm	181 @ 3200	221 @ 3100

EPA city/highway mpg

4-speed OD automatic	19/27	17/26

Built in Canada.

PRICES

Dodge Intrepid	Retail Price	Dealer Invoice	Fair Price
4-door notchback	$19445	$17836	$18636

Prices are accurate at time of publication; subject to manufacturer's change.

DODGE

	Retail Price	Dealer Invoice	Fair Price
ES 4-door notchback	$22910	$20920	21720
Destination charge	550	550	550

Standard Equipment:

3.3-liter V-6 engine, 4-speed automatic transmission, driver- and passenger-side air bags, power steering, air conditioning, cruise control, cloth front bucket seats, console with armrest and cupholders, solar-control glass, heated power mirrors, power windows and door locks, rear defogger, tilt steering column, intermittent wipers, AM/FM cassette with six speakers, tachometer, coolant-temperature gauge, headlamp shut-off delay, trip odometer, AM/FM radio, reading lights, visor mirrors, remote decklid release, touring suspension, fog lamps, floormats, 225/60R16 touring tires, wheel covers. **ES** adds: 3.5-liter OHC V-6 engine, anti-lock 4-wheel disc brakes, variable-assist power steering, premium cloth front bucket seats with lumbar support adjustment, power driver seat, leather-wrapped steering wheel, eight speakers, Message Center, fold-away outside mirrors, remote keyless entry, remote decklid release, illuminated visor mirrors, dual exhaust outlets, alloy wheels.

Optional Equipment:

Pkg. 22E, base	800	712	760

3.5-liter OHC V-6 engine, autostick transmission, 8-way power driver seat, leather-wrapped steering wheel, Message Center.

Pkg. 26R, ES	1400	1246	1330

Autostick transmission, traction control, automatic temperature control, overhead console (compass/temperature/traveler displays, front and rear reading lamps, storage compartment, automatic day/night mirror, illuminated visor mirrors), Chrysler/Infinity cassette system, security alarm, cargo net, conventional spare tire.

Convenience Group, base	420	374	399
base w/Pkg. 26E	395	352	363

Message center, illuminated visor mirrors, remote keyless entry, remote decklid release.

Anti-lock 4-wheel disc brakes, base	625	556	594
base w/Pkg. 22E or Convenience Group	600	534	570
Traction control, ES	175	156	166
Automatic temperature control, ES	155	138	147
Overhead console, ES	385	343	366

Compass/temperature/traveler displays, front and rear reading lamps, storage compartment, automatic day/night mirror, illuminated visor mirrors. NA with power sunroof.

	Retail Price	Dealer Invoice	Fair Price
AM/FM/cassette, base	$350	$312	$333
Includes amplifier and eight speakers.			
Chrysler/Infinity Spatial Imaging Cassette Sound System, ES	215	191	198
AM/FM cassette with equalizer, amplifier, 11 Infinity speakers.			
Chrysler/Infinity Spatial Imaging Cassette/Compact Disc Sound System, ES	515	458	474
ES w/Pkg. 26R	300	267	285
AM/FM stereo, compact disc player, equalizer, amplifier.			
Power moonroof, base w/Pkg. 22E, ...	1275	1135	1211
base w/Convenience Group, ES	1100	979	1045
ES w/Pkg. 26R	720	641	684
Includes mini overhead console (compass/temperature/traveler displays, front and rear reading lamps, automatic day/night mirror, illuminated visor mirrors).			
Cloth 50/50 front bench seat, base	NC	NC	NC
NA with Pkg. 26E.			
8-way power driver seat, base	380	338	361
Power passenger's seat, ES	380	338	361
Leather front bucket seats, ES	1015	903	964
Includes power front seats, leather-wrapped shift knob.			
Security alarm, ES	155	138	147
Requires automatic temperature control.			
Performance Handling Group, ES	220	196	209
Performance suspension, 225/60VR16 performance tires.			
Conventional spare tire	125	111	119
Metallic paint	200	178	190
Engine block heater	20	18	19
Polycast wheel, base	150	134	143

Chrysler Concorde	Retail Price	Dealer Invoice	Fair Price
LX 4-door notchback $20435	$18717	$19517
Destination charge	550	550	550

Standard Equipment:

LX: 3.5-liter V-6 engine, 4-speed automatic transmission, driver- and passenger-side air bags, touring suspension, power steering, air conditioning, tilt steering wheel, cruise control, cloth front bucket seats w/power driver seat, lumbar support adjuster, front console with armrest, power windows and door locks, tachometer, trip odometer, coolant-temperature gauge, tinted glass with solar-control front and rear windows, AM/FM/cassette with six speakers, rear

DODGE

defogger, intermittent wipers, heated power mirrors, power decklid release, reading lights, floormats, dual exhaust outlets, 225/60R16 tires, wheel covers.

Optional Equipment:

	Retail Price	Dealer Invoice	Fair Price
Anti-lock brakes	$600	$534	$570
Pkg. 26C	1280	1139	1216

Automatic temperature control, eight speakers, remote keyless entry, overhead console (trip computer, compass, outside temperature readout, automatic day/night mirror), illuminated visor mirrors, cargo net.

LXi Pkg. 26D	4230	3765	4018

Pkg. 26C plus anti-lock brakes, variable-assist power steering, Infinity cassette system, traction control, leather front bucket seats, power passenger seat, leather-wrapped steering wheel and shifter, foldaway outside mirrors, security alarm, sparkle-gold alloy wheels.

Luxury Appearance Pkg., LX w/Pkg. 26C	1135	1010	1078

Leather bench seats, power passenger seat, leather-wrapped steering wheel, alloy wheels. Deletes overhead console.

Traction control, Pkg. 26C	175	156	166
Power front passenger seat			
Pkg. 26C	380	338	361
Cloth 50/50 split bench front seat, LX	NC	NC	NC
Pkg. 26C (credit)	(155)	(138)	(138)

Overhead console is deleted when ordered with Pkg. 26C.

Power moonroof, w/Pkg. 26C or			
LXi Pkg. 26D	720	641	684

Includes mini overhead console. Mini console replaces full overhead console.

Security alarm, Pkg. 26C	150	134	143
Chrysler/Infinity cassette system,			
w/Pkg. 26C	215	191	204

Includes equalizer, 11 speakers, amplifier.

Chrysler/Infinity cassette/CD system,			
w/Pkg. 26C	515	458	489
w/LXi Pkg. 26D	300	267	285

Includes equalizer, 11 speakers, amplifier.

Alloy wheels, Pkg. 26C	365	325	347
Full-size spare tire	125	111	113
Bright platinum metallic paint	200	178	190
Engine block heater	20	18	19

Eagle Vision	Retail Price	Dealer Invoice	Fair Price
ESi 4-door notchback	$20305	$18591	$19191

	Retail Price	Dealer Invoice	Fair Price
TSi 4-door notchback	$24485	$22347	$22947
Destination charge	550	550	550

Standard Equipment:

ESi: 3.5-liter V-6 engine, 4-speed automatic transmission, driver- and passenger-side air bags, air conditioning, power steering, cruise control, touring suspension, reclining front bucket seats with lumbar support adjustment, floor console, tilt steering wheel, rear defogger, solar-control tinted glass, power windows and door locks, power mirrors, AM/FM/cassette with six speakers, visor mirrors, intermittent wipers, remote decklid release, floormats, 225/60R16 touring tires, polycast wheels. **TSi** adds: Autostick 4-speed automatic transmission, anti-lock 4-wheel disc brakes, traction control, variable-assist power steering, automatic climate control, power driver seat, overhead console, automatic day/night rearview mirror, remote keyless entry system, AM/FM/cassette with eight speakers, trip computer, leather-wrapped steering wheel, illuminated visor mirrors, fog lamps, dual exhaust outlets, 225/60R16 tires, alloy wheels.

Optional Equipment:

Pkg. 26C, ESi	600	534	570
Power driver seat, remote keyless entry system, illuminated visor mirrors.			
Pkg. 26M, TSi	1155	1028	1097
Chrysler/Infinity cassette system, leather/vinyl bucket seats, security alarm, cargo net, full-size spare tire.			
Anti-lock brakes, ESi	600	534	570
Power moonroof, ESi w/Pkg. 26C	1100	979	1045
TSi	720	641	684
Mini overhead console replaces full console (TSi).			
Leather/vinyl bucket seats, TSi	620	552	589
Power driver's seat, ESi	380	338	361
Performance Handling Group,			
TSi w/Pkg. 26M	220	196	209
Performance suspension, 225/60VR16 performance tires. Requires full-size spare tire.			
AM/FM/cassette with eight speakers, ESi ...	350	312	333
Chrysler/Infinity cassette system, ESi	565	503	537
TSi	215	191	204
Includes equalizer, amplifier, 11 speakers. ESi requires Pkg. 26C.			
Chrysler/Infinity cassette/CD system, TSi ...	515	458	489
TSi w/Pkg. 26M	300	267	285
Includes equalizer, amplifier, 11 speakers.			

Prices are accurate at time of publication; subject to manufacturer's change.

DODGE

	Retail Price	Dealer Invoice	Fair Price
Security alarm, TSi	$150	$134	$143
Full-size spare tire	125	111	119
Bright platinum metallic paint	200	178	190
Engine block heater	20	18	19

DODGE/PLYMOUTH NEON

Dodge Neon 2-door

Specifications

	2-door notchback	4-door notchback
Wheelbase, in.	104.0	104.0
Overall length, in.	171.8	171.8
Overall width, in.	67.5	67.5
Overall height, in.	53.0	52.8
Curb weight, lbs.	2385	2428
Cargo vol., cu. ft.	11.8	11.8
Fuel capacity, gals.	12.5	12.5
Seating capacity	5	5

Engines

	ohc I-4	dohc I-4
Size, liters/cu. in.	2.0/122	2.0/122
Horsepower @ rpm	132 @ 6000	150 @ 6500
Torque (lbs./ft.) @ rpm	129 @ 5000	133 @ 5500
EPA city/highway mpg		
5-speed OD manual	29/39	29/39
3-speed automatic	25/34	25/34

Built in Belvidere, Ill., and Mexico.

PRICES

Dodge/Plymouth Neon	Retail Price	Dealer Invoice	Fair Price
Base 2-door notchback	$10800	$10131	$10300
Base 4-door notchback	11000	10315	10500
Highline 2-door notchback	12470	11418	11970
Highline 4-door notchback	12670	11598	12170
Destination charge	500	500	500

Standard Equipment:

Base: 2.0-liter 4-cylinder engine, 5-speed manual transmission, driver- and passenger-side air bags, power steering, cloth reclining bucket seats, storage armrest with cupholders, trip odometer, tinted glass, AM/FM radio with four speakers, dual remote mirrors, passenger-side visor mirror, variable intermittent wipers, 175/70R14 tires, wheel covers. **Highline** adds: air conditioning, 60/40 split folding rear seat, dual visor mirrors, remote decklid release, bodyside moldings, 185/65R14 touring tires.

Optional Equipment:

2.0-liter DOHC 4-cylinder engine, Highline w/option pkg.	NC	NC	NC
3-speed automatic transmission	600	534	570
Air conditioning, Base	1000	890	950
Anti-lock 4-wheel disc brakes	565	503	537

NA with Competition Pkg.

Competition Pkg., Base 2-door	1730	1592	1644
Base 4-door	1560	1435	1549

2.0-liter DOHC 4-cylinder engine (2-door), 5-speed manual performance transmission, 4-wheel disc brakes, dual remote mirrors, heavy duty radiator, 16:1 ratio power steering, competition suspension, tachometer with low fuel light, Power Bulge hood, 175/65HR14 tires (4-door), 185/60HR14 tires (2-door), alloy wheels.

National Champion Interior Pkg., base	500	460	475

Tango cloth upholstery, 60/40 split folding rear seat, leather-wrapped steering wheel and shift knob. Requires Competition Pkg.

Highline Sport Pkg. 21G/22G/23G/24G, Highline	300	267	285

Tango cloth upholstery, tachometer, interior assist handles, Sport graphics, power bulge hood, rear spoiler, fog lamps, sport wheel covers. Pkg. 22G requires 3-speed automatic transmission. Pkg. 23G requires 2.0-liter DOHC 4-cylinder engine. Pkg. 24G requires 2.0-liter DOHC 4-cylinder engine and 3-speed automatic transmission.

Deluxe Convenience Group, Highline	350	312	333

Cruise control, tilt steering.

Prices are accurate at time of publication; subject to manufacturer's change.

	Retail Price	Dealer Invoice	Fair Price
Power Convenience Group,			
Highline 4-door	$300	$267	$285
Highline 2-door	260	231	247
Power mirrors and door locks.			
Light Group, Highline	130	116	124
Illuminated visor mirrors, courtesy/reading lights.			
Power moonroof, Highline	595	530	565
Rear defogger, Base	205	182	195
Remote keyless entry, Highline	155	138	147
Requires Power Convenience Group.			
Bodyside moldings, Base	60	53	58
NA with Competition Pkg.			
Dual manual remote mirrors, Base	70	62	67
NA with Competition Pkg.			
AM/FM/cassette with eight speakers	260	231	247
NA with Competition Pkg.			
Premium AM/FM/cassette w/eight speakers,			
Highline	285	254	271
Premium AM/FM/CD player w/eight speakers,			
Highline	395	352	375
Integrated child seat, Highline	100	89	95
Includes fixed rear seat back.			
Tilt steering wheel, Base	150	134	143
NA with Competition Pkg.			
Power front door windows, Highline	265	236	252
Tachometer with low fuel light, Highline	100	89	95
Front and rear floormats	50	45	48
NA Competition Pkg.			
Alloy wheels, Highline w/option pkg.	355	316	337

DODGE STRATUS/ CHRYSLER CIRRUS/ PLYMOUTH BREEZE

Specifications

	4-door notchback
Wheelbase, in.	108.0
Overall length, in.	186.0
Overall width, in.	71.7
Overall height, in.	52.4

Dodge Stratus

	4-door notchback
Curb weight, lbs.	2922
Cargo vol., cu. ft.	15.7
Fuel capacity, gals.	16.0
Seating capacity	5

Engines

	ohc I-4	dohc I-4	ohc V-6
Size, liters/cu. in.	2.0/122	2.4/148	2.5/152
Horsepower @ rpm	132 @ 6000	150 @ 5200	168 @ 5800
Torque (lbs./ft.) @ rpm	129 @ 5000	165 @ 4000	170 @ 4350

EPA city/highway mpg

	ohc I-4	dohc I-4	ohc V-6
5-speed OD manual	26/37		
4-speed OD automatic		20/30	20/29

Built in Sterling Heights, Mich.

PRICES

Dodge Stratus	Retail Price	Dealer Invoice	Fair Price
4-door notchback	$14990	$13771	$14271
ES 4-door notchback	16785	15396	15796
Destination charge	535	535	535

Standard Equipment:

Base: 2.0-liter 4-cylinder engine, 5-speed manual transmission, driver- and passenger-side air bags, air conditioning, power steering, cloth reclining front bucket seats, console, folding rear bench seat, AM/FM/cassette, digital clock, trip odometer, oil-pressure and coolant-temperature gauges, tachometer, voltmeter, cruise control, tilt steering column, rear defogger, tinted glass with solar-control

Prices are accurate at time of publication; subject to manufacturer's change.

DODGE

windshield, dual remote mirrors, intermittent wipers, remote decklid release, visor mirrors, front floormats, 195/70R14 tires, wheel covers. **ES** adds: anti-lock brakes, touring suspension, variable-assist power steering, 4-way manual driver seat with height and lumbar-support adjusters, power windows and door locks, heated power mirrors, reading lights, fog lights, illuminated visor mirrors, rear floormats, alloy wheels, 195/65HR15 touring tires.

Optional Equipment:

	Retail Price	Dealer Invoice	Fair Price
2.4-liter DOHC 4-cylinder engine	$450	$401	$414
Requires 4-speed automatic transmission. NA ES w/Pkg. 26S.			
2.5-liter V-6 engine, ES	1250	1113	1150
Requires 4-speed automatic transmission.			
4-speed automatic transmission, base	1050	935	966
ES	825	734	759
Includes cruise control. Requires 2.4-liter DOHC 4-cylinder engine or 2.5-liter V-6 engine.			
Autostick transmission, ES	150	134	138
Requires 2.5-liter V-6 engine and 4-speed automatic transmission.			
Anti-lock brakes, Base	565	503	520
Pkg. 21B/24B, Base	685	609	630
Power windows and door locks, heated power mirrors, 4-way manual driver seat with height adjuster, rear floormats. Pkg. 24B requires 2.4-liter DOHC 4-cylinder engine and 4-speed automatic transmission.			
Pkg. 21K/24K, ES	1805	1606	1661
Premium cassette player, Personal Security Group, anti-theft alarm, 8-way power driver seat, leather upholstery, leather-wrapped steering wheel, trunk net. Pkg. 24K requires 2.4-liter DOHC 4-cylinder engine and 4-speed automatic transmission. NA w/2.5-liter V-6 engine.			
Pkg. 26S, ES	1955	1740	1799
Pkg. 21K/24K plus autostick transmission. Requires 2.5-liter V-6 engine and 4-speed automatic transmission.			
Personal Security Group	170	151	156
Remote keyless entry, illuminated entry, panic alarm, headlamp time delay. Base requires Pkg. 21B/24B.			
Anti-theft alarm, ES	149	132	137
Requires Personal Security Group.			
Integrated child safety seat	100	89	92
Includes fixed rear seatback. NA ES w/Pkg. 26S.			
Premium cassette player	340	303	313
Includes eight speakers and power amplifier.			
CD player	200	178	184
NA on ES with option pkg.			

	Retail Price	Dealer Invoice	Fair Price
6-disc CD changer and premium cassette player	$550	$490	$506
NA on ES with option pkg.			
6-disc CD changer, ES	500	445	460
Candy apple red metallic paint	200	178	184
Full-size spare tire	125	111	115
Engine-block and battery heater	30	27	28
Smoker's Group	20	18	18
Ashtray, lighter.			

Chrysler Cirrus	Retail Price	Dealer Invoice	Fair Price
LX 4-door notchback	$18160	$16637	$17137
Destination charge	535	535	535

Standard Equipment:

2.4-liter DOHC 4-cylinder engine, 4-speed automatic transmission, anti-lock brakes, driver- and passenger-side air bags, variable-assist power steering, air conditioning, cloth reclining front bucket seats with driver-side manual height and lumbar adjusters, folding rear bench seat, console, AM/FM/cassette with four speakers, digital clock, trip odometer, oil-pressure and coolant-temperature gauges, voltmeter, tachometer, cruise control, tilt steering column, rear defogger, power windows and door locks, tinted glass with solar-control windshield, heated power mirrors, speed-sensitive intermittent wipers, illuminated remote keyless entry, remote decklid release, universal garage-door opener, reading lights, auxiliary power outlet, color-keyed bodyside moldings, illuminated visor mirrors, fog lights, floormats, 195/65R15 tires, wheel covers.

Optional Equipment:

2.5-liter V-6 engine	800	712	736
LXi Pkg.	2335	2078	2148
Firm Feel suspension, leather upholstery, leather-wrapped steering wheel and shift lever, 8-way power driver's seat, premium cassette player w/eight speakers and power amplifier, remote keyless entry w/security alarm, color-keyed grille, cargo net, 195/65HR15 touring tires, chromed alloy wheels. Requires 2.5-liter V-6 engine.			
Gold Pkg.	450	264	414
Gold trim and badging, alloy wheels. NA w/LXi Pkg.			
8-way power driver seat	380	338	350
Integrated child safety seat	100	89	92
Includes fixed rear seatback. NA w/LXi Pkg.			

DODGE

	Retail Price	Dealer Invoice	Fair Price
Premium cassette player	$340	$303	$313
Includes eight speakers and power amplifier.			
Premium CD player	200	178	184
NA w/LXi Pkg.			
Premium cassette and 6-disc CD changer .	550	490	506
6-disc CD changer	500	445	460
Remote keyless entry w/security alarm	150	134	138
Trip computer	160	142	147
Metallic candy-apple-red paint	200	178	184
Full-size spare tire	125	111	113
Alloy wheels	320	285	294
NA w/LXi Pkg.			
Engine block and battery heater	30	27	28

Plymouth Breeze	Retail Price	Dealer Invoice	Fair Price
4-door notchback $14825	$13599	$14099
Destination charge	535	535	535

Standard Equipment:

2.0-liter 4-cylinder engine, 5-speed manual transmission, driver- and passenger-side air bags, air conditioning, power steering, cloth reclining front bucket seats, folding rear seat, center storage console, tilt steering column, dual remote mirrors, trip odometer, tachometer, voltmeter, oil-pressure gauge, coolant-temperature gauge, tinted glass, 4-speaker AM/FM radio, digital clock, cupholders, rear defogger, speed-sensitive intermittent wipers, auxiliary power outlet, remote decklid release, tinted glass, visor mirrors, front floormats, 195/70R14 tires, wheel covers.

Optional Equipment:

4-speed automatic transmission	1050	935	966
Includes cruise control.			
Pkg. 21B/22B	676	609	622
4-way manual driver-seat height adjuster, power heated mirrors, power door locks and windows, rear floormats.			
Cold Weather Pkg.	30	27	28
Engine-block heater, battery heater.			
Anti-lock 4-wheel disc brakes	565	503	520
Integrated child seat	100	89	92
Includes fixed rear seat.			
Personal Security Pkg.	170	151	156
Remote keyless entry w/alarm, illuminated entry. Requires Pkg. 21B/22B.			

	Retail Price	Dealer Invoice	Fair Price
Cassette player	$180	$160	$166
Premium CD player	380	338	350
Premium AM/FM/cassette and 6-disc CD changer	730	650	672
Smoker's Pkg.	20	18	18
Lighter, ashtray.			
Full-size spare	125	111	115
Candy-apple red paint	200	178	184

1998 FORD CONTOUR/ MERCURY MYSTIQUE

1998 Ford Contour LX

Specifications

	4-door notchback
Wheelbase, in.	106.5
Overall length, in.	184.7
Overall width, in.	69.1
Overall height, in.	54.5
Curb weight, lbs.	2772
Cargo vol., cu. ft.	13.9
Fuel capacity, gals.	14.5
Seating capacity	5

Engines

	dohc I-4	dohc V-6
Size, liters/cu. in.	2.0/121	2.5/155
Horsepower @ rpm	125 @ 5500	170 @ 6250

Prices are accurate at time of publication; subject to manufacturer's change.

FORD

	dohc I-4	dohc V-6
Torque (lbs./ft.) @ rpm	130 @ 4000	165 @ 4250
EPA city/highway mpg		
5-speed OD manual	24/33	20/30
4-speed OD automatic	23/32	21/30

Built in Kansas City, Mo., and Mexico.

PRICES

1998 Ford Contour	Retail Price	Dealer Invoice	Fair Price
4-door notchback	$13460	$12614	—
GL 4-door notchback	14645	13399	—
LX 4-door notchback	15195	13889	—
SE 4-door notchback	17535	15971	—
Destination charge	535	535	535

Fair price not available at time of publication All models require a Preferred Pkg., pricing and contents may vary in some regions.

Standard Equipment:

Base: 2.0-liter DOHC 4-cylinder engine, 5-speed manual transmission, driver- and passenger-side air bags, power steering, cloth reclining front bucket seats, console w/cupholder, tilt steering wheel, dual remote mirrors, digital clock, trip odometer, coolant temperature gauge, solar-control tinted glass, intermittent wipers, visor mirrors, AM/FM radio, remote decklid releases, interior air filter, 185/70R14 tires, wheel covers. **GL** adds: upgraded console with armrest, cloth door-trim panel. **LX** adds: split folding rear seat, heated power mirrors, tachometer, illuminated entry, cassette player, illuminated visor mirrors, variable intermittent wipers, rear passenger grab handles, fog lamps, 205/60R15 tires. **SE** adds: 2.5-liter DOHC V-6 engine, 4-wheel disc brakes, sport suspension, air conditioning, leather-wrapped steering wheel, rear spoiler, alloy wheels.

Optional Equipment:

2.5 liter DOHC V-6 engine, GL	1235	1099	—
LX	1200	1066	—

Includes sport suspension, anti-theft system, 4-wheel disc brakes w/manual transmission, 195/65R tires (GL), tachometer (GL). Requires Preferred Pkg.

4-speed automatic transmission	815	725	—
Air conditioning	795	708	—
Group 1, base, GL	185	165	—

Cassette player

	Retail Price	Dealer Invoice	Fair Price
Group 2, GL	$1065	$948	—
LX	985	877	—
SE	190	168	—
Rear defogger, air conditioning (GL, LX), power mirrors (GL).			
Group 3,	345	307	—
Power door locks plus Light Group (front reading light and footwell illumination, rear-door courtesy-light switches). NA base.			
Preferred Pkg. 230A, base	375	334	—
Upgraded console with armrest, cassette player, rear defogger.			
Preferred Pkg. 236A, GL	1310	1166	—
Air conditioning, cruise control, power mirrors, power door locks, cassette player, rear defogger, Light Group (front reading light and footwell illumination, rear-door courtesy-light switches).			
Preferred Pkg. 240A, GL	2685	2390	—
Pkg. 236A plus 2.5-liter DOHC V-6 engine (tachometer), power windows, 195/65R14 performance tires.			
Preferred Pkg. 238A, LX	2415	2150	—
2.5-liter V-6 engine, air conditioning, rear defogger, Light Group, power door locks and windows, cruise control.			
Preferred Pkg. 239A, SE	590	525	—
Air conditioning, rear defogger, power mirrors, Light Group, power door locks and windows, cruise control.			
Sport Pkg., GL	525	468	—
LX	450	401	—
Alloy wheels, 205/60R15 tires (GL), leather-wrapped steering wheel and shift knob, sport floormats, tachometer (GL), fog lamps (GL).			
Leather upholstery, LX,SE	895	797	—
Requires power windows and power driver seat. LX includes leather-wrapped steering wheel.			
Anti-lock brakes	600	534	—
10-way power driver's seat, LX, SE	350	312	—
Split folding rear seat, GL	205	182	—
Includes armrest and side bolsters.			
Integrated child seat, LX, SE	135	120	—
Cruise control	215	191	—
NA base.			
Cassette player with Premium Sound, GL	315	280	—
GL w/Group 1, LX, SE	130	116	—
Includes amplifier.			
CD player with Premium Sound, GL	455	405	—
GL w/Group 1, LX, SE	270	240	—
Includes amplifier.			
Power antenna	90	80	—
NA base.			

Prices are accurate at time of publication; subject to manufacturer's change.

FORD

	Retail Price	Dealer Invoice	Fair Price
Remote keyless entry	$190	$169	—
Requires Pkg. 236A and power windows. NA base.			
Power windows, GL with Pkg. 236A	340	302	—
Power moonroof	595	530	—
NA base.			
Rear defogger	190	169	—
Rear Spoiler..	245	218	—
Alloy wheels, GL, LX	425	379	—
Includes 205/60R15 tires.			

1998 Mercury Mystique	Retail Price	Dealer Invoice	Fair Price
Base 4-door notchback	$13960	$13084	—
GS 4-door notchback	15320	14015	—
LS 4-door notchback	17270	15750	—
Destination charge	535	535	535

Fair price not available at time of publication.

Standard Equipment:

Base: 2.0-liter DOHC 4-cylinder engine, 5-speed manual transmission, driver- and passenger-side air bags, power steering, cloth reclining front bucket seats, 60/40 split folding rear seat, front storage console, tilt steering wheel, coolant-temperature gauge, trip odometer, solar-control tinted glass, AM/FM radio, dual outside mirrors, day/night rearview mirror, intermittent wipers, remote decklid release, interior air filter, visor mirrors, 185/70R14 tires, wheel covers. **GS adds:** tachometer, color-keyed power mirrors, cloth door trim. **LS adds:** 2.5 liter DOHC V-6 engine, 10-way power driver seat, cassette player, rear defogger, power antenna, variable intermittent wipers, fog lights, floormats, 205/60R15 tires, polished Mach alloy wheels. GS and LS require a Preferred Pkg.

Optional Equipment:

4-speed automatic transmission	815	725	—
Anti-lock brakes	600	534	—
Air conditioning, base	795	708	—
Preferred Pkg. 371A, GS	1560	1389	—
Group 1 (air conditioner, rear defogger, cassette player), Group 2 (power windows and door locks, Light Group [illuminated visor mirrors, map lights, illuminated entry]), cruise control.			
Preferred Pkg. 381A, LS	675	601	—
Group 1 (air conditioner), Group 2 (power windows and door locks, Light Group [illuminated passenger-side visor mirror, map lights, illuminated entry], remote keyless entry), cruise control, steering wheel.			

	Retail Price	Dealer Invoice	Fair Price
Group 1, base	$1170	$1041	—
Air conditioner, rear defogger, cassette player.			
Spree Pkg., GS	525	468	—
Leather-wrapped steering wheel and shifter, unique interior trim, fog lights, Spree floormats, Spree badging, polished Mach alloy wheels, 205/60R15 performance tires.			
Leather upholstery, LS	895	797	—
10-way power driver seat, GS	350	312	—
Integrated child seat	135	120	—
Power moonroof, GS, LS	595	530	—
Premium cassette player, base	315	280	—
GS, LS	130	116	—
Includes amplifier.			
CD player, GS, LS	270	240	—
Includes amplifier.			
Mach alloy wheels, GS	475	423	—
Includes 205/60R15 tires. NA with Spree Pkg.			
Polished Mach alloy wheels	475	423	—
Includes 205/60R15 tires.			

FORD ESCORT/ MERCURY TRACER

Ford Escort

Specifications

	4-door notchback	4-door wagon
Wheelbase, in.	98.4	98.4
Overall length, in.	174.7	172.7
Overall width, in.	66.2	66.2

Prices are accurate at time of publication; subject to manufacturer's change.

FORD

	4-door notchback	4-door wagon
Overall height, in.	53.3	53.9
Curb weight, lbs.	2457	2525
Cargo vol., cu. ft.	12.8	63.4
Fuel capacity, gals.	12.7	12.7
Seating capacity	5	5

Engines

	ohc I-4
Size, liters/cu. in.	2.0/121
Horsepower @ rpm	110 @ 5000
Torque (lbs./ft.) @ rpm	125 @ 3800
EPA city/highway mpg	
5-speed OD manual	28/37
4-speed OD automatic	26/34

Built in Wayne, Mich., and Mexico.

PRICES

Ford Escort	Retail Price	Dealer Invoice	Fair Price
4-door notchback	$11015	$10313	$10815
LX 4-door notchback	11795	11024	11524
LX 4-door wagon	12505	11669	12169
Destination charge	415	415	415

Standard Equipment:

2.0-liter 4-cylinder engine, 5-speed manual transmission, driver- and passenger-side air bags, power steering, cloth and vinyl reclining bucket seats, folding rear seat, center console with cupholders, tinted glass, dual mirrors, coolant temperature gauge, trip odometer, AM/FM radio, digital clock, variable intermittent wipers, door pockets, 185/65R14 tires, wheel covers. **LX** adds: upgraded upholstery, 60/40 split rear seatback, tachometer, passenger-side visor mirror, color-keyed bodyside moldings, bolt-on full wheel covers. **Wagon** adds: cargo cover.

Optional Equipment:

4-speed automatic transmission	815	725	758
Anti-lock brakes	570	507	530
Air conditioning, base	795	708	739
Preferred Equipment Pkg. 317A, LX	765	681	711

Air conditioning, driver-side remote keyless entry, rear defogger.

	Retail Price	Dealer Invoice	Fair Price
Preferred Equipment Pkg. 318A, LX	$1390	$1237	$1293

Pkg. 317A plus dual power mirrors, power door locks w/anti-theft system, all-door remote keyless entry, power windows.

	Retail Price	Dealer Invoice	Fair Price
Group 1, LX	910	810	846

Air conditioning, driver-side remote keyless entry.

Group 2, LX	725	646	674

Power mirrors, power door locks w/anti-theft system, all-door remote keyless entry, power windows.

Group 3, LX w/Preferred Equipment Pkg. ...	465	414	432

Cruise control, tachometer, tilt steering column, map lights, visor mirrors.

Sport Pkg., LX notchback	495	441	460

Sport seats w/rear integrated headrests, tachometer, liftgate spoiler, bright exhaust outlets, alloy wheels. Requires Preferred Equipment Pkg.

Wagon Group, LX w/Preferred Equipment Pkg.	240	213	223

Rear wiper/washer, roof rack.

Rear defogger	190	169	177
Power mirror, LX w/Pkg. 317A	95	85	88
Integrated child seat, LX	135	120	126
AM/FM/cassette	165	147	153

Requires rear defroster or air conditioning.

AM/FM/cassette w/6-disc CD changer, LX notchback w/Preferred Equipment Pkg. .	515	458	479

Includes premium sound system.

Alloy wheels, LX	265	236	246

Requires Preferred Equipment Pkg,

Floormats	45	40	42
Engine block heater	20	18	19

Mercury Tracer	Retail Price	Dealer Invoice	Fair Price
GS 4-door notchback	$11145	$10442	—
LS 4-door notchback	11950	11175	—
LS 4-door wagon	12660	11821	—
Destination charge	415	415	415

Fair price not available at time of publication. LS requires Preferred Pkg.

Standard Equipment:

GS: 2.0-liter 4-cylinder engine, 5-speed manual transmission, driver- and passenger-side air bags, power steering, cloth and vinyl reclining bucket seats, folding rear seat, center console with cupholders, tinted glass, dual mirrors, coolant temperature gauge, trip odometer, AM/FM radio, digital clock, variable intermittent wipers, door pockets, 185/65R14 tires, wheel covers. **LS** adds: upgraded upholstery, 60/40 split rear seatback, tachometer, passenger-side visor mirror, color-keyed bodyside moldings, bolt-on full wheel covers. **Wagon** adds: cargo cover.

Optional Equipment:

	Retail Price	Dealer Invoice	Fair Price
4-speed automatic transmission	$815	$725	—
Anti-lock 4-wheel disc brakes	570	507	—
Air conditioning, GS	795	708	—
Preferred Pkg. 541A, LS	835	743	—
Air conditioning, rear defogger, power mirrors, driver-side remote keyless entry.			
Preferred Pkg. 542A, LS	1530	1361	—
Pkg. 541A plus power windows, power door locks w/anti-theft system, cassette player.			
Convenience Group, LS	355	316	—
Cruise control, tilt steering wheel, dual visor mirrors, map lights, floormats.			
Trio Pkg., LS notchback	495	441	—
Fog lamps, decklid spoiler, bright exhaust outlets, alloy wheels.			
Wagon Group, wagon	240	213	—
Rear wiper/washer, roof rack.			
Rear defogger, GS	190	169	—
Integrated child seat, LS	135	120	—
AM/FM/cassette	165	147	—
Requires rear defroster or air conditioning.			
AM/FM/cassette w/6-disc CD changer, LS ..	515	458	—
LS w/Preferred Equipment Pkg. 542A	350	312	—
Includes premium sound system.			
Engine block heater	20	18	—
Floormats	45	40	—
Alloy wheels, LS	265	236	—

FORD EXPLORER/ MERCURY MOUNTAINEER

Specifications

	2-door wagon	4-door wagon
Wheelbase, in.	101.7	111.5
Overall length, in.	178.6	188.5
Overall width, in.	70.2	70.2

Ford Explorer Eddie Bauer

	2-door wagon	4-door wagon
Overall height, in.	67.0	67.0
Curb weight, lbs.	3981	4189
Cargo vol., cu. ft.	69.4	81.6
Fuel capacity, gals.	17.5	21.0
Seating capacity	4	6

Engines

	ohv V-6	ohc V-6	ohv V-8
Size, liters/cu. in.	4.0/245	4.0/245	5.0/302
Horsepower @ rpm	160 @ 4200	205 @ 5250	210 @ 4500
Torque (lbs./ft.) @ rpm	225 @ 2800	245 @ 2800	280 @ 3500

EPA city/highway mpg

	ohv V-6	ohc V-6	ohv V-8
5-speed OD manual	14/19		
4-speed OD automatic			14/18
5-speed OD automatic	15/20	15/19	

Built in Louisville, Ky., and St. Louis, Mo.

PRICES

Ford Explorer	Retail Price	Dealer Invoice	Fair Price
XL 2-door wagon, 2WD	$20085	$18285	—
XL 2-door wagon, 4WD	22050	20015	—
XL 4-door wagon, 2WD	21485	19517	—
XL 4-door wagon, 4WD	23405	21206	—
Sport 2-door wagon, 2WD	21265	19323	—
Sport 2-door wagon, 4WD	23095	20934	—
XLT 4-door wagon, 2WD	24220	21924	—
XLT 4-door wagon, 4WD	26225	23688	—

Prices are accurate at time of publication; subject to manufacturer's change.

FORD

	Retail Price	Dealer Invoice	Fair Price
XLT 4-door wagon, AWD	$26225	$23688	—
Eddie Bauer 4-door wagon, 2WD	29065	26187	—
Eddie Bauer 4-door wagon, 4WD	31070	27952	—
Eddie Bauer 4-door wagon, AWD	30730	27653	—
Limited 4-door wagon, 2WD	32720	29404	—
Limited 4-door wagon, 4WD	35005	31414	—
Limited 4-door wagon, AWD	34670	31120	—
Destination charge	525	525	525

Fair price not available at time of publication.

Standard Equipment:

XL: 4.0-liter V-6 engine, 5-speed manual transmission, anti-lock 4-wheel disc brakes, driver- and passenger-side air bags, power steering, air conditioning, vinyl front bucket seats, split folding rear bench seat with headrests, solar-control tinted windshield, intermittent wipers, auxiliary power outlet, illuminated entry, trip odometer, tachometer, AM/FM radio with digital clock, map light, cargo hooks, chrome bumpers, passenger-side visor mirror, 3.27 ratio axle, 225/70R15 tires, full-size spare tire. **Sport and XLT** add: cloth front captain's chairs (XLT), console (XLT), Power Equipment Group (power window, door, and liftgate locks, power mirrors, upgraded door-panel trim, delayed-off accessory power), speed-sensitive intermittent wipers, rear privacy glass, rear wiper/washer and defogger, power rear-liftgate lock, power mirrors, leather-wrapped steering wheel, color-keyed grille (Sport), color-keyed bodyside moldings, black painted bumpers (Sport), cruise control, tilt steering wheel, striping (XLT), cargo cover (Sport), illuminated visor mirrors, alloy wheels. **Eddie Bauer** deletes full-size spare tire and adds: 4.0-liter SOHC V-6 engine, 5-speed automatic transmission, 6-way power sport cloth front bucket seats with power lumbar adjusters, roof rack, cassette player, 2-tone paint, cargo cover, floormats, 4.10 ratio axle, 255/70R16 outline-white-letter all-terrain tires, chrome wheels. **Limited** deletes 2-tone paint, 4.10 ratio axle, chrome wheels, and adds to Eddie Bauer: automatic air conditioning, Electronics Group (remote keyless entry, anti-theft system, automatic door locks, door keypad), leather upholstery and door trim, Ford JBL Audio System with cassette player, power antenna, console with rear climate and radio controls, systems message center, overhead console with electronic compass and outside temperature indicator, heated power mirrors, running boards, automatic day/night rearview mirror, automatic headlights, fog lights, color-keyed grille and bumpers, 235/75R15 outline-white-letter all-terrain tires, full-size spare tire (2WD, 4WD). **4WD** models have Control Trac part-time 4WD, transfer-case skid plate. **AWD** models have permanent 4-wheel drive and require 5.0-liter V-8 engine and 4-speed automatic transmission.

Optional Equipment:

	Retail Price	Dealer Invoice	Fair Price
4.0-liter SOHC V-6 engine, XL, XLT, Sport .	$425	$362	—
Requires 5-speed automatic transmission.			
5.0-liter V-8 engine, XLT w/Pkg. 941A	1545	1313	—
XLT w/Pkg. 945B	1425	1212	—
Eddie Bauer 2WD	790	672	—
Eddie Bauer AWD	1140	969	—
Limited 2WD	965	820	—
Limited AWD	1315	1117	--

NA 4WD. Requires 4-speed automatic transmission. Includes limited-slip 3.73 ratio axle with Trailer Towing Pkg., 235/75R15 all-terrain outline-white-letter tires (includes full-size spare on XLT 2WD only).

4-speed automatic transmission,			
XLT w/Pkg. 941A	945	803	—
XLT w/Pkg. 945B, Eddie Bauer, Limited ..	NC	NC	NC

NA 4WD. Requires 5.0-liter V-8 engine.

5-speed automatic transmission,			
XL, XLT, Sport	1065	905	—

NA with 5.0-liter engine.

Limited-slip axle (3.73 ratio)			
and Trailer Tow Pkg.	355	302	—

NA with Eddie Bauer.

Limited-slip axle (4.10 ratio) and Trailer Tow			
Pkg., Sport w/Pkg. 934B, Eddie Bauer	310	263	—
Automatic Ride Control,			
Eddie Bauer w/Pkg. 946A, Limited	650	553	—

NA 2WD.

Preferred Equipment Pkg. 931A, Sport	145	123	—

Cloth front captain's chairs, premium cassette player, 235/75R15 all-terrain outline-white-letter tires.

Preferred Equipment Pkg. 934B, Sport	2275	1933	—

4.0-liter SOHC V-6 engine, 5-speed automatic transmission, 6-way power sport cloth bucket seats with power lumbar adjusters, Luxury Group (floor console with rear climate and radio controls, overhead console with electronic compass and outside-temperature indicator, Electronics Group [remote keyless entry, anti-theft system, automatic door locks, door keypad], fog lights), premium cassette player, floormats, 235/75R15 all-terrain outline-white-letter tires.

Preferred Equipment Pkg. 941A, XLT	NC	NC	NC

Roof rack, cassette player.

Preferred Equipment Pkg. 945B, XLT	2130	1812	—

Pkg. 941A plus 4.0-liter SOHC V-6 engine, 5-speed automatic transmission, 6-way power sport cloth bucket seats with power lumbar adjusters, Luxury Group, cargo cover, floormats.

FORD

	Retail Price	Dealer Invoice	Fair Price

Preferred Equipment Pkg. 942A,

Eddie Bauer .... NC NC NC
6-way power leather bucket seats with power lumbar adjusters. Requires Ford JBL Audio System.

Preferred Equipment Pkg. 946A,

Eddie Bauer .... $1815 $1544 —
Pkg. 942A plus Ford JBL Audio System, automatic temperature control, systems message center, Luxury Group.

Decor Group, XL .... 370 314 —
Privacy glass, bodyside molding. Requires rear wiper/washer and defogger.

Power Equipment Group, XL 2-door .... 685 583 —
XL 4-door .... 1020 867 —
Power window, door, and liftgate locks, power mirrors, upgraded door-panel trim, delayed-off accessory power. Requires cruise control, and rear wiper/washer and defogger.

Electronics Group, Eddie Bauer .... 370 314 —
Remote keyless entry, anti-theft system, automatic door locks, door keypad.

Sport Appearance Pkg.,

Sport 4WD w/Pkg. 934B .... 995 846 —
Includes 4.0-liter SOHC V-6 engine, 5-speed automatic transmission, 4.10 ratio axle, medium-graphite bumpers, moldings, and side-step bar, roof rack, rear tow hook, chrome wheels, 255/70R16 all-terrain outline-white-letter tires.

Cloth captain's chairs, XL.............................. 280 238 —
Includes console.

Cloth 60/40 bench seat, XL 4-door .... 290 247 —
XLT w/Pkg. 941A .... 10 8 —
Includes storage consolette. Requires automatic transmission.

6-way power cloth bucket seats, Sport .... 1020 867 —
XLT w/Pkg. 941A .... 955 812 —
Includes power lumbar adjusters and console. Requires Premium Sound stereo.

6-way power leather bucket seats,

Sport w/Pkg. 934B, XLT w/Pkg. 945B ..... 655 557 —
Includes floor console (XLT).

Integrated rear child seat, 4-door .... 200 170 —
Includes rear-seat recliner. NA with vinyl bucket seats.

Console with rear climate and radio controls,

Eddie Bauer .... 390 332 —
Requires Electronics Group.

Rear wiper/washer and defogger, XL .... 280 238 —
Includes speed-sensitive front wipers. Requires cruise control.

	Retail Price	Dealer Invoice	Fair Price
Automatic day/night mirror, Sport w/Pkg. 934B, XLT w/Pkg. 945B, Eddie Bauer w/Pkg. 946A	$185	$158	—
Includes automatic headlights.			
Cruise control and leather-wrapped tilt-steering wheel, XL	385	328	—
Requires rear wiper/washer and defogger.			
Power moonroof, Sport w/Pkg. 934B, XLT w/Pkg. 945B, Eddie Bauer w/Pkg. 946A, Limited	800	680	—
Includes front overhead console with rear reading lamps. Sport requires roof rack.			
Side-step bar, Sport	295	251	—
Running boards, XLT, Eddie Bauer	395	336	—
Cassette player w/Premium Sound, XL	210	178	—
Includes amp. Requires rear wiper/washer and defogger, cruise control.			
Ford JBL Audio System with cassette, Sport w/Pkg. 934B, XLT w/Pkg. 945B, Eddie Bauer	830	706	—
Includes sub-woofer, digital signal processor, and power antenna. Eddie Bauer and XLT require console with rear climate and radio controls, Electronics Group.			
CD changer, Sport w/Pkg. 934B, XLT w/Pkg. 945B, Eddie Bauer, Limited	370	314	—
Cellular telephone, Eddie Bauer w/Pkg. 946A, Limited	690	587	—
Roof rack, XL, Sport	140	119	—
2-tone paint, XLT	120	102	—
Floormats and cargo cover, XLT	125	107	—
Floormats, Sport with Pkg. 931A	45	38	—
Deep-dish alloy wheels, XLT	NC	NC	NC
235/75R15 all-terrain outline-white-letter tires, XLT	230	195	—
Includes full-size spare tire on 2WD only.			
Engine-block heater	35	30	—

Mercury Mountaineer	Retail Price	Dealer Invoice	Fair Price
4-door wagon, 2WD	$27240	$24591	—
4-door wagon, AWD	29240	26351	—
Destination charge	525	525	525

Fair price not available at time of publication. All models require a Preferred Equipment Pkg.

Prices are accurate at time of publication; subject to manufacturer's change.

FORD

Standard Equipment:

5.0-liter V-8 engine, 4-speed automatic transmission, limited-slip differential, anti-lock 4-wheel disc brakes, driver- and passenger-side air bags, air conditioning, power steering, cruise control, cloth front bucket seats w/leather headrests, split folding rear seat, floor console, tilt leather-wrapped steering wheel, power mirrors, power windows and door locks, tachometer, trip odometer, front solar-tinted glass, rear privacy glass, rear wiper/washer, rear defogger, AM/FM/cassette, digital clock, visor mirrors, speed-sensitive intermittent wipers, auxiliary power outlets, dual-note horn, door map pockets, map lights, bright grille, scuff plates, skid plate (AWD), fog lamps, 235/75R15 all-terrain outline-white-letter tires, full-size spare, alloy wheels.

Optional Equipment:

	Retail Price	Dealer Invoice	Fair Price
Preferred Equipment Pkg. 650A	$230	$195	—
Running boards, roof rack, floormats			
Preferred Equipment Pkg. 655A	1415	1203	—
Pkg. 650A plus 6-way power front seats w/power lumbar support, upgraded floor console (includes rear climate and radio controls, cupholders), overhead console (includes outside temperature gauge, compass, reading lamps, storage), Electronics Group, cargo cover.			
6-way power front seats	955	812	—
Includes power lumbar support.			
Leather upholstery	655	557	—
Requires Pkg. 655A.			
Integrated child seats	200	170	—
Requires Pkg. 655A and leather upholstery.			
Electronics Group	370	314	—
Includes remote keyless entry, anti-theft system, auto-locking. Requires 6-way power seats.			
Automatic day/night rearview mirror	185	158	—
Includes automatic on/off headlamps. Requires Pkg. 655A.			
Power moonroof	800	680	—
Requires Pkg. 655A.			
JBL Sound System w/Luxury Cassette	830	706	—
Requires Pkg. 655A.			
AM/FM/CD	65	55	
6-disc CD changer	370	314	—
Requires Pkg. 655A.			
Cargo cover	80	68	—
Engine block heater	35	30	—

FORD MUSTANG

Ford Mustang GT convertible

Specifications

	2-door notchback	2-door conv.
Wheelbase, in.	101.3	101.3
Overall length, in.	181.5	181.5
Overall width, in.	71.8	71.8
Overall height, in.	53.2	53.2
Curb weight, lbs.	3084	3264
Cargo vol., cu. ft.	10.9	7.7
Fuel capacity, gals.	15.4	15.4
Seating capacity	4	4

Engines

	ohv V-6	ohc V-8	dohc V-8
Size, liters/cu. in.	3.8/232	4.6/282	4.6/282
Horsepower @ rpm	150 @ 4000	215 @ 4400	305 @ 5800
Torque (lbs./ft.) @ rpm	215 @ 2750	285 @ 3500	300 @ 4800
EPA city/highway mpg			
5-speed OD manual	20/30	18/26	17/26
4-speed OD automatic	20/30	17/24	

Built in Dearborn, Mich.

PRICES

Ford Mustang	Retail Price	Dealer Invoice	Fair Price
2-door notchback	$15355	$14107	$14607
2-door convertible	20755	18912	19755
GT 2-door notchback	18000	16460	17260
GT 2-door convertible	23985	21787	22985

Prices are accurate at time of publication; subject to manufacturer's change.

FORD

	Retail Price	Dealer Invoice	Fair Price
Cobra 2-door notchback	$25335	$22988	—
Cobra 2-door convertible	28135	25480	—
Destination charge	525	525	525

Cobra fair prices not available at time of publication.

Standard Equipment:

3.8-liter V-6 engine, 5-speed manual transmission, driver- and passenger-side air bags, 4-wheel disc brakes, power steering, reclining cloth bucket seats, split folding rear seat (notchback), storage console with armrest and cupholder, power mirrors, AM/FM radio, digital clock, visor mirrors, tachometer, trip odometer, coolant-temperature and oil-pressure gauges, voltmeter, tilt steering wheel, tinted glass, intermittent wipers, auxiliary power outlet, passive anti-theft system, 205/65R15 all-season tires, wheel covers. **Convertible** adds: power convertible top, power door locks, remote decklid release, power windows, illuminated visor mirrors. **GT** adds to base notchback: 4.6-liter OHC V-8 engine, split folding rear seat (notchback), GT Suspension Pkg., dual exhaust, 225/55ZR16 all-season tires, alloy wheels. **GT Convertible** adds GT and base convertible: GT bucket seats, leather-wrapped steering wheel, fog lamps, rear decklid spoiler. **Cobra** adds: 4.6-liter DOHC V-8 engine, anti-lock 4-wheel disc brakes, air conditioning, sport bucket seats, power driver seat, cruise control, cassette player with Premium Sound, rear defogger, remote keyless entry, front floormats, performance suspension, 245/45ZR17 tires.

Optional Equipment:

4-speed automatic transmission	815	725	774
Requires air conditioning. NA Cobra.			
Anti-lock brakes, base, GT	570	507	542
Anti-theft system	145	129	138
Requires Group 1 and remote keyless entry. Base requires Pkg. 243A. NA Cobra.			
Optional axle ratio, GT	200	178	190
Preferred Pkg. 241A, base	615	548	584
Air conditioning, cassette player.			
Preferred Pkg. 243A, base notchback	2115	1882	2009
base convertible	1615	1437	1534
Air conditioning, Group 1 (power windows and door locks, remote decklid release), Group 2 (cruise control, cassette player with Premium Sound, alloy wheels), 4-way power driver seat, illuminated visor mirrors, remote keyless entry.			
Preferred Pkg. 248A, GT notchback	670	596	637
Air conditioning, cassette player.			

	Retail Price	Dealer Invoice	Fair Price
Preferred Pkg. 249A, GT notchback	$2940	$2616	$2770
GT convertible	1685	1500	1601

Anti-lock brakes, air conditioning, Groups 1, 2, and 3 (GT bucket seats, leather-wrapped steering wheel, illuminated visor mirrors, fog lamps, rear spoiler), 4-way power driver seat.

	Retail Price	Dealer Invoice	Fair Price
Preferred Pkg. 250A, Cobra	1335	1189	180

Leather upholstery, Mach 460 cassette/CD player, anti-theft system.

	Retail Price	Dealer Invoice	Fair Price
Group 1, GT notchback w/Pkg. 248A	565	503	537

Power windows and door locks, remote decklid release.

	Retail Price	Dealer Invoice	Fair Price
Sport Appearance Group, base w/Pkg. 243A	345	306	328

Leather-wrapped steering wheel, rear decklid spoiler, striping, alloy wheels.

	Retail Price	Dealer Invoice	Fair Price
4-way power driver seat	210	187	200

NA Cobra.

	Retail Price	Dealer Invoice	Fair Price
Leather upholstery, base convertible, GT with Pkg. 249A	500	445	475

Includes power lumbar support.

	Retail Price	Dealer Invoice	Fair Price
Cruise control, GT w/Pkg. 248A	215	191	204
Rear defogger, base, GT	190	169	180
Cassette player w/Premium Sound, GT w/Pkg. 248A	130	116	124
Mach 460 cassette player, Base w/Pkg. 243A, GT w/Pkg. 249A	395	352	375

Includes 460 watts peak power, AM/FM stereo, 60-watt equalizer, CD-changer compatibility, soft-touch tape controls, ten speakers.

	Retail Price	Dealer Invoice	Fair Price
CD player, base, GT	295	263	280

Requires cassette player w/Premium Sound, Mach 460 cassette player, Group 1, or Group 2. NA on base with Pkg. 241A.

	Retail Price	Dealer Invoice	Fair Price
Alloy wheels, base	265	236	252
Front floormats	30	27	29
Remote keyless entry	270	240	257

NA on base with Pkg. 241A. Requires Group 1.

	Retail Price	Dealer Invoice	Fair Price
Rear decklid spoiler, base, GT w/Pkg. 248A, Cobra	195	174	185
Engine block heater, base, GT	20	18	19
15-inch alloy wheels, base	265	236	252
17-inch alloy wheels and 245/45ZR17 tires, GT with Pkg. 249A	500	445	475

Prices are accurate at time of publication; subject to manufacturer's change.

FORD PROBE/ MAZDA MX-6

Ford Probe

Specifications

	2-door hatchback
Wheelbase, in.	102.8
Overall length, in.	178.7
Overall width, in.	69.8
Overall height, in.	51.6
Curb weight, lbs.	2690
Cargo vol., cu. ft.	18.8
Fuel capacity, gals.	15.5
Seating capacity	4

Engines

	dohc I-4	dohc V-6
Size, liters/cu. in.	2.0/122	2.5/153
Horsepower @ rpm	118 @ 5500	164 @ 5600
Torque (lbs./ft.) @ rpm	127 @ 4500	160 @ 4800

EPA city/highway mpg

5-speed OD manual	26/33	21/27
4-speed OD automatic	23/31	20/26

Built in Flat Rock, Mich.

PRICES

Ford Probe	Retail Price	Dealer Invoice	Fair Price
2-door hatchback	$14355	$13151	$13551
GT 2-door hatchback	16855	15377	15977

	Retail Price	Dealer Invoice	Fair Price
Destination charge	$400	$400	$400

Standard Equipment:

2.0-liter DOHC 4-cylinder engine, 5-speed manual transmission, power steering, driver- and passenger-side air bags, cloth reclining front bucket seats with memory, split folding rear seat, tachometer, coolant-temperature and oil-pressure gauges, voltmeter, trip odometer, tinted rear and quarter windows, AM/FM radio, passenger-side visor mirror, center console, dual remote mirrors, remote hatch and fuel-door releases, 195/65R14 tires, wheel covers. **GT** adds: 2.5-liter DOHC V-6 engine, 4-wheel disc brakes, handling suspension, full console with storage armrest and cupholders, multi-adjustable front seats with driver-side lumbar support and side bolsters, leather-wrapped steering wheel and shifter, fog lights, lower bodyside cladding, 225/50VR16 tires, alloy wheels.

Optional Equipment:

4-speed automatic transmission	895	797	806
GT requires anti-lock brakes.			
Anti-lock brakes, base	820	730	738
GT	650	579	585
Base includes 4-wheel disc brakes.			
Preferred Pkg. 253A, base	740	660	666
Air conditioning (includes tinted glass), AM/FM/cassette.			
Preferred Pkg. 263A, GT	740	660	666
Air conditioning (includes tinted glass), AM/FM/cassette.			
GTS Sport Appearance Group, GT	745	663	671
Rear spoiler, chrome wheels, striping.			
Convenience Group, base	430	383	387
GT	375	334	338
Tilt steering column, cruise control, full console with storage armrest and cupholders (SE), rear wiper/washer, intermittent wipers.			
Luxury Group	615	547	554
Power windows and door locks, power mirrors, remote keyless entry, illuminated entry.			
Rear defogger	190	169	171
Power driver seat	290	258	261
Leather front bucket seats	500	445	450
Requires power driver seat and Luxury Group.			
Cassette player w/Premium Sound	170	152	153
Requires Preferred Equipment Pkg.			
CD player	620	553	558
ordered with Preferred Pkg.	455	406	410
Includes Premium Sound and subwoofer.			

Prices are accurate at time of publication; subject to manufacturer's change.

FORD

	Retail Price	Dealer Invoice	Fair Price
Rear spoiler	$235	$209	$212
Color-keyed bodyside moldings	60	54	55
Sliding power roof	615	547	554
Includes dome light and map lights.			
Alloy wheels, base	470	418	423
Includes 205/55HR15 tires and handling suspension.			
Chrome wheels, GT	390	347	351
Floormats	30	27	28
Engine block heater	20	18	19

Mazda MX-6	Retail Price	Dealer Invoice	Fair Price
2-door notchback	$20195	$18011	—
LS 2-door notchback	23950	21391	—
Destination charge	450	450	450

Fair price not available at time of publication. Prices are for vehicles distributed by Mazda Motor of America, Inc. Prices may be higher in areas served by independent distributors.

Standard Equipment:

Base: 2.0-liter DOHC 4-cylinder engine, 5-speed manual transmission, variable-assist power steering, driver- and passenger-side air bags, cloth reclining front bucket seats, driver-seat thigh support adjustment, 60/40 folding rear seat with armrest, console with storage, power windows and door locks, cruise control, power mirrors, visor mirrors, AM/FM/cassette, tachometer, coolant temperature gauge, trip odometer, tilt steering column, intermittent wipers, door pockets, tinted glass, remote fuel door and decklid releases, rear defogger, cargo lights, reading lights, front and rear stabilizer bars, 195/65SR14 tires, full wheel covers. **LS** adds: 2.5-liter DOHC V-6 engine, 4-wheel disc brakes, air conditioning, power steel sunroof, anti-theft alarm, variable intermittent wipers, 6-speaker audio system, leather-wrapped steering wheel, power antenna, remote keyless entry, fog lights, mud guards, floormats, 205/55VR15 tires, alloy wheels.

Optional Equipment:

4-speed automatic transmission	800	696	760
Anti-lock brakes, base	950	808	903
LS	800	680	760
Base includes 4-wheel disc brakes and requires Popular Equipment Group.			
Air conditioning, base	900	720	854

	Retail Price	Dealer Invoice	Fair Price
Popular Equipment Group, base	$2575	$2163	$2446

Air conditioning, power steel sunroof, anti-theft alarm, variable intermittent wipers, 6-speaker audio system, power antenna, remote keyless entry, rear spoiler, floormats, alloy wheels.

Leather Pkg., LS	1095	876	1045

Leather/vinyl sport bucket seats, power driver's seat, heated outside mirrors.

Rear spoiler, base, LS	375	300	356
Floormats, base	80	56	75

FORD TAURUS/ MERCURY SABLE

Ford Taurus LX 4-door

Specifications

	4-door notchback	4-door wagon
Wheelbase, in..	108.5	108.5
Overall length, in.	197.5	199.6
Overall width, in..	73.0	73.0
Overall height, in.	55.1	57.6
Curb weight, lbs..	3326	3480
Cargo vol., cu. ft.	15.8	81.3
Fuel capacity, gals..	16.0	16.0
Seating capacity	6	8

Engines

	ohv V-6	dohc V-6	dohc V-8
Size, liters/cu. in.	3.0/182	3.0/181	3.4/207
Horsepower @ rpm	145 @ 5250	200 @ 5750	235 @ 6100

Prices are accurate at time of publication; subject to manufacturer's change.

FORD

	ohv V-6	dohc V-6	dohc V-8
Torque (lbs./ft.) @ rpm......................	170 @ 3250	200 @ 4500	230 @ 4800
EPA city/highway mpg			
4-speed OD automatic......................	20/28	19/28	17/26

Built in Atlanta, Ga., and Chicago, Ill.

PRICES

Ford Taurus	Retail Price	Dealer Invoice	Fair Price
G 4-door notchback	$17995	$16636	—
GL 4-door notchback	18985	17337	—
LX 4-door notchback	21610	19673	—
SHO 4-door notchback	26460	23990	—
GL 5-door wagon	20195	18414	—
LX 5-door wagon	22715	20656	—
Destination charge	550	550	550

Fair price not available at time of publication.

Standard Equipment:

G: 3.0-liter V-6 engine, 4-speed automatic transmission, air conditioning, variable-assist power steering, 4-wheel disc brakes (wagon), driver- and passenger-side air bags, 6-passenger seating with dual recliners, front center seating console and cupholders, 60/40 split/folding rear seat, tilt steering wheel, power windows, black power mirrors, visor mirrors, tinted glass, intermittent wipers, rear defogger, rear heat ducts, AM/FM radio, power antenna (wagon), digital clock, coolant-temperature gauge, trip odometer, wheel covers, luggage rack (wagon), 205/65R15 tires. **GL** adds: tachometer, color-keyed exterior mirrors and roof, remote decklid release (notchback), map pockets. **LX** adds: 3.0-liter DOHC V-6 engine, rear-seat air conditioning, 5-passenger seating with reclining front bucket seats and floor console, 6-way power driver seat with driver-side power lumbar support, leather-wrapped steering wheel, floor shifter, anti-theft system, power door locks, illuminated visor mirrors, cassette player with six speakers, automatic headlights, bodyside cladding, illuminated entry, reading lights, dual exhaust outlets, alloy wheels. **SHO** adds: 3.4-liter DOHC V-8 engine, anti-lock 4-wheel disc brakes, cruise control, sport front bucket seats, rear spoiler, semi-active handling suspension, aerodynamic wipers, interior air filter, floormats, 225/55VR16 tires, 5-spoke alloy wheels.

Optional Equipment:

Anti-lock 4-wheel disc brakes,			
G, GL	600	534	—

	Retail Price	Dealer Invoice	Fair Price
Automatic air conditioning, LX, SHO	$210	$187	—

Includes heated power mirrors and outside temperature indicator. Requires Mach audio system.

Preferred Pkg. 204A, GL	250	223	—

Groups 1 (cruise control, interior air filter, floormats) and 2 (cassette player, power door locks).

Preferred Pkg. 205A, GL	850	757	—

Groups 1, 2, and 3 (power driver seat, alloy wheels, Light Group [front courtesy reading, map, and dome lights]).

Preferred Pkg. 209A, LX	720	641	—

Group 1A (cruise control, leather-wrapped steering wheel, interior air filter, floormats), anti-lock 4-wheel disc brakes, remote keyless entry with perimeter anti-theft.

Preferred Pkg. 210A, LX notchback	1710	1522	—
LX wagon	1630	1451	—

Group 1A, anti-lock 4-wheel disc brakes, remote keyless entry with perimeter anti-theft, automatic air conditioning, outside-temperature indicator, Mach audio system w/power antenna, heated power mirrors, power antenna, chrome alloy wheels.

Preferred Pkg. 211A, SHO	1210	1076	—

Automatic air conditioning, power moonroof, remote keyless entry with perimeter anti-theft, heated power mirrors, outside-temperature indicator, Mach audio system w/power antenna.

Group 2, G	460	410	—

Cassette player, power door locks.

Wagon group, wagon	295	263	—

Rear wiper/washer, cargo area cover and net. Requires Group 2.

Cloth bucket seats w/center seating console,			
LX	NC	NC	NC
Leather upholstery, GL	1040	926	—
LX	990	881	—
SHO	1190	1059	—
6-way power driver seat,			
GL with Pkg. 204A	340	302	—
Rear-facing third seat, wagon	200	178	—
Integrated child seat, GL and LX wagon	135	120	—
Cassette player, G	185	165	—
Mach Audio System, LX notchback	400	356	—
LX wagon	320	285	—

Requires automatic air conditioning. Notchback includes power antenna.

6-disc CD changer, GL	350	312	—
LX, SHO	595	530	—

LX requires Mach sound system.

FORD

	Retail Price	Dealer Invoice	Fair Price
Interior air filter, G	$30	$27	—
Voice-activated cellular telephone	650	579	—
NA with G.			
Remote keyless entry, GL	190	169	—
Power moonroof, GL, LX	740	658	—
Includes overhead map lights.			
Daytime running lights	40	35	—
Includes heavy-duty battery.			
Light Group, GL with Pkg. 204A	45	41	—
Map and courtesy lights.			
Floormats, G	45	40	—
Alloy wheels, GL with Pkg. 204A	315	280	—
Chrome wheels, LX, SHO	580	516	—
Full-size spare tire	125	112	—
NA on wagon, G, or SHO.			
Heavy-duty suspension, GL and LX wagon	25	23	—
Engine block heater	35	31	—
Floormats	45	40	—

Mercury Sable

	Retail Price	Dealer Invoice	Fair Price
GS 4-door notchback $19555		$17864	—
LS 4-door notchback 22140		20164	—
GS 4-door wagon 19555		17864	—
LS 4-door wagon 22140		20164	—
Destination charge	550	550	550

Fair price not available at time of publication.

Standard Equipment:

GS notchback: 3.0-liter V-6 engine, 4-speed automatic transmission, power steering, driver- and passenger-side air bags, air conditioning, 6-passenger seating (cloth upholstery, reclining front bucket seats w/center seating console, 60/40 split folding rear seat), cupholders, front armrest, solar-control tinted glass, tachometer, coolant temperature gauge, trip odometer, digital clock, power mirrors, power windows, tilt steering wheel, AM/FM radio, variable intermittent wipers, rear defogger, remote decklid release, visor mirrors, rear heat ducts, 205/65R15 tires, wheel covers. **GS wagon** deletes remote decklid release, and adds: 4-wheel disc brakes, power antenna, luggage rack, cargo tie-downs, cargo-area light. **LS notchback** adds to GS notchback: 3.0-liter DOHC V-6 engine, 5-passenger seating (cloth/leather upholstery, reclining front bucket seats w/6-way power driver seat, 60/40 split folding rear seat), rear armrest, floor console, leather-wrapped shifter, cassette player w/six speakers, power door locks, theft-deterrent system, remote fuel-door release, illuminated visor mirrors, automatic headlamps, Light Group (courtesy, reading, map, and dome lights), bright exhaust outlets, 5-spoke alloy wheels. **LS wagon** deletes bright exhaust outlets, and includes LS notchback and GS wagon standard equipment.

Optional Equipment:	Retail Price	Dealer Invoice	Fair Price
Anti-lock 4-wheel disc brakes, GS	$600	$534	—
Automatic air conditioning and heated power mirrors, LS w/Pkg. 461A	210	187	—
Requires Ford Mach audio system.			
Preferred Pkg. 450A, GS	250	223	—
Group 1 (cruise control, interior air filter, floormats), Group 2 (cassette player, power door locks).			
Preferred Pkg. 451A, GS	850	757	—
Pkg. 450A plus Group 3 (6-way power driver seat, Light Group [courtesy, reading, map, and dome lights], alloy wheels).			
Preferred Pkg. 461A, LS	720	641	—
Anti-lock 4-wheel disc brakes, Group 1 (cruise control, leather-wrapped steering wheel, interior air filter, floormats), remote keyless entry w/theft-deterrent system.			
Preferred Pkg. 462A, LS	1710	1522	—
Pkg. 461A plus automatic air conditioning, heated power mirrors, Ford Mach audio system, chrome wheels.			
Luxury Group 68T, GS	1780	1584	—
6-disc CD changer, power moonroof, leather upholstery. Requires Pkg. 451A.			
Wagon Group, wagon	295	263	—
Cargo-area cover, rear wiper/washer, cargo net.			
Light Group, GS w/Pkg. 450A	45	41	—
Courtesy, reading, map, and dome lights.			
Remote keyless entry, GS	190	169	—
Power moonroof, LS	740	658	—
Ford Mach audio system, LS w/Pkg. 461 A	400	357	—
Requires automatic air conditioning and heated power mirrors.			
6-disc CD changer, LS	350	312	—
Requires Ford Mach audio system.			
Rear-facing third seat, wagon	200	178	—
Integrated child seat, wagon	135	120	—
Leather upholstery, GS	1040	925	—
LS	990	881	—
Cloth/leather bucket seats with center seating console, LS	NC	NC	NC
Power driver seat	340	302	—

Prices are accurate at time of publication; subject to manufacturer's change.

	Retail Price	Dealer Invoice	Fair Price
Cellular telephone	$650	$579	—
Heavy-duty suspension, wagon	25	23	—
Rear wiper/washer, wagon	255	227	—
Includes cargo-area cover.			
Daytime running lights	40	36	—
Cargo net, sedan	40	35	—
Full-size spare tire, notchback	125	112	—
Alloy wheels, GS w/Pkg. 450A	315	280	—
Chrome wheels, LS w/Pkg. 461A	580	516	—
Heavy-duty battery	30	27	—
Engine-block heater	35	31	—

FORD THUNDERBIRD/ MERCURY COUGAR

Ford Thunderbird LX

Specifications

	2-door notchback
Wheelbase, in.	113.0
Overall length, in.	200.3
Overall width, in.	72.7
Overall height, in.	52.5
Curb weight, lbs.	3561
Cargo vol., cu. ft.	15.1
Fuel capacity, gals.	18.0
Seating capacity	5

Engines

	ohv V-6	ohc V-8
Size, liters/cu. in.	3.8/232	4.6/281

	ohv V-6	ohc V-8
Horsepower @ rpm	145 @ 4000	205 @ 4250
Torque (lbs./ft.) @ rpm	215 @ 2750	280 @ 3000
EPA city/highway mpg		
4-speed OD automatic	18/26	17/25

Built in Lorain, Ohio.

PRICES

Ford Thunderbird	Retail Price	Dealer Invoice	Fair Price
LX 2-door notchback	$17885	$16318	$16818
Destination charge	510	510	510

Standard Equipment:

3.8-liter V-6 engine, 4-speed automatic transmission, driver- and passenger-side air bags, 4-wheel disc brakes, power steering, air conditioning, cruise control, cloth front bucket seats, center storage console with cupholders, rear seat center armrest, rear heat ducts, remote outside mirrors, visor mirrors, tinted glass, coolant-temperature gauge, tachometer, trip odometer, tilt steering wheel, AM/FM/cassette, digital clock, power windows and door locks, remote fuel-door and decklid releases, intermittent wipers, map/dome lights, lower bodyside cladding, 205/70R15 tires, wheel covers.

Optional Equipment:

Anti-lock brakes	570	507	513
Preferred Pkg. 155A	NC	NC	NC
Group 1 (rear defogger, alloy wheels, 215/70R15 tires).			
Preferred Pkg. 157A	840	747	756
4.6-liter V-8 engine, Groups 1 and 2 (6-way power driver seat, illuminated entry, leather-wrapped steering wheel and shifter), variable-assist steering, heavy-duty battery.			
Luxury Group	395	352	356
Semi-automatic air conditioning, autolamp system, power antenna, illuminated visor mirrors. Requires Preferred Pkg.			
Sport Option, Pkg. 157A	450	401	405
Performance suspension and brakes, rear spoiler, 9-spoke alloy wheels, 225/65R16 touring tires.			
Leather upholstery	490	436	441
Includes leather-wrapped steering wheel and shifter. Requires Preferred Pkg.			

Prices are accurate at time of publication; subject to manufacturer's change.

FORD

	Retail Price	Dealer Invoice	Fair Price
Leather-wrapped steering wheel, Pkg. 155A	$90	$80	$81
Includes leather-wrapped shifter.			
6-way power driver seat, Pkg. 155A	290	258	261
Traction-Assist	210	187	189
Requires anti-lock brakes. NA with Traction-Lok axle.			
Traction-Lok axle	95	85	86
NA with Traction-Assist.			
Premium Sound cassette player	290	258	261
Premium Sound CD player	430	383	387
Remote keyless entry/Illuminated entry,			
Pkg. 155A	270	240	243
Pkg. 157A	190	169	171
Power moonroof	740	658	666
Requires Preferred Pkg. and Luxury Group.			
Anti-theft system	145	129	131
Requires remote keyless entry.			
Rear spoiler	250	223	225
Front floormats	30	27	28
Tri-coat paint	225	201	203
Chrome wheels	580	517	522
Requires alloy wheels (in Group 1).			
Engine block heater	20	18	19

Mercury Cougar	Retail Price	Dealer Invoice	Fair Price
XR7 2-door notchback	$17830	$16279	$16779
Destination charge	510	510	510

Standard Equipment:

3.8-liter V-6 engine, 4-speed automatic transmission, power steering, driver- and passenger-side air bags, 4-wheel disc brakes, air conditioning, cloth/leather upholstery, reclining front bucket seats, front storage console w/armrest and cupholders, rear armrest, tilt steering wheel, coolant-temperature gauge, tachometer, power windows and mirrors, AM/FM/cassette, tinted glass, intermittent wipers, rear heat ducts, visor mirrors, map lights, 205/70R15 tires, wheel covers. Requires Preferred Equipment Pkg.

Optional Equipment:

Traction-Lok axle	95	85	86
NA with Traction Assist.			
Anti-lock brakes	570	507	513
Semi-automatic air conditioning	155	138	140

	Retail Price	Dealer Invoice	Fair Price
Traction Assist	$210	$187	$189
Requires anti-lock brakes. NA with Traction Assist.			
Preferred Equipment Pkg. 260A	505	450	455
Group 1 (rear defogger, front floormats), Group 2 (cruise control, Power Lock Group [power door locks, remote decklid release], 215/70R15 tires, alloy wheels).			
Preferred Equipment Pkg. 262A	1345	1196	1211
Pkg. 260A plus 4.6-liter V-8 engine (includes variable-assist power steering, heavy-duty battery), Group 3 (power driver seat, leather-wrapped steering wheel and shifter, illuminated entry).			
30th Anniversary Feature Car	495	441	446
Upgraded front brakes, sport-tuned suspension, unique front bucket seats w/driver-seat power lumbar support, automatic day/night inside mirror, interior and exterior 30th Anniversary logos, front floormats, Dark Toreador Red paint, 225/60R16 tires, unique wheels. NA with Luxury Appearance Group or Sport Edition.			
Luxury Appearance Group	115	102	104
Decorative luggage rack, geometric spoke wheels. NA with rear decklid spoiler, Sport Edition.			
Sport Edition	450	401	405
Sport-tuned suspension, upgraded front brakes, rear decklid spoiler, 225/60R16 touring tires, 7-spoke alloy wheels.			
Power moonroof	740	658	666
Includes dual reading lights, illuminated entry (with Pkg. 260A), pop-up air deflector, sunshade, rear tilt-up. Requires illuminated visor mirrors.			
Premium electronic AM/FM/cassette	290	258	261
Includes amplifier and premium speakers.			
Premium electronic AM/FM/CD player	430	383	387
Includes amplifier and premium speakers.			
Power antenna	85	76	77
Power driver seat, Pkg. 260A	290	258	261
Power passenger seat	290	258	261
Requires power driver seat.			
Leather upholstery	490	436	441
Requires leather-wrapped steering wheel and shifter, power driver seat.			
Leather-wrapped steering wheel and shifter, Pkg. 260A	90	80	81
Requires cruise control.			
Automatic headlamps	70	62	63
Remote keyless entry, Pkg. 260A	270	240	243
Pkg. 262A	190	169	171
Includes illuminated entry.			

	Retail Price	Dealer Invoice	Fair Price
Illuminated visor mirrors	$95	$85	$86
Theft-deterrent system	145	129	131
Requires remote keyless entry.			
Rear decklid spoiler	250	223	225
NA w/Luxury Appearance Group.			
Heavy-duty battery, Pkg. 260A	25	23	24
Tri-coat paint	225	201	203

1998 FORD WINDSTAR

1998 Ford Windstar Limited

Specifications

	3-door van
Wheelbase, in.	120.7
Overall length, in.	201.2
Overall width, in.	75.4
Overall height, in.	68.0
Curb weight, lbs.	3762
Cargo vol., cu. ft.	144.0
Fuel capacity, gals.	20.0
Seating capacity	7

Engines

	ohv V-6	ohv V-6
Size, liters/cu. in.	3.0/182	3.8/232
Horsepower @ rpm	150 @ 5000	200 @ 5000
Torque (lbs./ft.) @ rpm......................	170 @ 3250	230 @ 3000

EPA city/highway mpg

	ohv V-6	ohv V-6
4-speed OD automatic....................................	17/25	17/23

Built in Canada.

PRICES

Ford Windstar	Retail Price	Dealer Invoice	Fair Price
Base 3-door van	$19085	$17697	$18497
GL 3-door van	20655	18697	19497
LX 3-door van	25905	23316	24116
Limited 3-door van...................................	29205	26220	27020
Destination charge	580	580	580

Standard Equipment:

Base: 3.0-liter V-6 engine, 4-speed automatic transmission, driver- and passenger-side air bags, anti-lock brakes, power steering, 7-passenger seating (cloth high-back front buckets, 2-place middle and 3-place rear bench seats), solar-tinted windshield and front door glass, dual outside mirrors, AM/FM radio, digital clock, intermittent wipers, rear wiper/washer, cupholders, coolant-temperature gauge, front-door map pockets, storage bins, 205/70R15 tires, full wheel covers. **GL** adds: reclining middle bench seat, adjustable rear seat track. **LX** adds: 3.8-liter V-6 engine, front air conditioning, low-back front bucket seats with adjustable headrests, tip-slide driver seat with 6-way power adjustment, AM/FM/cassette, Light Group (front map/dome light, glovebox and instrument-panel lights), Power Convenience Group (power windows, power door locks and mirrors), power rear vent windows, tilt steering wheel, leather-wrapped steering wheel, cruise control, tachometer, illuminated visor vanity mirrors, closed cargo bins, map pockets on front seatbacks, bodyside molding, cargo net, 25-gallon fuel tank, 215/70R15 tires, alloy wheels. **Limited** adds: rear air conditioning, rear defogger, quad bucket seats, leather upholstery, premium AM/FM/cassette, automatic headlamps, fog lamps, remote entry system, electrochromatic rearview mirror, overhead console (includes rear seat radio controls, compass, thermometer, conversation mirror, coin holder, and garage door opener/sunglasses holder), storage drawer under front passenger seat, 225/60R16 tires, polished alloy wheels.

Optional Equipment:

3.8-liter V-6 engine, GL	685	583	617
Includes tachometer.			
Traction control, GL, LX, Limited	395	336	355
Preferred Pkg. 470A, base	1010	859	910
Front air conditioning, Power Convenience Group (power windows, power door locks and mirrors).			
Preferred Pkg. 472A, GL	2165	1841	1950
3.8-liter V-6 engine, front air conditioning, tip-slide driver seat, cassette player, cruise control, tachometer, Power Convenience Group, tilt steering wheel, rear defogger, bodyside molding.			

Prices are accurate at time of publication; subject to manufacturer's change.

FORD

	Retail Price	Dealer Invoice	Fair Price
Preferred Pkg. 473A, GL	$3075	$2614	$2770

Pkg. 472A plus rear air conditioning, Light Group (front map/dome light, glovebox and instrument panel lights), overhead console, privacy glass, luggage rack.

Preferred Pkg. 477A, LX	1580	1340	1420

Rear air conditioning, rear defogger, quad bucket seats, overhead console, privacy glass, front and rear floormats, luggage rack, 2-tone paint, remote entry system.

Preferred Pkg. 479A, Limited	680	578	610

Privacy glass, front and rear floormats, luggage rack.

Front air conditioning, base, GL	855	727	770
Rear air conditioning, GL, LX	475	404	450

Includes rear heater.

Load-levelling air suspension, LX, Limited	290	247	261
Rear defogger	170	144	162
Cruise control and tilt steering wheel, Base, GL	370	314	352
Floor console, GL, LX, Limited	155	132	140

Includes cupholders and covered storage bin. Requires rear air conditioning. GL requires Power Convenience Group.

Overhead console, GL	100	85	90
LX	180	153	160

Includes rear seat radio controls, compass and thermometer (LX), conversation mirror, coin holder, and garage door opener/sunglasses holder). GL requires Light Group

Light Group, Base, GL	75	63	68

Front map/dome light, glovebox and instrument panel lights.

Premium Light Group, LX	295	251	265

Includes fog lamps, automatic headlamps, electrochromatic mirror.

Interior Convenience Group, GL	50	43	45

Left rear storage bin, covered center bin, cargo net.

Power Convenience Group, Base, GL	670	569	603

Power windows, power door locks and mirrors. GL requires 3.8-liter engine, cruise control/tilt steering wheel.

Trailer Towing Pkg.	435	370	392
with front and rear A/C	410	347	369

Includes heavy-duty battery, engine-oil and power-steering coolers, auxiliary transmission-oil cooler, trailer wiring harness, full-size spare tire. NA base. GL requires 3.8-liter engine.

Fog lamps, LX	110	93	105
Luggage rack, GL, LX, Limited	175	149	158
Remote entry, GL, LX	175	149	158

Remote entry system and illuminated entry. Requires Power Convenience Group.

	Retail Price	Dealer Invoice	Fair Price
Privacy glass, GL, LX, Limited	$415	$352	$394
Security Group, LX, Limited	200	171	180
Includes programmable garage-door opener, anti-theft system. Requires remote entry.			
Cassette player, base, GL	170	144	153
Premium AM/FM/cassette, LX	155	132	140
Premium AM/FM/CD player, GL	495	420	446
LX,	325	276	293
Limited	170	144	153
Requires cruise control, tilt steering wheel, Light Group.			
JBL Audio System, LX, Limited	510	433	485
Seat bed, GL w/Pkg. 472A or 473A	615	522	566
Quad bucket seats, GL	745	633	670
LX	625	532	565
Tip-slide driver seat, GL	150	128	135
Leather upholstery, LX	865	735	779
Requires quad bucket seats.			
Integrated child seats (two), GL, LX	225	191	214
Base	285	214	255
Replacing quad bucket seats, Pkg. 477A (credit)	(510)	(433)	(433)
Floormats, front and rear	90	77	81
2-tone paint, LX	235	200	212
2-tone paint delete, LX w/Pkg. 477A (credit)	(135)	(115)	(115)
Bodyside molding, GL	80	68	72
25-gallon fuel tank, GL	30	26	27
Engine block heater	35	30	33
Alloy wheels, GL w/Pkg. 472A or 473A	415	352	374
Includes 215/70R15 tires.			
215/70R15 self-sealing tires, GL, LX	245	208	220
Requires alloy wheels.			
Full-size spare tire	110	93	105

GEO METRO

Specifications	2-door hatchback	4-door notchback
Wheelbase, in.	93.1	93.1
Overall length, in.	149.4	164.0
Overall width, in.	62.6	62.6
Overall height, in.	54.7	55.7
Curb weight, lbs.	1832	1962

Prices are accurate at time of publication; subject to manufacturer's change.

GEO

Geo Metro LS 4-door

	2-door hatchback	4-door notchback
Cargo vol., cu. ft.	21.9	10.3
Fuel capacity, gals.	10.6	10.6
Seating capacity	4	4

Engines

	ohc I-3	ohc I-4
Size, liters/cu. in.	1.0/61	1.3/79
Horsepower @ rpm	55 @ 5700	70 @ 5500
Torque (lbs./ft.) @ rpm	58 @ 3300	74 @ 3000

EPA city/highway mpg

5-speed OD manual	44/49	39/43
3-speed automatic		30/34

Built in Canada.

PRICES

Geo Metro	Retail Price	Dealer Invoice	Fair Price
Base 2-door hatchback	$8580	$8082	8382
LSi 2-door hatchback	9180	8556	8856
LSi 4-door notchback	9850	9180	9480
Destination charge	340	340	340

Standard Equipment:

Base: 1.0-liter 3-cylinder engine, 5-speed manual transmission, driver- and passenger-side air bags, cloth/vinyl reclining front bucket seats, folding rear seat, console with cupholders and storage tray, dual outside mirrors, coolant-temperature gauge, 155/80R13 tires. **LSi 2-door** adds: 1.3-liter 4-cylinder engine, easy-entry passenger seat, upgraded cloth/vinyl upholstery, intermittent wipers, trip odometer, passenger-side visor mirror, color-keyed bumpers, body-side moldings, wheel covers. **LSi 4-door** deletes easy-entry passenger seat and adds: cargo-area lighting.

Optional Equipment:

	Retail Price	Dealer Invoice	Fair Price
3-speed automatic transmission, LSi	$595	$530	$565
Air conditioning	785	699	746
Anti-lock brakes	565	503	537
Preferred Equipment Group 2, base	179	159	170
Easy-entry passenger seat, remote outside mirrors, bodyside moldings, floormats, wheel covers.			
Preferred Equipment Group 3, base	1265	1126	1202
Group 2 plus air conditioning, AM/FM radio with digital clock.			
Preferred Equipment Group 2, LSi 2-door ..	1346	1198	1279
Air conditioning, AM/FM/cassette with digital clock, floormats.			
Preferred Equipment Group 2, LSi 4-door ..	1616	1438	1535
Air conditioning, power steering, AM/FM/cassette with digital clock, floormats.			
Convenience Pkg., LSi	125	111	119
Split folding rear seat (4-door), remote outside mirrors, remote hatch release (2-door), remote decklid release (4-door), passenger seat-back pocket, cargo cover (2-door).			
Power steering, 4-door	270	240	257
AM/FM radio	301	268	286
Includes seek and scan, digital clock, and four speakers.			
AM/FM/cassette	521	464	495
base w/Group 3	220	196	209
AM/FM/cassette and CD players, LSi	799	711	759
LSi w/Group 2	278	247	264
Power door locks, 4-door	220	196	209
Rear defogger	160	142	152
Rear wiper/washer, LSi 2-door	125	111	119
Requires rear defogger.			
Tachometer	70	62	67
Includes trip odometer on base.			
Floormats	40	35	38
Bodyside moldings, base	50	45	48

GEO PRIZM

Specifications

	4-door notchback
Wheelbase, in.	97.1
Overall length, in.	173.0

Prices are accurate at time of publication; subject to manufacturer's change.

GEO

Geo Prizm

	4-door notchback
Overall width, in.	66.3
Overall height, in.	53.3
Curb weight, lbs.	2359
Cargo vol., cu. ft.	12.7
Fuel capacity, gals.	13.2
Seating capacity	5

Engines

	dohc I-4	dohc I-4
Size, liters/cu. in.	1.6/97	1.8/110
Horsepower @ rpm	100 @ 5600	105 @ 5200
Torque (lbs./ft.) @ rpm	105 @ 4400	117 @ 2800

EPA city/highway mpg
5-speed OD manual	30/34	29/35
3-speed automatic	25/29	
4-speed OD automatic		27/34

Built in Fremont, Calif.

PRICES

Geo Prizm	Retail Price	Dealer Invoice	Fair Price
4-door notchback	$12840	$12224	$12524
LSi 4-door notchback	13485	12433	12933
Destination charge	405	405	405

Standard Equipment:

1.6-liter DOHC 4-cylinder engine, 5-speed manual transmission, driver- and passenger-side air bags, power steering, reclining front bucket seats, cloth/vinyl upholstery, center console with storage tray and cupholders, left remote and right manual mirrors, daytime running lights, remote fuel-door and decklid release, tinted glass, rear heat ducts, bodyside moldings, 175/65R14 tires. **LSi** adds: tilt steering column, upgraded full cloth upholstery, center console with covered storage box, split-folding rear seat, visor mirrors, wheel covers.

Optional Equipment:

	Retail Price	Dealer Invoice	Fair Price
1.8-liter 4-cylinder engine, LSi	$352	$303	$308
Includes rear stabilizer bar and 185/65R14 tires. Requires option group.			
3-speed automatic transmission	495	426	433
Requires 1.6-liter engine and Preferred Equipment Group.			
4-speed automatic transmission, LSi	800	688	700
Requires 1.8-liter engine.			
Anti-lock brakes	645	555	564
Air conditioning	795	684	696
Preferred Equipment Group 2, base	1222	1051	1088
Air conditioning, AM/FM radio with digital clock, floormats, wheel covers.			
Preferred Equipment Group 2, LSi	1450	1247	1291
Air conditioning, AM/FM/cassette with digital clock, dual power mirrors, floormats.			
Preferred Equipment Group 3, LSi	2210	1901	1967
Group 2 plus Convenience Pkg. (power windows and door locks, cruise control), variable intermittent wipers.			
Convenience Pkg., LSi	705	606	627
Power windows and door locks, cruise control. Requires Preferred Equipment Group.			
Cruise control, LSi with Group 2	185	159	165
Leather upholstery, LSi	595	512	521
Requires Convenience Pkg.			
Integrated child safety seat, LSi	125	108	111
NA leather upholstery. Includes fixed rear seat.			
Rear defogger	180	155	160
Power door locks	220	189	193
Power sunroof, LSi	675	581	601
Includes map light.			
Tachometer	70	60	62
AM/FM radio	335	288	293
Includes seek and scan, digital clock, and four speakers.			
AM/FM/cassette player	555	477	486
with option group	220	189	193
Includes seek and scan, theft deterrent, tone select, digital clock, and four speakers.			
AM/FM radio with CD and cassette players, LSi with option group	195	168	174
Includes seek and scan, theft deterrent, tone select, digital clock, and six speakers.			

Prices are accurate at time of publication; subject to manufacturer's change.

	Retail Price	Dealer Invoice	Fair Price
Alloy wheels, LSi	$335	$288	$293
Requires Preferred Equipment Group.			
Wheel covers, base	52	45	46
Floormats	40	34	35

GEO TRACKER

Geo Tracker 4-door

Specifications

	2-door conv.	4-door wagon
Wheelbase, in.	86.6	97.6
Overall length, in.	143.7	158.7
Overall width, in.	64.2	64.4
Overall height, in.	64.3	65.7
Curb weight, lbs.	2339	2619
Cargo vol., cu. ft.	32.9	45.9
Fuel capacity, gals.	11.1	14.5
Seating capacity	4	4

Engines

	ohc I-4
Size, liters/cu. in.	1.6/97
Horsepower @ rpm	95 @ 5600
Torque (lbs./ft.) @ rpm	98 @ 4000

EPA city/highway mpg

5-speed OD manual	24/26
3-speed automatic	23/24
4-speed OD automatic	22/25

Built in Canada.

PRICES

Geo Tracker	Retail Price	Dealer Invoice	Fair Price
2-door convertible, 2WD	$13415	$12771	$12971
2-door convertible, 4WD	14450	13756	13956
4-door wagon, 2WD	14570	13871	14371
4-door wagon, 4WD	15320	14585	15085
LSi 4-door wagon, 2WD	14970	14251	14751
LSi 4-door wagon, 4WD	15710	14956	15456
Destination charge	340	340	340

Standard Equipment:

1.6-liter 4-cylinder engine, 5-speed manual transmission, driver- and passenger-side air bags, power steering (wagon, 4WD convertible), rear defogger (wagon), cloth/vinyl reclining front bucket seats, folding rear bench seat (convertible), split folding rear bench seat (wagon), center console with storage tray and cupholders, tachometer, trip odometer, dual mirrors, passenger-side visor mirror, intermittent wipers, daytime running lights, fuel-tank skid plate, full-size lockable spare tire, spare-tire cover, front and rear tow hooks, 195/75R15 tires (2WD) or 205/75R15 tires (4WD). **LSi** adds: upgraded cloth/vinyl upholstery, adjustable rear bucket seats, color-keyed bumpers, bodyside moldings, floormats, hub caps.

Optional Equipment:

	Retail	Dealer	Fair
3-speed automatic transmission, convertibles	625	556	566
4-speed automatic transmission, wagons	950	846	860
Air conditioning	745	663	674
Anti-lock brakes	595	530	538
Preferred Group 2, base 4WD convertible	1254	1116	1135
base 2WD convertible	1544	1374	1397
base wagon	1261	1122	1141
Air conditioning, AM/FM radio with digital clock, power steering (2WD convertible), bodyside moldings, floormats.			
Preferred Group 2, LSi wagon	1536	1367	1390
Air conditioning, cruise control, AM/FM/cassette player with digital clock.			
Preferred Group 3, LSi 2WD wagon	2481	2208	2245
LSi 4WD wagon	2681	2386	2436
Group 2 plus automatic locking front hubs (4WD), Convenience Pkg. (power windows and door locks, power mirrors), alloy wheels.			
Convenience Pkg., LSi wagon	580	516	525
Power windows and door locks, power mirrors.			
Power steering, 2WD convertible	290	258	262

	Retail Price	Dealer Invoice	Fair Price
Cruise control	$175	$156	$158
Automatic locking front hubs, 4WD	200	178	181
AM/FM radio	306	272	277
Includes digital clock.			
AM/FM/cassette	526	468	476
with preferred group	220	196	199
Includes digital clock.			
AM/FM/cassette and CD players	835	743	752
base with preferred group	529	471	479
LSi with preferred group	309	275	280
Includes digital clock.			
Expression color-appearance pkg.,			
convertible	249	222	225
convertible with preferred group	164	146	148
Adjustable rear bucket seats, custom upholstery, bodyside moldings, special tan exterior color treatments.			
Rear wiper/washer, wagon	125	111	113
Transfer-case and front-differential			
skid plates, 4WD	75	67	68
Alloy wheels	365	325	330
Floormats, base convertible	28	25	26
base wagon	35	31	32
Bodyside moldings, base	85	76	77

HONDA ACCORD

Honda Accord LX V-6

Specifications

	2-door notchback	4-door notchback	4-door wagon
Wheelbase, in.	106.9	106.9	106.9
Overall length, in.	185.6	185.6	188.4

	2-door notchback	4-door notchback	4-door wagon
Overall width, in.	70.1	70.1	70.1
Overall height, in.	54.7	55.1	55.9
Curb weight, lbs.	2855	2855	3053
Cargo vol., cu. ft.	13.0	13.0	25.7
Fuel capacity, gals.	17.0	17.0	17.0
Seating capacity	5	5	5

Engines

	ohc I-4	ohc I-4	ohc V-6
Size, liters/cu. in.	2.2/132	2.2/132	2.7/163
Horsepower @ rpm	130 @ 5300	145 @ 5500	170 @ 5600
Torque (lbs./ft.) @ rpm	139 @ 4200	147 @ 4500	165 @ 4500

EPA city/highway mpg

5-speed OD manual	25/32	25/31	
4-speed OD automatic	23/30	23/29	19/25

Built in Marysville, Ohio.

PRICES

Honda Accord	Retail Price	Dealer Invoice	Fair Price
LX 2-door notchback, 5-speed	$17990	$15897	$16397
LX 2-door notchback, automatic	18790	16604	17104
SE 2-door notchback, automatic	20200	17849	18349
EX 2-door notchback, 5-speed	20500	18114	18614
EX 2-door notchback, automatic	21300	18821	19321
EX 2-door notchback w/leather, 5-speed	21650	19131	19931
EX 2-door notchback w/leather, automatic	22450	19838	20638
DX 4-door notchback, 5-speed	15100	13343	14143
DX 4-door notchback, automatic	15900	14050	14850
LX 4-door notchback, 5-speed	18190	16074	16574
LX 4-door notchback, automatic	18990	16780	17280
LX 4-door notchback w/ABS, automatic	19840	17531	18031
LX V-6 4-door notchback, automatic	22500	19882	20682
SE 4-door notchback, automatic	20400	18026	18526
EX 4-door notchback, 5-speed	20700	18291	19091
EX 4-door notchback, automatic	21500	18998	19798
EX 4-door notchback w/leather, 5-speed	21850	19307	20107
EX 4-door notchback w/leather, automatic	22650	20014	20814
EX V-6 4-door notchback, automatic	25100	22179	22979
LX 4-door wagon, 5-speed	19090	16869	17369
LX 4-door wagon, automatic	19890	17576	18076
EX 4-door wagon, automatic	22530	19909	20709

Prices are accurate at time of publication; subject to manufacturer's change.

	Retail Price	Dealer Invoice	Fair Price
Destination charge	$395	$395	$395

Fair price not available at time of publication. ABS denotes anti-lock 4-wheel disc brakes.

Standard Equipment:

DX: 2.2-liter 4-cylinder engine, 5-speed manual or 4-speed automatic transmission, variable-assist power steering, driver- and passenger-side air bags, cloth reclining front bucket seats, folding rear seat, storage console with armrest, tachometer, coolant-temperature gauge, trip odometer, maintenance interval indicator, digital clock, tinted glass, tilt steering column, cupholder, intermittent wipers, rear defogger, dual remote outside mirrors, remote fuel-door and decklid releases, passenger-side visor mirror, rear heat ducts, 185/70R14 tires. **LX notchback** adds: air conditioning, cruise control, power windows and door locks, power mirrors, rear armrest, trunk pass-through, AM/FM/cassette, integrated antenna, illuminated visor mirrors, variable intermittent wipers, wheel covers. **LX wagon** adds: rear wiper/washer, split folding rear seatback, power antenna, cargo cover, 195/60HR15 tires, full-size spare tire. **LX V-6** adds to LX notchback: 2.7-liter V-6 engine, 4-speed automatic transmission, anti-lock 4-wheel disc brakes, 6-way power driver seat, 205/60R15 tires. **SE** adds to LX notchback: 4-speed automatic transmission, leather-wrapped steering wheel, power moonroof, AM/FM/CD player, remote keyless entry, theft-deterrent system, color-keyed bodyside moldings, alloy wheels. **EX notchback** adds to LX notchback: 2.2-liter 4-cylinder high-output VTEC engine, anti-lock 4-wheel disc brakes, driver-seat lumbar support and power height adjusters, leather upholstery and leather-wrapped steering wheel (leather model), 6-way power driver seat (leather model), power moonroof, upgraded audio system, color-keyed bodyside moldings, 195/60HR15 tires, alloy wheels. **Wagon** adds to EX notchback and LX wagon: remote keyless entry, roof rack. **EX V-6** adds to EX notchback: 2.7-liter V-6 engine, 4-speed automatic transmission, leather upholstery, 8-way power driver seat, leather-wrapped steering wheel, 205/60R15 tires.

Options are available as dealer-installed accessories.

HONDA CIVIC

Specifications	2-door notchback	2-door hatchback	4-door notchback
Wheelbase, in.	103.2	103.2	103.2
Overall length, in.	175.1	164.5	175.1

Honda Civic EX 4-door

	2-door notchback	2-door hatchback	4-door notchback
Overall width, in.	67.1	67.1	67.1
Overall height, in.	54.1	54.1	54.7
Curb weight, lbs.	2262	2222	2319
Cargo vol., cu. ft.	11.9	13.4	11.9
Fuel capacity, gals.	11.9	11.9	11.9
Seating capacity	5	5	5

Engines

	ohc I-4	ohc I-4	ohc I-4
Size, liters/cu. in.	1.6/97	1.6/97	1.6/97
Horsepower @ rpm	106 @ 6200	115 @ 6300	127 @ 6600
Torque (lbs./ft.) @ rpm	103 @ 4600	104 @ 5400	107 @ 5500

EPA city/highway mpg

5-speed OD manual	32/38	37/44	30/36
4-speed OD automatic	29/35		28/35
CVT automatic		34/38	

Built in East Liberty, Ohio; Canada; and Japan.

PRICES

Honda Civic	Retail Price	Dealer Invoice	Fair Price
CX 2-door hatchback, 5-speed	$10550	$9896	—
CX 2-door hatchback, automatic	11550	10834	—
DX 2-door hatchback, 5-speed	11800	10587	—
DX 2-door hatchback, automatic	12800	11484	—
DX 2-door notchback, 5-speed	12280	11018	—
DX 2-door notchback, automatic	13280	11915	—
HX 2-door notchback, 5-speed	13400	12022	—
HX 2-door notchback, CVT	14400	12920	—
EX 2-door notchback, 5-speed	15250	13682	—

Prices are accurate at time of publication; subject to manufacturer's change.

	Retail Price	Dealer Invoice	Fair Price
EX 2-door notchback, automatic	$16050	$14400	—
EX 2-door notchback w/ABS, automatic	16650	14938	—
DX 4-door notchback, 5-speed	12635	11336	—
DX 4-door notchback, automatic	13435	12054	—
LX 4-door notchback, 5-speed	14650	12898	—
LX 4-door notchback, automatic	15450	13616	—
EX 4-door notchback, 5-speed	16480	14786	—
EX 4-door notchback, automatic	17280	15504	—
Destination charge	395	395	395

Fair price not available at time of publication. ABS denotes anti-lock brakes.

Standard Equipment:

CX: 1.6-liter 4-cylinder engine (106 horsepower), 5-speed manual or 4-speed automatic transmission, driver- and passenger-side air bags, power steering (requires automatic transmission), reclining cloth front bucket seats, 50/50 split folding rear seats, remote fuel-door and hatch releases, tinted glass, rear defogger, dual remote outside mirrors, cupholder, intermittent wipers, visor mirrors, 185/65R14 tires. **DX hatchback** adds: rear wiper/washer, AM/FM stereo w/clock, rear map pocket, cargo cover, wheel covers. **DX notchback** adds to CX: power steering (2-door requires automatic transmission), lockable 60/40 fold-down rear seat, AM/FM stereo w/clock, tilt steering column, rear heat ducts, remote trunk release, rear map pocket, full wheel covers. **HX** adds to DX notchback: 1.6-liter 4-cylinder VTEC engine (115 horsepower), 5-speed manual or Continuously Variable Transmission (CVT), power steering, power windows and door locks, power mirrors, tachometer, cargo-area light, alloy wheel covers. **LX** adds to DX notchback: air conditioning, power steering, power mirrors, power windows and door locks, cruise control, tachometer, front storage console with armrest, cargo-area light. **EX** adds to LX: 1.6-liter 4-cylinder VTEC engine (127 horsepower), anti-lock brakes (4-door), power moonroof, six-speakers (2-door), remote keyless entry, color-keyed bodyside molding.

Options are available as dealer-installed accessories.

HONDA CR-V

Specifications

	4-door wagon
Wheelbase, in.	103.2
Overall length, in.	177.6

Honda CR-V

	4-door wagon
Overall width, in.	68.9
Overall height, in.	65.9
Curb weight, lbs.	3150
Cargo vol., cu. ft.	34.3
Fuel capacity, gals.	15.3
Seating capacity	5

Engines

	dohc I-4
Size, liters/cu. in.	2.0/122
Horsepower @ rpm	126 @ 5400
Torque @ rpm	133 @ 4300

EPA city/highway mpg

4-speed OD automatic	NA

Built in Japan.

PRICES

Honda CR-V	Retail Price	Dealer Invoice	Fair Price
4-door wagon	$19300	17513	—
4-door wagon w/ABS	20300	18420	—
Destination charge	395	395	395

Fair price not available at time of publication.

Standard Equipment:

2.0-liter 4-cylinder engine, 4-speed automatic transmission, variable-assist power steering, Real Time 4-wheel drive, air conditioning, driver- and passenger-side air bags, cruise control, reclining front bucket seats w/driver-seat height adjustment, split folding and reclining 50/50 rear bench seat, cupholders, power windows and door locks, power mirrors,

HONDA

tilt steering column, tachometer, solar-control tinted glass, AM/FM radio w/clock, rear defogger, intermittent rear wiper/washer, rear heat ducts, visor mirrors, interior air filter, map lights, remote hatch release, lift-out folding picnic table, auxiliary power outlet, rear mud guards, outside spare-tire carrier w/cover, 205/70R15 tires. **ABS** adds: 4-wheel anti-lock brakes, alloy wheels.

Options are available as dealer-installed accessories.

HONDA DEL SOL

Honda del Sol VTEC

Specifications

	2-door notchback
Wheelbase, in.	93.3
Overall length, in.	157.3
Overall width, in.	66.7
Overall height, in.	49.4
Curb weight, lbs.	2301
Cargo vol., cu. ft.	10.5
Fuel capacity, gals.	11.9
Seating capacity	2

Engines

	ohc I-4	ohc I-4	dohc I-4
Size, liters/cu. in.	1.6/97	1.6/97	1.6/97
Horsepower @ rpm	106 @ 6200	125 @ 6600	160 @ 7600
Torque (lbs./ft.) @ rpm	103 @ 4600	106 @ 5200	111 @ 7000
EPA city/highway mpg			
5-speed OD manual	33/39	30/36	26/30
4-speed OD automatic	28/35	28/35	

Built in Japan.

PRICES

Honda del Sol	Retail Price	Dealer Invoice	Fair Price
S 2-door notchback, 5-speed	$15080	$13530	—
S 2-door notchback, automatic	16080	14427	—
Si 2-door notchback, 5-speed	17300	15522	—
Si 2-door notchback, automatic	18100	16239	—
VTEC 2-door notchback, 5-speed	19600	17585	—
Destination charge	395	395	395

Fair price not available at time of publication.

Standard Equipment:

S: 1.6-liter 4-cylinder engine, 5-speed manual or 4-speed automatic transmission, driver- and passenger-side air bags, power steering (with automatic transmission), reclining bucket seats, center armrest with storage, lockable rear storage compartments, removable roof panel, power windows, rear defogger, intermittent wipers, tilt steering column, tachometer, digital clock, dual outside mirrors, passenger-side visor mirror, remote fuel door and decklid releases, 175/70R13 tires, wheel covers. **Si adds:** 1.6-liter SOHC VTEC engine, power steering, 4-wheel disc brakes, sport suspension, cruise control, AM/FM/cassette, power mirrors and door locks, 185/60HR14 tires, alloy wheels. **VTEC adds:** 1.6-liter DOHC VTEC engine, 5-speed manual transmission, anti-lock brakes, front and rear stabilizer bars, 195/60VR14 tires.

Options are available as dealer-installed accessories.

HONDA ODYSSEY

Honda Odyssey LX

Specifications

	4-door van
Wheelbase, in.	111.4

HONDA

	4-door van
Overall length, in.	187.2
Overall width, in.	70.6
Overall height, in.	64.6
Curb weight, lbs.	3450
Cargo vol., cu. ft.	102.5
Fuel capacity, gals.	17.2
Seating capacity	7

Engines

	ohc I-4
Size, liters/cu. in.	2.2/132
Horsepower @ rpm	140 @ 5600
Torque (lbs./ft.) @ rpm	145 @ 4500

EPA city/highway mpg

4-speed OD automatic	21/26

Built in Japan.

PRICES

Honda Odyssey	Retail Price	Dealer Invoice	Fair Price
LX 4-door van, 7-passenger	$23560	$20818	—
LX 4-door van, 6-passenger	23970	21180	—
EX 4-door van	25550	22577	—
Destination charge	395	395	395

Fair price not available at time of publication.

Standard Equipment:

LX: 2.2-liter 4-cylinder engine, 4-speed automatic transmission, anti-lock 4-wheel disc brakes, driver- and passenger-side air bags, variable-assist power steering, front and rear air conditioning, cloth front bucket seats, split folding middle bench seat (7-passenger seating) or removable captain's chairs (6-passenger seating), folding third bench seat, cupholders, cruise control, tilt steering column, power windows and door locks, power mirrors, AM/FM/cassette, digital clock, remote fuel-door release, rear defogger, variable intermittent wipers, visor mirrors, rear wiper/washer, bodyside moldings, 205/65R15 tires. **EX** adds: 6-passenger seating, driver seat w/power height adjustment, power sunroof, remote keyless entry, 6-speaker sound system, map lights, color-keyed bodyside moldings and mirrors, alloy wheels.

Options are available as dealer-installed accessories.

HONDA PRELUDE

Honda Prelude SH

Specifications

	2-door notchback
Wheelbase, in.	101.8
Overall length, in.	178.0
Overall width, in.	69.0
Overall height, in.	51.8
Curb weight, lbs.	2954
Cargo vol., cu. ft.	8.7
Fuel capacity, gals.	15.9
Seating capacity	4

Engines

	dohc I-4
Size, liter/ cu. in.	2.2/132
Horsepower @ rpm	195 @ 7000
Torque (lbs./ft.) @ rpm	156 @ 5250

EPA city/highway mpg
5-speed OD manual	22/26
4-speed OD automatic	21/26

Built in Japan.

PRICES

Honda Prelude	Retail Price	Dealer Invoice	Fair Price
2-door notchback, 5-speed	$23200	$20578	—
2-door notchback, automatic	24200	21465	—
SH 2-door notchback, 5-speed	25700	22796	—

Prices are accurate at time of publication; subject to manufacturer's change.

	Retail Price	Dealer Invoice	Fair Price
Destination charge	$395	$395	$395

Fair price not available at time of publication.

Standard Equipment:

2.2-liter 4-cylinder VTEC engine, 5-speed manual or 4-speed Sequential SportShift automatic transmission, anti-lock 4-wheel disc brakes, variable-assist power steering, air conditioning, driver- and passenger-side air bags, cruise control, cloth upholstery, reclining front bucket seats w/driver-seat height adjustment, folding rear seat, storage console w/armrest, front and rear cupholders, adjustable steering column, power windows and door locks, power outside mirrors, power moonroof, leather-wrapped steering wheel, tachometer, digital clock, AM/FM/CD player w/Acoustic Feedback Control, integrated rear-window antenna, visor mirrors, map lights, rear defogger, remote fuel-door and decklid release, variable intermittent wipers, theft-deterrent system, auxiliary power outlet, dual exhaust outlets, 205/50R16 tires, alloy wheels. **SH** adds: 5-speed manual transmission, Active Torque Transfer System, leather-wrapped shifter, rear spoiler.

Options are available as dealer-installed accessories.

HYUNDAI ACCENT

Hyundai Accent 4-door

Specifications

	2-door hatchback	4-door notchback
Wheelbase, in.	94.5	94.5
Overall length, in.	161.5	162.1
Overall width, in.	63.8	63.8
Overall height, in.	54.9	54.9

	2-door hatchback	4-door notchback
Curb weight, lbs.	2101	2105
Cargo vol., cu. ft.	16.2	10.7
Fuel capacity, gals.	11.9	11.9
Seating capacity	5	5

Engines

	ohc I-4	dohc I-4
Size, liters/cu. in.	1.5/191	1.5/191
Horsepower @ rpm	92 @ 5500	105 @ 6000
Torque (lbs./ft.) @ rpm	97 @ 3000	101 @ 4500

EPA city/highway mpg

5-speed OD manual	28/37	27/35
4-speed OD automatic	27/36	26/34

Built in South Korea.

PRICES

Hyundai Accent	Retail Price	Dealer Invoice	Fair Price
L 2-door hatchback, 5-speed	$8599	$8104	—
GS 2-door hatchback, 5-speed	9399	8664	—
GS 2-door hatchback, automatic	10154	9348	—
GL 4-door notchback, 5-speed	9799	9033	—
GL 4-door notchback, automatic	10554	9717	—
GT 2-door hatchback, 5-speed	10199	9402	—
GT 2-door hatchback, automatic	10954	10086	—
Destination charge	415	415	415

Fair price not available at time of publication.

Standard Equipment:

L: 1.5-liter 4-cylinder engine, 5-speed manual transmission, driver- and passenger-side air bags, cloth reclining front bucket seats, folding rear seat, front and rear center consoles, remote outside mirrors, coolant-temperature gauge, trip odometer, rear defogger, remote fuel-door release, passenger-side visor mirror, intermittent wipers, cargo-area cover, 155/80R13 tires. **GS** and **GL** add: 5-speed manual or 4-speed automatic transmission, adjustable driver seat w/lumbar support, 60/40 split folding rear seat (GS), fixed rear seat (GL), tinted glass, tachometer, digital clock, remote hatch/decklid release, rear wiper/washer (GS), cargo-area cover (GS), bodyside moldings, 175/70R13 tires, wheel covers. **GT** adds to GS: 1.5-liter DOHC 4-cylinder engine, power steering, sports-tuned suspension, AM/FM radio, leather-wrapped steering wheel and shifter, rear spoiler, lower bodyside cladding, fog lamps, 175/70R14 performance tires, alloy wheels.

Optional Equipment:

	Retail Price	Dealer Invoice	Fair Price
Option Pkg. 2, GS, GL	$710	$582	—
Power steering, AM/FM/cassette.			
Option Pkg. 3, GS, GL	1605	1352	—
Air conditioner, power steering, AM/FM/cassette.			
Option Pkg. 4, GS, GL	2080	1739	—
Air conditioning, power steering, pop-up sunroof, AM/FM/CD player.			
Option Pkg. 5, GS, GL	2630	2249	—
Anti-lock brakes, air conditioning, power steering, pop-up sunroof, AM/FM/CD player.			
Option Pkg. 6, GS, GL	2005	1682	—
Air conditioner, power steering, AM/FM/cassette, pop-up sunroof.			
Option Pkg. 7, GS, GL	2555	2192	—
Anti-lock brakes, air conditioner, power steering, AM/FM/cassette, pop-up sunroof.			
Option Pkg. 15, GT	1525	1278	—
Air conditioning, cassette player, pop-up sunroof.			
Option Pkg. 16, GT	2075	1788	—
Anti-lock brakes, air conditioning, cassette player, pop-up sunroof.			
Option Pkg. 17, GT	1600	1335	—
Air conditioning, CD player, pop-up sunroof.			
Option Pkg. 18, GT	2150	1845	—
Anti-lock brakes, air conditioning, CD player, pop-up sunroof.			

HYUNDAI ELANTRA

Hyundai Elantra 4-door

Specifications

	4-door notchback	4-door wagon
Wheelbase, in.	100.4	100.4

	4-door notchback	4-door wagon
Overall length, in.	174.0	175.2
Overall width, in.	66.9	66.9
Overall height, in.	54.9	58.8
Curb weight, lbs.	2458	2619
Cargo vol., cu. ft.	11.4	63.0
Fuel capacity, gals.	14.5	14.5
Seating capacity	5	5

Engines

	dohc I-4
Size, liters/cu. in.	1.8/110
Horsepower @ rpm	130 @ 6000
Torque (lbs./ft.) @ rpm	122 @ 5000

EPA city/highway mpg

5-speed OD manual	24/32
4-speed OD automatic	23/31

Built in South Korea.

PRICES

Hyundai Elantra	Retail Price	Dealer Invoice	Fair Price
4-door notchback, 5-speed	$11099	$10117	—
4-door notchback, automatic	11899	10842	—
4-door wagon, 5-speed	11999	10938	—
4-door wagon, automatic	12799	11663	—
GLS 4-door notchback, 5-speed	12549	11181	—
GLS 4-door notchback, automatic	13349	11906	—
GLS 4-door wagon, automatic	13999	12472	—
Destination charge	415	415	415

Fair price not available at time of publication.

Standard Equipment:

1.8-liter DOHC 4-cylinder engine, 5-speed manual transmission or 4-speed automatic transmission, driver- and passenger-side air bags, variable-assist power steering, cloth reclining front bucket seats, 60/40 split folding rear seat (wagon), front storage console, tilt steering column, remote outside mirrors, digital clock, trip odometer, coolant-temperature gauge, passenger-side visor mirror, tinted glass, variable intermittent wipers, rear defogger, remote fuel-door and decklid release, rear heat ducts, roof rack (wagon), cargo-area cover (wagon), 175/65R14 tires, wheel covers. **GLS** adds: 4-wheel disc brakes, upgraded cloth upholstery, 6-way adjustable driver seat, 60/40 split

HYUNDAI

folding rear seat, deluxe front storage console w/armrest, power windows and door locks, power mirrors, tachometer, AM/FM/cassette, rear wiper/washer (wagon), driver-side visor mirror, map lights, full cargo-area trim, 194/60HR14 tires, deluxe wheel covers.

Optional Equipment:	Retail Price	Dealer Invoice	Fair Price
Option Pkg. 2, base	$450	$348	—
AM/FM/cassette.			
Option Pkg. 3, base	1345	1085	—
Air conditioning, AM/FM/cassette.			
Option Pkg. 4, base	1565	1266	—
Air conditioning, cruise control, AM/FM/cassette.			
Option Pkg. 5, base	1640	1323	—
Air conditioning, cruise control, CD player.			
Option Pkg. 13, GLS	2320	1895	—
Pkg. 14 plus rear spoiler, alloy wheels.			
Option Pkg. 14, GLS	1840	1507	—
Air conditioning, cruise control, power moonroof, AM/FM/CD player.			
Option Pkg. 15, GLS	1590	1301	—
Air conditioning, cruise control, AM/FM/CD player, alloy wheels.			
Option Pkg. 19, GLS	1115	918	—
Air conditioning, cruise control.			
Option Pkg. 20, GLS	1890	1636	—
Air conditioning, cruise control, anti-lock brakes.			
Option Pkg. 21, GLS	1595	1306	—
Air conditioning, cruise control, rear spoiler, alloy wheels.			

HYUNDAI SONATA

Hyundai Sonata

Specifications

	4-door notchback
Wheelbase, in.	106.3

	4-door notchback
Overall length, in.	185.0
Overall width, in.	69.7
Overall height, in.	55.9
Curb weight, lbs.	3025
Cargo vol., cu. ft.	13.2
Fuel capacity, gals.	17.2
Seating capacity	5

Engines

	dohc I-4	ohc V-6
Size, liters/cu. in.	2.0/122	3.0/181
Horsepower @ rpm	137 @ 5800	142 @ 5000
Torque (lbs./ft.) @ rpm	129 @ 4000	168 @ 2400

EPA city/highway mpg

5-speed OD manual	21/28	
4-speed OD automatic	20/27	18/24

Built in South Korea.

PRICES

Hyundai Sonata	Retail Price	Dealer Invoice	Fair Price
4-door notchback, 5-speed	$14749	$13368	$13868
4-door notchback, automatic	15549	14159	14659
GL 4-door notchback, automatic	16349	14650	15150
GL 4-door notchback, V-6 automatic	17349	15546	16046
GLS 4-door notchback, V-6 automatic	18549	16240	16740
Destination charge	415	415	415

Standard Equipment:

2.0-liter DOHC 4-cylinder engine, 5-speed manual or 4-speed automatic transmission, air conditioning, power steering, driver- and passenger-side air bags, cloth reclining front bucket seats w/4-way adjustable driver seat, 60/40 split folding rear seat, front storage console, cupholders, tilt steering wheel, remote outside mirrors, tinted glass, tachometer, coolant-temperature gauge, trip odometer, digital clock, AM/FM/cassette w/6-speakers, remote fuel-door and decklid releases, rear defogger, rear heat ducts, variable intermittent wipers, visor mirrors, 195/70R14 tires, wheel covers. **GL** adds: 2.0-liter DOHC 4-cylinder or 3.0-liter V-6 engine, 4-speed automatic transmission, power windows and door locks, power mirrors, deluxe wheel covers. **GLS** adds to GL: 3.0-liter V-6 engine, 4-wheel disc brakes, cruise control, upgraded cloth upholstery, 6-way adjustable driver seat, console armrest, rear armrest, upgraded audio system w/6-speakers, power antenna, passenger-side visor mirror, seat-back pockets, map lights, 205/60HR15 tires, alloy wheels.

Optional Equipment:	Retail Price	Dealer Invoice	Fair Price
Option Pkg. 3, GL	$965	$767	$849
Cruise control, console armrest, power moonroof, reading lights.			
Option Pkg. 4, GL	1245	1107	1195
Anti-lock 4-wheel disc brakes, cruise control, console armrest.			
Option Pkg. 6, GL	365	273	321
Cruise control, console armrest.			
Option Pkg. 10, GLS	600	494	570
Power moonroof, reading lights.			
Option Pkg. 11, GLS	1350	1112	1283
Power moonroof, AM/FM/cassette/CD player.			
Option Pkg. 12, GLS	1400	1226	1330
AM/FM/cassette/CD player, Leather Pkg. (leather upholstery, leather-wrapped steering wheel).			
Option Pkg. 13, GLS	2000	1720	1900
Power moonroof, AM/FM/cassette/CD player, Leather Pkg. (leather upholstery, leather-wrapped steering wheel), reading lights.			
Option Pkg. 14, GLS	2880	2554	2736
Anti-lock brakes, power moonroof, AM/FM/cassette/CD player, Leather Pkg. (leather upholstery, leather-wrapped steering wheel), reading lights.			
Option Pkg. 15, GLS	880	834	845
Anti-lock brakes.			

HYUNDAI TIBURON

Hyundai Tiburon

Specifications	2-door hatchback
Wheelbase, in..	97.4

	2-door hatchback
Overall length, in.	170.9
Overall width, in.	68.1
Overall height, in.	51.3
Curb weight, lbs.	2570
Cargo vol., cu. ft.	12.8
Fuel capacity, gals.	14.5
Seating capacity	4

Engines

	dohc I-4	dohc I-4
Size, liters/cu. in.	1.8/110	2.0/122
Horsepower @ rpm	130 @ 6000	140 @ 6000
Torque (lbs./ft.) @ rpm	122 @ 5000	133 @ 4800
EPA city/highway mpg		
5-speed OD manual	22/30	22/29
4-speed OD automatic	23/31	21/28

Built in South Korea.

PRICES

Hyundai Tiburon	Retail Price	Dealer Invoice	Fair Price
2-door hatchback, 5-speed	$13499	$12166	—
2-door hatchback, automatic	14299	12891	—
FX 2-door hatchback, 5-speed	14899	13121	—
FX 2-door hatchback, automatic	15699	13846	—
Destination charge	415	415	415

Fair price not available at time of publication.

Standard Equipment:

1.8-liter 4-cylinder engine, 5-speed manual or 4-speed automatic transmission, driver- and passenger-side air bags, power steering, cloth reclining front bucket seats, split folding rear seat, front storage console, cupholders, tilt steering column, power windows, remote outside mirrors, tinted glass, coolant-temperature gauge, trip odometer, tachometer, digital clock, AM/FM/cassette, rear defogger, remote hatch and fuel-door releases, variable intermittent wipers, map lights, rear heat ducts, cargo-area cover, bright exhaust outlets, 195/60R14 performance tires, wheel covers. **FX** adds: 2.0-liter 4-cylinder engine, 4-wheel disc brakes, upgraded seat trim, 6-way adjustable driver seat, deluxe front storage console, power door locks, power mirrors, passenger-side visor mirror, fog lights, rear spoiler, rear wiper/washer, alloy wheels.

Optional Equipment:	Retail Price	Dealer Invoice	Fair Price
Option Pkg. 2, base	$895	$737	—
Air conditioning.			
Option Pkg. 3, base	1245	1025	—
Air conditioning, upgraded audio system.			
Option Pkg. 4, base	1745	1419	—
Air conditioning, upgraded audio system, rear spoiler, fog lights.			
Option Pkg. 5, base	2140	1735	—
Air conditioning, upgraded audio system, rear spoiler, fog lights, 195/HR15 performance tires, alloy wheels.			
Option Pkg. 6, FX	1425	1174	—
Air conditioning, cruise control, upgraded audio system.			
Option Pkg. 7, FX	2050	1689	—
Air conditioning, cruise control, power sunroof, upgraded audio system.			
Option Pkg. 8, FX	2425	1998	—
Air conditioning, cruise control, power sunroof, AM/FM/cassette/CD player.			
Option Pkg. 9, FX	3125	2647	—
Anti-lock brakes, air conditioning, cruise control, power sunroof, AM/FM/cassette/CD player.			
Option Pkg. 10, FX	3910	3364	—
Anti-lock brakes, air conditioning, cruise control, leather upholstery, leather-wrapped steering wheel, power sunroof, AM/FM/cassette/CD player, 195/55HR15 performance tires.			
Option Pkg. 11, FX	3210	2715	—
Air conditioning, cruise control, leather upholstery, leather-wrapped steering wheel, power sunroof, AM/FM/cassette/CD player, 195/55HR15 performance tires.			
Option Pkg. 12, FX	1885	1551	—
Air conditioning, cruise control, AM/FM/cassette/CD player, 195/55HR15 performance tires.			
Option Pkg. 13, FX	2510	2066	—
Air conditioning, cruise control, power sunroof, AM/FM/cassette/CD player, 195/55HR15 performance tires.			
Option Pkg. 14, FX	1510	1242	—
Air conditioning, cruise control, upgraded audio system, 195/55HR15 performance tires.			
Option Pkg. 15, FX	2135	1757	—
Air conditioning, cruise control, power sunroof, upgraded audio system, 195/55HR15 performance tires.			
Option Pkg. 16, FX	3210	2715	—
Anti-lock brakes, air conditioning, cruise control, power sunroof, AM/FM/cassette/CD player, 195/55HR15 performance tires.			

INFINITI J30

Infiniti J30t

Specifications

	4-door notchback
Wheelbase, in.	108.7
Overall length, in.	191.3
Overall width, in.	69.7
Overall height, in.	54.7
Curb weight, lbs.	3527
Cargo vol., cu. ft.	10.1
Fuel capacity, gals.	19.0
Seating capacity	5

Engines

	dohc V-6
Size, liters/cu. in.	3.0/181
Horsepower @ rpm	210 @ 6400
Torque (lbs./ft.) @ rpm	193 @ 4800

EPA city/highway mpg

4-speed OD automatic	18/23

Built in Japan.

PRICES

Infiniti J30	Retail Price	Dealer Invoice	Fair Price
4-door notchback	$33500	$29771	—
J30t with Touring Package	35500	31548	—
Destination charge	455	455	455

Fair price not available at time of publication.

Prices are accurate at time of publication; subject to manufacturer's change.

Standard Equipment:

3.0-liter DOHC V-6 engine, 4-speed automatic transmission, anti-lock 4-wheel disc brakes, variable-assist power steering, limited-slip differential, driver- and passenger-side air bags, 8-way heated power front bucket seats, driver's seat power lumbar adjuster, leather upholstery, walnut inlays, automatic climate control, cruise control, tilt steering column, AM/FM/cassette and CD player with six speakers, power sunroof, tinted glass, power windows and locks, heated power mirrors, remote fuel door and decklid releases, remote keyless entry and anti-theft alarm systems, intermittent wipers, tachometer, trip odometer, leather-wrapped steering wheel, automatic day/night mirror, rear folding armrest, floormats, 215/60R15 all-season tires, cast alloy wheels. **J30t** adds: Touring Pkg. (rear spoiler, firmer suspension, larger stabilizer bars, forged alloy wheels), 215/60HR15 performance tires.

Options are available as dealer-installed accessories.

INFINITI Q45

Infiniti Q45

Specifications

	4-door notchback
Wheelbase, in.	111.4
Overall length, in.	199.2
Overall width, in.	71.7
Overall height, in.	56.9
Curb weight, lbs.	3879
Cargo vol., cu. ft.	12.6
Fuel capacity, gals.	21.1
Seating capacity	5

Engines

	dohc V-8
Size, liters/cu. in.	4.1/252

	dohc V-8
Horsepower @ rpm	266 @ 5600
Torque (lbs./ft.) @ rpm	278 @ 4000

EPA city/highway mpg

4-speed OD automatic	18/24

Built in Japan.

PRICES

Infiniti Q45	Retail Price	Dealer Invoice	Fair Price
Q45 4-door notchback	$47900	$42569	—
Q45t 4-door notchback	49900	44346	—
Destination charge	495	495	495

Fair price not available at time of publication.

Standard Equipment:

Q45: 4.1-liter DOHC V-8 engine, 4-speed automatic transmission, anti-lock 4-wheel disc brakes, variable-assist power steering, traction control system, limited-slip differential, driver- and passenger-side air bags, cruise control, automatic climate control, leather upholstery, 10-way power front bucket seats, memory driver seat, folding rear seat with armrest, front storage console with auxiliary power outlet, cupholders, wood interior trim, leather-wrapped steering wheel and shifter, tilt/telescopic steering wheel, Nissan/Bose AM/FM/CD player, power antenna, integrated diversity antenna, power sunroof, green tinted glass, power windows and door locks, remote keyless entry, heated power mirrors, tachometer, coolant-temperature gauge, digital clock, outside temperature indicator, automatic day/night inside mirror, interior air filter, rear air ducts, rear defogger, remote fuel-door and decklid releases, illuminated visor mirrors, map lights, variable intermittent wipers, theft-deterrent system, automatic headlamps, Homelink universal garage-door opener, floormats, fog lights, cargo net, 215/60R16 tires, alloy wheels. **Q45t** adds: sport-tuned suspension, leather-wrapped sport steering wheel, heated front seats, 6-disc CD changer, rear spoiler, performance alloy wheels.

Optional Equipment:

Heated front seats, Q45	400	355	—

Prices are accurate at time of publication; subject to manufacturer's change.

ISUZU RODEO/ HONDA PASSPORT

Isuzu Rodeo

Specifications

	4-door wagon
Wheelbase, in.	108.7
Overall length, in.	176.5
Overall width, in.	66.5
Overall height, in.	65.4
Curb weight, lbs.	3545
Cargo vol., cu. ft.	74.9
Fuel capacity, gals.	21.9
Seating capacity	5

Engines

	dohc I-4	dohc I-4
Size, liters/cu. in.	2.6/156	3.2/193
Horsepower @ rpm	120 @ 4600	190 @ 5200
Torque (lbs./ft.) @ rpm	150 @ 2600	188 @ 4000

EPA city/highway mpg

5-speed OD manual	19/22	16/19
4-speed OD automatic		15/18

Built in Lafayette, Ind.

PRICES

Isuzu Rodeo	Retail Price	Dealer Invoice	Fair Price
S 4-cylinder 2WD 4-door wagon, 5-speed	$17340	$16300	—
S V-6 2WD 4-door wagon, 5-speed	20650	18895	—

	Retail Price	Dealer Invoice	Fair Price
S V-6 2WD 4-door wagon, automatic	$21620	$19783	—
LS V-6 2WD 4-door wagon, automatic	25990	23781	—
S V-6 4WD 4-door wagon, 5-speed	22690	20648	—
S V-6 4WD 4-door wagon, automatic	23840	21695	—
LS V-6 4WD 4-door wagon, 5-speed	27260	24806	—
LS V-6 4WD 4-door wagon, automatic	28410	25853	—
Destination charge	445	445	445

Fair price not available at time of publication.

Standard Equipment:

S: 2.6-liter 4-cylinder engine, 5-speed manual transmission, anti-lock rear brakes, driver- and passenger-side air bags, variable-assist power steering, cloth reclining front bucket seats with folding armrest, folding rear seat, center storage console, 4-speaker AM/FM/cassette, rear defogger, dual outside mirrors, tinted glass, coolant-temperature gauge, trip odometer, cargo rope hooks, fuel-tank skid plate, 225/75R16 all-season tires, styled steel wheels with bright center caps, full-size spare tire. **S V-6** adds: 3.2-liter V-6 engine, 5-speed manual or 4-speed automatic transmission, 4-wheel disc brakes, tachometer, intermittent rear wiper/washer, voltmeter, oil-pressure gauge, radiator skid plate, floormats, outside spare-tire carrier. **LS** adds: air conditioning, moquette upholstery, tilt steering wheel, split folding rear seat, power windows and door locks, heated power mirrors, cruise control, 6-speaker premium audio system, visor mirrors, leather-wrapped steering wheel, intermittent front wipers, power hatchgate release, front-door map pockets, map and courtesy lights, roof rack, privacy rear quarter and rear side glass, bright exterior trim, dual note horn, cargo net and cover, mud guards, 245/70R16 tires, alloy wheels. **4WD** adds: part-time 4WD, automatic locking hubs, tow hooks, transfer-case skid plate.

Optional Equipment:

4-wheel anti-lock brakes	800	712	—
Air conditioning, S	950	845	—
Preferred Equipment Pkg., S	2150	1913	—

Air conditioning, tilt steering wheel, power windows and door locks, power mirrors, cruise control, power tailgate release, intermittent front wipers, intermittent rear wiper/washer, visor mirrors, roof rack, 6-speaker AM/FM/cassette, cargo net and cover.

LX Luxury/Security Pkg., LX	1875	1669	—

Front anti-lock brakes, leather upholstery, 12-disc CD changer, remote keyless entry.

Appearance Pkg., S 4-cylinder	349	276	—

Roof rack, bodyside moldings, striping, wheel trim rings.

Prices are accurate at time of publication; subject to manufacturer's change.

	Retail Price	Dealer Invoice	Fair Price
Leather upholstery, LS	$1195	$1063	—
Limited-slip differential, 4WD	280	249	—
Sunroof, LS	350	311	—
Outside spare-tire carrier, S 4-cylinder	275	245	—
Alloy wheels, S 4WD	800	712	—
S 2WD	400	356	—

Requires Preferred Equipment Pkg.

JAGUAR XJ SEDAN

Jaguar XJ6

Specifications

	4-door notchback	4-door notchback
Wheelbase, in.	113.0	117.9
Overall length, in.	197.8	202.7
Overall width, in.	70.8	70.8
Overall height, in.	53.1	53.1
Curb weight, lbs.	4080	4110
Cargo vol., cu. ft.	11.1	11.1
Fuel capacity, gals.	23.1	23.1
Seating capacity	5	5

Engines

	dohc I-6	Supercharged dohc I-6
Size, liters/cu. in.	4.0/243	4.0/243
Horsepower @ rpm	245 @ 4700	322 @ 5000
Torque (lbs./ft.) @ rpm	289 @ 4000	378 @ 3050

EPA city/highway mpg

4-speed OD automatic	17/23	12/20

Built in England.

PRICES

Jaguar XJ Sedan	Retail Price	Dealer Invoice	Fair Price
XJ6 4-door notchback	$54400	$47524	—
XJ6 L 4-door notchback	59400	51892	—
Vanden Plas 4-door notchback	63800	55736	—
XJR 4-door notchback	67400	55881	—
Destination charge	580	580	580

Fair price not available at time of publication. Gas guzzler tax is included in the retail price of the XJR.

Standard Equipment:

XJ6: 4.0-liter DOHC 6-cylinder engine, 4-speed automatic transmission, driver- and passenger-side side air bags, anti-lock 4-wheel disc brakes, variable-assist power steering, automatic climate control, cruise control, leather upholstery, 12-way power front bucket seats with power lumbar adjusters, contoured rear bench seat, front storage console, overhead console, cupholders, walnut interior trim and shifter, power sunroof, power tilt/telescopic steering wheel, automatic power door locks, power windows, power heated mirrors w/memory feature, trip computer, outside-temperature indicator, AM/FM/cassette, rear defogger, remote keyless entry, theft-deterrent system, remote fuel-door and decklid releases, illuminated visor mirrors, map lights, intermittent wipers, chrome hood ornament, carpeted floormats, front and rear fog lamps, 225/60ZR16 tires, full-size spare tire, dimple-style alloy wheels. **Vanden Plas** adds: wood and leather-wrapped steering wheel, walnut picnic trays on front seatbacks, automatic day/night inside mirror, universal garage-door opener, lambswool floormats, 20-spoke alloy wheels. **XJR** deletes walnut picnic trays and lambswool floormats, and adds: supercharged 4.0-liter DOHC 6-cylinder engine, traction control, limited-slip differential, sport suspension, Harman/Kardon audio system w/CD changer, heated front seats, maple or walnut interior trim and shifter, carpeted floormats, 255/45ZR17 tires, sport-style alloy wheels.

Optional Equipment:

Convenience Group, XJ6	350	294	—

Universal garage-door opener; automatic day/night inside mirror; memory feature for driver seat, driver-side outside mirror, and steering wheel.

All-weather Pkg., XJ6,			
Vanden Plas	2000	1680	—

Traction control, heated front and rear seats.

CD changer, XJ6,			
Vanden Plas	800	672	—

Prices are accurate at time of publication; subject to manufacturer's change.

	Retail Price	Dealer Invoice	Fair Price
Harman/Kardon audio system w/CD changer, XJ6, Vanden Plas	$1800	$1512	—
Chrome wheels, XJ6, Vanden Plas	1000	840	—
Extra-cost paint	1000	840	—

JAGUAR XK8

Jaguar XK8

Specifications

	2-door notchback	2-door conv.
Wheelbase, in.	101.9	101.9
Overall length, in.	187.4	187.4
Overall width, in.	72.0	72.0
Overall height, in.	51.0	51.4
Curb weight, lbs.	3673	3867
Cargo vol., cu. ft.	11.1	6.8
Fuel capacity, gals.	19.9	19.9
Seating capacity	4	4

Engines

	dohc V-8
Size, liters/cu. in.	4.0/244
Horsepower @ rpm	290 @ 6100
Torque (lbs./ft.) @ rpm	290 @ 4200

EPA city/highway mpg

5-speed OD automatic	17/25

Built in England.

PRICES

Jaguar XK8	Retail Price	Dealer Invoice	Fair Price
2-door notchback	$64900	$57104	—
2-door convertible	69900	61472	—
Destination charge	580	580	580

Fair price not available at time of publication.

Standard Equipment:

4.0-liter DOHC 6-cylinder engine, 5-speed automatic transmission, anti-lock 4-wheel disc brakes, Automatic Stability Control, driver- and passenger-side air bags, automatic climate control, variable-assist power steering, cruise control, power top (convertible), leather upholstery, 4-way power front bucket seats w/power lumbar support, memory driver seat, cupholders, walnut interior trim and shifter, power tilt/telescopic steering wheel, leather-wrapped steering wheel, tachometer, voltmeter, oil-pressure gauge, trip computer, outside-temperature indicator, AM/FM/cassette, automatic power door locks, power windows, heated power mirrors w/memory feature, remote keyless entry, universal garage-door opener, theft-deterrent system, illuminated visor mirrors, automatic day/night rearview mirror, rear defogger, remote fuel-door and decklid release, variable intermittent windshield wipers, map lights, front and rear fog lights, 245/50ZR17 tires, full-size spare tire, alloy wheels.

Optional Equipment:

All-Weather Pkg.	2000	1680	—
Traction Control, heated front seats, headlamp washers.			
CD changer	800	672	—
Harmon Kardon sound system w/CD changer	1800	1512	—
Chrome wheels	1000	840	—
Extra-cost paint	1000	840	—

JEEP CHEROKEE

Specifications	2-door wagon	4-door wagon
Wheelbase, in.	101.4	101.4
Overall length, in.	167.5	167.5
Overall width, in.	67.9	67.9
Overall height, in.	63.9	64.0
Curb weight, lbs.	2947	2993
Cargo vol., cu. ft.	71.0	71.0

Prices are accurate at time of publication; subject to manufacturer's change.

JEEP

Jeep Cherokee Country

	2-door wagon	4-door wagon
Fuel capacity, gals.	20.0	20.0
Seating capacity	5	5

Engines

	ohv I-4	ohv I-6
Size, liters/cu. in.	2.5/150	4.0/242
Horsepower @ rpm	125 @ 5400	190 @ 4600
Torque (lbs./ft.) @ rpm	150@ 3250	225 @ 3000

EPA city/highway mpg

	ohv I-4	ohv I-6
5-speed OD manual	19/23	18/23
4-speed OD automatic		15/21

Built in Toledo, Ohio.

PRICES

Jeep Cherokee	Retail Price	Dealer Invoice	Fair Price
SE 2-door 2WD	$15300	$14383	—
SE 2-door 4WD	16815	15782	—
SE 4-door 2WD	16340	15349	—
SE 4-door 4WD	17850	16744	—
Sport 2-door 2WD	17915	16225	—
Sport 2-door 4WD	19425	17574	—
Sport 4-door 2WD	18950	17156	—
Sport 4-door 4WD	20460	18505	—
Country 4-door 2WD	21905	19756	—
Country 4-door 4WD	23420	21110	—
Destination charge	525	525	525

Fair price not available at time of publication.

Standard Equipment:

SE: 2.5-liter 4-cylinder engine, 5-speed manual transmission, driver- and passenger-side air bags, power steering, vinyl upholstery, front bucket seats, folding rear seat, floor console, remote outside mirrors, AM/FM radio w/two speakers, tinted glass, intermittent wipers, 215/75R15 tires. **Sport** adds: 4.0-liter 6-cylinder engine, cloth/vinyl upholstery, tachometer, cassette player w/four speakers, Sport Decor Group, lower bodyside molding, spare-tire cover, 225/75R15 outline-white-letter all-terrain tires. **Country** adds: 4-speed automatic transmission, upgraded cloth upholstery, power windows and door locks, power mirrors, leather-wrapped steering wheel, Light Group (Sentinel headlamp delay, illuminated visor mirrors, courtesy lights, map/dome lights, cargo-area light), remote keyless entry, intermittent rear wiper/washer, cloth door trim and map pockets, floormats, Country Decor Group, striping, roof rack, underhood light, 225/70R15 outline-white-letter tires, alloy wheels. **4WD** adds: Command-Trac part-time 4-wheel drive.

Optional Equipment:

	Retail Price	Dealer Invoice	Fair Price
Air conditioning	NC	NC	NC
4.0-liter 6-cylinder engine, SE	$995	$846	—
4-speed automatic transmission, SE, Sport	945	803	—
SE requires 4.0-liter 6-cylinder engine.			
Selec-Trac full-time 4-wheel drive,			
Sport 4WD, Country 4WD	395	336	—
Sport requires automatic transmission.			
Trac-Lok rear differential	285	242	—
Requires full-size spare tire.			
Anti-lock brakes	600	510	—
SE requires 4.0-liter 6-cylinder engine.			
Quick Order Pkg. 23B/25B/26B, SE	275	234	—
Cloth upholstery, power mirrors, rear wiper/washer. Pkg. 25B requires 4.0-liter 6-cylinder engine and manual transmission. Pkg. 26B requires 4.0-liter 6-cylinder engine and automatic transmission.			
Quick Order Pkg. 25E/26E, Sport	110	93	—
Air conditioning, power mirrors, leather-wrapped tilt steering column, rear wiper/washer, floormats, roof rack. Pkg. 26E requires 4-speed automatic transmission.			
Quick Order Pkg. 26H, Country (credit)	(385)	(327)	—
Air conditioning, cruise control, tilt steering column.			
Cloth upholstery, SE	145	123	—
Leather upholstery, Country	835	710	—
Includes 6-way power driver seat.			
6-way power driver seat, Sport, Country	300	255	—
Sport requires Power Equipment Group.			

Prices are accurate at time of publication; subject to manufacturer's change.

	Retail Price	Dealer Invoice	Fair Price
Overhead console, Sport, Country	$235	$200	—
Sport requires Power Equipment Group or Light Group.			
Tilt steering column	140	119	—
Cruise control	250	213	—
SE and Sport require leather-wrapped steering wheel.			
Leather-wrapped steering wheel, SE, Sport	50	43	—
Power Equipment Group, Sport 2-door	630	536	—
Sport 2-door w/Quick Order Pkg.	500	425	—
Sport 4-door	805	684	—
Sport 4-door w/Quick Order Pkg.	675	574	—
Includes remote keyless entry, power windows and door locks, power mirrors. Requires Light Group, rear wiper/washer.			
Power mirrors, SE, Sport	130	111	—
Heated power mirrors, SE	175	149	—
SE and Sport w/Quick Order Pkg., Country	45	38	—
Requires rear defogger.			
Cassette player, SE	300	255	—
Includes four speakers.			
Cassette/CD player, SE	710	604	—
Sport, Country	410	349	—
SE includes four speakers.			
Infinity speakers	350	298	—
Includes power amplifier, cargo-area light. Requires cassette/CD player.			
Rear defogger	165	140	—
SE and Sport require rear wiper/washer.			
Intermittent rear wiper/washer, SE, Sport ...	150	128	—
Sunscreen glass, Sport 2-door	375	319	—
Sport 4-door, Country	270	230	—
Light Group, SE	200	170	—
SE w/cassette player or cassette/CD player, Sport	160	136	—
Sentinel headlamp delay, illuminated visor mirrors, underhood light, courtesy lights, map/dome lights, cargo-area light.			
Trailer Tow Group	365	310	—
4WD w/Up Country Suspension Group ...	245	208	—
Equalizer hitch, 7-wire receptacle, 4-wire trailer adapter, maximum engine cooling. SE and Sport require automatic transmission and full-size spare tire. Country requires full-size spare tire.			
Up Country Suspension Group,			
SE 4WD	1060	901	—
Sport 4WD	770	655	—
Sport 4WD w/alloy wheels	835	710	—

	Retail Price	Dealer Invoice	Fair Price
Country 4WD	$750	$638	—

Trac-Lok rear differential, maximum engine cooling, off-road suspension, tow hooks, Skid Plate Group, rear stabilizer bar delete, 225/75R15 outline-white-letter all-terrain tires, full-size spare tire.

Skid Plate Group, 4WD	145	123	—

Fuel-tank, transfer-case, and front-suspension skid plates.

Fog lamps, Sport, Country	110	94	—

Sport requires rear defogger and rear wiper/washer. Country requires rear defogger.

Cargo-area cover	75	64	—
Roof rack, SE, Sport	140	110	—
Floormats, SE, Sport	50	43	—
225/75R15 outline-white-letter tires, SE	315	268	—

Requires full-size spare tire.

Full-size spare tire,

SE w/std. 215/75R15 tires	75	64	—
SE w/225/75R15 outline-white-letter tires.	120	102	—
Sport	145	123	—
Sport w/alloy wheels	210	179	—
Country	210	179	—
Spare-tire cover, SE	50	43	—
Alloy wheels, SE	440	374	—
Sport	245	208	—

Requires full-size spare tire.

JEEP GRAND CHEROKEE

Jeep Grand Cherokee Orvis

Specifications

	4-door wagon
Wheelbase, in.	105.9
Overall length, in.	177.2

Prices are accurate at time of publication; subject to manufacturer's change.

JEEP

	4-door wagon
Overall width, in.	69.3
Overall height, in.	64.9
Curb weight, lbs.	3609
Cargo vol., cu. ft.	79.3
Fuel capacity, gals.	23.0
Seating capacity	5

Engines

	ohv I-6	ohv V-8
Size, liters/cu. in.	4.0/242	5.2/318
Horsepower @ rpm	185 @ 4600	220 @ 4400
Torque (lbs./ft.) @ rpm	220 @ 2400	300 @ 2800

EPA city/highway mpg

4-speed OD automatic	15/20	14/17

Built in Detroit, Mich.

PRICES

Jeep Grand Cherokee	Retail Price	Dealer Invoice	Fair Price
Laredo 4-door 2WD	$25545	$23155	$23955
Laredo 4-door 4WD	27515	24923	25723
TSi 4-door 2WD	27695	25047	25847
TSi 4-door 4WD	29665	26815	27615
Limited 4-door 2WD	31360	28272	29072
Limited 4-door 4WD	33790	30445	31245
Destination charge	525	525	525

Standard Equipment:

Laredo: 4.0-liter 6-cylinder engine, 4-speed automatic transmission, driver- and passenger-side air bags, anti-lock 4-wheel disc brakes, power steering, cloth reclining front bucket seats, split folding rear seat, air conditioning, power windows, leather-wrapped tilt steering wheel, cruise control, tachometer, voltage and temperature gauges, trip odometer, illuminated entry system, storage console with armrest and cupholders, tinted glass, rear defogger, intermittent front and rear wiper/washer, remote keyless entry system, power mirrors, lighted visor mirrors, roof rack, floormats, cargo cover, net, and tiedown hooks, 215/75R15 tires, alloy wheels. 4WD system is Selec-Trac full-time 4WD. **TSi** adds: body-color grille, AM/FM/cassette with eight speakers, leather reclining front bucket seats, leather-wrapped tilt steering wheel with automatic speed controls and remote audio buttons. 4WD system is Quadra-Trac permanent 4WD. **Limited** adds: automatic temperature control, leather front seats, Luxury Group (power front seats, automatic day/night rearview mirror, automatic headlamp system, vehicle information system), remote keyless entry w/memory feature, heated memory outside mirrors, fog lamps, deep-tinted side and rear glass, flip-up liftgate glass, universal garage-door opener, steering wheel w/radio controls, overhead console (compass, trip computer, map/reading lights), security system, Infinity Gold speakers, gold or silver badging and graphics, 225/70R16 outline-white -etter tires, gold- or silver-accented alloy wheels.

Optional Equipment:

	Retail Price	Dealer Invoice	Fair Price
5.2-liter V-8 engine,			
2WD Laredo w/option pkg., TSi, Limited .	$880	$748	$836
4WD Laredo w/option pkg.	1325	1126	1258
4WD Limited w/Orvis Pkg.	760	646	722

Includes Trailer Tow Prep Group (std. with Orvis Pkg.). 4WD includes Quadra-Trac permanent 4WD.

Quadra-Trac permanent 4WD,			
Laredo 4WD	445	378	423

Requires full-size spare tire.

Trac-Lok rear differential	285	242	271
Pkg. 26S/28S, 2WD TSi	1650	1402	—

Overhead console, flip-up liftgate glass, fog lamps, deep-tinted glass, Luxury Group, heated outside mirrors, AM/FM/cassette with Infinity Gold speakers, 225/70R16 outline-white-letter tires, security system, alloy wheels.

Pkg. 26S/28S, 4WD TSi	2255	1916	—

Package 26S/28S, 2WD plus full-size spare tire, Quadra-Trac permanent 4WD.

Pkg. 26X/28X, Laredo	55	47	53

Overhead console (compass, trip computer, map/reading lights), tinted glass, 225/75R15 outline-white-letter tires. Pkg. 28X requires 5.2-liter V-8 engine.

Pkg. 26Y/28Y, Laredo	1530	1300	1460

Package 26X/28X plus Luxury Group, security system, cassette player with Infinity Gold speakers, heated outside mirrors, flip-up liftgate glass. Pkg. 28F requires 5.2-liter V-8 engine.

Pkg. 26K/28K, Limited	1290	1097	1226

Power sunroof, heated front seats, CD player, mini overhead console. Pkg. 28K requires 5.2-liter V-8 engine.

Orvis Pkg. 26L/28L,			
4WD Limited	1210	1029	1150

Heated front seats, Up Country Suspension Group, CD player, Orvis badging and graphics, Orvis floormats, front and rear tow hooks, Trailer Tow Prep Group, 225/70R16 Wrangler all-terrain outline-white-letter tires, full-size spare, green-accented alloy wheels. Pkg. 28L requires 5.2-liter V-8 engine.

Prices are accurate at time of publication; subject to manufacturer's change.

	Retail Price	Dealer Invoice	Fair Price
Luxury Group, Laredo w/Pkg. 26X/28X	$965	$820	$917
Power front seats, automatic day/night rearview mirror, automatic headlamp system, vehicle information system.			
Trailer Tow Prep Group	105	89	100
Trailer Tow Group III, TSi, Limited	360	306	342
Includes Trailer Tow Prep Group. NA with 5.2-liter V-8.			
Trailer Tow Group IV, Laredo w/option pkg., TSi, Limited	245	208	233
Includes Trailer Tow Prep Group. Requires 5.2-liter V-8.			
Fog lamps, 2WD Laredo	120	102	108
Skid Plate/Tow Hook Group, 4WD	200	170	190
Up Country Suspension Group (4WD only),			
Base Laredo..	825	701	784
Laredo w/option pkg.	575	489	549
TSi..	230	196	—
Limited	390	332	371
Skid Plate Group, tow hooks, high-pressure gas shocks, 245/70R15 outline-white-letter all-terrain tires (Laredo), 225/70R16 Wrangler outline-white-letter all-terrain tires (TSi, Limited), conventional spare tire, matching fifth wheel.			
Security system, Laredo	150	128	143
Power sunroof, TSi, Limited	760	646	722
Includes mini overhead console.			
Leather seats, Laredo	580	493	550
Requires Luxury Group.			
Heated front seats, TSi, Limited	250	213	238
Deep-tinted glass, base Laredo	270	230	257
Flip-up liftgate glass,			
Laredo Pkg. 26X/28X	100	85	95
AM/FM/cassette/CD player, Laredo	560	476	532
NA with Pkg. 26F/28F.			
AM/FM/cassette with Infinity Gold speakers,			
Laredo	660	561	627
AM/FM/cassette/CD with Infinity Gold speakers,			
Laredo Pkg. 26X/28X and base	940	799	893
Laredo Pkg. 26F/28F, TSi, Limited	280	238	266
Full-size spare tire	160	136	152
225/75R15 outline-white-letter tires,			
Base Laredo..	250	213	238
225/75R15 outline-white-letter all-terrain			
tires, Base Laredo	315	268	299
Laredo with option pkg.	65	55	62
NA with Skid Plate/Tow Hook Group.			
Engine block heater	40	34	38

JEEP WRANGLER

Jeep Wrangler Sahara

Specifications

	2-door conv.
Wheelbase, in.	93.4
Overall length, in.	151.8
Overall width, in.	66.7
Overall height, in.	70.2
Curb weight, lbs.	3092
Cargo vol., cu. ft.	55.7
Fuel capacity, gals.	15.0
Seating capacity	4

Engines

	ohv I-4	ohv I-6
Size, liters/cu. in.	2.5/151	4.0/242
Horsepower @ rpm	120 @ 5400	181 @ 4600
Torque (lbs./ft.) @ rpm	140 @ 3500	222 @ 2800
EPA city/highway mpg		
5-speed OD manual	19/20	15/18
3-speed automatic	17/18	15/17

Built in Toledo, Ohio.

PRICES

Jeep Wrangler	Retail Price	Dealer Invoice	Fair Price
SE 2-door convertible	$13470	$12927	—

Prices are accurate at time of publication; subject to manufacturer's change.

JEEP

	Retail Price	Dealer Invoice	Fair Price
Sport 2-door convertible	$17140	$15483	—
Sahara 2-door convertible	19210	17305	—
Destination charge	525	525	525

Fair price not available at time of publication.

Standard Equipment:

SE: 2.5-liter 4-cylinder engine, 5-speed manual transmission, Command-Trac part-time 4WD, driver- and passenger-side air bags, reclining front vinyl bucket seats, dual outside, mirrors, tachometer, voltmeter, trip odometer, oil pressure and coolant temperature gauge, front carpeting, mini floor console w/cupholder, dual horn, fender flares, rear bumper, front and rear stabilizer bars, 205/75R15 all-terrain tires, styled steel wheels. **Sport:** 4.0-liter 6-cylinder engine, power steering, folding rear bench seat, 2-speaker AM/FM radio, clock, rear carpeting, front and rear bumper extensions, cargo net, 215/75R15 all-terrain tires. **Sahara:** heavy-duty suspension, tilt steering wheel, cloth upholstery, Convenience Group, 4-speaker cassette player with rear sound bar and lamp, intermittent wiper, leather-wrapped steering wheel, map pockets, front floormats, fog lamps, Heavy Duty Electrical Group, bodyside steps, upgraded fender flares, extra-capacity fuel tank, front tow hooks, 225/75R15 outline-white-letter tires, alloy wheels, spare-tire cover.

Optional Equipment:

3-speed automatic transmission	625	531	—
Anti-lock brakes,			
Sport, Sahara	599	509	—
Trac-Loc rear differential	285	242	—

   Requires full-size spare tire. SE and Sport require anti-lock brakes. NA with SE when ordered with 3-speed automatic transmission.

Dana 44 rear axle, Sport, Sahara	595	506	—

   Requires full-size spare. NA with anti-lock brakes. Includes Trac-Loc rear differential.

Air conditioning	895	761	—

   SE requires power steering.

Hard top, SE, Sport	755	642	—
Sahara	923	785	—

   Includes full metal doors with roll-up windows, rear wiper/washer, glass sunscreen, cargo light.

Pkg. 22B/23B, SE	895	761	—

   Power steering, folding rear bench seat. 22B requires 3-speed automatic transmission.

	Retail Price	Dealer Invoice	Fair Price
Pkg. 24D/25D, Sport	$540	$459	—
Tilt steering wheel, intermittent wipers, Convenience Group, extra-capacity fuel tank, full-size spare tire. Pkg. 24D requires automatic transmission.			
Convenience Group, SE, Sport	165	140	—
Full storage console w/cupholders, courtesy lights.			
Heavy Duty Electrical Group,			
SE, Sport	135	115	—
with A/C or rear defogger	NC	NC	—
Heavy-duty battery and alternator.			
Heavy-duty suspension, SE, Sport	90	77	—
SE requires optional tires.			
Side steps...	75	64	—
Rear seat, SE	592	503	—
Includes rear carpeting.			
Pueblo cloth reclining front bucket seats			
with rear seat, SE, Sport	110	94	—
Power steering, SE	300	255	—
Tilt steering wheel, SE, Sport	195	166	—
Includes intermittent wipers.			
Leather-wrapped steering wheel,			
SE, Sport	50	43	—
Rear defogger for hardtop	165	140	—
Requires Heavy Duty Electrical Group or air conditioning.			
Full metal doors w/roll-up windows	125	106	—
Sunscreen glass, SE, Sport	170	145	—
Requires hardtop.			
Add-A-Trunk lockable storage	125	106	—
SE requires rear seat.			
AM/FM radio with 2 speakers, SE	270	230	—
AM/FM/cassette, SE	715	608	—
Sport	423	360	—
SE includes Sound Group. Sport includes rear sound bar and lamp.			
Sound Group, SE	535	455	—
AM/FM radio, four speakers w/rear sound bar and lamp.			
Four speakers w/rear sound bar and lamp,			
Sport	245	208	—
Bodyside steps, SE, Sport	73	62	—
Fog lamps, Sport	120	102	—
Requires Heavy Duty Electrical Group or air conditioning.			
Front tow hooks, SE, Sport	40	34	—
19 gal. fuel tank, SE, Sport	65	55	—
Front floormats, SE, Sport	30	26	—

Prices are accurate at time of publication; subject to manufacturer's change.

	Retail Price	Dealer Invoice	Fair Price
Engine block heater	$35	$30	—
Five 215/75R15 outline-white-letter all-terrain			
tires, SE	275	234	—
Sport w/Pkg. 24C/25C	230	196	—
Sport w/Pkg. 24D/25D	120	102	—
SE requires 5-spoke steel wheels.			
Five 225/75R15 outline-white-letter all-terrain			
tires, SE	465	395	—
Sport w/Pkg. 24C/25C	420	357	—
Sport w/Pkg. 24D/25D	310	264	—
SE requires 5-spoke steel or alloy wheels.			
Full-size spare tire, SE, Sport	115	98	—
Sahara	205	174	—
Tire and Wheel Pkg., Sport	785	667	—
Sport w/Pkg. 24D/25D	670	570	—
Sahara	355	302	—
Five alloy wheels, full-size spare, 30×95R15 outline-white-letter tires. Sport includes heavy-duty suspension. NA with optional tires or 5-spoke alloy wheels. Deletes spare-tire cover on Sahara.			
Five 5-spoke steel wheels, SE	230	196	—
Requires optional tires.			
15X7 alloy wheels, Sport	265	225	—
Requires full-size spare or optional tires.			

KIA SPORTAGE

Kia Sportage EX

Specifications

	4-door wagon
Wheelbase, in.	104.4
Overall length, in.	159.4
Overall width, in.	68.2

	4-door wagon
Overall height, in.	65.2
Curb weight, lbs.	3280
Cargo vol., cu. ft.	55.4
Fuel capacity, gals.	15.8
Seating capacity	5

Engines

	dohc I-4
Size, liters/cu. in.	2.0/122
Horsepower @ rpm	130 @ 5500
Torque (lbs./ft.) @ rpm	127 @ 4000

EPA city/highway mpg

5-speed OD manual	19/23
4-speed OD automatic	19/22

Built in South Korea.

PRICES

Kia Sportage	Retail Price	Dealer Invoice	Fair Price
Base 4-door wagon, 2WD	$14495	$13177	—
Base 4-door wagon, 4WD	15995	14410	—
EX 4-door wagon, 2WD	15390	13865	—
EX 4-door wagon, 4WD	16615	14835	—
Destination charge	425	425	425

Fair price not available at time of publication.

Standard Equipment:

2.0-liter DOHC 4-cylinder engine, 5-speed manual transmission, anti-lock rear brakes, driver-side air bag and knee bag, power steering, cloth reclining front bucket seats w/driver-side lumbar adjuster, split folding rear bench seat, cupholders, tinted glass, power windows and door locks, power mirrors, digital clock, tachometer, rear defogger, remote fuel-door release, passenger-side visor mirror, intermittent wipers, full-size spare with cover, rear spare-tire carrier, 205/75R15 tires, alloy wheels. **4WD** adds: part-time 4WD, automatic locking hubs, alloy wheels. **EX** adds: cruise control, rear wiper/washer, bright door handles, color-keyed outside mirrors, roof rack.

Optional Equipment:

4-speed automatic transmission	1000	910	—
Air conditioning	900	763	—

Prices are accurate at time of publication; subject to manufacturer's change.

	Retail Price	Dealer Invoice	Fair Price
AM/FM/cassette	$400	$305	—
AM/FM/CD	545	430	—
Leather upholstery, EX	1000	865	—
Includes leather door-panel inserts, leather-wrapped steering wheel.			
Sport appearance graphics	95	60	—
Rear spoiler	189	143	—
Roof rack, base	185	142	—
Floormats	64	43	—
Alloy wheels, base 2WD	340	274	—

LAND ROVER DISCOVERY

Land Rover Discovery SE7

Specifications

	4-door wagon
Wheelbase, in.	100.0
Overall length, in.	178.7
Overall width, in.	70.6
Overall height, in.	77.4
Curb weight, lbs.	4465
Cargo vol., cu. ft.	69.8
Fuel capacity, gals.	23.4
Seating capacity	7

Engines

	ohv V-8
Size, liters/cu. in.	4.0/241

	ohv V-8
Horsepower @ rpm	182 @ 4750
Torque (lbs./ft.) @ rpm	233 @ 3000

EPA city/highway mpg

5-speed OD manual	13/17
4-speed OD automatic	14/17

Built in England.

PRICES

Land Rover Discovery	Retail Price	Dealer Invoice	Fair Price
SD 4-door wagon, 5-speed	$32000	$28480	—
SD 4-door wagon, automatic	32000	28480	—
SD 4-door wagon w/leather interior, automatic	34000	30260	—
SE 4-door wagon, automatic	36000	32040	—
SE7 4-door wagon, 5-speed	38500	34265	—
SE7 4-door wagon, automatic	38500	34265	—
Destination charge	625	625	625

Fair price not available at time of publication.

Standard Equipment:

SD: 4.0-liter V-8 engine, 5-speed manual or 4-speed automatic transmission, permanent 4-wheel drive, anti-lock 4-wheel disc brakes, driver- and passenger-side air bags, dual-zone climate control, power steering, cruise control, cloth upholstery, front bucket seats w/adjustable lumbar support, 60/40 split folding rear seat, front storage console, cupholders, leather-wrapped tilt steering wheel, power windows and door locks, heated power mirrors, tachometer, coolant-temperature gauge, AM/FM/cassette/CD player with amplifier, power diversity antenna, rear defogger, remote keyless entry, illuminated visor mirrors, automatic day/night inside mirror, variable intermittent wipers, rear wiper/washer, headlamp washers, theft-deterrent system, burled-walnut interior trim, cargo cover, Class III towing hitch receiver, rear-mounted full-size spare tire, 235/70HR16 mud and snow tires, Freestyle alloy wheels. **SD w/leather interior** adds: leather upholstery, heated power front seats. **SE** adds: 4-speed automatic transmission, dual power sunroofs, Homelink universal garage-door opener, additional wood interior trim, front fog lights, dished alloy wheels. **SE7** adds: 5-speed manual or 4-speed automatic transmission, rear air conditioning, rear jump seats, hydraulic rear step.

Optional Equipment:

	Retail Price	Dealer Invoice	Fair Price
Rear jump seats,			
SD w/cloth upholstery	$875	$735	—
SD w/leather upholstery, SE	975	825	—
6-disc			
CD changer	625	525	—
Beluga			
black paint	300	250	—

LEXUS GS 300

Lexus GS 300

Specifications

	4-door notchback
Wheelbase, in.	109.4
Overall length, in.	194.9
Overall width, in.	70.7
Overall height, in.	55.9
Curb weight, lbs.	3660
Cargo vol., cu. ft.	13.0
Fuel capacity, gals.	21.1
Seating capacity	5

Engines

	dohc I-6
Size, liters/cu. in.	3.0/183
Horsepower @ rpm	220 @ 5800
Torque (lbs./ft.) @ rpm	210 @ 4800

EPA city/highway mpg

5-speed OD automatic	18/24

Built in Japan.

PRICES

Lexus GS 300	Retail Price	Dealer Invoice	Fair Price
4-door notchback	$45700	$39233	$40733
Destination charge	495	495	495

Standard Equipment:

3.0-liter DOHC 6-cylinder engine, 5-speed automatic transmission, anti-lock 4-wheel disc brakes, automatic climate control, driver- and passenger-side air bags, variable-assist power steering, cruise control, cloth upholstery, power front bucket seats with power lumbar support, front storage console, rear folding armrest, cupholder, power tilt/telescopic steering column, power windows and door locks, power heated outside mirrors, Lexus/Pioneer Audio System with AM/FM/cassette and seven speakers, power antenna, diversity antenna, digital clock, two trip odometers, outside-temperature indicator, walnut wood trim, remote keyless entry, color-keyed tinted glass, rear defogger, variable intermittent wipers, theft-deterrent system, illuminated visor mirrors, remote fuel-door and trunk releases, front and rear reading lights, automatic headlamps, fog lamps, tool kit, first-aid kit, dual exhaust, 215/60VR16 tires, alloy wheels.

Optional Equipment:

Traction Control System	1870	1496	1777
Includes heated front seats. Requires Leather Trim Pkg. and all-season tires.			
Leather Trim Pkg.	1400	1120	1330
Leather upholstery, leather-wrapped steering wheel and shifter.			
Lexus/Nakamichi Premium Audio System	1200	900	1140
Requires Leather Trim Pkg. and 12-disc CD changer .			
12-disc CD changer	1050	840	998
Power moonroof	1000	800	950
215/60VR16 all-season tires	NC	NC	NC
Chrome wheels	1700	850	1615

LEXUS LS 400

Specifications	4-door notchback
Wheelbase, in.	112.2
Overall length, in.	196.7
Overall width, in.	72.0
Overall height, in.	56.5

Prices are accurate at time of publication; subject to manufacturer's change.

LEXUS

Lexus LS 400

	4-door notchback
Curb weight, lbs.	3726
Cargo vol., cu. ft.	13.9
Fuel capacity, gals.	22.5
Seating capacity	5

Engines

	dohc V-8
Size, liters/cu. in.	4.0/242
Horsepower @ rpm	260 @ 5300
Torque (lbs./ft.) @ rpm	270 @ 4500

EPA city/highway mpg

4-speed OD automatic	19/25

Built in Japan.

PRICES

Lexus LS 400	Retail Price	Dealer Invoice	Fair Price
4-door notchback	$52900	$44880	—
Destination charge	495	495	495

Fair price not available at time of publication.

Standard Equipment:

4.0-liter DOHC V-8 engine, 4-speed automatic transmission, anti-lock 4-wheel disc brakes, driver- and passenger-side front and side air bags, variable-assist power steering, automatic dual-zone climate control, cruise control, leather upholstery, power front bucket seats with power lumbar support, rear folding armrest, front storage console with auxiliary power outlet, cupholders, leather-wrapped steering wheel and shifter, power windows and door locks, heated power mirrors, automatic day/night inside and outside mirrors, power tilt/telescopic steering wheel, Lexus/Pioneer AM/FM/cassette with seven speakers, power antenna, diversity antenna, digital clock, tachometer, two trip odometers, coolant-temperature gauge, outside-temperature indicator, interior air filter, color-keyed tinted glass, rear defogger, remote fuel-door and decklid releases, illuminated visor mirrors, remote keyless entry, front and rear reading lights, walnut interior trim, theft-deterrent system, speed-sensitive variable intermittent wipers, automatic headlamps, fog lights, dual exhaust outlets, tool kit, first-aid kit, full-size spare tire, 225/60VR16 tires, alloy wheels.

Optional Equipment:

	Retail Price	Dealer Invoice	Fair Price
Power moonroof	$1100	$880	—
Traction control	2020	1616	—
Includes heated front seats. Requires memory system and all-season tires.			
Electronic air suspension	1850	1480	—
Requires power moonroof, memory system, Lexus/Nakamichi Premium Audio System, and traction control.			
Memory system	800	640	—
Memory driver seat, outside mirrors, and steering wheel.			
Lexus/Nakamichi Premium Audio System	1200	900	—
Requires 6-CD auto changer.			
6-disc CD changer	1050	840	—
Chrome wheels	1700	850	—

LEXUS SC 300/400

Lexus SC 300

Specifications

	2-door notchback
Wheelbase, in.	105.9

Prices are accurate at time of publication; subject to manufacturer's change.

LEXUS

	2-door notchback
Overall length, in.	192.5
Overall width, in.	70.9
Overall height, in.	53.1
Curb weight, lbs.	3516
Cargo vol., cu. ft.	9.3
Fuel capacity, gals.	20.6
Seating capacity	4

Engines

	dohc I-6	dohc V-8
Size, liters/cu. in.	3.0/183	4.0/242
Horsepower @ rpm	225 @ 6000	260 @ 5300
Torque (lbs./ft.) @ rpm	210 @ 4800	270 @ 4500
EPA city/highway mpg		
5-speed OD manual	19/24	
4-speed OD automatic	18/24	18/23

Built in Japan.

PRICES

Lexus SC 300/400	Retail Price	Dealer Invoice	Fair Price
300 2-door notchback, 5-speed	$39000	$33875	—
300 2-door notchback, automatic	39900	34657	—
400 2-door notchback, automatic	50800	43612	—
Destination charge	495	495	495

Fair price not available at time of publication.

Standard Equipment:

300: 3.0-liter 6-cylinder engine, 5-speed manual or 4-speed automatic transmission, anti-lock 4-wheel disc brakes, variable-assist power steering, driver- and passenger-side air bags, automatic climate control, cloth upholstery, power front bucket seats, cruise control, tilt/telescoping steering column, power windows and door locks, heated power mirrors, tachometer, trip computer w/outside-temperature indicator, solar-control tinted glass, Pioneer Audio System with AM/FM/cassette and seven speakers, power and diversity antennas, rear defogger, illuminated visor mirrors, remote fuel-door and deck-lid releases, variable intermittent wipers, automatic day/night inside mirror, remote keyless entry, theft-deterrent system, maple wood interior trim, cellular phone pre-wiring, automatic on/off headlamps, fog lamps, tool kit, first aid kit, 225/55VR16 performance tires, alloy wheels. **400** adds: 4.0-liter V-8 engine, 4-speed automatic transmission, leather upholstery and trim, memory driver seat, power tilt/telescoping steering column w/memory, automatic day/night outside mirrors w/memory.

Optional Equipment:	Retail Price	Dealer Invoice	Fair Price
Traction control system w/heated front seats	$1870	$1496	—
Requires automatic transmission, 225/55VR16 all-season tires. 300 also requires Leather Trim Pkg.			
Leather Trim Pkg., 300	2050	1640	—
Leather upholstery and trim, automatic day/night outside mirrors w/memory, power tilt/telescoping steering column w/memory, memory driver seat.			
Heated front seats, 300 with manual transmission	420	336	—
Requires Leather Trim Pkg.			
Power glass moonroof	1000	800	—
Remote 12-disc CD changer	1050	840	—
Lexus/Nakamichi Premium Sound System	1200	900	—
Requires remote 12-disc CD changer. 300 also requires Leather Trim Pkg.			
Rear spoiler	420	336	—
225/55VR16 all-season tires	NC	NC	NC
Chrome wheels	1700	850	—

LINCOLN CONTINENTAL

Lincoln Continental

Specifications

	4-door notchback
Wheelbase, in.	109.0
Overall length, in.	206.3

Prices are accurate at time of publication; subject to manufacturer's change.

LINCOLN

	4-door notchback
Overall width, in.	73.3
Overall height, in.	56.0
Curb weight, lbs.	3911
Cargo vol., cu. ft.	18.1
Fuel capacity, gals.	18.0
Seating capacity	6

Engines

	dohc V-8
Size, liters/cu. in.	4.6/281
Horsepower @ rpm	260 @ 5750
Torque (lbs./ft.) @ rpm	265 @ 4750

EPA city/highway mpg

4-speed OD automatic	17/25

Built in Wixom, Mich.

PRICES

Lincoln Continental	Retail Price	Dealer Invoice	Fair Price
4-door notchback	$37280	$33999	$34999
Destination charge	670	670	670

Standard Equipment:

4.6-liter DOHC V-8 engine, 4-speed automatic transmission, anti-lock 4-wheel disc brakes, driver- and passenger-side air bags, programmable variable-assist power steering, traction control, adjustable suspension system, automatic load leveling, cruise control, automatic climate control, leather upholstery, reclining front bucket seats with power lumbar adjusters, 6-way power front seats, center console, power windows, heated power mirrors, automatic power door locks, 2-driver memory system, rear defogger, automatic day/night rearview mirror w/compass, variable intermittent wipers, solar-control tinted glass, tachometer, coolant temperature gauge, AM/FM/cassette, digital clock, anti-theft alarm system, remote keyless entry, remote fuel-door and decklid releases, overhead console, systems message center, interior air-filtration system, burl walnut interior trim, leather-wrapped tilt steering wheel, reading lights, automatic day/night rearview mirror, illuminated visor mirrors, automatic headlights, floormats, cargo net, 225/60R16 tires, alloy wheels.

Optional Equipment:

Programmable garage-door opener	120	104	108

	Retail Price	Dealer Invoice	Fair Price
Personal Security Pkg.	$750	$646	$675
Securitire with pressure alert, programmable garage-door opener. NA with chrome wheels.			
RESCU Pkg.	2245	1930	2021
ordered w/Personal Security Pkg.	2125	1828	1913
Global-positioning satellite, JBL Audio System, programmable garage-door opener, and voice-activated cellular telephone.			
Power moonroof	1515	1302	1364
Requires programmable garage-door opener.			
Heated seats	290	250	261
Voice-activated cellular telephone	690	594	621
Requires JBL Audio System.			
Automatic day/night outside mirrors	110	94	99
JBL Audio System	565	486	509
Digital signal processing, subwoofer amplifier, additional speakers.			
CD changer	595	512	536
Requires JBL Audio System.			
Tri-coat paint	300	258	270
Double-window chrome wheels	845	726	761
NA with Personal Security Pkg.			
5-spoke chrome wheels	845	726	761
Includes 225/60VR16 tires. NA with Personal Security Pkg.			
Engine block heater	60	52	54

LINCOLN MARK VIII

Lincoln Mark VIII

Specifications

	2-door notchback
Wheelbase, in.	113.0

Prices are accurate at time of publication; subject to manufacturer's change.

LINCOLN

	2-door notchback
Overall length, in.	207.3
Overall width, in.	74.8
Overall height, in.	53.6
Curb weight, lbs.	3768
Cargo vol., cu. ft.	14.4
Fuel capacity, gals.	18.0
Seating capacity	5

Engines

	dohc V-8	dohc V-8
Size, liters/cu. in.	4.6/281	4.6/281
Horsepower @ rpm	280 @ 5500	290 @ 5500
Torque (lbs./ft.) @ rpm	285 @ 4500	295 @ 4500

EPA city/highway mpg
4-speed OD automatic	18/26	18/26

Built in Wixom, Mich.

PRICES

Lincoln Mark VIII	Retail Price	Dealer Invoice	Fair Price
2-door notchback	$37280	$33994	$34794
LSC 2-door notchback	38880	35418	36218
Destination charge	670	670	670

Standard Equipment:

4.6-liter DOHC V-8 engine (280 horsepower), 4-speed automatic transmission (3.07 final drive ratio), anti-lock 4-wheel disc brakes, driver- and passenger-side air bags, automatic climate control, variable-assist power steering, leather upholstery, reclining 6-way power front seats with power lumbar supports and driver-side memory, rear armrest, console with cupholder and storage bin, tilt/telescopic steering wheel, analog instrumentation with message center and programmable trip functions, tachometer, service interval reminder, leather-wrapped steering wheel, solar-control tinted glass, anti-theft system, cruise control, power windows and locks, heated power mirrors with remote 3-position memory, automatic day/night inside/outside mirrors, illuminated visor mirrors, rear defogger, remote decklid and fuel-door releases, remote keyless entry, JBL audio system with AM/FM/CD player, integrated antenna, intermittent wipers, automatic headlamps, dual exhaust, bright grille, bright exterior trim, 225/60VR16 tires, lacy-spoke alloy wheels. **LSC** adds: 4.6-liter DOHC V-8 engine (290 horsepower), 4-speed automatic transmission (3.27 final drive ratio), upgraded suspension, perforated-leather upholstery, color-keyed grille, color-keyed exterior trim, chrome directional wheels with locking lug nuts.

Optional Equipment:

	Retail Price	Dealer Invoice	Fair Price
Traction control	NC	NC	NC
Heated seats	$290	$250	$261
Child restraint tether	NC	NC	NC
Power moonroof	1515	1302	1364
Portable voice-activated cellular telephone	790	680	711
Premium cassette player	NC	NC	NC
Replaces standard CD player.			
CD changer	670	576	603
Tri-coat paint	300	258	270
Cast-alloy wheels, base	NC	NC	NC
Chrome octastar wheels, base	845	726	761
LSC	NC	NC	NC
Floormats	NC	NC	NC
Engine block heater	60	52	54

LINCOLN TOWN CAR

Lincoln Town Car

Specifications

	4-door notchback
Wheelbase, in.	117.4
Overall length, in.	218.9
Overall width, in.	76.7
Overall height, in.	56.9
Curb weight, lbs.	4040
Cargo vol., cu. ft.	22.3
Fuel capacity, gals.	20.0
Seating capacity	6

Prices are accurate at time of publication; subject to manufacturer's change.

LINCOLN

Engines

	ohc V-8
Size, liters/cu. in.	4.6/281
Horsepower @ rpm	190 @ 4250
Torque (lbs./ft.) @ rpm	265 @ 3250

EPA city/highway mpg

4-speed OD automatic	17/25

Built in Wixom, Mich.

PRICES

Lincoln Town Car	Retail Price	Dealer Invoice	Fair Price
Executive 4-door notchback	$37280	$32890	$33690
Signature Series 4-door notchback	39640	34920	35720
Cartier Designer Series 4-door notchback	43200	37982	38782
Destination charge	670	670	670

Standard Equipment:

Executive: 4.6-liter V-8, 4-speed automatic transmission, anti-lock 4-wheel disc brakes, variable-assist power steering, driver- and passenger-side air bags, automatic climate control, 6-way power twin-comfort lounge seats with 2-way front headrests, front and rear armrests, power windows and door locks, tilt steering wheel, leather-wrapped steering wheel, cruise control, heated power mirrors, rear defogger, AM/FM/cassette, diversity antenna, coolant-temperature gauge, solar-control tinted glass, remote fuel-door and decklid releases, power decklid pulldown, remote keyless entry, auxiliary power outlet, automatic headlights, anti-theft alarm system, cornering lamps, intermittent wipers, digital clock, illuminated visor mirrors, floormats, trunk net, 215/70R15 whitewall tires, alloy wheels. **Signature Series** adds: dual shade paint, memory driver-seat, power lumbar support, power front recliners, memory mirrors, dual footwell lights, front-seat storage with cupholders, premium sound system, steering-wheel radio and climate controls, programmable garage-door opener, striping. **Cartier Designer Series** adds: traction assist, leather upholstery, heated front seat, 4-way front-seat headrests, Ford JBL Audio System, compass, automatic day/night mirror, rear-seat vanity mirrors, upgraded door trim panels, dual exhaust, 225/60R16 whitewall tires.

Optional Equipment:

Traction Assist, Executive, Signature	215	184	194
Leather upholstery, Executive, Signature	770	662	693

	Retail Price	Dealer Invoice	Fair Price
Heated front seats, Signature	$290	$250	$261
Requires leather upholstery.			
Automatic day/night mirror	330	284	297
Power moonroof	1515	1302	1364
NA Executive. Deletes rear-seat vanity mirrors on Cartier.			
Ford JBL Audio System, Signature	565	486	509
Trunk-mounted CD changer	815	700	734
Requires Ford JBL Audio System. NA on Executive.			
Touring Pkg., Signature	1825	1570	1643
Power moonroof, traction assist, Ride Control Pkg., JBL Audio System, automatic day/night mirror.			
Ride Control Pkg., Signature	300	258	270
Cartier	100	89	90
Auxiliary power steering fluid cooler, 3.27 rear axle ratio, 225/60R16 whitewall tires (Signature), 16-inch alloy wheels (Signature). NA with Livery/Heavy Duty Trailer Towing Pkg.			
Special Value Pkg., Signature	610	524	549
Traction Control System, Ford JBL Audio System, automatic day/night mirror.			
Trailer Wiring Pkg.	80	68	72
Voice-activated cellular telephone	690	594	621
NA on Executive.			
Tri-coat paint, Signature	300	258	270
Cartier	NC	NC	NC
Monotone paint, Signature	NC	NC	NC
Striping delete	NC	NC	NC
Engine block heater	60	52	54
Y-spoke alloy wheels, Signature	NC	NC	NC
Chrome wheels, Cartier,			
Signature w/Ride Control Pkg.	845	726	761
Signature	1045	896	941
Signature includes 225/60R16 whitewall tires			
Full-size spare tire	220	190	198
w/chrome wheels, Signature, Cartier	430	370	387

MAZDA MIATA

Specifications

	2-door conv.
Wheelbase, in.	89.2
Overall length, in.	155.4
Overall width, in.	65.9

Prices are accurate at time of publication; subject to manufacturer's change.

MAZDA

Mazda Miata

	2-door conv.
Overall height, in.	48.2
Curb weight, lbs.	2293
Cargo vol., cu. ft.	3.6
Fuel capacity, gals.	12.7
Seating capacity	2

Engines

	dohc I-4
Size, liters/cu. in.	1.8/112
Horsepower @ rpm	133 @ 6500
Torque (lbs./ft.) @ rpm	114 @ 5500
EPA city/highway mpg	
5-speed OD manual	23/29
4-speed OD automatic	22/28

Built in Japan.

PRICES

Mazda Miata	Retail Price	Dealer Invoice	Fair Price
2-door convertible	$19125	$17248	—
Destination charge	450	450	450

Fair price not available at time of publication. Prices are for vehicles distributed by Mazda Motor of America, Inc. Prices may be higher in areas served by independent distributors.

Standard Equipment:

1.8-liter DOHC 4-cylinder engine, 5-speed manual transmission, 4-wheel disc brakes, driver- and passenger-side air bags, cloth reclining bucket seats, front storage console w/cupholder, tachometer, coolant-temperature gauge, trip odometer, AM/FM/cassette, digital clock, dual outside mirrors, remote fuel-door and decklid releases, intermittent wipers, cargo light, 185/60HR14 tires, bright center caps.

Optional Equipment:

	Retail Price	Dealer Invoice	Fair Price
4-speed automatic transmission	$850	$739	—
Requires Popular Equipment Pkg. or Leather Pkg.			
Anti-lock brakes	900	765	—
Requires Popular Equipment Pkg. or Leather Pkg.			
Air conditioning, base	900	720	—
Power Steering Pkg.	300	252	—
Variable-assist power steering, wheel trim rings.			
Touring Pkg.	1100	924	—
Power steering, power windows and mirrors, leather-wrapped steering wheel, door map pockets, alloy wheels.			
Popular Equipment Pkg.,			
ordered w/5-speed	2090	1756	—
ordered w/automatic	1700	1428	—
Touring Pkg. plus limited-slip differential (5-speed), cruise control, headrest speakers, power antenna.			
Leather Pkg., ordered w/5-speed	2985	2507	—
ordered w/automatic	2595	2108	—
Popular Equipment Pkg. plus tan interior with leather seating surfaces, tan vinyl top.			
R Pkg., ordered w/5-speed	1500	1260	—
Limited-slip differential, sport suspension, front and rear spoilers, alloy wheels. NA with Popular Equipment Pkg., Power Steering Pkg., or Leather Pkg.			
Detachable hardtop	1500	1215	—
Includes rear defogger. Base requires Popular Equipment Pkg. or Leather Pkg.			
Premium sound system w/AM/FM/cassette/			
CD player	675	540	—
Requires Popular Equipment or Leather Pkg.			
Floormats	80	56	—

MAZDA MILLENIA

Specifications

	4-door notchback
Wheelbase, in...	108.3
Overall length, in.	189.8
Overall width, in.	69.7

Prices are accurate at time of publication; subject to manufacturer's change.

MAZDA

Mazda Millenia S

	4-door notchback
Overall height, in.	54.9
Curb weight, lbs.	3220
Cargo vol., cu. ft.	13.3
Fuel capacity, gals.	18.0
Seating capacity	5

Engines

	dohc V-6	Supercharged dohc V-6
Size, liters/cu. in.	2.5/152	2.3/138
Horsepower @ rpm	170 @ 5800	210 @ 4800
Torque (lbs./ft.) @ rpm	160 @ 4800	210 @ 3500

EPA city/highway mpg

	dohc V-6	Supercharged dohc V-6
4-speed OD automatic	20/27	20/28

Built in Japan.

PRICES

Mazda Millenia	Retail Price	Dealer Invoice	Fair Price
4-door notchback	$28995	$25562	—
L 4-door notchback	32995	28751	—
S 4-door notchback	36595	31514	—
Destination charge	450	450	450

Fair price not available at time of publication. Prices are for vehicles distributed by Mazda Motor America, Inc. Prices may be higher in areas served by independent distributors.

Standard Equipment:

Base: 2.5-liter DOHC V-6 engine, 4-speed automatic transmission, anti-lock 4-wheel disc brakes, driver- and passenger-side air bags, automatic climate control, variable-assist power steering, cruise control, cloth reclining front bucket seats, 8-way power driver seat, front storage console w/cupholder, folding rear armrest, leather-wrapped power tilt steering wheel, tachometer, trip odometer, outside-temperature indicator, power windows and door locks, heated power mirrors, variable intermittent wipers, theft-deterrent system, tinted glass, AM/FM/cassette/CD player, integrated diversity antenna, digital clock, illuminated visor mirrors, rear defogger, auxiliary power outlet, remote fuel-door and decklid releases, fog lamps, floormats, rear heat ducts, dual exhaust outlets, 205/65HR15 tires, alloy wheels w/locks. **L** adds: leather upholstery, 8-way power front passenger seat, remote keyless entry, power moonroof. **S** adds: 2.3-liter DOHC supercharged V-6 engine, traction control, heavy-duty starter, Bose audio system, 215/55VR16 tires.

Optional Equipment:	Retail Price	Dealer Invoice	Fair Price
4-Seasons Package, base, L	$600	$504	—
S	300	252	—
Traction control (base, L), heated front seats, heavy-duty wipers, heavy-duty battery, extra-capacity windshield-washer tank.			
Bose audio system, L	700	560	—
White pearl metallic paint, L, S	350	294	—

MAZDA MPV

Mazda MPV All-Sport

Specifications	4-door van	4WD 4-door van
Wheelbase, in.	110.4	110.4

Prices are accurate at time of publication; subject to manufacturer's change.

MAZDA

	4-door van	4WD 4-door van
Overall length, in.	183.5	183.5
Overall width, in.	71.9	71.9
Overall height, in.	68.9	71.5
Curb weight, lbs.	3790	4045
Cargo vol., cu. ft.	42.1	42.1
Fuel capacity, gals.	19.6	19.8
Seating capacity	8	8

Engines

	ohc V-6
Size, liters/cu. in.	3.0/180
Horsepower @ rpm	155 @ 5000
Torque (lbs./ft.) @ rpm	169 @ 4000

EPA city/highway mpg

4-speed OD automatic	16/21

Built in Japan.

PRICES

Mazda MPV	Retail Price	Dealer Invoice	Fair Price
LX 2WD 4-door van	$23095	$20834	$21334
ES 2WD 4-door van	26395	23807	24307
LX 4WD 4-door van	26895	24258	24758
ES 4WD 4-door van	28895	26060	26560
Destination charge	480	480	480

Prices are for vehicles distributed by Mazda Motor of America, Inc. Prices may be higher in areas served by independent distributors.

Standard Equipment:

LX 2WD: 3.0-liter V-6 engine, 4-speed automatic transmission, anti-lock 4-wheel disc brakes, driver- and passenger-side air bags, variable-assist power steering, cruise control, velour upholstery, 8-passenger seating (reclining front bucket seats, 3-passenger reclining and folding middle bench seat, 3-passenger rear bench seat), tilt steering wheel, power mirrors, power windows and door locks, tachometer, AM/FM/cassette, digital clock, tinted glass, variable intermittent wipers, intermittent rear wiper/washer, rear defogger, remote fuel-door release, rear heat ducts, wheel covers, 195/75R15 tires. **LX 4WD** adds: part-time 4-wheel drive, 4-Seasons Pkg. (rear heater, large-capacity washer tank, heavy-duty battery), high-capacity cooling fan, All-Sport Pkg. (grille guard, stone guard, eyebrow fender flares, rear bumper guard, roof rack, All-Sport graphics, alloy wheels, 225/70R15 mud and snow tires), special 2-tone paint, full-size spare tire. **ES 2WD** deletes middle bench seat and adds to LX 2WD: leather upholstery, 7-passenger seating (quad captain's chairs, 3-passenger rear bench seat), leather-wrapped steering wheel, Load Leveling Pkg. (automatic load leveling, transmission-oil cooler, high-capacity cooling fan, full-size spare), All-Sport Pkg. (includes 215/65R15 tires), special 2-tone paint. **ES 4WD** adds: part-time 4-wheel drive, 4-Seasons Pkg., All-Sport Pkg. (includes 225/70R15 mud and snow tires).

Optional Equipment:	Retail Price	Dealer Invoice	Fair Price
LX Preferred Equipment Group 1, LX	$795	$676	$731
Front air conditioning, remote keyless entry, rear privacy glass, floormats.			
LX Preferred Equipment Group 2, LX	1495	1271	1375
Front and rear air conditioning, remote keyless entry, rear privacy glass, floormats.			
ES Preferred Equipment Group 1, ES	1395	1186	1283
Front and rear air conditioning, remote keyless entry, rear privacy glass, floormats.			
Load leveling Pkg., LX 2WD	595	506	547
LX 4WD	495	421	455
Automatic load leveling, transmission-oil cooler, high-capacity cooling fan (2WD), full-size spare (2WD).			
All-Sport Pkg., LX 2WD	880	748	810
Grille guard, stone guard, eyebrow fender flares, rear bumper guard, roof rack, All-Sport graphics, alloy wheels, 215/65R15 tires (2WD).			
4-Seasons Pkg., 2WD	350	298	322
Rear heater, large-capacity washer tank, heavy-duty battery.			
Quad captain's chairs, LX	400	340	368
Power moonroof, ES	1200	1020	1104
CD Player, LX, EX	350	298	322
Alloy Wheel Pkg., LX 2WD	495	421	455
215/65R15 tires, alloy wheels.			
Special 2-tone paint, LX 2WD	350	298	322

MAZDA PROTEGE

Specifications	4-door notchback
Wheelbase, in.	102.6
Overall length, in.	174.8

Prices are accurate at time of publication; subject to manufacturer's change.

Mazda Protege LX

	4-door notchback
Overall width, in.	67.3
Overall height, in.	55.9
Curb weight, lbs.	2385
Cargo vol., cu. ft.	13.1
Fuel capacity, gals.	14.5
Seating capacity	5

Engines

	dohc I-4	dohc I-4
Size, liters/cu. in.	1.5/191	1.8/110
Horsepower @ rpm	92 @ 5500	122 @ 6000
Torque (lbs./ft.) @ rpm	96 @ 4000	117 @ 4000

EPA city/highway mpg

5-speed OD manual	30/37	26/32
4-speed OD automatic	25/33	23/30

Built in Japan.

PRICES

Mazda Protege	Retail Price	Dealer Invoice	Fair Price
DX 4-door notchback	$12145	$11455	$11955
LX 4-door notchback	13545	12498	12998
ES 4-door notchback	15295	13956	14456
Destination charge	450	450	450

Prices are for vehicles distributed by Mazda Motor of America, Inc. Prices may be higher in areas served by independent distributors.

Standard Equipment:

DX: 1.5-liter DOHC 4-cylinder engine, 5-speed manual transmission, driver- and passenger-side air bags, variable-assist power steering, cloth/vinyl reclining front bucket seats, cupholders, tilt steering wheel, storage console, remote outside mirrors, green tinted glass, rear defogger, remote fuel-door release, coolant-temperature gauge, trip odometer, intermittent wipers, auxiliary power outlet, 175/70R13 tires. **LX** adds: cruise control, AM/FM/cassette, velour upholstery, split folding rear seat, remote decklid release, tachometer, digital clock, power windows and door locks, power mirrors, map lights, passenger-side vanity mirror, front side storage trays, 185/65R14 tires, full wheel covers. **ES** adds: 1.8-liter DOHC 4-cylinder engine, 4-wheel disc brakes, air conditioning, sport front bucket seats with thigh-support and height adjustment, rear stabilizer bar.

Optional Equipment:	Retail Price	Dealer Invoice	Fair Price
4-speed automatic transmission	$800	$720	$760
Anti-lock brakes, LX, ES	800	680	760
Convenience Pkg., DX	1575	1292	1496
Air conditioning, AM/FM/cassette, floormats.			
Luxury Pkg., LX	1145	939	1088
Air conditioning, raised console armrest (automatic transmission-equipped models), floormats.			
Premium Pkg., ES	1195	956	1135
Alloy wheels with locks, power sunroof.			
Touring Pkg., ES	105	84	100
Floormats, raised console armrest. Requires automatic transmission.			
Power sunroof, LX	700	560	665
Remote keyless entry, LX, ES	200	160	190
Includes theft-deterrent system.			
Floormats	80	64	76

MAZDA 626

Specifications

	4-door notchback
Wheelbase, in.	102.8
Overall length, in.	184.4
Overall width, in.	68.9
Overall height, in.	55.1
Curb weight, lbs.	2749
Cargo vol., cu. ft.	13.8
Fuel capacity, gals.	15.9
Seating capacity	5

Prices are accurate at time of publication; subject to manufacturer's change.

Mazda 626 ES

Engines

	dohc I-4	dohc V-6
Size, liters/cu. in.	2.0/122	2.5/153
Horsepower @ rpm	114 @ 5500	164 @ 5500
Torque (lbs./ft.) @ rpm	124 @ 4500	160 @ 4800
EPA city/highway mpg		
5-speed OD manual	26/34	21/26
4-speed OD automatic	23/31	20/26

Built in Flat Rock, Mich.

PRICES

Mazda 626	Retail Price	Dealer Invoice	Fair Price
DX 4-door notchback	$15695	$14481	$15081
LX 4-cylinder 4-door notchback	17895	16172	16772
LX V-6 4-door notchback	19995	18064	18664
ES V-6 4-door notchback	22995	20546	21146
Destination charge	450	450	450

Prices are for vehicles distributed by Mazda Motor of America, Inc. Prices may be higher in areas served by independent distributors.

Standard Equipment:

DX: 2.0-liter DOHC 4-cylinder engine, 5-speed manual transmission, variable-assist power steering, driver- and passenger-side air bags, velour upholstery, reclining front bucket seats w/adjustable thigh support, 60/40 folding rear seat w/folding armrest, storage console with armrest, cupholders, tachometer, coolant-temperature gauge, trip odometer, tilt steering wheel, intermittent wipers, remote outside mirrors, green tinted glass, remote fuel-door and decklid releases, rear defogger, passenger-side visor mirror, rear heat ducts, front mud guards, 195/65R14 tires, full wheel covers. **LX** adds: air conditioning, upgraded velour upholstery, power windows and door locks, cruise control, power mirrors, AM/FM/cassette, digital clock, dual visor mirrors w/illuminated passenger-side mirror. **LX V-6** adds: 2.5-liter DOHC V-6 engine, 4-wheel disc brakes, variable intermittent wipers, rear stabilizer bar, floormats, dual bright exhaust outlets, 205/55HR15 tires, alloy wheels. **ES** adds: anti-lock brakes, leather upholstery, 8-way power driver seat, leather-wrapped steering wheel and shifter, 6-speaker sound system, power antenna, theft-deterrent system, remote keyless entry, power moonroof, illuminated visor mirrors, heated power mirrors, map lights, fog lamps.

Optional Equipment:	Retail Price	Dealer Invoice	Fair Price
4-speed automatic transmission	$800	$696	$760
Deletes leather-wrapped shifter on ES.			
Anti-lock brakes, LX 4-cylinder	950	808	903
LX V-6	800	680	760
LX 4-cylinder includes 4-wheel disc brakes.			
Convenience Pkg., DX	1215	972	1154
Air conditioning, AM/FM/cassette, floormats.			
Luxury Pkg., LX 4-cylinder	1750	1400	1663
Power moonroof, heated power mirrors, theft-deterrent system, 6-speaker sound system, power antenna, remote keyless entry, floormats, alloy wheels.			
LX Appearance Pkg., LX 4-cylinder	1895	1630	1800
Leather upholstery, power moonroof, remote keyless entry, theft deterrent system, floormats, 2-tone paint, chrome wheel covers. Requires automatic transmission.			
Premium Pkg., LX V-6	2095	1676	1990
Anti-lock brakes, power driver seat, power moonroof, heated power mirrors, theft-deterrent system, 6-speaker sound system, power antenna, remote keyless entry.			
Floormats, DX, LX 4-cylinder	80	56	76

MERCEDES-BENZ C-CLASS

Specifications	4-door notchback
Wheelbase, in.	105.9
Overall length, in.	177.4
Overall width, in.	67.7
Overall height, in.	56.1
Curb weight, lbs.	3195

Prices are accurate at time of publication; subject to manufacturer's change.

MERCEDES-BENZ

Mercedes-Benz C280

	4-door notchback
Cargo vol., cu. ft.	11.6
Fuel capacity, gals.	16.4
Seating capacity	5

Engines

	dohc I-4	dohc I-6	dohc I-6
Size, liters/cu. in.	2.3/140	2.8/171	3.6/220
Horsepower @ rpm	148 @ 5500	194 @ 5500	276 @ 5750
Torque (lbs./ft.) @ rpm	162 @ 4000	199 @ 3750	284 @ 4000
EPA city/highway mpg			
5-speed OD automatic	23/30	20/27	18/24

Built in Germany.

PRICES

Mercedes-Benz C-Class	Retail Price	Dealer Invoice	Fair Price
C230 4-door notchback	$30450	$26490	—
C280 4-door notchback	35400	30800	—
C36 4-door notchback	51925	45170	—
Destination charge	595	595	595

Fair price not available at time of publication.

Standard Equipment:

C230: 2.3-liter DOHC 4-cylinder engine, 5-speed automatic transmission, anti-lock 4-wheel disc brakes, driver- and passenger-side air bags, power steering, automatic climate control, cruise control, cloth 10-way power driver seat, 10-way manual adjustable passenger seat, center storage console, folding rear armrest, cupholders, power windows and door locks, heated power mirrors, leather-wrapped steering wheel and shifter, remote AM/FM/cassette, tachometer, coolant-temperature gauge, trip odometer, outside-temperature indicator, digital clock, remote keyless entry, remote deck-lid release, tinted glass, illuminated visor mirrors, rear defogger, Homelink universal garage-door opener, fog lamps, burl walnut interior trim, first-aid kit, floormats, 195/65HR15 all-season tires, alloy wheels. **C280** adds: 2.8-liter DOHC 6-cylinder engine, 10-way power passenger seat, Bose sound system. **C36** adds: 3.6-liter DOHC 6-cylinder engine, leather upholstery, power sunroof, 225/45ZR17 front and 245/40ZR17 rear performance tires.

Optional Equipment:

	Retail Price	Dealer Invoice	Fair Price
C1 Option Pkg., C230	$950	$826	—
C280, C36	1875	1631	—
Electronic Traction System (C230), ASR acceleration slip control (C280, C36), heated front seats, headlamp washer/wipers.			
C2 Option Pkg., C230, C280	550	478	—
Multi-contour power driver seat, split folding rear seat. NA w/Sport Pkg.			
C3 Option Pkg., C230	2190	1905	—
C280	1990	1731	—
Leather upholstery, 10-way power passenger seat, power sunroof, telescopic steering wheel (C280), automatic day/night inside and driver-side outside mirrors (C280). NA Sport Pkg.			
C4 Option Pkg., C230	650	565	—
Bose sound system, telescopic steering wheel, automatic day/night inside mirror.			
C5 Option Pkg.	1495	1087	—
Integrated cellular telephone, 6-disc CD changer.			
Sport Pkg., C280	790	687	—
Leather upholstery, sport front bucket seats, sport steering and suspension, telescopic steering wheel, sport interior trim, special exterior trim, 205/60R15 Pirelli summer tires, monoblock alloy wheels. NA w/C2 or C3 option pkg., multi-contour power passenger seat.			
Theft-deterrent system	610	531	—
Headlamp washer/wipers	335	291	—
Power glass sunroof, C230, C280	1090	948	—
Telescopic steering wheel	160	139	—
10-way power passenger seat, C230	600	522	—
Multi-contour passenger seat, C230, C280 .	380	331	—
Split folding rear seat	350	304	—
Ski sack	170	148	—

Prices are accurate at time of publication; subject to manufacturer's change.

MERCEDES-BENZ

	Retail Price	Dealer Invoice	Fair Price
Automatic day/night inside and driver-side outside mirrors	$125	$109	—
Metallic paint	600	522	—

MERCEDES-BENZ E-CLASS

Mercedes-Benz E420

Specifications

	4-door notchback
Wheelbase, in.	111.5
Overall length, in.	189.4
Overall width, in.	70.8
Overall height, in.	56.7
Curb weight, lbs.	3605
Cargo vol., cu. ft.	18.5
Fuel capacity, gals.	17.2
Seating capacity	5

Engines	Diesel dohc I-6	dohc I-6	dohc V-8
Size, liters/cu. in.	3.0/183	3.2/195	4.2/256
Horsepower @ rpm	134 @ 5000	217 @ 5500	275 @ 5700
Torque (lbs./ft.) @ rpm	155 @ 2600	229 @ 3750	295 @ 3900
EPA city/highway mpg			
5-speed OD automatic	26/33	20/27	18/25

Built in Germany.

PRICES

Mercedes-Benz E-Class	Retail Price	Dealer Invoice	Fair Price
E300D 4-door notchback	$39900	$34710	—
E320 4-door notchback	44800	38980	—
E420 4-door notchback	49900	43410	—
Destination charge	595	595	595

Fair price not available at time of publication.

Standard Equipment:

E300D/E320: 3.0-liter DOHC 6-cylinder diesel engine (E300D), 3.2-liter DOHC 6-cylinder engine (E320), 5-speed automatic transmission, front and side air bags, anti-lock 4-wheel disc brakes, Electronic Traction System, variable-assist power steering, automatic climate control, cruise control, leather upholstery (E320), cloth upholstery (E300D), 10-way power front bucket seats with memory feature, split folding rear seats, cupholders, power tilt/telescopic steering wheel with memory feature, leather-wrapped steering wheel, power windows and door locks, tachometer, outside-temperature indicator, AM/FM/cassette, power heated outside mirrors with memory feature, automatic day/night inside and driver-side outside mirrors, tinted glass, rear defogger, illuminated visor mirrors, theft-deterrent system, remote keyless entry, remote decklid release, Homelink universal garage-door opener, variable intermittent wipers, reading lights, walnut interior trim, interior air filter, first-aid kit, fog lamps, floormats, 215/55R16 tires, alloy wheels. **E420** adds to E320: 4.2-liter DOHC V-8 engine, ASR acceleration slip control, Bose sound system, full-size spare tire.

Optional Equipment:

E1 Option Pkg., E300D, E420	760	661	—
E320	1750	1522	—
Heated front seats, headlamp wiper/washer, ASR acceleration slip control (E320).			
E2 Option Pkg., E300D, E320	1065	927	—
Bose sound system, multi-contour power front seats.			
E3 Option Pkg., E300D	1980	1723	—
Leather upholstery, power glass sunroof.			
E4 Option Pkg.	1630	1418	—
Multi-contour power front seats, headlamp wiper/washer, Xenon headlamps.			
E5 Option Pkg.	1495	1087	—
Integrated cellular telephone and 6-disc CD changer.			

Prices are accurate at time of publication; subject to manufacturer's change.

MERCEDES-BENZ

	Retail Price	Dealer Invoice	Fair Price
E6 Sport Pkg., E420	$3900	$3393	—
Ground effects, 235/45ZR17 performance tires, monoblock alloy wheels.			
E7 Option Pkg., E420	1950	1696	—
Electronic stability program, headlamp wiper/washers, Xenon headlamps.			
Power glass sunroof	1090	948	—
Leather upholstery, E300D	1695	1475	—
Multicontour power driver seat	380	331	—
Multicontour power passenger seat	380	331	—
Heated front seats	595	518	—
Bose Premium Sound System, E300D, E320	560	487	—
Headlamp washers/wipers	335	291	—
Power rear window sunshade	395	344	—
Xenon headlamps	950	826	—
Requires headlamp washer/wipers or E1 Option Pkg.			
Metallic paint, E300D, E320	695	605	—
E420	NC	NC	NC

MERCEDES-BENZ S-CLASS

Mercedes-Benz S500 4-door

Specifications	2-door notchback	4-door notchback	4-door notchback
Wheelbase, in.	115.9	119.7	123.6
Overall length, in.	199.4	201.3	205.2
Overall width, in.	74.6	74.3	74.3
Overall height, in.	57.1	58.7	58.9
Curb weight, lbs.	4785	4630	4760

	2-door notchback	4-door notchback	4-door notchback
Cargo vol., cu. ft.	14.2	15.6	15.6
Fuel capacity, gals.	26.3	26.4	26.4
Seating capacity	4	5	5

Engines	dohc I-6	dohc V-8	dohc V-8	dohc V-12
Size, liters/cu. in.	3.2/195	4.2/156	5.0/303	6.0/365
Horsepower @ rpm	228 @ 5600	275 @ 5700	315 @ 5600	389 @ 5200
Torque (lbs./ft.) @ rpm	232 @ 3750	295 @ 3900	345 @ 3900	421 @ 3800

EPA city/highway mpg				
5-speed OD automatic	17/24	16/22	15/21	13/19

Built in Germany.

PRICES

Mercedes-Benz S-Class	Retail Price	Dealer Invoice	Fair Price
S320 4-door notchback (119.7-inch wheelbase)	$63300	$55070	—
S320 4-door notchback (123.6-inch wheelbase)	66600	57940	—
S420 4-door notchback	73900	64290	—
S500 4-door notchback	87500	76120	—
S500 2-door notchback	91900	79950	—
S600 4-door notchback	130300	113360	—
S600 2-door notchback	133300	115970	—
Destination charge	595	595	595
Gas Guzzler Tax, S420,			
S500 2-door	1300	1300	1300
S500 4-door	1700	1700	1700
S600 2-door	2600	2600	2600
S600 4-door	3000	3000	3000

Fair price not available at time of publication.

Standard Equipment:

S320: 3.2-liter 6-cylinder engine, 5-speed automatic transmission, anti-lock 4-wheel disc brakes, ASR traction control, variable-assist power steering, front and side air bags, power windows and door locks, dual-zone automatic climate control, cruise control, leather upholstery, 12-way power front bucket seats w/memory feature, power tilt/telescopic steering column w/memory feature, front storage console, leather-wrapped steering wheel and shift knob, power

Prices are accurate at time of publication; subject to manufacturer's change.

MERCEDES-BENZ

glass sunroof, power memory mirrors, automatic day/night inside and driver-side outside mirror, Bose AM/FM/cassette, power antenna, tachometer, oil-pressure gauge, trip odometer, rear defogger, headlamp wipers/washers (123.6-inch wheelbase), automatic windshield wipers, remote keyless entry and decklid release, Homelink universal garage-door opener, theft-deterrent system, front reading lights, rear reading lights (4-door), illuminated front and rear visor mirrors, front and rear fog lights, floormats, cargo net, 225/60HR16 tires, full-size spare tire, alloy wheels. **S420** adds: 4.2-liter DOHC V-8 engine, 235/60HR16 tires. **S500** adds: 5.0-liter DOHC V-8 engine, automatic rear leveling system, upgraded leather upholstery (2-door), heated front seats, heated rear seats (4-door), Parktronic system (2-door), rear storage console (2-door), Xenon headlamps. **S600** adds: 6.0-liter DOHC V-12 engine, Adaptive Damping System, Electronic Stability Program, power rear seats (4-door), rear dual-zone air conditioner (4-door), 6-disc CD changer, portable cellular telephone, power rear-window sunshade, upgraded leather upholstery, multi-contour power front seats.

Optional Equipment:

	Retail Price	Dealer Invoice	Fair Price
Rear air conditioner, S320, S420, S500	$1980	$1723	—
NA 2-door models.			
Adaptive Damping System, S500	2235	1944	—
Includes automatic rear leveling system.			
Automatic rear leveling system, S320, S420	925	805	—
Electronic Stability Program, S420, S500	1290	1122	—
Parktronic system (std. 2-door)	960	835	—
Power rear-window sunshade (std. S600)	495	431	—
Multi-contour power front seats, each (std. S600)	380	331	—
4-place power seating, S500 4-door, S600 4-door	5460	4750	—
Power rear seat, S500 4-door	1725	1501	—
Heated front seats, S320, S420	595	518	—
Xenon headlamps, S320, S420	950	826	—
Headlamp washers, S320 119.7-inch wheelbase	335	291	—

MERCURY GRAND MARQUIS/ FORD CROWN VICTORIA

Mercury Grand Marquis

Specifications

	4-door notchback
Wheelbase, in.	114.4
Overall length, in.	211.8
Overall width, in.	77.8
Overall height, in.	56.8
Curb weight, lbs.	3796
Cargo vol., cu. ft.	20.6
Fuel capacity, gals.	20.0
Seating capacity	6

Engines

	ohc V-6
Size, liters/cu. in.	4.6/281
Horsepower @ rpm	190 @ 4250
Torque (lbs./ft.) @ rpm	265 @ 3250

EPA city/highway mpg

4-speed OD automatic	17/25

Built in Canada.

PRICES

Mercury Grand Marquis	Retail Price	Dealer Invoice	Fair Price
GS 4-door notchback	$22495	$21001	$21501

Prices are accurate at time of publication; subject to manufacturer's change.

MERCURY

Ford Crown Victoria

	Retail Price	Dealer Invoice	Fair Price
LS 4-door notchback	$23930	$22294	$22794
Destination charge	605	605	605

Standard Equipment:

GS: 4.6-liter SOHC V-8 engine, 4-speed automatic transmission, 4-wheel disc brakes, variable-assist power steering, driver- and passenger-side air bags, air conditioning, cloth bench seats, 6-way power driver seat, front and rear folding armrests, power windows and mirrors, solar-control tinted glass, tilt steering wheel, oil-pressure and coolant-temperature gauges, voltmeter, trip odometer, digital clock, AM/FM/cassette, integrated rear-window antenna, intermittent wipers, rear defogger, passenger-side visor mirror, automatic headlamps, rear heat ducts, 215/70R15 whitewall tires, wheel covers. **LS** adds: upgraded upholstery, rear-seat headrests, power driver-seat lumbar adjuster. Both models require a Preferred Equipment Pkg.

Optional Equipment:

Anti-lock brakes			
w/Traction-Assist	695	619	626
Automatic climate			
control, LS	175	156	158
Includes outside-temperature indicator.			
Preferred Pkg. 157A,			
GS (credit)	(860)	(764)	(764)

  Group 1 (cruise control, floormats, radial-spoke wheel covers), Group 2 (Power Lock Group [power door locks, remote decklid release], illuminated entry).

	Retail Price	Dealer Invoice	Fair Price
Preferred Pkg. 172A, LS (credit)	($80)	($71)	($71)

Group 1 (cruise control, floormats), Group 2, Group 3 (Luxury Light Group [includes underhood light, dual dome/map lights, rear reading lights, dual secondary sun visors, illuminated visor mirrors], striping, leather-wrapped steering wheel, remote keyless entry, cornering lamps, alloy wheels).

	Retail Price	Dealer Invoice	Fair Price
Preferred Pkg. 173A, LS	1755	1559	1580

Pkg. 172A plus Group 4 (anti-lock brakes with Traction-Assist, Electronic Group [includes digital instrumentation, tripminder computer, heavy-duty battery], automatic climate control, outside-temperature indicator, automatic day/night mirror, premium cassette player w/upgraded speakers and amplifier, power passenger seat).

Luxury Light Group, GS	190	169	171

Includes dual dome/map lights, rear reading lights, dual secondary sun visors, illuminated visor mirrors.

Electronic Group, LS	455	405	410

Digital instrumentation, tripminder computer. Requires Automatic climate control, premium cassette player w/upgraded speakers and amplifier.

Keyless entry system, GS	240	213	216
Handling Pkg., GS	600	534	540
LS	1020	908	918

Includes rear air suspension, tuned suspension, larger stabilizer bars, power steering fluid cooler, dual exhaust, 3.27 axle ratio, 225/60R16 handling whitewall tires, alloy wheels.

Power front passenger seat, LS	360	321	324
Leather upholstery, LS	735	654	661

Requires power front passenger seat.

Premium cassette player, LS	360	321	324

Includes upgraded speakers, amplifier. Requires automatic climate control.

Full-size spare tire, LS	185	165	167
LS w/Handling Pkg.	240	213	216
Cast alloy wheels, LS	NC	NC	NC
Striping, GS	60	54	55
Engine-block heater	25	23	24

Ford Crown Victoria	Retail Price	Dealer Invoice	Fair Price
4-door notchback	$21575	$20139	$20639
LX 4-door notchback	23295	21691	22191
Destination charge	605	605	605

Prices are accurate at time of publication; subject to manufacturer's change.

MERCURY

Standard Equipment:

4.6-liter V-8 engine, 4-speed automatic transmission, 4-wheel disc brakes, variable-assist power steering, driver- and passenger-side air bags, air conditioning, cloth reclining split bench seat, AM/FM radio, digital clock, power windows and mirrors, voltmeter, oil-pressure and coolant-temperature gauges, trip odometer, tilt steering wheel, rear defogger, intermittent wipers, 215/70R15 all-season tires, wheel covers. **LX** adds: upgraded interior trim, power driver seat with power recliner and power lumbar support, carpeted spare tire cover.

### Optional Equipment:	Retail Price	Dealer Invoice	Fair Price
Anti-lock brakes			
w/Traction Assist	$695	$619	$626
Automatic air conditioning,			
LX w/Pkg. 113A	175	156	158
Preferred Equipment Pkg. 111A,			
base (credit)	(840)	(747)	(747)
Group 1 (Power Lock Group [power door locks, remote decklid release], cruise control, illuminated entry, spare tire cover) plus floormats, radial-spoke wheel covers.			
Preferred Equipment			
Pkg. 113A, LX (credit)..............................	(360)	(321)	(321)
Pkg. 111A plus Group 2 (cassette player, Light/Decor Group [illuminated visor mirrors, map and dome lights, striping], leather-wrapped steering wheel, cornering lamps, cast or 12-spoke alloy wheels).			
Preferred Equipment			
Pkg. 114A, LX	1890	1681	1701
Pkg. 113A plus Group 3 (automatic air conditioning, anti-lock brakes w/Traction Assist, high-level audio system, electronic instruments, automatic day/night mirror, remote keyless entry, 6-way power passenger seat).			
Keyless remote entry, LX	240	213	216
Requires Group 1.			
Leather upholstery,			
LX	735	654	662
Requires power front passenger seat.			
6-way power passenger seat,			
LX w/Pkg. 113A...	360	321	324
6-way power			
driver seat, base	360	321	324
Handling and			
Performance Pkg.	1100	979	990
LX w/Pkg. 113A	680	605	612

	Retail Price	Dealer Invoice	Fair Price
LX w/Pkg. 114A	$410	$365	$369

Includes performance springs, shocks and stabilizer bars, alloy wheels, anti-lock brakes w/Traction Assist, dual exhaust, 3.27 axle ratio, power-steering cooler, rear air suspension, 225/60R16 tires.

Light/Decor Group, base	225	201	203

Illuminated visor mirrors, map and dome lights, striping.

Cassette player, base	185	165	167
High-level audio system, LX	360	321	324

Cassette player, upgraded amplifier and speakers. Requires automatic air conditioning.

215/70R15 whitewall tires	80	71	72
Full-size spare tire	80	71	72
w/Handling and Performance Pkg.	260	232	234
Engine block heater	25	23	24

MERCURY VILLAGER

Mercury Villager Nautica

Specifications

	3-door van
Wheelbase, in.	112.2
Overall length, in.	190.2
Overall width, in.	73.8
Overall height, in.	66.0
Curb weight, lbs.	3815
Cargo vol., cu. ft.	126.4
Fuel capacity, gals.	20.0
Seating capacity	7

Prices are accurate at time of publication; subject to manufacturer's change.

MERCURY

Engines

ohc V-6

Size, liters/cu. in.	3.0/181
Horsepower @ rpm	151 @ 4800
Torque (lbs./ft.) @ rpm	174 @ 4400

EPA city/highway mpg

4-speed OD automatic	17/23

Built in Avon Lake, Ohio.

PRICES

Mercury Villager	Retail Price	Dealer Invoice	Fair Price
GS 3-door van	$20215	$18299	$19099
LS 3-door van	25085	22585	23385
Nautica 3-door van	26915	24174	24974
Destination charge	580	580	580

Standard Equipment:

GS: 3.0-liter V-6 engine, 4-speed automatic transmission, driver- and passenger-side air bags, power steering, cloth upholstery, 5-passenger seating (reclining front bucket seats, 3-passenger second-row bench seat), front and rear cupholders, tilt steering column, AM/FM/cassette, tachometer, coolant-temperature gauge, trip odometer, solar-tinted glass, dual outside mirrors, visor mirrors, variable-intermittent wipers, rear wiper/washer, cornering lamps, rear auxiliary power outlet, rear storage bin, color-keyed bodyside molding, floormats, 205/75R15 tires, wheel covers. **LS** adds: front air conditioning, anti-lock brakes, 7-passenger seating (reclining front bucket seats, 3-passenger second-row bench seat, 2-passenger rear bench seat), cruise control, power windows and door locks, power mirrors, Light Group (overhead dual map lights, dual liftgate lights, front door step lights, power rear vent windows, under instrument panel lights with time delay), privacy glass, rear defogger, luggage rack, illuminated visor mirrors, seatback map pockets, automatic headlamps, lockable underseat storage bin, 2-tone paint, color-keyed bodyside molding w/chrome strip. **Nautica** adds: leather quad captain's chairs, unique exterior paint, color-keyed bodyside molding w/yellow Mylar insert, unique grille, white alloy wheels. All models require Preferred Equipment Pkg.

Optional Equipment:

Rear air conditioning and heater, GS w/Pkg. 691A	465	395	428

	Retail Price	Dealer Invoice	Fair Price
Anti-lock brakes, GS w/Pkg. 691A	$590	$503	$543
Automatic temperature control, LS	180	153	166
Includes front and rear air conditioning and heater.			
Preferred Equipment Pkg. 691A, GS	1600	1359	1472
Front air conditioning, cruise control, quad captain's chairs, power windows and door locks, power mirrors, rear defogger.			
Preferred Equipment Pkg. 692A, GS	3400	2891	3128
Pkg. 691A plus anti-lock brakes, 8-way power driver seat, rear air conditioning and heater, remote keyless entry, flip-open liftgate window, privacy glass, luggage rack, underseat storage bin, alloy wheels.			
Preferred Equipment Pkg. 696A, LS	1930	1639	1776
Rear air conditioning and heater, cruise control, leather quad captain's chairs, 8-way power driver seat, 4-way power front passenger seat, leather-wrapped steering wheel w/radio controls, heated power mirrors, Premium Sound cassette player (rear radio controls with front-seat lockout, dual mini headphone jacks, cassette/CD storage console), remote keyless entry, illuminated visor mirrors, flip-open liftgate window, deluxe alloy wheels.			
Preferred Equipment Pkg. 697A, Nautica ...	1500	1275	1380
Automatic front and rear air conditioning and heater, cruise control, 8-way power driver seat, 4-way power front passenger seat, Premium Sound cassette player (rear radio controls with front-seat lockout, dual mini headphone jacks, cassette/CD storage console), leather-wrapped steering wheel w/radio controls, flip-open liftgate window, heated power mirrors, electronic instrumentation, remote keyless entry, illuminated visor mirrors.			
Light Group, GS w/Pkg. 692A	165	140	152
Overhead dual map lights, dual liftgate lights, front-door step lights, power rear vent windows, under instrument panel lights with time delay.			
Handling suspension	85	73	79
Includes 215/70R15 performance tires, firm-ride suspension, rear stabilizer bar. GS requires deluxe alloy wheels. NA GS w/Pkg. 691A.			
Trailer Towing Pkg.	250	213	230
Includes heavy-duty battery, full-size spare tire, 3500-pound trailer rating.			
Power moonroof, LS, Nautica	775	659	714
7-passenger seating,			
GS, LS	NC	NC	NC
Cloth upholstery, reclining front bucket seats, 3-passenger second-row bench seat, 2-passenger rear bench seat.			
Cloth quad captain's chairs, LS	NC	NC	NC

Prices are accurate at time of publication; subject to manufacturer's change.

	Retail Price	Dealer Invoice	Fair Price
8-way power driver seat, GS w/Pkg. 691A	$395	$336	$363
Integrated child seats, GS, LS	240	204	221
Requires 7-passenger seating.			
Premium Sound cassette player, GS w/Pkg. 692A	310	263	285
Includes rear radio controls with front seat lockout, dual mini headphone jacks, cassette/CD storage console.			
Premium Sound cassette/6-disc CD changer, GS w/Pkg. 692A	680	578	626
LS, Nautica	370	314	340
Includes rear radio controls with front seat lockout, dual mini headphone jacks, cassette/CD storage console.			
Supersound CD/cassette player, LS, Nautica	865	735	796
Premium Sound cassette/6-disc CD changer plus subwoofer speaker.			
Electronic instrumentation, LS	245	208	225
Requires automatic temperature control.			
Remote keyless entry, GS w/Pkg. 691A	175	149	161
Flip-open liftgate window, GS w/Pkg. 691A	115	97	106
Requires rear defogger.			
Privacy glass, GS w/Pkg. 691A	415	352	382
Requires rear defogger.			
Theft-deterrent system	100	85	92
Requires remote keyless entry. GS w/Pkg. 691A requires anti-lock brakes.			
Luggage rack, GS w/Pkg. 691A	175	149	161
Cargo net	30	26	28
Monotone paint, LS (credit)	(135)	(115)	(115)
2-tone paint, GS	295	251	271
Deluxe alloy wheels, GS w/Pkg. 692A	40	34	37

MITSUBISHI DIAMANTE

Specifications

	4-door notchback
Wheelbase, in.	107.1
Overall length, in.	194.1
Overall width, in.	70.3
Overall height, in.	56.5
Curb weight, lbs.	3363

MItsubishi Diamante LS

	4-door notchback
Cargo vol., cu. ft.	14.2
Fuel capacity, gals.	19.0
Seating capacity	5

Engines

	ohc V-6
Size, liters/cu. in.	3.5/213
Horsepower @ rpm	210 @ 5000
Torque (lbs./ft.) @ rpm	231 @ 4000

EPA city/highway mpg

4-speed OD automatic	18/26

Built in Australia.

PRICES

Mitsubishi Diamante	Retail Price	Dealer Invoice	Fair Price
ES 4-door notchback	$25900	$22274	—
LS 4-door notchback	29990	25492	—
Destination charge	470	470	470

Fair price not available at time of publication.

Standard Equipment:

ES: 3.5-liter V-6 engine, 4-speed automatic transmission, 4-wheel disc brakes, power steering, driver- and passenger-side air bags, automatic climate control, cruise control, velour upholstery, 7-way adjustable front bucket seats, front console with armrest, cupholders, folding rear armrest, power windows and door locks, power mirrors, tilt steering column, tinted glass, remote fuel-door and decklid releases, tachometer, coolant-temperature gauge, trip odometer,

MITSUBISHI

variable intermittent wipers, AM/FM/cassette, power and diversity antenna, digital clock, rear defogger, theft-deterrent system, front map light, rear heat ducts, 205/65VR15 tires, wheel covers, full-size spare tire. **LS** adds: power driver seat, leather upholstery, leather-wrapped steering wheel, AM/FM/cassette/CD player, rear map light, wood interior trim, 215/60VR16 tires, alloy wheels.

Optional Equipment:	Retail Price	Dealer Invoice	Fair Price
Anti-lock brakes	$732	$600	—
Premium Pkg., ES	2000	1640	—
Leather upholstery, power driver seat, leather-wrapped steering wheel, remote keyless entry, cargo net, fog lights, 215/60VR16 tires, alloy wheels.			
Luxury Group, LS	2287	1875	—
Power sunroof, Homelink universal garage-door opener, high-contrast instrument panel w/two trip odometers.			
Convenience Group, LS	2561	2100	—
Anti-lock brakes, power passenger seat, integrated child seat, Infinity AM/FM/cassette/CD player, remote keyless entry, automatic day/night inside mirror, steering-wheel controls, power fuel door release.			
Power sunroof	963	790	—
Includes Homelink universal garage-door opener.			
Integrated child seat	195	160	—
CD player, ES	399	299	—
10-disc CD changer	758	522	—
Includes trunk mat.			
Remote keyless entry	216	150	—
Floormats	90	58	—
Trunk mat	71	46	—
Cargo net	36	23	—
Wheel locks, LS	39	27	—
Mud guards	125	87	—

MITSUBISHI ECLIPSE/ EAGLE TALON

Specifications	2-door hatchback	2-door conv.
Wheelbase, in.	98.8	98.8
Overall length, in.	172.2	172.2
Overall width, in.	68.3	68.3

Mitsubishi Eclipse GS-T

	2-door hatchback	2-door conv.
Overall height, in.	50.2	51.6
Curb weight, lbs.	2767	2888
Cargo vol., cu. ft.	16.6	5.1
Fuel capacity, gals.	16.9	16.9
Seating capacity	4	4

Engines	dohc I-4	dohc I-4	Turbo dohc I-4
Size, liters/cu. in.	2.0/122	2.4/143	2.0/122
Horsepower @ rpm	140 @ 6000	141 @ 5500	210 @ 6000
Torque (lbs./ft.) @ rpm	130 @ 4800	148 @ 3000	214 @ 3000

EPA city/highway mpg

5-speed OD manual	22/33	22/30	23/31
4-speed OD automatic	21/31	20/28	20/27

Built in Normal, III.

PRICES

Mitsubishi Eclipse	Retail Price	Dealer Invoice	Fair Price
Base 2-door hatchback, 5-speed	$13830	$12440	$12940
Base 2-door hatchback, automatic	14510	13051	13551
RS 2-door hatchback, 5-speed	15140	13156	13656
RS 2-door hatchback, automatic	15830	13768	14268
GS 2-door hatchback, 5-speed	17550	15255	15755
GS 2-door hatchback, automatic	18240	15866	16366
Spyder GS 2-door convertible, 5-speed	19940	17340	—
Spyder GS 2-door convertible, automatic	20650	17957	—

Prices are accurate at time of publication; subject to manufacturer's change.

Eagle Talon TSi

	Retail Price	Dealer Invoice	Fair Price
GS-T 2-door hatchback, 5-speed	$21190	$18424	$18924
GS-T 2-door hatchback, automatic	22020	19154	19654
Spyder GS-T 2-door convertible, 5-speed	25780	22422	—
Spyder GS-T 2-door convertible, automatic	26630	23160	—
GSX 2-door hatchback, 5-speed	23220	19963	20763
GSX 2-door hatchback, automatic	24070	20694	21494
Destination charge	420	420	420

Fair price for Spyder models not available at time of publication.

Standard Equipment:

Base: 2.0-liter DOHC 4-cylinder engine, 5-speed manual or 4-speed automatic transmission, driver- and passenger-side air bags, power steering, cloth upholstery, reclining front bucket seats, folding rear seat, 5-way adjustable driver seat w/memory feature, front storage console w/cupholders, tilt steering column, coolant-temperature gauge, trip odometer, digital clock, tinted glass, dual outside mirrors, map lights, remote fuel-door release, 185/70HR14 tires. **RS** adds: tachometer, AM/FM radio w/4-speakers, rear defogger, remote hatch release, cargo light, 195/70HR14 tires, wheel covers. **GS** adds: 4-wheel disc brakes, 6-way adjustable driver seat w/memory feature, split folding rear seat, cassette player w/6-speakers, power mirrors, Homelink universal garage-door opener, rear wiper/washer, low rear spoiler, fog lights, cargo cover and net, 205/55HR16 tires. **Spyder GS** adds to RS: 2.4-liter SOHC 4-cylinder engine, variable-assist power steering, power insulated soft top with glass rear window, vinyl tonneau cover, 6-way adjustable driver seat w/memory feature, power windows and door locks, power mirrors, CD player, alloy wheels. **GS-**

T adds to GS: 2.0-liter DOHC 4-cylinder turbocharged and intercooled engine, air conditioning, sport suspension, cruise control, oil-pressure gauge, turbo-boost gauge, Infinity 8-speaker AM/FM/cassette/CD player w/amplifier, power windows and door locks, dual bright exhaust outlets, high rear spoiler, 205/55HR16 tires, alloy wheels. **Spyder GS-T** adds: variable-assist power steering, sport suspension, power insulated soft top with glass rear window, vinyl tonneau cover, leather upholstery, remote keyless entry, theft-deterrent system, leather-wrapped steering wheel and shifter, 205/55VR16 tires. **GSX** adds to GS-T: all-wheel drive, 215/50VR17 tires.

Optional Equipment:

	Retail Price	Dealer Invoice	Fair Price
Air conditioning, base, RS, GS, Spyder GS .	$891	$731	$802
Anti-lock brakes, Spyder GS, GS-T, Spyder GS-T, GSX	716	587	644
Limited-slip differential, GSX	266	218	239
Preferred Value Pkg. P1, GS	1963	1930	1963
Air conditioning, power moonroof, power windows and door locks, cruise control, alloy wheels.			
Premium Value Pkg. P2, GS	3031	2889	3031
Pkg. P1 plus Infinity AM/FM/cassette, leather upholstery, theft-deterrent system, remote keyless entry.			
Premium Plus Value Pkg. P3, GS	3747	3476	3747
Pkg. P2 plus anti-lock brakes.			
Preferred Equipment Pkg. PM, RS	1529	1254	1376
Air conditioning, rear spoiler, cargo cover, alloy wheels.			
Preferred Equipment Pkg. PU, GSX	789	647	710
Leather upholstery, power driver seat.			
Appearance Pkg., Spyder GS	924	758	832
Rear spoiler, lower bodyside cladding, fog lamps, alloy wheels.			
Convenience Pkg., Spyder GS	1551	1272	1396
Air conditioning, cruise control, remote keyless entry, theft-deterrent system, Homelink universal garage-door opener.			
Power moonroof, RS, GS-T, GSX	731	599	658
Power Pkg., RS	755	619	680
Power windows and door locks, cruise control.			
Leather upholstery, GS-T	457	375	411
Spyder GS	567	465	510
AM/FM radio, base	234	192	211
Cassette player, RS	323	265	287
CD player, base, RS, GS, Spyder GS..........	399	299	359
Base requires AM/FM radio			
Infinity 8-speaker AM/FM/cassette with amplifier, Spyder GS	720	590	648
10 disc CD changer:.....................................	675	465	608
Base requires AM/FM radio			

Prices are accurate at time of publication; subject to manufacturer's change.

MITSUBISHI

	Retail Price	Dealer Invoice	Fair Price
Rear defogger, base	$162	$133	$146
Remote keyless entry, RS, GS, Spyder GS, GS-T, GSX..	136	89	122
RS requires Power Pkg. GS requires Preferred Value Pkg. 1.			
Remote keyless entry/theft-deterrent system, GS, GS-T, GSX	334	274	301
Mud guards...	93	61	84
Wheel locks, RS, GS, Spyder GS	33	23	30
Floormats..	49	32	44

Eagle Talon	Retail Price	Dealer Invoice	Fair Price
Base 2-door hatchback	$14059	$13023	$13523
ESi 2-door hatchback	14830	13762	14262
TSi 2-door hatchback	18015	16659	17159
TSi AWD 2-door hatchback	20271	18709	19509
Destination charge	535	535	535

Standard Equipment:

Base: 2.0-liter DOHC 4-cylinder engine, 5-speed manual transmission, driver- and passenger-side air bags, variable-assist power steering, cloth reclining front bucket seats, folding rear seat, front console with storage and armrest, tinted glass, tachometer, coolant temperature gauge, trip odometer, map lights, dual remote mirrors, visor mirrors, digital clock, remote fuel-door and hatch releases, tilt steering column, intermittent wipers, 195/70R14 tires, wheel covers. **ESi** adds: AM/FM radio, variable intermittent wipers, color-keyed bodyside moldings, rear spoiler. **TSi** adds: turbocharged engine, 4-wheel disc brakes, sport-tuned exhaust system, upgraded suspension, driver-seat lumbar support adjustment, split folding rear seat, leather-wrapped steering wheel and manual gearshift handle, power mirrors, turbo-boost and oil-pressure gauges, cassette player, rear wiper/washer, illuminated visor mirrors, rear defogger, cargo-area cover, cargo net, fog lamps, 205/55R16 tires, painted alloy wheels. **TSi AWD** adds: permanent 4-wheel drive, cruise control, power door locks and windows, 215/50VR17 tires, alloy wheels.

Optional Equipment:

4-speed automatic transmission, base, ESi	745	633	671
TSi	891	757	802
TSi AWD	891	757	757
TSi AWD includes 215/55VR17 tires.			

MITSUBISHI

	Retail Price	Dealer Invoice	Fair Price
Anti-lock brakes	$649	$552	$584
Requires option pkg. NA base.			
Limited-slip differential,			
TSi AWD w/option pkg.	266	226	239
Air conditioning	860	731	774
Pkg. 21B/22B, ESi	1688	1435	1519
Air conditioning, cruise control, rear defogger, power mirrors, cassette player, front floormats. Pkg. 22B requires 4-speed automatic transmission.			
Pkg. 21C/22C, ESi	2222	1889	2000
Pkg. 21B/22B plus power windows and door locks, cargo net, upgraded interior trim. Pkg. 22C requires 4-speed automatic transmission.			
Pkg. 23P/24P, TSi	1614	1372	1453
Air conditioning, cruise control, power windows and door locks, front floormats. Pkg. 24P requires automatic transmission.			
Pkg. 25S/26S, TSi AWD	1223	1040	1101
Air conditioning, remote keyless entry with security alarm, front floormats. Pkg. 26S requires automatic transmission.			
Pkg. 25L/26L, TSi AWD	4184	3556	3766
Pkg. 25S/26S plus anti-lock brakes, power driver seat, leather/vinyl front upholstery, CD/cassette player with graphic equalizer, power sunroof. Pkg. 26L requires automatic transmission.			
Remote keyless entry with security alarm,			
ESi w/Pkg. 21C/22C, TSi w/option pkg. ..	334	284	301
Rear defogger, base, ESi	162	138	146
AM/FM radio, base	234	199	211
AM/FM/cassette, base	502	427	452
Cassette/CD player,			
ESi w/Pkg. 21C/22C, TSi w/option pkg.,			
TSi AWD w/Pkg. 25S/26S	390	332	351
Cassette/CD player with graphic equalizer,			
TSi w/option pkg.,			
TSi AWD w/Pkg. 25S/26S	793	674	714
Includes eight Infinity speakers.			
Power sunroof, ESi w/Pkg. 21C/22C,			
TSi w/option pkg.,			
TSi AWD w/Pkg. 25S/26S	730	621	657
Leather/vinyl upholstery, TSi w/option pkg.,			
TSi AWD w/Pkg. 25S/26S	457	388	411
Universal garage-door opener,			
TSi AWD w/Pkg. 25L/26L	113	96	102
Power driver seat, TSi w/option pkg.			
TSi AWD w/Pkg. 25S/26S	332	282	299

Prices are accurate at time of publication; subject to manufacturer's change.

	Retail Price	Dealer Invoice	Fair Price
Alloy wheels, ESi	$507	$431	$456

Includes 205/55HR16 tires.

MITSUBISHI GALANT

Mitsubishi Galant ES

Specifications

	4-door notchback
Wheelbase, in.	103.7
Overall length, in.	187.6
Overall width, in.	68.1
Overall height, in.	53.1
Curb weight, lbs.	2777
Cargo vol., cu. ft.	12.5
Fuel capacity, gals.	16.9
Seating capacity	5

Engines

	ohc I-4
Size, liters/cu. in.	2.4/144
Horsepower @ rpm	143 @ 5500
Torque (lbs./ft.) @ rpm	148 @ 3000

EPA city/highway mpg

5-speed OD manual	23/30
4-speed OD automatic	22/28

Built in Normal, Ill., and Japan.

PRICES

Mitsubishi Galant	Retail Price	Dealer Invoice	Fair Price
DE 4-door notchback, 5-speed	$15420	$13717	$14217
DE 4-door notchback, automatic	16290	14493	14993
ES 4-door notchback, automatic	18115	15958	16458
LS 4-door notchback, automatic	23980	20380	20880
Destination charge	420	420	420

Standard Equipment:

DE: 2.4-liter SOHC 4-cylinder engine, 5-speed manual or 4-speed automatic transmission, driver- and passenger-side air bags, power steering, cloth upholstery, 5-way adjustable driver seat, front storage console w/armrest, tilt steering column, cupholders, radio prep pkg., digital clock, tinted glass, driver-side visor mirror, tachometer, coolant-temperature gauge, remote fuel-door and decklid releases, rear defogger, intermittent wipers, remote outside mirrors, 185/70HR14 tires, wheel covers. **ES** adds: 4-speed automatic transmission, air conditioning, cruise control, upgraded cloth upholstery, folding rear seat with center armrest, power windows and door locks, AM/FM/cassette, power diversity antenna, power mirrors, variable intermittent wipers, passenger-side visor mirror, door map pockets, woodgrain interior trim, floormats, cargo net. **LS** adds: automatic climate control, power driver seat, leather upholstery, power sunroof, Infinity audio system w/amplifier, Homelink universal garage-door opener, fog lamps, illuminated visor mirrors, seatback map pockets, 195/60HR15 tires, alloy wheels.

Optional Equipment:

Anti-lock brakes, ES, LS	965	791	869
Air conditioning, DE	902	740	812
Premium Pkg., ES	1787	1465	1608

Power sunroof, Homelink universal garage-door opener, illuminated visor mirrors, remote keyless entry, fog lamps, 195/60R15 tires, alloy wheels.

MITSUBISHI MIRAGE

Specifications	2-door notchback	4-door notchback
Wheelbase, in.	95.1	98.4
Overall length, in.	168.1	173.6
Overall width, in.	66.5	66.5
Overall height, in.	51.4	52.6

Prices are accurate at time of publication; subject to manufacturer's change.

MITSUBISHI

Mitsubishi Mirage 4-door

	2-door notchback	4-door notchback
Curb weight, lbs.	2127	2227
Cargo vol., cu. ft.	11.5	11.5
Fuel capacity, gals.	13.2	13.2
Seating capacity	5	5

Engines

	ohc I-4	ohc I-4
Size, liters/cu. in.	1.5/90	1.8/112
Horsepower @ rpm	92 @ 5500	113 @ 5500
Torque (lbs./ft.) @ rpm	93 @ 3000	116 @ 4500

EPA city/highway mpg

5-speed OD manual	33/40	29/37
4-speed OD automatic	29/36	27/33

Built in Japan.

PRICES

Mitsubishi Mirage	Retail Price	Dealer Invoice	Fair Price
DE 2-door notchback, 5-speed	$10520	$9566	$9889
DE 2-door notchback, automatic	11230	10178	10444
DE 4-door notchback, 5-speed	12220	10878	—
DE 4-door notchback, automatic	12920	11490	—
LS 2-door notchback, 5-speed	13350	11857	12149
LS 2-door notchback, automatic	14020	12469	12758
LS 4-door notchback, 5-speed	13150	11707	—
LS 4-door notchback, automatic	13830	12319	—
Destination charge	420	420	420

4-door fair price not available at time of publication.

Standard Equipment:

DE: 1.5-liter 4-cylinder engine, 5-speed manual or 4-speed automatic transmission, driver- and passenger-side air bags, power steering (4-door), vinyl/cloth upholstery (2-door), cloth upholstery (4-door), highback front bucket seats (2-door), sport front bucket seats (4-door), front and rear armrests, front storage console, coolant-temperature gauge, tachometer (4-door w/5-speed), rear defogger, dual outside mirrors, tinted glass, remote fuel-door and decklid release, 175/70R13 tires, wheel covers (4-door). **LS** adds: 1.8-liter 4-cylinder engine, air conditioning (4-door), power steering, cloth upholstery, sport front bucket seats, height-adjustable driver seat, split folding rear seat (2-door), tilt steering column, tachometer (5-speed), digital clock, AM/FM/cassette with CD controls (2-door), intermittent wipers, cloth door-trim panels, rear spoiler (2-door), 175/70R13 tires (4-door), 185/65R14 tires (2-door), alloy wheels (2-door).

Optional Equipment:	Retail Price	Dealer Invoice	Fair Price
Air conditioning, DE	$880	$720	$792
Anti-lock brakes, LS	732	600	659
Power steering, DE 2-door	262	215	236
Preferred Equipment Pkg. PE, DE 2-door ..	166	136	149
Tilt steering wheel, intermittent wipers, wheel covers.			
Value Pkg. VE, DE 4-door	1070	960	963
Air conditioning, split folding rear seat, tilt steering wheel, AM/FM/cassette, remote outside mirrors, visor mirrors, cargo-area light, intermittent wipers, cloth door-trim panels, floormats.			
Value Pkg. VM, LS 2-door	1017	901	915
Air conditioner, CD player, cargo net, floormats, wheel locks.			
Appearance Pkg., LS 2-door	207	170	186
Fog lamps, air dam.			
Convenience Pkg., LS 2-door	744	610	670
Cruise control, power windows and door locks, power mirrors, variable intermittent wipers, visor mirrors.			
Premium Pkg PR, LS 4-door	1190	976	1071
Power sunroof, alloy wheels, wheel locks.			
Value Pkg. VL, LS 4-door	1637	1477	1477
Air conditioning, cruise control, split folding rear seat, power windows and door locks, AM/FM/cassette with CD controls, power mirrors, variable intermittent wipers, 185/65R14 tires, floormats.			
AM/FM/cassette, DE	352	247	317
AM/FM/cassette with CD controls, DE 2-Door	470	330	423
CD player, DE 2-Door, LS 4-Door	399	299	359
DE 2-Door requires AM/FM/cassette. LS 4-Door requires Value Pkg. VL.			

MITSUBISHI

	Retail Price	Dealer Invoice	Fair Price
Remote keyless entry, LS	$254	$165	$229
Requires Convenience Pkg.			
Mud guards	71	46	64
Floormats, DE	65	43	59

MITSUBISHI MONTERO

Mitsubishi Montero LS

Specifications

	4-door wagon
Wheelbase, in.	107.3
Overall length, in.	185.2
Overall width, in.	66.7
Overall height, in.	74.4
Curb weight, lbs.	4385
Cargo vol., cu. ft.	67.1
Fuel capacity, gals.	24.3
Seating capacity...	7

Engines

	ohc V-6
Size, liters/cu. in.	3.5/213
Horsepower @ rpm	200 @ 5000
Torque (lbs./ft.) @ rpm	228 @ 3500

EPA city/highway mpg

4-speed OD automatic.................................	16/19

Built in Japan.

PRICES

Mitsubishi Montero	Retail Price	Dealer Invoice	Fair Price
LS 4-door wagon	$29290	$25028	$25528
SR 4-door wagon	36460	30436	31136
Destination charge	445	445	445

Standard Equipment:

LS: 3.5-liter V-6 engine, 4-speed automatic transmission, Active-Trac 4-wheel drive, 4-wheel disc brakes, driver- and passenger-side air bags, power steering, engine oil cooler, cruise control, cloth reclining front bucket seats, split folding second-row seat with headrests, tilt steering column, front storage console w/cupholders, leather-wrapped steering wheel, power windows and door locks, power mirrors, digital clock, trip odometer, tachometer, coolant-temperature gauge, AM/FM/cassette, power diversity antenna, rear defogger, variable intermittent wipers, intermittent rear wiper/washer, remote fuel-door release, auxiliary power outlets, map/spot lights, visor mirrors w/illuminated passenger-side mirror, cargo tie-down hooks, tool kit, rear heat ducts, front and rear tow hooks, skid plates, mud guards, full-size spare tire, 235/75R15 tires. **SR adds:** rear differential lock, leather upholstery, power driver seat, split folding third-row seat, Infinity AM/FM/cassette/CD player w/amplifier, power sunroof, multi-meter (oil-pressure gauge, compass, outside-temperature indicator, voltmeter), illuminated driver-side visor mirror, rear privacy glass, sliding rear quarter window, headlamp washers, 265/70R15 tires, alloy wheels.

Optional Equipment:

Air conditioning/ alloy wheels, LS	1305	1070	1175
Preferred Equipment Pkg. #2, LS	1654	1356	1489

Split folding third-row seat, seat, power moonroof, multi-meter (oil-pressure gauge, compass, outside-temperature indicator, voltmeter), sliding rear-quarter windows, rear privacy glass.

All-Weather Pkg., LS	1402	1150	1262
SR	1585	1300	1427

Anti-lock brakes, heated front seats. SR also includes adjustable shock absorbers.

Luxury Pkg., LS	1933	1585	1740

Leather upholstery, power driver seat, Infinity sound system w/amplifier.

MITSUBISHI MONTERO SPORT

Mitsubishi Montero Sport XLS

Specifications

	4-door wagon
Wheelbase, in.	107.3
Overall length, in.	178.3
Overall width, in.	66.7
Overall height, in.	67.3
Curb weight, lbs.	3945
Cargo vol., cu. ft.	79.3
Fuel capacity, gals.	19.5
Seating capacity	5

Engines

	ohc I-4	ohc V-6
Size, liters/cu. in.	2.4/143	3.0/181
Horsepower @ rpm	134 @ 5500	173 @ 5250
Torque (lbs./ft.) @ rpm	148 @ 2750	188 @ 4000
EPA city/highway mpg		
5-speed OD manual	NA	NA
4-speed OD automatic		NA

Built in Japan.

PRICES

Mitsubishi Montero Sport	Retail Price	Dealer Invoice	Fair Price
ES 2WD 4-door wagon, 5-speed	$17620	$15858	—
LS 2WD 4-door wagon, automatic	21820	18983	—
LS 4WD 4-door wagon, 5-speed	23130	20123	—
LS 4WD 4-door wagon, automatic	23970	20854	—
XLS 4WD 4-door wagon, automatic	31110	27064	—
Destination charge	445	445	445

Fair price not available at time of publication.

Standard Equipment:

ES: 2.4-liter 4-cylinder engine, 5-speed manual transmission, driver- and passenger-side air bags, power steering, cloth upholstery, front bucket seats, reclining folding rear seat, front cupholders, tilt steering column, trip odometer, coolant-temperature gauge, tinted glass, dual outside mirrors, AM/FM/CD player w/four speakers, digital clock, rear defogger, intermittent wipers, visor mirrors, map lights, auxiliary power outlet, carpeting, mud guards, front and rear tow hooks, front-end and fuel-tank skid plates, 225/75R15 mud and snow tires. **LS 2WD** adds: 3.0-liter V-6 engine, 4-speed automatic transmission, split folding rear seat, rear cupholders, rear privacy glass, AM/FM/cassette w/six speakers, power antenna, variable intermittent wipers, rear wiper/washer, chrome grille accent. **LS 4WD** adds: 4-speed automatic or 5-speed manual transmission, 4-wheel disc brakes, part-time 4-wheel drive, automatic locking front hubs, transfer-case skid plates. **XLS** adds: 4-speed automatic transmission, air conditioning, cruise control, leather upholstery, power windows and door locks, power outside mirrors, power sunroof, Infinity AM/FM/cassette player w/eight speakers, fender flares, side steps, 2-tone paint, 265/70R15 mud and snow tires.

Optional Equipment:

Air conditioning,			
ES, LS	915	750	—
Anti-lock brakes,			
LS, XLS	610	500	—
Preferred Pkg. 3, ES, LS	1037	825	—
Air conditioning, cargo net, floormats.			
Preferred Pkg. 4, ES, LS	755	505	—
Roof rack, rear wind deflector, side steps. NA w/Premium Pkg., Appearance Pkg., or power sunroof.			
Convenience Pkg., LS	829	680	—
Cruise control, power windows and door locks, power mirrors.			

Prices are accurate at time of publication; subject to manufacturer's change.

	Retail Price	Dealer Invoice	Fair Price
All-Weather Pkg., LS 4WD, XLS	$744	$610	—

Limited-slip differential, rear heater, multi-meter (includes compass, outside-temperature indicator, voltmeter, oil-pressure gauge).

Off-Road Pkg., LS 4WD	1037	850	—

All-Weather Pkg plus rear-mounted spare-tire cover.

Appearance Pkg., LS	1793	1470	—

Leather-wrapped steering wheel, side steps, bright grille, fender flares, 265/70R15 tires, alloy wheels.

Premium Pkg., LS	3070	2517	—

Appearance Pkg. plus power sunroof, Infinity AM/FM/cassette.

Leather upholstery, LS 2WD	1220	1000	—
Power sunroof, LS	793	650	—
CD player, LS, XLS	399	299	—
10-disc CD changer, LS, XLS	675	465	—
Rear wind deflector	145	95	—
Trailer hitch w/harness	252	164	—
Side steps, ES, LS	350	245	—
Floormats	85	51	—
Cargo net	37	24	—
Roof rack, ES, LS w/o sunroof	260	165	—
Spare tire carrier, LS 4WD	75	50	—

Requires Off-Road Pkg.

Wheel trim rings, ES, LS	70	45	—
Four wheel locks, LS, XLS	50	33	—
Five wheel locks, LS 4WD	60	40	—

Requires Off-Road Pkg.

Alloy wheels, LS	427	350	—
Rear wiper/washer, ES	195	160	—

NISSAN ALTIMA

Specifications

	4-door notchback
Wheelbase, in.	103.1
Overall length, in.	180.5
Overall width, in.	67.1
Overall height, in.	55.9
Curb weight, lbs.	2853
Cargo vol., cu. ft.	14.0
Fuel capacity, gals.	15.9
Seating capacity	5

Nissan Altima GXE

Engines

	dohc I-4
Size, liters/cu. in.	2.4/146
Horsepower @ rpm	150 @ 5600
Torque (lbs./ft.) @ rpm	154 @ 4400

EPA city/highway mpg

5-speed OD manual	24/30
4-speed OD automatic	21/29

Built in Smyrna, Tenn.

PRICES

Nissan Altima	Retail Price	Dealer Invoice	Fair Price
XE 4-door notchback, 5-speed	$15849	$14272	$14772
XE 4-door notchback, automatic	16649	14992	15492
GXE 4-door notchback, 5-speed	17399	15577	16077
GXE 4-door notchback, automatic	18199	16293	16793
SE 4-door notchback, 5-speed	19699	17534	18034
SE 4-door notchback, automatic	20499	18246	18746
GLE 4-door notchback, automatic	20899	18602	18746
Destination charge	420	420	420

Standard Equipment:

XE: 2.4-liter DOHC 4-cylinder engine, 5-speed manual or 4-speed automatic transmission, driver- and passenger-side air bags, power steering, tilt steering column, rear defogger, cupholders, remote fuel door and decklid releases, cloth reclining bucket seats, tachometer,

NISSAN

coolant-temperature gauge, trip odometer, digital clock, tinted glass, power mirrors, variable intermittent wipers, visor mirrors, 205/60R15 tires, wheel covers. **GXE** adds: power windows, power door locks, front storage console with armrest, rear center armrest with trunk pass-through. **SE** adds: anti-lock 4-wheel disc brakes, sport-tuned suspension, air conditioning, cruise control, front sport seats, AM/FM/cassette, power antenna, fog lights, cornering lamps, rear spoiler, leather-wrapped steering wheel and manual shift knob, alloy wheels. **GLE** adds to GXE: 4-speed automatic transmission, air conditioning, cruise control, leather upholstery, adjustable lumbar support, cornering lamps, power diversity antenna, illuminated visor mirrors, alloy wheels.

Optional Equipment:

	Retail Price	Dealer Invoice	Fair Price
Anti-lock 4-wheel disc brakes	$499	$450	$449
XE and GXE require option pkg.			
XE option pkg.	1899	1632	1709
Air conditioning, AM/FM/cassette with digital clock, cruise control.			
GXE value option pkg.	1299	1116	1169
AM/FM/cassette with digital clock, air conditioning, cruise control, power antenna.			
Limited Edition, GXE w/option pkg.............	499	428	449
Remote keyless entry, anti-theft alarm, floormats, alloy wheels.			
Cruise control, XE	249	214	224
Requires automatic transmission.			
CD player, XE, GXE	469	349	422
Requires option pkg.			
3-disc CD changer, XE, GXE	669	511	602
Requires option pkg.			
CD/cassette player, GLE	399	343	359
Leather Trim Pkg., SE	1049	901	944
Includes adjustable lumbar support.			
Power sunroof, GXE, SE, GLE	849	730	764
GXE requires option pkg.			
Rear spoiler, XE, GXE, GLE	419	302	377
Floormats	79	52	71

NISSAN MAXIMA/ INFINITI I30

Specifications

	4-door notchback
Wheelbase, in.	106.3
Overall length, in.	187.7

Nissan Maxima GLE

	4-door notchback
Overall width, in.	69.7
Overall height, in.	55.7
Curb weight, lbs.	3001
Cargo vol., cu. ft.	14.5
Fuel capacity, gals.	18.5
Seating capacity	5

Engines

	dohc V-6
Size, liters/cu. in.	3.0/181
Horsepower @ rpm	190 @ 5600
Torque (lbs./ft.) @ rpm	205 @ 4000

EPA city/highway mpg

5-speed OD manual	22/27
4-speed OD automatic	21/28

Built in Japan.

PRICES

Nissan Maxima	Retail Price	Dealer Invoice	Fair Price
GXE 4-door notchback, 5-speed	$21499	$19470	—
GXE 4-door notchback, automatic	23249	20814	—
SE 4-door notchback, 5-speed	23299	20739	—
SE 4-door notchback, automatic	24299	21628	—
GLE 4-door notchback, automatic	26899	23943	—
Destination charge	420	420	420

Fair price not available at time of publication.

Prices are accurate at time of publication; subject to manufacturer's change.

Infiniti I30

Standard Equipment:

GXE: 3.0-liter DOHC V-6 engine, 5-speed manual or 4-speed automatic transmission, driver- and passenger-side air bags, 4-wheel disc brakes, air conditioning, power steering, cruise control, cloth reclining front bucket seats, multi-adjustable driver seat w/lumbar support, front storage console, cupholders, folding rear armrest w/trunk pass-through, power windows and door locks, power mirrors, tilt steering column, tinted glass, tachometer, coolant-temperature gauge, trip odometer, digital clock, 4-speaker AM/FM/cassette, diversity antenna, visor mirrors, intermittent wipers, rear defogger, remote decklid and fuel-door releases, map light, bright grille, 205/65R15 tires, wheel covers. **SE** adds: sport-tuned suspension, deluxe 6-speaker audio system with AM/FM/cassette/CD player, leather-wrapped steering wheel and shifter, fog lamps, rear spoiler, bright exhaust outlet, color-keyed grille, 215/55R15 tires, alloy wheels. **GLE** adds to GXE: 4-speed automatic transmission, automatic air conditioning, 8-way power driver seat, 4-way power passenger seat, leather upholstery, leather-wrapped steering wheel and shifter, simulated-wood interior trim, remote keyless entry, illuminated visor mirrors, variable intermittent wipers, remote keyless entry system with trunk release, theft-deterrent system, Bose 6-speaker audio system with AM/FM/cassette/CD player, Homelink universal garage-door opener, simulated-leather door panels, bright exhaust outlet, 205/65HR15 tires, alloy wheels.

Optional Equipment:	Retail Price	Dealer Invoice	Fair Price
Anti-lock brakes	$499	$450	—

	Retail Price	Dealer Invoice	Fair Price
Leather Trim Pkg., SE	$1349	$1159	—

Includes leather seats, 4-way power front passenger seat, automatic temperature control, simulated-leather door panels. Requires Security and Convenience Pkg. and power sunroof.

Cold Weather Pkg.	199	175	—

Includes heated front seats, heated outside mirrors, heavy-duty battery, low-windshield-washer-fluid warning light. GLE requires anti-lock brakes. SE and GXE require anti-lock brakes and Security and Convenience Pkg. NA GXE with 5-speed manual transmission.

Security and Convenience Pkg., GXE	699	615	—
SE	799	703	—

Includes 8-way power driver seat, remote keyless entry system, power trunk release, security system, illuminated visor vanity mirrors, variable intermittent wipers, Homelink universal garage-door opener (SE), 205/65HR15 high performance tires (GXE). SE requires power sunroof. NA GXE with 5-speed manual transmission.

Deluxe audio system with AM/FM/cassette/ CD player, GXE w/automatic	399	343	—

Requires Security and Convenience Pkg.

Bose audio system, SE	899	790	—

Requires Security and Convenience and power sunroof.

Power sunroof	899	772	—

GXE requires automatic transmission and Security and Convenience Pkg.

Infiniti I30	Retail Price	Dealer Invoice	Fair Price
4-door notchback, 5-speed	$28800	$25885	—
4-door notchback, automatic	28800	25885	—
Leather-Appointed 4-door notchback, automatic	29900	26270	—
I30t with Touring Package, 5-speed	31500	27676	—
I30t with Touring Package, automatic	32500	28555	—
Destination charge	495	495	495

Fair price not available at time of publication.

Standard Equipment:

Base: 3.0-liter DOHC V-6 engine, 5-speed manual or 4-speed automatic transmission, anti-lock 4-wheel disc brakes, variable-assist power steering, driver- and passenger-side air bags, automatic climate control, cloth power front bucket seats, console with armrest, cruise control, tilt steering column, AM/FM/cassette and CD player with six speakers, power antenna, tinted glass, rear defogger, power windows and door locks, power mirrors, remote fuel-door and deck-lid releases, remote keyless entry, anti-theft alarm, intermittent wipers, tachometer, coolant-temperature gauge, trip odometer, digital clock, leather-wrapped steering wheel, shifter knob, and parking brake handle, rear folding armrest, illuminated visor mirrors, map lights, fog lights, floormats, 205/65R15 all-season tires, cast alloy wheels. **Leather-Appointed** model adds: 4-speed automatic transmission, leather upholstery, power glass sunroof, Homelink remote control transmitter, automatic day/night inside mirror. **I30t** adds: 5-speed manual or 4-speed automatic transmission, limited-slip differential, sport suspension, Heated Seat Pkg. (heated front seats and mirrors, low-windshield-washer-fluid warning light, heavy-duty battery), decklid spoiler, 215/60HR15 touring tires, forged alloy wheels.

Optional Equipment:

	Retail Price	Dealer Invoice	Fair Price
Power glass sunroof, base	$950	$835	—
Requires 4-speed automatic transmission.			
Heated Seat Pkg., Leather-Appointed	400	351	—
Heated front seats and mirrors, low-windshield-washer-fluid warning light, heavy-duty battery.			
Heated Seat Pkg. delete, I30t (credit)	(400)	(351)	(351)
Limited-slip differential, Leather-Appointed .	830	729	—
Includes Heated Front Seat Pkg.			

NISSAN PATHFINDER/ INFINITI QX4

Specifications

	4-door wagon
Wheelbase, in.	106.3
Overall length, in.	178.3
Overall width, in.	68.7
Overall height, in.	67.1
Curb weight, lbs.	3675
Cargo vol., cu. ft.	85.0
Fuel capacity, gals.	20.8
Seating capacity	5

Engines

	ohc V-6
Size, liters/cu. in.	3.3/201

Nissan Pathfinder LE

	ohc V-6
Horsepower @ rpm	168 @ 4800
Torque (lbs./ft.) @ rpm	196 @ 2800
EPA city/highway mpg	
5-speed OD manual	16/18
4-speed OD automatic	15/19

Built in Japan.

PRICES

Nissan Pathfinder	Retail Price	Dealer Invoice	Fair Price
XE 2WD 4-door wagon, 5-speed	$22899	$20619	—
XE 2WD 4-door wagon, automatic	23899	21520	—
XE 4WD 4-door wagon, 5-speed	24899	22420	—
XE 4WD 4-door wagon, automatic	25899	23321	—
SE 4WD 4-door wagon, 5-speed	27949	25167	—
SE 4WD 4-door wagon, automatic	28949	26068	—
LE 2WD 4-door wagon, automatic	30449	27418	—
LE 4WD 4-door wagon, automatic	32849	29580	—
Destination charge	420	420	420

Fair price not available at time of publication.

Standard Equipment:

XE: 3.3-liter V-6 engine, 5-speed manual transmission or 4-speed automatic transmission, driver- and passenger-side air bags, power steering, anti-lock brakes, cloth upholstery, reclining front bucket seats, 60/40 split folding rear seat with reclining seatback and head

NISSAN

Infiniti QX4

restraints, center storage console with armrest, cupholders, tilt steering column, AM/FM/CD player, diversity antenna, digital clock, tachometer, coolant-temperature gauge, trip odometer, tinted glass, dual outside mirrors, passenger-side visor mirror, rear defogger, variable intermittent wipers, rear intermittent wiper/washer, remote fuel-door release, auxiliary power outlets, concealed storage bin, rear heat ducts (4WD), map lights, cargo cover (4WD), front and rear tow hooks, 235/70R15 tires, chromed steel wheels, full-size spare tire. **SE** adds: cruise control, moquette upholstery, multi-adjustable driver seat, rear folding armrest, heated power mirrors, power door locks and windows, remote keyless entry, theft-deterrent system, power antenna, privacy glass, illuminated visor mirrors, luggage rack, tubular step rail, fog lamps, rear wind deflector, fender flares, bright grille and bumper, mud guards, cargo net and cover, 265/70R15 tires, 6-spoke alloy wheels. **LE** deletes fender flares, tubular step rail, and adds: 4-speed automatic transmission, limited-slip differential (4WD), automatic air conditioning, leather upholstery, heated front seats (4WD), leather-wrapped steering wheel, wood-grain interior trim, simulated-leather door trim, digital compass and outside-temperature gauge, Bose AM/FM/cassette/CD player, Homelink universal garage-door opener, bright running boards, 235/70R15 tires, lacy-spoke alloy wheels.

Optional Equipment:

	Retail Price	Dealer Invoice	Fair Price
Air conditioning, XE	$999	$858	—
Automatic air conditioning, SE	1199	1030	—
Convenience Pkg., XE	1499	1288	—

Cruise control, power windows and door locks, heated power mirrors, remote keyless entry and vehicle security system, cargo cover and net, luggage rack. Requires air conditioning.

	Retail Price	Dealer Invoice	Fair Price
Sport Pkg., XE 2WD	$499	$428	—
XE 4WD	699	601	—

Includes limited-slip differential (4WD), black fender flares, fog lights, rear wind deflector. Requires Convenience Pkg.

Leather Trim Pkg., SE 4WD	1399	1201	—

Includes leather upholstery, leather-wrapped steering wheel, heated front seats, simulated leather door trim, compass, outside temperature gauge. Requires automatic air conditioning.

Off-Road Pkg., SE 4WD	249	214	—

Limited-slip rear differential, black bumpers. Requires Bose/Moonroof Pkg.

Luxury Pkg., LE	1299	1116	—

Power moonroof, power front seats.

Bose/Moonroof Pkg., SE	1549	1331	—

Power moonroof, Bose AM/FM/cassette/CD player, power antenna, Homelink universal garage-door opener. Requires automatic air conditioning.

Cassette player, XE, SE	389	287	—
Rear wind deflector, XE	89	68	—
Woodgrain interior trim, XE, SE	299	212	—
Alloy wheels, XE	849	588	—
Spare tire carrier, XE, SE	299	257	—

XE requires Sport Pkg. SE requires Off-Road Pkg.

Infiniti QX4	Retail Price	Dealer Invoice	Fair Price
4-door wagon	$35550	$31666	—
Destination charge	495	495	495

Fair price not available at time of publication.

Standard Equipment:

3.3-liter V-6 engine, 4-speed automatic transmission, All-Mode 4-wheel drive, anti-lock brakes, automatic climate control, driver- and passenger-side air bags, variable-assist power steering, cruise control, leather upholstery, power front bucket seats, reclining 60/40 split folding rear seat, rear armrest, center storage console w/armrest, overhead storage console (includes outside-temperature indicator, compass, map lights), cupholders, tilt steering column, power windows, heated power mirrors, leather-wrapped steering wheel and shifter, tachometer, trip odometer, tinted glass, 6-speaker Bose audio system with AM/FM/cassette/CD player, integrated diversity antenna, remote keyless entry w/theft-deterrent system, variable intermittent wipers, intermittent rear wiper, rear defogger, remote

NISSAN

fuel-door and hatch releases, auxiliary power outlet, illuminated visor mirrors, wood interior trim, cargo net and cover, rear storage bin, floormats, fog lights, step rail, roof rack, mud guards, fuel-tank skid plates, 245/70R16 tires, alloy wheels.

Optional Equipment:

	Retail Price	Dealer Invoice	Fair Price
Premium Sport Pkg.	$1650	$1467	—
Limited-slip rear differential, heated front seats, power sunroof.			
Heated front seats	400	355	—
Requires sunroof.			
Power sunroof	950	845	—

NISSAN QUEST

Nissan Quest XE

Specifications

	3-door van
Wheelbase, in.	112.2
Overall length, in.	189.9
Overall width, in.	73.7
Overall height, in.	65.6
Curb weight, lbs.	3865
Cargo vol., cu. ft.	114.8
Fuel capacity, gals.	20.0
Seating capacity	7

Engines

	ohc V-6
Size, liters/cu. in.	3.0/181
Horsepower @ rpm	151 @ 4800
Torque (lbs./ft.) @ rpm	174 @ 4400

EPA city/highway mpg

4-speed OD automatic 17/23

Built in Avon Lake, Ohio.

PRICES

Nissan Quest	Retail Price	Dealer Invoice	Fair Price
XE 3-door van	$21249	$18913	$19713
GXE 3-door van	26049	23186	23986
Destination charge	470	470	470

Standard Equipment:

XE: 3.0-liter V-6 engine, 4-speed automatic transmission, driver- and passenger-side air bags, front air conditioning, power steering, cloth upholstery, reclining front bucket seats, 2-passenger second-row bench seat and 3-passenger rear bench seat, front storage console, tilt steering column, tachometer, trip odometer, coolant-temperature gauge, AM/FM/cassette/CD player, diversity antenna, digital clock, tinted glass, dual outside mirrors, rear defogger, visor mirrors, variable intermittent wipers, intermittent rear wiper/washer, cornering lamps, floormats, 205/75R15 tires, wheel covers. **GXE** adds: anti-lock 4-wheel disc brakes, rear air conditioning, rear climate controls, cruise control, upgraded cloth upholstery, 8-way power driver seat, second row captain's chairs, power windows and door locks, heated power mirrors, illuminated visor mirrors, rear audio controls, power antenna, leather-wrapped steering wheel w/audio controls, remote keyless entry, theft-deterrent system, roof rack, side and rear privacy glass, map lights, automatic headlamps, rear auxiliary power outlets, lockable underseat storage, cargo net, alloy wheels.

Optional Equipment:

Rear air conditioning,			
XE	649	558	597
Requires Convenience Pkg., Power and Glass Pkg.			
Anti-lock 4-wheel			
disc brakes, XE	499	428	459
Handling Pkg., GXE	549	472	505
Tuned springs and shock absorbers, rear stabilizer bar, trailer wiring harness, full-size spare tire, 215/70R15 tires. Requires Luxury Pkg.			
Power and Glass			
Pkg., XE	1249	1074	1149
Power windows and door locks, heated mirrors, side and rear privacy glass.			

Prices are accurate at time of publication; subject to manufacturer's change.

	Retail Price	Dealer Invoice	Fair Price
Convenience Pkg., XE	$649	$558	$597

Cruise control, remote keyless entry, theft-deterrent system, illuminated passenger-side visor mirror, lockable underseat storage, roof rack, cargo net. Requires Power and Glass Pkg.

	Retail Price	Dealer Invoice	Fair Price
Touring Pkg., XE	999	858	919

6-disc CD changer, leather-wrapped steering wheel w/radio controls, trailer wiring harness, full-size spare tire, alloy wheels. Requires rear air conditioning, Convenience Pkg., and Power and Glass Pkg.

Leather Trim Pkg., GXE	1299	1116	1195

Leather upholstery, 4-way power passenger seat. NA w/integrated child seats. Requires Luxury Pkg.

Luxury Pkg., GXE	1249	1074	1149

6-disc CD changer, semi-automatic air conditioning, power sunroof.

Second-row captain's chairs, XE	599	514	569

Requires rear air conditioning, Convenience Pkg., Power and Glass Pkg.

Integrated child seats, XE	199	170	183

Requires rear air conditioning, Convenience Pkg., and Power and Glass Pkg. Middle bench seat replaces captain's chairs on GXE. NA with Leather Trim Pkg.

2-tone paint	299	257	275

NISSAN SENTRA/200SX

Nissan Sentra XE

Specifications

	2-door notchback	4-door notchback
Wheelbase, in.	99.8	99.8

Nissan 200SX SE

	2-door notchback	4-door notchback
Overall length, in.	170.1	170.1
Overall width, in.	66.6	66.6
Overall height, in.	54.2	54.5
Curb weight, lbs.	2330	2315
Cargo vol., cu. ft.	10.4	10.7
Fuel capacity, gals.	13.2	13.2
Seating capacity	4	5

Engines

	dohc I-4	dohc I-4
Size, liters/cu. in.	1.6/97	2.0/122
Horsepower @ rpm	115 @ 6000	140 @ 6400
Torque (lbs./ft.) @ rpm	108 @ 4000	132 @ 4800

EPA city/highway mpg

5-speed OD manual	29/39	23/31
4-speed OD automatic	27/36	23/30

Built in Smyrna, Tenn.

PRICES

Nissan Sentra	Retail Price	Dealer Invoice	Fair Price
4-door notchback, 5-speed	$11499	$10950	$11450
XE 4-door notchback, 5-speed	13649	12714	13214
XE 4-door notchback, automatic	14449	13459	13959
GXE 4-door notchback, 5-speed	14799	13402	13902
GXE 4-door notchback, automatic	15599	14127	14627
GLE 4-door notchback, 5-speed	15649	14172	14672

Prices are accurate at time of publication; subject to manufacturer's change.

NISSAN

	Retail Price	Dealer Invoice	Fair Price
GLE 4-door notchback, automatic	$16199	$14670	$15170
Destination charge	420	420	420

Standard Equipment:

1.6-liter DOHC 4-cylinder engine, 5-speed manual transmission, driver- and passenger-side air bags, cloth reclining front bucket seats, front console, cupholders, tinted glass, tilt steering column, driver-side outside mirror, coolant-temperature gauge, trip odometer, rear defogger, auxiliary power outlet, 155/80R13 tires. **XE** adds: 5-speed manual or 4-speed automatic transmission, power steering, air conditioning, AM/FM/cassette, digital clock, intermittent wipers, remote decklid and fuel-door releases, dual outside mirrors, 175/70R13 tires, wheel covers. **GXE** adds: cruise control, split folding rear seat, upgraded cloth upholstery, power windows and door locks, power mirrors, passenger-side visor mirror, bodyside moldings, cargo light. **GLE** adds: velour upholstery, fold front armrest (w/automatic), remote keyless entry, theft-deterrent system, tachometer, 175/65R14 tires, alloy wheels.

Optional Equipment:

Anti-lock brakes, GXE, GLE	499	450	474
Includes 4-wheel disc brakes.			
Power moonroof, GLE	449	386	427
3-disc CD changer	669	511	636
CD player	469	349	446
Rear spoiler	339	246	322

Nissan 200SX	Retail Price	Dealer Invoice	Fair Price
2-door notchback, 5-speed	$12999	$12377	$12877
2-door notchback, automatic	13799	13139	13639
SE 2-door notchback, 5-speed	15349	13980	14480
SE 2-door notchback, automatic	16149	14708	15208
SE-R 2-door notchback, 5-speed	16749	15255	15755
SE-R 2-door notchback, automatic	17549	15984	16484
Destination charge	470	470	470

Standard Equipment:

1.6-liter DOHC 4-cylinder engine, 5-speed manual or 4-speed automatic transmission, power steering, driver- and passenger-side air bags, cloth upholstery, reclining front bucket seats, cupholders, power mirrors, tinted glass, tilt steering column, tachometer, coolant-temperature gauge, trip odometer, rear defogger, intermittent wipers, remote decklid and fuel-door releases, rear spoiler, 175/70R13 tires, wheel covers. **SE** adds: air conditioning, cruise control, upgraded cloth upholstery, front sport bucket seats, split folding rear seat, AM/FM/cassette, digital clock, power windows and door locks, fog lights, color-keyed bodyside moldings and door handles, 175/65R14 tires, alloy wheels. **SE-R** adds: 2.0-liter DOHC 4-cylinder engine, 4-wheel disc brakes, limited-slip differential, remote keyless entry, theft-deterrent system, leather-wrapped steering wheel and shifter, 195/55R15 tires.

Optional Equipment:

	Retail Price	Dealer Invoice	Fair Price
Anti-lock brakes, SE, SE-R	$499	$450	$474
SE includes 4-wheel disc brakes.			
Value Option Pkg., base	999	858	950
Air conditioning, AM/FM/cassette.			
Power sunroof, SE, SE-R	449	386	427
3-disc CD changer	669	511	636
CD player	469	349	446
Floormats	79	52	75

NISSAN 240SX

Nissan 240SX SE

Specifications

	2-door notchback
Wheelbase, in.	99.4
Overall length, in.	177.2
Overall width, in.	68.1
Overall height, in.	51.0
Curb weight, lbs.	2800
Cargo vol., cu. ft.	8.6

Prices are accurate at time of publication; subject to manufacturer's change.

NISSAN

	2-door notchback
Fuel capacity, gals.	17.2
Seating capacity	4

Engines

	dohc I-4
Size, liters/cu. in.	2.4/146
Horsepower @ rpm	155 @ 5600
Torque (lbs./ft.) @ rpm	160 @ 4400

EPA city/highway mpg

5-speed OD manual	22/28
4-speed OD automatic	21/27

Built in Japan.

PRICES

Nissan 240SX	Retail Price	Dealer Invoice	Fair Price
Base 2-door notchback, 5-speed	$18359	$16437	$16737
Base 2-door notchback, automatic	19159	17153	17453
SE 2-door notchback, 5-speed	21999	19695	19995
SE 2-door notchback, automatic	22799	20411	20711
LE 2-door notchback, 5-speed	24449	21888	22188
LE 2-door notchback, automatic	25249	22605	22905
Destination charge	470	470	470

Standard Equipment:

Base: 2.4-liter 4-cylinder engine, 5-speed manual or 4-speed automatic transmission, 4-wheel disc brakes, driver- and passenger-side air bags, power steering, cloth reclining front bucket seats, folding rear seat w/trunk pass-through, center storage console, power windows, power mirrors, tachometer, trip odometer, digital clock, tinted glass, rear defogger, remote fuel-door release, 195/60HR15 tires, wheel covers. **SE** adds: air conditioning, cruise control, tilt steering column, power door locks, AM/FM/cassette w/four speakers, intermittent wipers, remote decklid release, passenger-side visor mirror, cloth door trim, rear spoiler, fog lamps, sport-tuned suspension, rear stabilizer bar, dual chrome exhaust outlets, 205/55VR16 tires, alloy wheels. **LE** adds: leather upholstery, leather-wrapped steering wheel and shifter, power sunroof, CD player w/six speakers, power diversity antenna, remote keyless entry w/theft-deterrent system.

Optional Equipment:

	Retail Price	Dealer Invoice	Fair Price
Air conditioning, base	$999	$858	$919
Anti-lock brakes, SE, LE	699	629	643
Includes limited-slip differential.			
Popular Equipment Pkg., base	1449	1245	1333
Air conditioning, cruise control, cassette player. Requires Power and Convenience Pkg.			
Power and Convenience Pkg., base	649	558	597
Tilt steering wheel, power door locks and mirrors, passenger-side visor mirror, cloth door trim, intermittent wipers, remote decklid release, alloy wheels.			
Power sunroof, base, SE	899	772	827
Base requires Popular Equipment Pkg. and Power and Convenience Pkg.			
CD player, base, SE	469	349	431
Base requires Popular Equipment Pkg.			
3-disc CD changer	669	511	615
Base requires Popular Equipment Pkg.			
Floormats	79	52	73
Pearlglow paint	399	343	367

OLDSMOBILE ACHIEVA/ BUICK SKYLARK

Oldsmobile Achieva 4-door

Specifications

	2-door notchback	4-door notchback
Wheelbase, in.	103.4	103.4
Overall length, in.	187.9	187.9

Prices are accurate at time of publication; subject to manufacturer's change.

OLDSMOBILE

Buick Skylark Limited 4-door

	2-door notchback	4-door notchback
Overall width, in.	68.6	68.1
Overall height, in.	53.4	53.4
Curb weight, lbs.	2886	2917
Cargo vol., cu. ft.	14.0	14.0
Fuel capacity, gals.	15.2	15.2
Seating capacity	5	5

Engines

	dohc I-4	ohv V-6
Size, liters/cu. in.	2.4/146	3.1/191
Horsepower @ rpm	150 @ 5600	155 @ 5200
Torque (lbs./ft.) @ rpm	155 @ 4400	185 @ 4000
EPA city/highway mpg		
5-speed OD manual	23/33	
4-speed OD automatic	22/32	20/29

Built in Lansing, Mich.

PRICES

Oldsmobile Achieva	Retail Price	Dealer Invoice	Fair Price
Series I 2-door notchback	$15425	$14114	—
Series I 4-door notchback	15225	13931	—
Series II 2-door notchback	16975	15532	—
Series II 4-door notchback	16775	15349	—
Destination charge	525	525	525

Fair price not available at time of publication.

Standard Equipment:

Series I: 2.4-liter DOHC 4-cylinder engine, 4-speed automatic transmission, anti-lock brakes, driver- and passenger-side air bags, air conditioning, Enhanced Traction System, cruise control (2-door), power steering, tilt steering wheel, cloth reclining front bucket seats w/driver-side lumbar support, front console (armrest, storage, cupholders, and auxiliary power outlet), power mirrors, power door locks, tachometer, coolant-temperature gauge, 4-speaker AM/FM radio, digital clock, rear-window grid antenna, tinted glass, PassLock theft-deterrent system, rear defogger, intermittent wipers, remote fuel-door and decklid releases, illuminated entry/exit, reading/map/courtesy lights, visor mirrors, daytime running lamps, floormats, 195/65R15 touring tires, bolt-on wheel covers. **Series II** adds: cruise control, split folding rear seat, power windows, cassette player w/automatic tone control, alloy wheels. **All 2-door models** add: Sport Pkg. (rear spoiler, leather-wrapped steering wheel and shifter, fog lights).

Optional Equipment:	Retail Price	Dealer Invoice	Fair Price
3.1-liter V-6	$457	$407	—
Includes variable-effort power steering. NA Series I 4-door.			
5-speed manual transmission (credit)	(550)	(490)	(490)
NA Series II 4-door.			
Economy Pkg., Series I (credit)	(755)	(521)	(521)
5-speed manual transmission, 195/70R14 all-season tires.			
Sport Pkg., Series II 4-door	224	193	—
Rear spoiler, leather-wrapped steering wheel and shifter, fog lights.			
Convenience Pkg., Series II	395	352	—
6-way power driver seat, remote keyless entry.			
Split folding rear seat, Series I	150	134	—
Power glass sunroof, Series II	595	530	—
Power windows, Series I 2-door	270	240	—
Series I 4-door	340	303	—
Cruise control, Series I 4-door	225	200	—
Cassette player, Series I	220	196	—
Includes automatic tone control.			
CD/cassette player, Series II	260	231	—
Includes automatic tone control, six speakers.			
Engine block heater	18	16	—

Buick Skylark	Retail Price	Dealer Invoice	Fair Price
Custom 2-door notchback	$15970	$15092	$15392
Custom 4-door notchback	15970	15092	15392
Destination charge	525	525	525

Prices are accurate at time of publication; subject to manufacturer's change.

OLDSMOBILE

Standard Equipment:

2.4-liter DOHC 4-cylinder engine, 4-speed automatic transmission, driver- and passenger-side air bags, anti-lock brakes, traction control, air conditioning, power steering, tilt steering wheel, cloth 55/45 split bench seat with seatback recliners, 4-way manual driver seat, front storage armrest with cupholders, trip odometer, coolant-temperature gauge, AM/FM radio with clock, tinted glass, intermittent wipers, rear defogger, automatic power door locks, Passlock theft-deterrent system, remote fuel door and decklid releases, remote mirrors, front and rear courtesy lights, visor mirrors, floormats, 195/70R14 tires, and wheel covers.

Optional Equipment:

	Retail Price	Dealer Invoice	Fair Price
3.1-liter V-6 engine	$395	$340	$352
Limited Pkg. SB	988	850	879

Cruise control, power mirrors (black), power windows, cassette player, cargo net, polycast wheels.

Gran Sport Pkg. SC	2306	1983	2052

Pkg. SK plus 3.1-liter V-6 engine, gran touring suspension, bucket seats, driver-side lumber support, analog gauge cluster (tachometer, trip odometer, voltmeter, oil-pressure and coolant-temperature gauges), deluxe headliner (assist handles, lighted visor vanity mirrors, extendable sunshade, reading lamps), color-keyed grille, blackout exterior trim, 205/55R16 tires, alloy wheels.

Cruise control, Custom	225	194	200
6-way power driver's seat	270	232	240

Requires rear-window antenna. Custom also requires power windows and mirrors.

Bucket seats with full console and driver-side lumbar support	175	151	156

Requires cruise control and analog gauge cluster.

Leather/cloth trim, Limited	620	533	552
Gran Sport	495	426	441

Includes leather-wrapped steering wheel and shifter and split folding rear seat. Limited includes analog gauge cluster.

Analog gauge cluster	126	108	112

Includes tachometer, trip odometer, voltmeter, oil-pressure and coolant-temperature gauges. Requires cruise control and bucket seats.

Deluxe headliner, Limited	135	116	120

Includes assist handles, lighted visor vanity mirrors, extendable sunshade, reading lamps. NA with power sunroof.

Power windows, Custom 2-door	290	249	258
Custom 4-door	355	305	316

4-door includes passenger lockout.

	Retail Price	Dealer Invoice	Fair Price
Power sunroof, Limited, Gran Sport	$595	$512	$530

Includes covered vanity mirrors, extendable sunshades, and reading lamps. NA with deluxe headliner. Deletes deluxe headliner on Gran Sport.

Power mirrors (black), Custom	78	67	69

Requires power windows.

Remote keyless entry system	135	116	120

Requires rear-window antenna. Custom also requires power windows and mirrors.

Cassette player, Custom	195	168	174
Cassette player with			
auto tone control	220	189	196
Limited, Gran Sport	25	22	23

Requires Concert Sound II speakers.

CD/cassette player,			
Custom	420	361	374
Limited, Gran Sport	225	194	200

Includes auto tone control. Requires Concert Sound II speakers.

Concert Sound II			
speakers	45	39	40

NA with with base AM/FM radio.

Steering-wheel-mounted			
radio controls	125	108	111

Requires cassette player with auto tone control or CD/cassette player.

Rear-window			
antenna	22	19	20

Requires power windows.

Cargo net	30	26	27
Engine block			
heater	18	15	16
15-inch styled wheel covers,			
Custom	28	24	25
Limited	(75)	(65)	(65)

Requires 195/65R15 tires.

14-inch polycast wheels,			
Custom	115	99	102

NA with optional tires.

195/65R15 tires, Custom,			
Limited	131	113	117

Requires 15-inch styled wheel covers.

195/70R14 whitewall tires,			
Custom, Limited	72	62	64

NA with 14-inch polycast wheels or 15-inch styled wheel covers.

OLDSMOBILE AURORA

Oldsmobile Aurora

Specifications

	4-door notchback
Wheelbase, in.	113.8
Overall length, in.	205.4
Overall width, in.	74.4
Overall height, in.	55.4
Curb weight, lbs.	3967
Cargo vol., cu. ft.	16.1
Fuel capacity, gals.	20.0
Seating capacity	5

Engines

	dohc V-8
Size, liters/cu. in.	4.0/244
Horsepower @ rpm	250 @ 5600
Torque (lbs./ft.) @ rpm	260 @ 4400

EPA city/highway mpg

4-speed OD automatic	17/26

Built in Orion, Mich.

PRICES

Oldsmobile Aurora	Retail Price	Dealer Invoice	Fair Price
4-door notchback	$35735	$32340	—

	Retail Price	Dealer Invoice	Fair Price
Destination charge	$665	$665	$665

Fair price not available at time of publication.

Standard Equipment:

4.0-liter DOHC V-8 engine, 4-speed automatic transmission, anti-lock 4-wheel disc brakes, driver- and passenger-side air bags, traction control, variable-assist power steering, automatic climate control system with inside/outside temperature indicator, leather upholstery, power front bucket seats with power lumbar support and driver-side 2-position memory, center storage console with leather-wrapped shifter and auxiliary power source, overhead storage console, folding rear armrest with trunk pass-through, solar-control tinted glass, cruise control, power windows, automatic programmable door locks, power memory mirrors with defoggers, automatic day/night rearview mirror with compass, AM/FM/cassette/CD player, integrated antenna, steering-wheel climate and radio controls, leather-wrapped steering wheel, interior wood trim, lighted visor mirrors, power fuel-door and deck-lid release, intermittent wipers, tilt steering wheel, Pass-Key theft-deterrent system, remote keyless illuminated entry/exit system, Driver Information System, tachometer, engine-coolant temperature gauge, trip odometer, oil-level sensor, universal garage-door opener, rear defogger, Twilight Sentinel automatic headlamp control, fog lamps, cornering lamps, dual exhaust outlets, cargo net, floormats, 235/60R16 tires, alloy wheels.

Optional Equipment:

Power sunroof	995	886	—
Cloth upholstery	NC	NC	NC
Heated driver and front passenger seats	295	263	—
Bose Acoustimass Sound System	871	775	—
12-disc CD changer	460	409	—
White diamond paint	395	352	—
Gold Graphics Pkg.	50	45	—
Autobahn Pkg.	395	352	—
Includes 3.71 axle ratio and 235/60VR16 tires.			
Chrome wheels	800	712	—
Engine block heater	18	16	—

Prices are accurate at time of publication; subject to manufacturer's change.

OLDSMOBILE CUTLASS SUPREME

Oldsmobile Cutlass Supreme 4-door

Specifications

	2-door notchback	4-door notchback
Wheelbase, in.	107.5	107.5
Overall length, in.	193.9	193.7
Overall width, in.	71.0	71.0
Overall height, in.	53.3	54.8
Curb weight, lbs.	3286	3388
Cargo vol., cu. ft.	15.5	15.5
Fuel capacity, gals.	17.1	17.1
Seating capacity	5	6

Engines

	ohv V-6
Size, liters/cu. in.	3.1/191
Horsepower @ rpm	160 @ 5200
Torque (lbs./ft.) @ rpm	185 @ 4000

EPA city/highway mpg

4-speed OD automatic	20/29

Built in Doraville, Ga.

PRICES

Oldsmobile Cutlass Supreme	Retail Price	Dealer Invoice	Fair Price
Series I 2-door notchback	$18950	$17339	—

	Retail Price	Dealer Invoice	Fair Price
Series I 4-door notchback	$18950	$17339	—
Series II 2-door notchback	19850	18163	—
Series II 4-door notchback	19850	18163	—
Series III 2-door notchback	20750	18986	—
Series III 4-door notchback	20750	18986	—
Destination charge	550	550	550

Fair price not available at time of publication.

Standard Equipment:

Series I: 3.1-liter V-6 engine, 4-speed automatic transmission, anti-lock brakes, driver- and passenger-side air bags, power steering, air conditioning, cruise control, cloth reclining front bucket seats, tilt steering wheel, tachometer, center console with storage armrest and cupholders, automatic programmable door locks, 4-speaker AM/FM/cassette, digital clock, power windows, power mirrors, rear defogger, intermittent wipers, illuminated entry system, courtesy/reading lights, Pass-Key theft-deterrent system, fog lamps, visor mirrors, remote decklid release, rear spoiler (2-door), floormats, 215/60R16 performance tires, alloy wheels. **Series II** adds: 6-way power driver seat, leather-wrapped steering wheel, remote keyless entry system, 6-speaker sound system, power antenna, illuminated visor mirrors. **Series III** adds: leather upholstery, split folding rear seat, automatic front/rear air conditioning with inside/outside thermometer, variable-assist steering, steering-wheel radio and air-conditioning controls.

Optional Equipment:

55/45 front seats, Series I and II 4-doors	NC	NC	NC
Cloth upholstery, Series III	NC	NC	NC
Power sunroof, Series III	695	619	—
CD/cassette player	200	178	—
Remote keyless entry, Series I	125	111	—
Engine block heater	18	16	—

PONTIAC BONNEVILLE

Specifications

	4-door notchback
Wheelbase, in.	110.8
Overall length, in.	200.5
Overall width, in.	74.5
Overall height, in.	55.7

Prices are accurate at time of publication; subject to manufacturer's change.

Pontiac Bonneville SSEi

Specifications

	4-door notchback
Curb weight, lbs.	3446
Cargo vol., cu. ft.	18.0
Fuel capacity, gals.	18.0
Seating capacity	6

Engines

	ohv V-6	Supercharged ohv V-6
Size, liters/cu. in.	3.8/231	3.8/231
Horsepower @ rpm	205 @ 4800	240 @ 5200
Torque (lbs./ft.) @ rpm	230 @ 3200	280 @ 3200

EPA city/highway mpg

	ohv V-6	Supercharged ohv V-6
4-speed OD automatic	19/28	18/28

Built in Flint, Mich.

PRICES

Pontiac Bonneville	Retail Price	Dealer Invoice	Fair Price
SE 4-door notchback sedan	$22234	$20122	$20622
SSE 4-door notchback sedan	27164	24583	25083
Destination charge	605	605	605

Standard Equipment:

SE: 3.8-liter V-6 engine, 4-speed automatic transmission, anti-lock brakes, air conditioning, driver- and passenger-side air bags, power steering, cruise control, cloth 45/55 split bench seat with storage armrest and cupholders, tilt steering wheel, power windows, power door locks, 4-speaker AM/FM radio, digital clock, tinted glass, left remote and right manual outside mirrors, coolant-temperature and oil-pressure gauges, voltmeter, tachometer, trip odometer, rear defogger, intermittent wipers, Pass-Key II theft-deterrent system, visor mirrors, daytime running lamps, Twilight Sentinel, Lamp Group (includes rear courtesy lights, rear assist handles, headlamp-on warning, trunk light), fog lights, floormats, 215/65R15 touring tires, bolt-on wheel covers. **SSE** adds: automatic climate control w/outside temperature indicator, electronic load leveling, variable-assist power steering, 45/45 cloth bucket seats with center storage console and rear vents, rear armrest w/cupholders, overhead console with power outlet, 6-way power driver seat, heated power mirrors, cassette player with equalizer and 6-speaker sound system, leather-wrapped steering wheel with radio controls, power antenna, Driver Information Center, remote keyless entry, remote decklid release, lower-body cladding, emergency road kit (includes spot light, first aid kit, air hose, windshield scraper, gloves), illuminated entry, illuminated visor mirrors, trunk net, decklid spoiler, dual exhaust, 225/60R16 touring tires, 3-spoke alloy wheels.

Optional Equipment:

	Retail Price	Dealer Invoice	Fair Price
Supercharged 3.8-liter V-6 engine, SE	$1362	$1212	$1226
SSE	1342	1194	1208
SSE with Group 1SB	1167	1039	1050

Includes traction control. SE requires Group 1SD. SSE includes SSEi Supercharger Pkg. (boost gauge, driver-selectable shift controls, 2.97 axle ratio, SSE badging and floormats, 225/60HR16 tires).

Option Group 1SB, SE	848	755	763

Variable-effort power steering, illuminated entry, cassette player, 6-way power driver's seat, power mirrors, remote decklid release, trunk net.

Option Group 1SC, SE	1314	1169	1183

Group 1SB plus automatic climate control, remote keyless entry system, leather-wrapped steering wheel, lighted visor mirrors.

Option Group 1SD, SE	3084	2745	2776

Group 1SC plus Sport Luxury Edition equipment (3.06 rear axle ratio, 6-speaker sound system, power antenna, 45/45 leather bucket seats, rear spoiler, 225/60R16 touring tires, 5-blade alloy wheels).

Option Group 1SB, SSE	1455	1295	1310

Traction control, 6-way power passenger seat, EYE-CUE head-up display, automatic day/night rearview mirror, CD player w/Bose 8-speaker system, anti-theft alarm.

PONTIAC

	Retail Price	Dealer Invoice	Fair Price
Computer Command Ride/Handling Pkg., SE			
with Group 1SC	$1183	$1053	$1065
with Group 1SD	775	690	698
with Group 1SD and supercharged 3.8-liter V-6 engine	600	534	540

Computer Command Ride, traction control, electronic load leveling, 3.06 rear axle ratio (with std. engine), 225/60R16 touring tires (with std. engine) or 225/60HR16 tires (with supercharged engine). Requires leather bucket seats and alloy wheels.

	Retail Price	Dealer Invoice	Fair Price
Traction control	175	156	158

SE requires option group, bucket seats, and alloy wheels.

	Retail Price	Dealer Invoice	Fair Price
Computer Command Ride, SSE with Group 1SB	380	338	342
Power glass sunroof, SE	995	886	896
SE with bucket seats, SSE	981	873	883

SE requires alloy wheels, option group.

	Retail Price	Dealer Invoice	Fair Price
Cloth 45/45 bucket seats, SE	314	279	283
with group 1SC	218	194	196
with group 1SD	NC	NC	NC

Includes center storage console and rear vents, lighted visor mirrors, overhead console with power outlet.

	Retail Price	Dealer Invoice	Fair Price
Leather 45/45 bucket seats, SE			
with group 1SB	1213	1080	1092
with group 1SC	1067	950	960
with group 1SB	NC	NC	NC

Includes center storage console and rear vents, rear seat storage armrest, leather-wrapped steering wheel, overhead console with power outlet.

	Retail Price	Dealer Invoice	Fair Price
45/45 leather bucket seats, SSE	779	693	701
45/45 articulating leather bucket seats, SSE	1329	1183	1196
SSE with Group 1SB	1024	911	922
6-way power driver's seat, SE	305	271	275
6-way power passenger seat	305	271	275

SE requires option group and alloy wheels when ordered with group 1SB or 1SC.

	Retail Price	Dealer Invoice	Fair Price
Remote keyless entry system, SE with Group 1SB	150	134	135
Cassette player, SE	195	174	176
SSE w/group 1SB (credit)	(100)	(89)	(89)

SSE includes Bose 8-speaker system.

	Retail Price	Dealer Invoice	Fair Price
CD player, SE	295	263	266

	Retail Price	Dealer Invoice	Fair Price
SE w/option group	$100	$89	$90
Cassette player with equalizer, SE			
with Group 1SB or 1SC	385	343	347
with leather upholstery and Group 1SB or 1SC	335	298	302
with Group 1SD	150	133	135

Includes leather-wrapped steering wheel with radio controls, power antenna. SE includes 6-speaker sound system. Requires alloy wheels when ordered with group 1SB or 1SC.

	Retail Price	Dealer Invoice	Fair Price
CD player with equalizer,			
SE with Group 1SB or 1SC	485	432	437
with leather upholstery and Group 1SB or 1SC	435	387	392
with Group 1SD	250	223	225
SSE	100	89	90

SE includes leather-wrapped steering wheel with radio controls, power antenna. SE includes 6-speaker sound system. SE requires alloy wheels when ordered with group 1SB or 1SC.

	Retail Price	Dealer Invoice	Fair Price
6-speaker sound system, SE	100	89	90

Requires alloy wheels.

Power antenna, SE	85	76	77

Requires option group.

Leather-wrapped steering wheel with radio controls, SE with Group 1SB	175	156	158
with leather upholstery, or with Group 1SC or 1SD	125	111	113
Anti-theft alarm	190	169	171

SE requires Group 1SC or 1SD.

Rear decklid spoiler, SE	110	98	99
Rear decklid spoiler delete (credit)	(110)	(98)	(98)

SE requires Group 1SD.

16-inch 5-blade alloy wheels, SE	324	288	292
SE w/1SC and Computer Command Ride/Handling Pkg., SSE	NC	NC	NC

Requires 225/60R16 tires.

16-inch gold or silver crosslace alloy wheels	324	288	292
SE w/Group 1SD, SE w/1SC and Computer Command Ride/Handling Pkg., SSE	NC	NC	NC

SE requires 225/60R16 tires.

16-inch Chrome Torque Star alloy wheels, SE	919	818	827

PONTIAC

	Retail Price	Dealer Invoice	Fair Price
SE w/Group 1SD, SE w/1SC and Computer Command Ride/Handling Pkg., SSE	$595	$530	$536
Requires 225/60R16 tires.			
225/60R16 blackwall touring tires, SE	84	75	76
Requires alloy wheels.			
Engine block heater	20	18	19

PONTIAC GRAND AM

Pontiac Grand Am GT 2-door

Specifications

	2-door notchback	4-door notchback
Wheelbase, in.	103.4	103.4
Overall length, in.	186.9	186.9
Overall width, in.	68.3	68.3
Overall height, in.	53.5	53.5
Curb weight, lbs.	2835	2877
Cargo vol., cu. ft.	13.4	13.4
Fuel capacity, gals.	15.2	15.2
Seating capacity	5	5

Engines

	dohc I-4	ohv V-6
Size, liters/cu. in.	2.4/146	3.1/191
Horsepower @ rpm	150 @ 6000	155 @ 5200
Torque (lbs./ft.) @ rpm	155 @ 4400	185 @ 4000

EPA city/highway mpg	dohc I-4	ohv V-6
5-speed OD manual	23/33	
4-speed OD automatic......................................	22/32	20/29

Built in Lansing, Mich.

PRICES

Pontiac Grand Am	Retail Price	Dealer Invoice	Fair Price
SE 2-door notchback	$14734	$13482	$13882
SE 4-door notchback	14734	13482	13882
GT 2-door notchback	15974	14616	15016
GT 4-door notchback	15974	14616	15016
Destination charge	525	525	525

Fair price not available at time of publication.

Standard Equipment:

SE: 2.4-liter DOHC 4-cylinder engine, 5-speed manual transmission, air conditioning, anti-lock brakes, driver- and passenger-side air bags, power steering, cloth reclining front bucket seats, center console (armrest, storage, and cupholders), overhead compartment, rear-seat headrests, left remote and right manual outside mirrors, AM/FM radio, tinted glass, power door locks, remote fuel-door and decklid release, tachometer, coolant-temperature gauge, trip odometer, illuminated entry, visor mirrors, daytime running lamps, fog lights, floormats, 195/70R14 tires, wheel covers. **GT** adds: leather-wrapped steering wheel, shifter, and parking-brake handle, tilt steering wheel, intermittent wipers, decklid spoiler, 205/55R16 performance tires, alloy wheels.

Optional Equipment:

3.1-liter V-6 engine	450	400	410

Requires 4-speed automatic transmission. SE requires 195/65R15 or 205/55R16 tires.

4-speed automatic transmission	810	721	737

Includes traction control.

Option Group 1SB,

SE	825	734	751

Cruise control, cassette player, intermittent wipers, rear defogger, tilt steering wheel.

Option Group 1SC,

SE 2-door	1582	1408	1440
SE 4-door...	1647	1466	1499

Group 1SB plus variable-effort power steering, power windows, power mirrors, split folding rear seat, remote keyless entry.

	Retail Price	Dealer Invoice	Fair Price
Option Group 1SB, GT	$672	$598	$612
Cruise control, cassette player, rear defogger, variable-effort power steering.			
Option Group 1SC, GT 2-door	1367	1217	1244
GT 4-door	1432	1274	1303
Group 1SB plus power windows, power mirrors, split folding rear seat, remote keyless entry.			
Power glass sunroof and			
CD player with equalizer, GT	600	534	546
GT w/option group	405	360	369
Sport Interior Group,			
SE	220	196	200
GT	170	151	155
Upgraded cloth upholstery, driver-seat lumbar adjuster, seat back pockets, 4-way manual seat adjuster, leather-wrapped steering wheel, shift knob, and parking-brake handle (SE), reading and courtesy lamps, sun visor extensions. Requires option group.			
Sport Interior Group w/leather upholstery,			
SE w/group 1SB	860	765	769
SE w/group 1SC	695	619	632
GT w/group 1SB	810	721	737
GT w/group 1SC	645	574	587
Split folding rear seat, driver-seat lumbar adjuster, seat back pockets, 4-way manual seat adjuster, leather-wrapped steering wheel, shift knob, and parking-brake handle (SE), reading and courtesy lamps, sun visor extensions.			
Cruise control	235	209	214
Rear defogger	180	160	164
6-way power driver's seat	340	303	309
Requires Group 1SC.			
Power windows, SE and			
GT with Group 1SB			
2-door	290	258	264
4-door	355	316	323
Power sunroof	595	530	536
Requires option group.			
Split folding rear seat,			
SE and GT with Group 1SB	165	147	150
Tilt steering wheel, SE	150	134	137
Intermittent wipers, SE	65	58	59
Remote keyless entry system,			
SE and GT with Group 1SB	150	134	137
Requires power windows.			
Cassette player	195	174	177

	Retail Price	Dealer Invoice	Fair Price
Cassette player with equalizer	$305	$271	$278
with option group	110	98	100
CD player with equalizer	405	360	369
with option group	210	187	191
Cassette and CD players			
with equalizer	600	534	546
with option group	405	360	369
with Power glass sunroof and CD player			
with equalizer	195	174	177
Steering wheel radio controls	125	111	114
Requires option group.			
Rear decklid spoiler, SE	170	151	155
Rear decklid spoiler delete,			
GT (credit)	(170)	(151)	(151)
195/65R15 touring tires, SE	131	117	119
205/55R16 touring tires,			
SE	223	198	203
15-inch crosslace alloy			
wheels, SE	300	267	273
16-inch alloy wheels, SE	325	289	296
Smoker's Pkg.	170	151	155
Lighter, ashtray.			

PONTIAC GRAND PRIX

Pontiac Grand Prix GT 4-door

Specifications

	2-door notchback	4-door notchback
Wheelbase, in.	110.5	110.5

Prices are accurate at time of publication; subject to manufacturer's change.

PONTIAC

	2-door notchback	4-door notchback
Overall length, in.	196.5	196.5
Overall width, in.	72.7	72.7
Overall height, in.	54.7	54.7
Curb weight, lbs.	3396	3414
Cargo vol., cu. ft.	16.0	16.0
Fuel capacity, gals.	18.0	18.0
Seating capacity	5	6

Engines

	ohv V-6	ohv V-6	Supercharged ohv V-6
Size, liters/cu. in.	3.1/191	3.8/231	3.8/231
Horsepower @ rpm	160 @ 5200	195 @ 5200	240 @ 5200
Torque (lbs./ft.) @ rpm	185 @ 4000	220 @ 4000	280 @ 3200

EPA city/highway mpg

4-speed OD automatic	20/29	19/30	18/28

Built in Kansas City, Kan.

PRICES

Pontiac Grand Prix	Retail Price	Dealer Invoice	Fair Price
SE 4-door notchback	$18219	$16670	—
GT 2-door notchback	19189	17558	—
GT 4-door notchback	20099	18391	—
Destination charge	550	550	550

Fair price not available at time of publication.

Standard Equipment:

SE: 3.1-liter V-6 engine, 4-speed automatic transmission, anti-lock 4-wheel disc brakes, driver- and passenger-side air bags, Enhanced Traction System, air conditioning, power steering, cloth front bucket seats, front floor console, auxiliary power outlet, integrated rear seat headrests, AM/FM radio, power windows and door locks, tachometer, trip odometer, coolant temperature gauge, Driver Information Center, tilt steering wheel, power mirrors, visor mirrors, door map pockets, tinted glass, intermittent wipers, Pass-Key II theft-deterrent system, fog lights, daytime running lights, bright exhaust outlets, 205/70R15 tires, wheel covers. **GT 2-door** adds: 3.8-liter V-6 engine, dual exhaust outlets, 225/60R16 tires, 5-spoke alloy wheels. **GT 4-door** adds: MAGNA-STEER variable-effort steering, cruise control, cassette player, leather-wrapped steering wheel with radio controls, remote decklid release.

Optional Equipment:

	Retail Price	Dealer Invoice	Fair Price
3.8-liter V-6 engine, SE w/option group	$415	$369	—
Option Group 1SB, SE 4-door, GT 2-door ..	670	596	—

Cruise control, rear defogger, cassette player, remote decklid release.

Option Group 1SC, SE 4-door, GT 2-door ..	1305	1161	—

Group 1SB plus power driver seat, steering wheel with radio controls, Leather Appointment Group (leather-wrapped steering wheel and shifter) (NA w/front bench seat), remote keyless entry, rear window antenna.

Option Group 1SD, GT 2-door	2099	1868	—

Group 1SC plus Custom Interior (overhead console, rear-seat pass-through [NA w/child seat], cargo net), Premium Lighting Pkg. (illuminated visor mirrors, day/night rearview mirror, courtesy lights), trip computer, EYECUE head-up display.

Option Group 1SB,

GT 4-door	765	681	—

Power driver seat, steering wheel with radio controls, rear defogger, Leather Appointment Group (leather-wrapped steering wheel and shifter) (NA w/front bench seat), remote keyless entry, rear window antenna.

Option Group 1SC,

GT 4-door	1589	1414	—

Group 1SB plus Custom Interior (overhead console, rear-seat pass-through [NA w/child seat], cargo net), Premium Lighting Pkg. (illuminated visor mirrors, day/night rearview mirror, courtesy lights, rear reading lights), trip computer, EYECUE head-up display.

GTP Performance Pkg., GT 2-door

w/Group 1SC	1526	1358	—
GT 2-door w/Group 1SD	1326	1180	—
GT 4-door w/Group 1SB	1433	1275	—
GT 4-door w/Group 1SC	1233	1097	—

3.8-liter supercharged V-6 engine, 4-speed automatic transmission, MAGNASTEER variable-effort steering (2-door), trip computer, rear decklid spoiler; 225/60R16 performance tires, 5-spoke alloy wheels. 4-door requires option group. 2-door requires option group 1SC or 1SD.

Automatic air conditioning	195	174	—

SE requires Group 1SC. GT 4-door requires option group. GT 2-door requires Group 1SC or 1SD.

Leather seats, SE w/Group 1SB,

GT 2-door w/Group 1SB	575	512	—

SE w/Group 1SC, GT 2-door w/Group 1SC,

GT 4-door w/Group 1SB	525	467	—

Prices are accurate at time of publication; subject to manufacturer's change.

	Retail Price	Dealer Invoice	Fair Price
SE w/option group and custom interior, GT 2-door w/Group 1SB or 1SC and custom interior, GT 2-door w/Group 1SD, GT 4-door w/Group 1SB and custom interior, GT 4-door w/Group 1SC	$475	$423	—
NA w/front bench seat.			
Custom Interior, SE and GT 2-door w/Group 1SB	210	187	—
SE and GT 2-door w/Group 1SB and child seat, SE and GT 2-door w/Group 1SC, GT 4-door w/Group 1SB	160	142	—
SE and GT 2-door w/Group 1SB and sunroof	130	116	—
SE and GT 2-door w/Group 1SC and child seat, GT 4-door w/Group 1SB and child seat	110	98	—
SE and GT 2-door w/Group 1SB, child seat, and sunroof; SE and GT 2-door w/Group 1SC and sunroof, GT 4-door w/Group 1SB and sunroof	80	71	—
SE and GT 2-door w/Group 1SC, child seat, and sunroof; GT 4-door w/Group 1SB, child seat, and sunroof	30	27	—
GT 4-door w/Group SC	NC	NC	NC
GT 2-door w/Group 1SD and sunroof, GT 4-door w/Group 1SC and sunroof (credit)	(80)	(71)	(71)

Leather Appointment Group (leather-wrapped steering wheel and shifter) (NA w/front bench seat), overhead console, rear-seat pass-through (NA w/child seat), cargo net. Requires option group.

45/55 split front bench seat, 4-door	NC	NC	NC
Heated driver seat	50	45	—
Requires option group, power driver seat w/power lumbar support, leather seats.			
Power driver seat, SE w/Group 1SB, GT 2-door w/Group 1SB	270	240	—
Power lumbar support	100	89	—
Requires option group, power driver seat, heated driver seat, leather seats.			
Rear-seat pass-through	50	45	—
Requires option group. NA with child seat.			
Child seat	125	111	—
Requires option group. NA with Group 1SD on GT 2-door. NA with rear-seat pass-through or leather seats.			
Rear defogger	180	160	—

	Retail Price	Dealer Invoice	Fair Price
Day/night rearview mirror	$60	$53	—
SE requires option group.			
EYECUE head-up display	250	223	—
Requires option group.			
Power sunroof	646	575	—
Requires option group, custom interior.			
Trip computer	200	178	—
SE requires Group 1SC. GT 4-door Group 1SB. GT 2-door require Group 1SC.			
Premium Lighting Pkg., 4-door	214	190	—
2-door	184	164	—
Illuminated visor mirrors, day/night rearview mirror, courtesy lights, rear reading lights (NA 2-door). Requires option group.			
Cassette player, GT 2-door	195	174	—
Cassette player w/graphic equalizer,			
SE and GT 2-door w/Group 1SB	325	289	—
SE and GT 2-door w/Group 1SB and leather			
bucket seats or custom interior group	275	245	—
SE w/Group 1SC, GT 2-door w/Group			
1SC or 1SD, GT 4-door	150	134	—
Includes steering-wheel radio controls, premium sound system. Requires option group.			
CD player	100	89	—
Requires option group.			
CD player w/graphic equalizer,			
SE and GT 2-door w/Group 1SB	425	378	—
SE and GT 2-door w/Group 1SB and leather			
bucket seats or custom interior group	375	334	—
SE w/Group 1SC, GT 2-door w/Group			
1SC or 1SD, GT 4-door	250	223	—
Includes steering-wheel radio controls, premium sound system. Requires option group.			
Multi-disc CD changer	595	530	—
Requires steering-wheel radio controls, premium sound system. Requires option group.			
Premium sound system	125	111	—
Requires cassette or CD player. SE requires option group.			
Steering-wheel radio controls, SE and GT			
2-door w/Group 1SB	175	156	—
SE and GT 2-door w/ Group 1SB and leather			
bucket seats or custom interior group	125	111	—
Includes leather-wrapped steering wheel and shifter. Requires cassette or CD player.			

Prices are accurate at time of publication; subject to manufacturer's change.

	Retail Price	Dealer Invoice	Fair Price
Remote keyless entry, SE w/Group 1SB, GT 2-door w/Group 1SB	$150	$134	—
Theft-deterrent system	60	53	—
Requires option group, remote keyless entry.			
MAGNASTEER variable-effort steering, SE, GT 2-door	93	83	—
SE requires option group, optional engine, alloy wheels.			
Rear window antenna	40	36	—
Requires rear defogger. SE requires option group.			
Rear decklid spoiler	175	156	—
SE and GT 2-door requires option group.			
Machine faced alloy wheels, SE	259	231	—
Requires option group.			
5-spoke high-polished alloy wheels, GT	285	254	—
5-spoke white alloy wheels, GT	NC	NC	NC
Requires white exterior paint.			
Crosslace alloy wheels, SE	259	231	—
GT	NC	NC	NC
SE requires option group, optional tires.			
225/60R16 tires, SE	160	142	—
Engine block heater	20	18	—
Requires Option Pkg.			

SAAB 900

Saab 900 SE Turbo 2-door

Specifications	2-door hatchback	4-door hatchback	2-door conv.
Wheelbase, in.	102.4	102.4	102.4

	2-door hatchback	4-door hatchback	2-door conv.
Overall length, in.	182.6	182.6	182.6
Overall width, in.	67.4	67.4	67.4
Overall height, in.	56.5	56.5	56.5
Curb weight, lbs.	2940	2980	3090
Cargo vol., cu. ft.	49.8	49.8	28.3
Fuel capacity, gals.	18.0	18.0	18.0
Seating capacity	5	5	4

Engines	dohc I-4	Turbo dohc I-4	dohc V-6
Size, liters/cu. in.	2.3/140	2.0/121	2.5/152
Horsepower @ rpm	150 @ 5700	185 @ 5500	170 @ 5900
Torque (lbs./ft.) @ rpm	155 @ 4300	194 @ 2100	167 @ 4200
EPA city/highway mpg			
5-speed OD manual	21/29	20/27	
4-speed OD automatic	19/27	18/26	19/25

Built in Sweden and Finland.

PRICES

Saab 900	Retail Price	Dealer Invoice	Fair Price
S 2-door hatchback	$24995	$22308	—
S 4-door hatchback	25995	23202	—
S 2-door convertible	34995	31234	—
SE Turbo 2-door hatchback	29995	26772	—
SE Turbo 4-door hatchback	30995	27663	—
SE V-6 4-door hatchback	32495	29002	—
SE Turbo 2-door convertible	40995	35973	—
SE V-6 2-door convertible	42495	37291	—
Destination charge	525	525	525

Fair price not available at time of publication.

Standard Equipment:

S: 2.3-liter DOHC 4-cylinder engine, 5-speed manual transmission, anti-lock 4-wheel disc brakes, driver- and passenger-side air bags, power steering, air conditioning, cruise control, power convertible top (convertible), velour upholstery (hatchbacks), leather upholstery (convertible), heated reclining front bucket seats, driver-seat lumbar adjustment, folding rear seat w/trunk pass-through, cupholder, leather-wrapped steering wheel and shifter (convertible), power win-

SAAB

dows and door locks, heated power mirrors, telescopic steering wheel, solar-control tinted glass, coolant temperature gauge, trip odometer, tachometer, analog clock, 6-speaker AM/FM/cassette w/weather band and anti-theft, power antenna, rear defogger, theft-deterrent system, intermittent wipers, illuminated visor mirrors, headlamp wipers/washers, rear wiper/washer (hatchbacks), front and rear fog lamps, daytime running lights, front spoiler, rear spoiler (2-door hatchback), floormats, tool kit, 195/60VR15 tires, alloy wheels. **SE Turbo** adds: 2.0-liter turbocharged DOHC 4-cylinder engine, lower sport chassis, automatic air conditioning, leather upholstery, power front seats w/driver-seat memory, leather-wrapped steering wheel and shifter, power sunroof (hatchbacks), turbo-boost gauge, 8-speaker upgraded audio system, 6-disc CD changer (convertible), Saab Car Computer, walnut-trimmed instrument panel, 205/50ZR16 tires. **SE V-6** delete turbo-boost gauge and lower sport chassis and add: 2.5-liter DOHC V-6 engine, 4-speed automatic transmission, traction control.

Optional Equipment:

	Retail Price	Dealer Invoice	Fair Price
4-speed automatic transmission, S, SE Turbo	$995	$851	—
Power sunroof, S hatchbacks	995	851	—
Leather Pkg., S hatchbacks	1295	1108	—
Leather upholstery, leather-wrapped steering wheel.			
Child booster seats, 4-doors	250	214	—
Extra-cost paint	180	154	—

SAAB 9000

Specifications

	4-door hatchback
Wheelbase, in.	105.2
Overall length, in.	187.4
Overall width, in.	70.0
Overall height, in.	55.9
Curb weight, lbs.	3130
Cargo vol., cu. ft.	56.5
Fuel capacity, gals.	17.4
Seating capacity	5

Engines

	Turbo dohc I-4	Turbo dohc I-4	dohc V-6
Size, liters/cu. in.	2.3/140	2.3/140	3.0/182

Saab 9000 CS

	Turbo dohc I-4	Turbo dohc I-4	dohc V-6
Horsepower @ rpm.............	170 @ 5700	200 @ 5500	210 @ 6100
Torque (lbs./ft.) @ rpm	192 @ 3200	238 @ 1800	200 @ 3300
EPA city/highway mpg			
5-speed OD manual...........	20/29	20/29	
4-speed OD automatic.........	17/26	17/26	18/26

Built in Sweden.

PRICES

Saab 9000	Retail Price	Dealer Invoice	Fair Price
CS 5-door hatchback	$31695	$28209	—
CSE Turbo 5-door hatchback	37995	33153	—
CSE V-6 5-door hatchback	40495	35331	—
Aero 5-door notchback	41495	36204	—
Destination charge	525	525	525

Fair price not available at time of publication.

Standard Equipment:

CS: 2.3-liter turbocharged DOHC 4-cylinder engine (170-horsepower), 5-speed manual transmission, anti-lock 4-wheel disc brakes, driver- and passenger-side air bags, power steering, automatic climate control, cruise control, velour upholstery, heated reclining front bucket seats, split folding rear seat, cupholders, overhead console w/map light, telescopic steering wheel, power windows and door locks, heated power mirrors, solar-control tinted glass, power antenna, removable analog clock, 8-speaker AM/FM/cassette w/weather band and anti-theft code, coolant-temperature gauge, tachometer, outside-temperature indicator, trip odometer, remote decklid release, rear defogger, intermittent wipers, rear wiper/washer, theft-deterrent system, rear reading lights, illuminated visor mirrors, headlamp wipers/washers, front and rear fog lamps, daytime running lights, front spoiler, tool kit, floormats, 195/65VR15 tires, 3-spoke alloy wheels. **CSE Turbo** adds: 2.3-liter turbocharged DOHC 4-cylinder engine (200-horsepower), leather upholstery, power front seats with driver-side memory, power sunroof, turbo-boost gauge, leather-wrapped steering wheel, leather-wrapped shifter and boot, Saab Car Computer with digital clock, 10-speaker Harmon/Kardon audio system with cassette/CD player, walnut-trimmed instrument panel, 205/50VR15 tires. **CSE V-6** adds: 3.0-liter DOHC V-6 engine, 4-speed automatic transmission, traction control, 8-spoke silver light-alloy wheels. **Aero** adds to CSE Turbo: 2.3-liter turbocharged DOHC 4-cylinder engine (225-horsepower w/5-speed, 200-horsepower w/automatic), lower sport chassis, sport suspension, leather sport seats, aerodynamic body trim, 205/55ZR16 tires, 3-spoke light-alloy wheels.

Optional Equipment:

	Retail Price	Dealer Invoice	Fair Price
4-speed automatic transmission, CS, CSE Turbo, Aero	$1045	$893	—
Power glass sunroof, CS	1115	953	—
Leather Pkg., CS	2095	1792	—
Leather upholstery, leather-wrapped steering wheel and shift boot cover, power front seats.			
Value Pkg., CS	2210	1967	—
Leather Pkg., power sunroof.			
Extra-cost paint	180	154	—

SATURN COUPE

Specifications

	2-door notchback
Wheelbase, in.	102.4
Overall length, in.	180.0
Overall width, in.	67.3
Overall height, in.	52.2
Curb weight, lbs.	2309
Cargo vol., cu. ft.	11.4
Fuel capacity, gals.	12.2
Seating capacity	4

Saturn SC1

Engines

	ohc I-4	dohc I-4
Size, liters/cu. in	1.9/116	1.9/116
Horsepower @ rpm	100 @	124 @
	5000	5600
Torque (lbs./ft.) @ rpm	114 @	122 @
	2400	4800
EPA city/highway mpg		
5-speed OD manual	28/40	27/37
4-speed OD automatic	27/37	24/34

Built in Spring Hill, Tenn.

PRICES

Saturn Coupe	Retail Price	Dealer Invoice	Fair Price
SC1 2-door notchback, 5-speed	$12495	$10871	—
SC1 2-door notchback, automatic	13335	11601	—
SC2 2-door notchback, 5-speed	13695	11915	—
SC2 2-door notchback, automatic	14535	12645	—
Destination charge	400	400	400

Fair price not available at time of publication.

Standard Equipment:

SC1: 1.9-liter 4-cylinder engine, 5-speed manual or 4-speed automatic transmission, driver- and passenger-side air bags, power steering, cloth reclining front bucket seats w/lumbar support, 60/40 folding rear seatback, front and rear consoles, cupholders, tilt steering wheel, tinted glass, coolant-temperature gauge, tachometer, trip odometer, AM/FM radio, digital clock, dual remote outside mirrors, rear defogger, intermittent wipers, remote fuel-door and decklid releases, passenger-side visor mirror, daytime running lights, 175/70R14 tires, wheel covers. **SC2** adds: 1.9-liter DOHC engine, variable-assist power steering, driver-seat height adjustment, sport suspension, locking storage armrest, rear spoiler, fog lights, striping, 195/60R15 tires.

Optional Equipment:	Retail Price	Dealer Invoice	Fair Price
Anti-lock brakes	$695	$605	—
Includes traction control. SC2 also includes 4-wheel disc brakes.			
Air conditioning	930	809	—
Option Pkg. 1, SC1	1860	1618	—
Air conditioning, cruise control, power windows and door locks, power passenger-side outside mirror, 185/65R15 touring tires, alloy wheels.			
Option Pkg. 2, SC2	2180	1897	—
Air conditioning, cruise control, power windows and door locks, power passenger-side outside mirror, alloy wheels.			
Power sunroof	695	605	—
Cassette player	245	213	—
Cassette player w/equalizer and premium speakers	375	326	—
CD player w/equalizer and premium speakers	495	431	—
Premium speakers	75	65	—
Cruise control	270	235	—
Leather upholstery, SC2	695	605	—
Includes leather-wrapped steering wheel.			
Rear spoiler, SC1	225	196	—
Floormats	55	48	—
Double-fin alloy wheels, SC1	430	374	—
Includes 185/65R15 touring tires.			
Teardrop II alloy wheels, SC2	320	278	—

SATURN SEDAN/ WAGON

Specifications	4-door notchback	4-door wagon
Wheelbase, in.	102.4	102.4
Overall length, in.	176.9	176.9
Overall width, in.	66.7	66.7
Overall height, in.	53.8	54.5
Curb weight, lbs.	2321	2391

Saturn SL1

	4-door notchback	4-door wagon
Cargo vol., cu. ft.	12.1	58.2
Fuel capacity, gals.	12.2	12.2
Seating capacity	5	5

Engines

	ohc I-4	dohc I-4
Size, liters/cu. in.	1.9/116	1.9/116
Horsepower @ rpm	100 @ 5000	124 @ 5600
Torque (lbs./ft.) @ rpm	114 @ 2400	122 @ 4800

EPA city/highway mpg

5-speed OD manual	28/40	27/37
4-speed OD automatic	27/37	24/34

Built in Spring Hill, Tenn.

PRICES

Saturn Sedan/Wagon	Retail Price	Dealer Invoice	Fair Price
SL 4-door notchback, 5-speed	$10595	$9218	—
SL1 4-door notchback, 5-speed	11595	10088	—
SL1 4-door notchback, automatic	12435	10818	—
SL2 4-door notchback, 5-speed	12495	10871	—
SL2 4-door notchback, automatic	13335	11601	—
SW1 4-door wagon, 5-speed	12195	10610	—
SW1 4-door wagon, automatic	13035	11340	—
SW2 4-door wagon, 5-speed	13095	11393	—
SW2 4-door wagon, automatic	13935	12123	—
Destination charge	400	400	400

Fair price not available at time of publication.

Prices are accurate at time of publication; subject to manufacturer's change.

SATURN

Standard Equipment:

SL: 1.9-liter 4-cylinder engine, 5-speed manual transmission, driver- and passenger-side air bags, cloth reclining front bucket seats w/lumbar support, 60/40 split folding rear seat, front console, cupholders, tilt steering wheel, tachometer, coolant-temperature gauge, trip odometer, tinted glass, AM/FM radio, digital clock, rear defogger, intermittent wipers, remote fuel-door and decklid releases, passenger-side visor mirror, daytime running lamps, 175/70R14 tires, wheel covers. **SL1** adds: 5-speed manual or 4-speed automatic transmission, power steering, dual outside mirrors, upgraded interior trim. **SL2** adds: 1.9-liter 4-cylinder DOHC engine, variable-assist power steering, sport suspension, upgraded upholstery, driver-seat height adjustment, 185/65R15 touring tires. **SW1** adds to SL1: rear wiper/washer, remote liftgate release. **SW2** adds to SW1: 1.9-liter DOHC engine, variable-assist power steering, sport suspension, upgraded upholstery, driver-seat height adjustment, cargo cover, 185/65R15 touring tires.

Optional Equipment:

	Retail Price	Dealer Invoice	Fair Price
Anti-lock brakes	$695	$605	—
Includes traction control. SL2 also includes 4-wheel disc brakes.			
Air conditioning	930	809	—
Option Pkg. 1, SL1, SW1, SW2	1985	1727	—
Air conditioning, cruise control, power windows and door locks, power passenger-side outside mirror.			
Option Pkg. 2, SL2	2305	2005	—
Option Pkg. 1 plus alloy wheels.			
Power sunroof, SL1, SL2	695	605	—
Cassette player, SL	275	239	—
SL1, SL2, SW1, SW2	245	213	—
Cassette player w/equalizer and premium speakers, SL	405	352	—
SL1, SL2, SW1, SW2	375	326	—
CD player w/equalizer and premium speakers, SL	525	457	—
SL1, SL2, SW1, SW2	495	431	—
Premium speakers	75	65	—
Power door locks	360	313	—
Includes remote keyless entry, theft-deterrent system. NA on SL.			
Cruise control	270	235	—
NA on SL.			
Passenger-side outside mirror, SL	40	35	—
Fog lamps, SL2, SW2	160	139	—
Leather upholstery, SL2, SW2	695	605	—
Includes leather-wrapped steering wheel.			

	Retail Price	Dealer Invoice	Fair Price
Rear spoiler, SL2	$205	$178	—
Cargo cover, SW1	75	65	—
Floormats	55	48	—
Alloy wheels, SL2, SW2	320	278	—

SUBARU IMPREZA

Subaru Impreza Outback Sport

Specifications

	2-door notchback	4-door notchback	4-door wagon
Wheelbase, in.	99.2	99.2	99.2
Overall length, in.	172.2	172.2	172.2
Overall width, in.	67.1	67.1	67.1
Overall height, in.	55.5	55.5	60.0
Curb weight, lbs.	2600	2690	2835
Cargo vol., cu. ft.	11.0	11.0	62.0
Fuel capacity, gals.	13.2	13.2	13.2
Seating capacity	5	5	5

Engines

	ohc flat-4	ohc flat-4
Size, liters/cu. in.	1.8/109	2.2/135
Horsepower @ rpm	115 @ 5600	137 @ 5400
Torque (lbs./ft.) @ rpm	120 @ 4000	145 @ 4000

EPA city/highway mpg

5-speed OD manual	24/30	23/30

Prices are accurate at time of publication; subject to manufacturer's change.

SUBARU

	ohc flat-4	ohc flat-4
4-speed OD automatic..		23/30

Built in Japan.

PRICES

Subaru Impreza	Retail Price	Dealer Invoice	Fair Price
Brighton 2-door notchback	$13795	$12818	$13218
L 2-door notchback	15895	14445	14845
L 4-door notchback	15895	14445	14845
L 4-door Sport Wagon	16295	14804	15204
Outback 4-door Sport Wagon	17995	16321	16721
Destination charge	495	495	495

Prices are for vehicles distributed by Subaru of America. Prices may be higher in areas served by independent distributors.

Standard Equipment:

Brighton: 1.8-liter SOHC 4-cylinder engine, 5-speed manual transmission, permanent all-wheel drive, driver- and passenger-side air bags, variable-assist power steering, air conditioning, cloth upholstery, reclining front bucket seats, front storage console, cupholders, tilt steering column, AM/FM/cassette w/2-speaker, tinted glass, driver-side outside mirror, rear defogger, intermittent wipers, remote decklid release, auxiliary power outlet, 175/70R14 tires, wheel covers. **L** adds: 2.2-liter SOHC 4-cylinder engine, 60/40 split folding rear seat (wagon), power windows and door locks, power mirrors, tachometer, upgraded AM/FM/cassette w/4-speakers, rear wiper/washer (wagon), remote decklid release (notchbacks), passenger-side visor mirror, front air dam, rear spoiler (2-door), rear stabilizer bar, 195/60HR15 tires. **Outback** adds to L wagon: anti-lock brakes, heavy-duty suspension, Outback cloth upholstery, cargo-area auxiliary power outlet, cargo tie-down hooks, roof rack, mud guards, 2-tone paint, hood scoop, 205/60R15 white-letter tires, Outback wheel covers.

Optional Equipment:

4-speed automatic transmission, L, Outback	800	718	722
Performance Group, Brighton	1000	916	900

2.2-liter 4-cylinder engine, 4-speed automatic transmission, rear stabilizer bar, 195/60HR15 tires.

SUBARU LEGACY

Subaru Legacy Outback Limited

Specifications

	4-door notchback	4-door wagon
Wheelbase, in.	103.5	103.5
Overall length, in.	180.9	183.9
Overall width, in.	67.5	67.5
Overall height, in.	55.3	57.1
Curb weight, lbs.	2885	2975
Cargo vol., cu. ft.	13.0	73.0
Fuel capacity, gals.	15.9	15.9
Seating capacity	5	5

Engines

	ohc flat-4	dohc flat-4
Size, liters/cu. in.	2.2/135	2.5/150
Horsepower @ rpm	137 @ 5400	165 @ 5600
Torque (lbs./ft.) @ rpm	145 @ 4000	162 @ 4000

EPA city/highway mpg

5-speed OD manual	23/30	21/27
4-speed OD automatic	23/30	21/27

Built in Lafayette, Ind.

PRICES

Subaru Legacy	Retail Price	Dealer Invoice	Fair Price
Brighton 4-door wagon, 5-speed	$16895	$15788	$16288

Prices are accurate at time of publication; subject to manufacturer's change.

SUBARU

	Retail Price	Dealer Invoice	Fair Price
Brighton 4-door wagon, automatic	$17695	$16502	$17002
L 4-door notchback, 5-speed	19195	17278	17778
L 4-door notchback, automatic	19995	17992	18492
L 4-door wagon, 5-speed	19895	17898	18398
L 4-door wagon, automatic	20695	18612	19112
Outback 4-door wagon, 5-speed	22495	20187	20687
Outback 4-door wagon, automatic	23295	20901	21401
Outback Limited 4-door wagon, 5-speed	24195	21694	22194
Outback Limited 4-door wagon, automatic	24995	22408	22908
GT 4-door notchback, 5-speed	22795	20453	20953
GT 4-door notchback, automatic	23595	21167	21667
GT 4-door wagon, 5-speed	23495	21073	21573
GT 4-door wagon, automatic	24295	21787	22287
LSi 4-door notchback, automatic	24995	22404	22904
LSi 4-door wagon, automatic	25695	23024	23524
Destination charge	495	495	495

Prices are for vehicles distributed by Subaru of America. Prices may be higher in areas served by independent distributors.

Standard Equipment:

Brighton: 2.2-liter 4-cylinder engine, 5-speed manual transmission or 4-speed automatic transmission, full-time all-wheel drive, driver- and passenger-side air bags, cloth reclining front bucket seats, air conditioning, storage console, variable-assist power steering, tilt steering column, 2-speaker AM/FM/cassette, digital clock, trip odometer, temperature gauge, tinted glass, rear defogger, intermittent wipers, remote fuel door and decklid releases, bodyside moldings, child safety rear door locks, 185/70SR14 tires, wheel covers. **L** adds: anti-lock 4-wheel disc brakes, cruise control, split folding rear seat (notchback), power mirrors, power windows and door locks, tachometer, 4-speaker AM/FM/cassette, right visor mirror. **Outback** adds: 2.5-liter DOHC 4-cylinder engine, hood scoop, roof rack, fog lights, 2-tone paint, upgraded cloth interior, rear headrests, map light, cargo hooks, cargo area power outlet, 205/70SR15 white-lettered tires, alloy wheels. **Outback Limited** adds: leather upholstery AM/FM/cassette with weather band, power antenna, Cold Weather Pkg. (heated front seats, heated power outside mirrors, engine-block heater), woodgrain interior trim, gold badging, special alloy wheels. **GT** adds to L: 2.5-liter DOHC 4-cylinder engine, power moonroof with sunshade, power antenna, leather-wrapped steering wheel and shifter, variable intermittent wipers, map light, fog lights, hood scoop, rear spoiler, ground effects, 205/55HR16 tires, alloy wheels. **GT wagon** adds roof rack. **LSi** adds to L: 2.5-liter DOHC 4-

cylinder engine, 4-speed automatic transmission, leather upholstery, rear armrest, power moonroof with sunshade, 6-speaker compact disc changer, power antenna, leather-wrapped steering wheel and shifter, security system, variable intermittent wipers, map light, 195/60HR15 tires, alloy wheels. **LSi wagon** deletes rear armrest and adds: rear headrests. **All wagons** add: rear wiper/washer, cargo cover (except Brighton), storage tray (except Brighton).

Optional Equipment:

	Retail Price	Dealer Invoice	Fair Price
Cold Weather Pkg., Outback	$400	$355	$360

Includes heated front seats, dual heated outside mirrors, engine-block heater.

SUZUKI ESTEEM

Suzuki Esteem GLX

Specifications

	2-door hatchback	4-door notchback
Wheelbase, in.	93.1	97.6
Overall length, in.	149.4	165.2
Overall width, in.	62.6	66.5
Overall height, in.	54.7	53.9
Curb weight, lbs.	1878	2183
Cargo vol., cu. ft.	22.5	12.0
Fuel capacity, gals.	10.6	13.5
Seating capacity	4	5

Engines

	ohc I-4	ohc I-4
Size, liters/cu. in.	1.3/79	1.6/97

Prices are accurate at time of publication; subject to manufacturer's change.

SUZUKI

	ohc I-4	ohc I-4
Horsepower @ rpm	70 @ 5500	98 @ 6000
Torque (lbs./ft.) @ rpm	74 @ 3000	94 @ 3200
EPA city/highway mpg		
5-speed OD manual	39/43	31/37
3-speed automatic	30/34	
4-speed OD automatic		27/34

Built in Canada and Japan.

PRICES

Suzuki Esteem	Retail Price	Dealer Invoice	Fair Price
GL 4-door notchback, 5-speed	$11899	$11304	—
GL 4-door notchback, automatic	12899	12254	—
GLX 4-door notchback, 5-speed	12999	12349	—
GLX 4-door notchback, automatic	13999	13299	—
GLX 4-door notchback w/option pkg., automatic	14799	14059	—
Destination charge	420	420	420

Fair price not available at time of publication.

Standard Equipment:

GL: 1.6-liter 4-cylinder engine, 5-speed manual or 4-speed automatic transmission, driver- and passenger-side air bags, air conditioning, power steering, cloth/vinyl upholstery, front bucket seats, folding rear seat, cupholders, dual outside mirrors, tinted glass, trip odometer, AM/FM/cassette, remote fuel-door and decklid releases, rear defogger, intermittent wipers, daytime running lights, 155/80R13 tires. **GLX adds**: cloth upholstery, split folding rear seat, power windows and door locks, power mirrors, tachometer, passenger-side visor mirror, mud guards, trunk light, 175/70R13 tires, wheel covers. **GLX with option pkg. adds**: anti-lock brakes, cruise control.

Options are available as dealer-installed accessories.

SUZUKI SIDEKICK

Specifications	2-door conv.	4-door wagon	Sport 4-door wagon
Wheelbase, in.	86.6	97.6	97.6

Suzuki Sidekick JLX Sport

	2-door conv.	4-door wagon	Sport 4-door wagon
Overall length, in.	143.7	158.7	162.4
Overall width, in.	64.2	64.4	66.7
Overall height, in.	64.3	65.7	66.3
Curb weight, lbs.	2339	2632	2917
Cargo vol., cu. ft.	32.9	45.0	45.0
Fuel capacity, gals.	11.1	14.5	18.5
Seating capacity	4	4	4

Engines

	ohc I-4	dohc I-4
Size, liters/cu. in.	1.6/97	1.8/112
Horsepower @ rpm	95 @ 5600	120 @ 6500
Torque (lbs./ft.) @ rpm	98 @ 4000	114 @ 3500

EPA city/highway mpg

	ohc I-4	dohc I-4
5-speed OD manual	23/26	22/25
3-speed automatic	23/24	
4-speed OD automatic	22/25	21/24

Built in Canada and Japan.

PRICES

Suzuki Sidekick	Retail Price	Dealer Invoice	Fair Price
JS 2WD 2-door convertible, 5-speed	$12899	$12254	$12454
JS 2WD 2-door convertible, automatic	13499	12824	13024
JX 4WD 2-door convertible, 5-speed	14669	13642	13842
JX 4WD 2-door convertible, automatic	15269	14200	14400

Prices are accurate at time of publication; subject to manufacturer's change.

SUZUKI

	Retail Price	Dealer Invoice	Fair Price
JS 2WD 4-door wagon, 5-speed	$14399	$13391	$13791
JS 2WD 4-door wagon, automatic	15349	14274	14674
JX 4WD 4-door wagon, 5-speed	15999	14559	14959
JX 4WD 4-door wagon, automatic	16949	15423	15823
JS Sport 2WD 4-door wagon, 5-speed	16699	—	—
JS Sport 2WD 4-door wagon, automatic	17699	—	—
JX Sport 4WD 4-door wagon, 5-speed	17699	16106	16506
JX Sport 4WD 4-door wagon, automatic	18699	17016	17416
JLX Sport 4WD 4-door wagon, 5-speed	19199	17471	17871
JLX Sport 4WD 4-door wagon, automatic	20199	18381	18781
Destination charge, 2-door	400	400	400
4-door	420	420	420

JS Sport dealer invoice and fair prices not available at time of publication.

Standard Equipment:

JS 2-door: 1.6-liter 4-cylinder engine, 5-speed manual or 3-speed automatic transmission, driver- and passenger-side air bags, folding canvas top, cloth reclining front bucket seats, folding rear seat, cupholders, dual outside mirrors, trip odometer, tinted glass, intermittent wipers, daytime running lights, fuel-tank skid plate, carpeting, spare-tire carrier w/full-size spare tire, 195/75R15 tires. **JX 2-door** adds: power steering, tachometer, 205/75R15 tires. **JS/JX 4-door** deletes folding canvas top and adds: 5-speed manual or 4-speed automatic transmission, split folding rear seat, AM/FM/cassette, rear defogger, 195/75R15 tires (JS), 205/75R15 tires (JX). **JS/JX Sport** adds: 1.8-liter DOHC 4-cylinder engine, air conditioning, power windows and door locks, power mirrors, passenger-side visor mirror, remote fuel-door release, theft-deterrent system, map lights, 215/65R16 tires. **JLX Sport** adds: anti-lock brakes, automatic locking front hubs, cruise control, cloth door trim, rear wiper/washer, spare-tire cover w/wheel lock, alloy wheels. **4WD models** add: part-time 4-wheel drive, 2-speed transfer case.

Optional Equipment:

Anti-lock brakes (std. JX/JLX Sport)	600	540	552

Other options are available as dealer-installed accessories.

TOYOTA AVALON

Toyota Avalon XLS

Specifications

	4-door notchback
Wheelbase, in.	107.1
Overall length, in.	190.2
Overall width, in.	70.3
Overall height, in.	55.9
Curb weight, lbs.	3263
Cargo vol., cu. ft.	15.4
Fuel capacity, gals.	18.5
Seating capacity	6

Engines

	dohc V-6
Size, liters/cu. in.	3.0/180
Horsepower @ rpm	200 @ 5200
Torque (lbs./ft.) @ rpm	214 @ 4400

EPA city/highway mpg

4-speed OD automatic	21/31

Built in Georgetown, Ky.

PRICES

Toyota Avalon	Retail Price	Dealer Invoice	Fair Price
XL 4-door notchback, front bucket seats	$23538	$20607	—

Prices are accurate at time of publication; subject to manufacturer's change.

TOYOTA

	Retail Price	Dealer Invoice	Fair Price
XL 4-door notchback, front bench seat	$24358	$21325	—
XLS 4-door notchback	27048	23401	—
Destination charge	420	420	420

Fair price not available at time of publication. Prices are for vehicles distributed by Toyota Motor Sales, U.S.A., Inc., and may be higher in areas served by independent distributors.

Standard Equipment:

XL: 3.0-liter DOHC V-6 engine, 4-speed automatic transmission, anti-lock 4-wheel disc brakes, driver- and passenger-side air bags, power steering, air conditioning, cruise control, cloth 6-way adjustable front bucket seats or power split bench seat with storage armrest, cupholders, tilt steering wheel, tachometer, AM/FM-cassette, power windows and door locks, power mirrors, tinted glass, remote fuel-door and decklid releases, illuminated visor mirrors, intermittent wipers, wheel covers, automatic headlamps, rear defogger, 205/65HR15 tires, full-size spare tire. **XLS** adds: automatic climate control, 7-way power front bucket seats or power split bench seat with storage armrest, leather-wrapped steering wheel, premium cassette player, heated power mirrors, theft-deterrent system, remote keyless entry, variable intermittent wipers, reading lights, alloy wheels.

Optional Equipment:

Leather Trim Pkg., XL with bucket seats	1910	1562	—
XL with bench seat	1060	848	—
XLS	1005	804	—
Leather upholstery, simulated-leather door trim. XL adds leather-wrapped steering wheel.			
7-way power front bucket seats,			
XL with bucket seats	850	714	—
Traction control	300	240	—
Power moonroof, XL	1000	800	—
XLS	980	784	—
Premium cassette player, XL	250	188	—
Premium cassette player and 12-disc CD changer,			
XL	1470	1103	—
XLS	1220	915	—
Includes equalizer.			
Heated power mirrors, XL	30	24	—
Theft-deterrent system, XL	220	176	—
Diamond white pearlescent paint	210	179	—
Mud guards	60	48	—

	Retail Price	Dealer Invoice	Fair Price
Alloy wheels, XL	$435	$348	—

TOYOTA CAMRY/ LEXUS ES 300

Toyota Camry LE

Specifications

	4-door notchback
Wheelbase, in.	105.2
Overall length, in.	188.5
Overall width, in.	70.1
Overall height, in.	55.4
Curb weight, lbs.	2976
Cargo vol., cu. ft.	14.1
Fuel capacity, gals.	18.5
Seating capacity	5

Engines

	dohc I-4	dohc V-6
Size, liter/ cu. in.	2.2/132	3.0/183
Horsepower @ rpm	133 @ 5400	194 @ 5200
Torque (lbs./ft.) @ rpm	147 @ 4400	209 @ 4400
EPA city/highway mpg		
5-speed OD manual	23/31	20/28
4-speed OD automatic	23/30	19/26

Built in Georgetown, Ky., and Japan.

Prices are accurate at time of publication; subject to manufacturer's change.

Lexus ES 300

PRICES

Toyota Camry	Retail Price	Dealer Invoice	Fair Price
CE 4-cylinder 4-door notchback, 5-speed	.$16398	$14525	—
CE 4-cylinder 4-door notchback, automatic	17198	15232	—
CE V-6 4-door notchback, 5-speed	19248	17049	—
LE 4-cylinder 4-door notchback, automatic	19868	17393	—
LE V-6 4-door notchback, automatic	22168	19407	—
XLE 4-cylinder 4-door notchback, automatic	21808	19092	—
XLE V-6 4-door notchback, automatic	24018	21027	—
Destination charge	420	420	420

Fair price not available at time of publication. Prices are for vehicles distributed by Toyota Motor Sales, U.S.A., Inc. The dealer invoice, fair price, and destination charge may be higher in areas served by independent distributors.

Standard Equipment:

CE: 2.2-liter 4-cylinder or 3.0-liter V-6 engine, 5-speed manual or 4-speed automatic transmission, anti-lock 4-wheel disc brakes (V-6), driver- and passenger-side air bags, power steering, cloth reclining front bucket seats, split folding rear seat w/armrest, front and rear storage consoles, overhead storage console, front and rear cupholders, tilt steering column, tachometer, coolant-temperature gauge, two trip odometers, AM/FM radio w/four speakers, tinted glass, dual remote outside mirrors, remote fuel-door and trunk releases, rear defogger, intermittent wipers, illuminated visor mirrors, auxiliary power outlet, 205/65HR15 tires (V-6), 195/70R14 tires (V-6), wheel covers. **LE adds:** 4-speed automatic transmission, anti-lock brakes, 4-wheel disc brakes

(V-6), air conditioning, cruise control, power windows and door locks, power mirrors, cassette player, integrated antenna. **XLE** adds to LE: power front seats, driver-seat manual lumbar support, theft-deterrent system, variable intermittent wipers, alloy wheels.

Optional Equipment:

	Retail Price	Dealer Invoice	Fair Price
Anti-lock 4-wheel brakes, CE w/4-cylinder engine	$550	$473	—
Air conditioning, CE	1005	804	—
Power Pkg., CE	780	624	—
Power windows, door locks, and mirrors.			
Leather Trim Pkg., LE	1100	880	—
Leather upholstery, driver-seat lumbar support, leather-wrapped steering wheel and shifter, seatback map pockets. NA with integrated child seat.			
Leather Power Seat Pkg., XLE	1005	804	—
Leather upholstery, leather-wrapped shifter. NA with integrated child seat.			
Traction control, LE V-6, XLE V-6	300	240	—
Cruise control, CE	290	232	—
Power moonroof, LE, XLE	1000	800	—
Includes map lights, sunshade.			
Heated power mirrors, XLE	30	24	—
Integrated child seat	125	100	—
NA w/Leather Trim Pkg. or Leather Power Seat Pkg.			
Cassette player, CE	225	169	—
Premium AM/FM/cassette, LE, XLE	250	188	—
Includes six speakers, diversity antenna.			
Premium cassette/CD player, LE, XLE	1195	896	—
Includes six speakers, equalizer, diversity antenna.			
Theft-deterrent system, LE	440	352	—
Variable intermittent wipers, CE, LE	20	16	—
Mud guards	60	48	—
Alloy wheels, LE 4-cylinder	415	332	—
LE V-6	435	348	—

Lexus ES 300	Retail Price	Dealer Invoice	Fair Price
4-door notchback	$29900	$25971	$26300
Destination charge	495	495	495

Standard Equipment:

3.0-liter DOHC V-6, 4-speed automatic transmission, anti-lock 4-wheel disc brakes, variable-assist power steering, driver- and passenger-side air bags, automatic climate control, cruise control, cloth upholstery, power front bucket seats, driver-side power lumbar support, split folding rear seat with trunk pass-through, front console with auxiliary power outlet, overhead console, rear cupholder, tilt steering wheel, power windows and door locks, heated power mirrors, AM/FM cassette, tachometer, outside-temperature indicator, solar-control tinted glass, rear defogger, variable intermittent wipers, illuminated visor mirrors, remote fuel-door and decklid releases, remote keyless entry, walnut interior trim, first-aid kit, theft-deterrent system, automatic headlamps, fog lamps, 205/65VR15 tires, full-size spare tire, alloy wheels.

Optional Equipment:	Retail Price	Dealer Invoice	Fair Price
Adaptive Variable Suspension	$600	$400	$570
Requires Leather Trim Pkg.			
Traction Control	300	240	285
Requires Leather Trim Pkg. and all-season tires.			
Leather Trim Pkg.	1650	1320	1568
Leather upholstery, memory driver seat.			
Heated front seats	420	336	399
Requires Leather Trim Pkg.			
Power moonroof	1000	800	950
6-disc CD changer	1050	840	998
205/65VR15			
all-season tires	NC	NC	NC
Chrome wheels	1700	850	1615

TOYOTA CELICA

Specifications	2-door notchback	2-door hatchback	2-door conv.
Wheelbase, in.	99.9	99.9	99.9
Overall length, in.	177.0	174.2	177.0
Overall width, in.	68.9	68.9	68.9
Overall height, in.	51.0	50.8	51.0
Curb weight, lbs.	2395	2415	2755
Cargo vol., cu. ft.	10.6	16.2	6.8
Fuel capacity, gals.	15.9	15.9	15.9
Seating capacity	4	4	4

Engines	dohc I-4	dohc I-4
Size, liters/cu. in.	1.8/108	2.2/132
Horsepower @ rpm	105 @ 5200	135 @ 5400

Toyota Celica GT 2-door

	dohc I-4	dohc I-4
Torque (lbs./ft.) @ rpm	117 @ 2800	145 @ 4400
EPA city/highway mpg		
5-speed OD manual	29/35	22/28
4-speed OD automatic	27/34	22/29

Built in Japan.

PRICES

Toyota Celica	Retail Price	Dealer Invoice	Fair Price
ST 2-door notchback, 5-speed	$17128	$15082	$15582
ST 2-door notchback, automatic	17928	15787	16387
ST 2-door hatchback, 5-speed	17488	15400	16000
ST 2-door hatchback, automatic	18288	16104	16704
Limited Edition ST 2-door hatchback 5-speed	19555	17316	—
Limited Edition ST 2-door hatchback automatic	20355	18019	—
GT 2-door hatchback, 5-speed	20178	17665	18265
GT 2-door hatchback, automatic	20978	18365	18965
GT 2-door convertible, 5-speed	24378	21585	22085
GT 2-door convertible, automatic	25178	22285	22885
Limited Edition GT 2-door convertible, 5-speed	25998	23087	—
Limited Edition GT 2-door convertible, automatic	26798	23785	—
Destination charge	420	420	420

Fair price for Limited Edition not available at time of publication.

TOYOTA

Prices are for vehicles distributed by Toyota Motor Sales, U.S.A., Inc. The dealer invoice, fair price, and destination charge may be higher in areas served by independent distributors.

Standard Equipment:

ST: 1.8-liter DOHC 4-cylinder engine, 5-speed manual or 4-speed automatic transmission, driver- and passenger-side air bags, variable-assist power steering, cloth front bucket seats, 4-way adjustable driver seat, front console with armrest, split folding rear seat, cupholders, tilt steering wheel, digital clock, coolant-temperature gauge, tachometer, trip odometer, intermittent wipers, tinted glass, power mirrors, AM/FM radio with four speakers, rear defogger, remote fuel-door and trunk/hatch releases, map lights, visor mirrors, automatic headlamps, cargo-area cover (hatchback), 185/70R14 tires, wheel covers. **Limited Edition ST** adds: air conditioning, power door locks and windows, rear wiper, rear spoiler, AM/FM/cassette/CD player with four speakers and diversity antenna, alloy wheels, black chrome trim, floormats. **GT hatchback** adds to ST: 2.2-liter DOHC 4-cylinder engine, 4-wheel disc brakes, upgraded door and interior trim, cassette player, power antenna, power windows and door locks, intermittent rear wiper, engine-oil cooler, fog lamps, 205/55R15 tires. **Convertible** deletes split folding rear seat and intermittent rear wiper, and adds: power top w/glass rear window, contoured rocker panels. **Limited Edition Convertible** adds: air conditioning, rear spoiler, premium AM/FM/cassette/CD player, six speakers and diversity antenna, cruise control, deep jewel green paint, alloy wheels, black chrome trim, floormats.

Optional Equipment:

	Retail Price	Dealer Invoice	Fair Price
Anti-lock brakes	$550	$473	$523
Requires cruise control. NA Limited Edition.			
Air conditioning	1005	804	955
Power Pkg., ST	525	420	499
Power windows and door locks. Requires cruise control.			
Leather Pkg., convertible	1085	868	1031
Leather sport seats, leather-wrapped steering wheel and manual shift knob, leather door trim. Requires cruise control.			
Sport Pkg., GT hatchback	970	776	922
Front sport suspension, front sport seats, leather-wrapped steering wheel and shifter, 205/55R15 summer tires, alloy wheels. Requires cruise control.			
Leather Sport Pkg., GT hatchback	1630	1304	1549
Sport Pkg. plus leather sport seats. Requires cruise control.			

	Retail Price	Dealer Invoice	Fair Price
Limited Edition Pkg, ST	NC	NC	NC
Air conditioning, power door locks and windows, rear wiper, rear spoiler, AM/FM/cassette/CD player with 6 speakers and diversity antenna, alloy wheels, black chrome trim, floormats.			
Rear spoiler, hatchbacks	$415	$332	$394
ST requires intermittent rear wiper.			
Intermittent rear wiper, ST hatchback	170	139	162
NA Limited Edition.			
Power moonroof	760	608	722
NA convertible or Limited Edition.			
Cruise control	290	232	276
Includes leather-wrapped steering wheel and shifter.			
Cassette player, ST	335	257	318
Includes power antenna.			
Premium cassette player, GT hatchback	250	190	238
convertible	195	146	185
Includes diversity antenna, graphic equalizer, and six speakers.			
Cassette and CD player,			
GT hatchback	1335	1004	1268
convertible	1280	960	1216
Includes diversity antenna, graphic equalizer, and eight speakers.			
Fog lamps, ST	100	80	95
NA Limited Edition.			
Contoured rocker panels			
(std. convertible)	200	160	190
NA Limited Edition ST 2-door hatchback.			
Alloy wheels, GT	435	348	413
ST	675	540	641

TOYOTA COROLLA

Specifications	4-door notchback
Wheelbase, in.	97.0
Overall length, in.	172.0
Overall width, in.	66.3
Overall height, in.	54.3
Curb weight, lbs.	2315
Cargo vol., cu. ft.	12.7
Fuel capacity, gals.	13.2
Seating capacity	5

Prices are accurate at time of publication; subject to manufacturer's change.

TOYOTA

Toyota Corolla DX

Engines

	dohc I-4	dohc I-4
Size, liters/cu. in.	1.6/97	1.8/110
Horsepower @ rpm	100 @	105 @
	5600	5200
Torque (lbs./ft.) @ rpm......................................	105 @	117 @
	4400	2800

EPA city/highway mpg

5-speed OD manual	31/35	29/35
3-speed automatic..	25/29	
4-speed OD automatic..		27/34

Built in Fremont, Calif., and Canada.

PRICES

Toyota Corolla	Retail Price	Dealer Invoice	Fair Price
Base 4-door notchback, 5-speed	$12998	$11914	$12414
Base 4-door notchback, automatic	13498	12373	12873
CE 4-door notchback, 5-speed	12998	11914	12414
CE 4-door notchback, automatic	13498	12373	12873
DX 4-door notchback, 5-speed	14188	12566	13066
DX 4-door notchback, automatic	14988	13273	13773
Destination charge	420	420	420

CE requires Classic Edition Pkg. Prices are for vehicles distributed by Toyota Motor Sales, U.S.A., Inc. The dealer invoice, fair price, and destination charge may be higher in areas served by independent distributors.

Standard Equipment:

Base and **CE:** 1.6-liter DOHC 4-cylinder engine, 5-speed manual or 3-speed automatic transmission, driver- and passenger-side air bags, cloth reclining front bucket seats w/lumbar support, front storage console with storage, cupholders, trip odometer, remote decklid release, 175/65R14 tires. **DX** adds: 1.8-liter DOHC 4-cylinder engine, 5-speed manual or 4-speed automatic transmission, power steering, upgraded cloth upholstery, 60/40 split folding rear seat w/headrests, cloth door trim w/map pockets, passenger-side visor mirror, dual remote mirrors, digital clock, intermittent wipers, rear defogger, bodyside moldings, cargo-area lamp, front stabilizer bar, 185/65R14 tires, wheel covers.

Optional Equipment:	Retail Price	Dealer Invoice	Fair Price
Anti-lock brakes	$550	$473	$506
Air conditioning, base, DX	950	760	855
Power steering, base	270	231	243
Value Pkg., base	892	803	847
Air conditioning, power steering, floormats.			
Value Pkg., DX	1837	1653	1745
Air conditioning, tilt steering column, Power Pkg., AM/FM/cassette with four speakers, floormats.			
Classic Edition Pkg., CE	1645	1480	1513
Air conditioning, power steering, Power Pkg., AM/FM radio w/four speakers, remote outside mirrors, floormats.			
Convenience Pkg., base	1220	991	1159
Includes power steering, air conditioning.			
Tilt steering column, DX	170	145	153
Power sunroof, DX	595	476	536
Includes map light.			
Radio Prep Pkg., base, DX	100	75	90
Includes two speakers, wiring harness, antenna.			
AM/FM radio with two speakers, base w/5-speed	245	184	225
AM/FM radio with four speakers, base, DX	390	293	351
AM/FM/cassette with four speakers base, DX	615	461	554
Power Pkg., DX	780	624	702
Power windows and door locks, power mirrors.			
Tachometer, DX	70	56	63
Cruise control, DX	290	232	261
Includes variable intermittent wipers.			

Prices are accurate at time of publication; subject to manufacturer's change.

	Retail Price	Dealer Invoice	Fair Price
All Weather Guard Pkg.,			
base and CE, 5-speed	$255	$207	$230
base and CE, automatic	265	215	244
DX	70	59	63
Heavy-duty rear defogger, battery, heater, and wiper motor, extra-capacity windshield-washer tank. Base w/automatic transmission and CE w/automatic transmission includes rear defogger.			
Integrated child seat, DX	125	100	113
Rear window defogger, base, CE	185	148	167
Bodyside molding, base, CE	50	40	45
DX	20	16	18
NA with black mud guards.			
Black mud guards, DX	60	48	54
NA with bodyside moldings.			
Color-keyed mud guards, DX	80	64	72
Requires bodyside moldings.			
Wheel covers, base, CE	120	96	108
Alloy wheels, DX	415	332	374

TOYOTA LAND CRUISER/ LEXUS LX 450

Toyota Land Cruiser

Specifications

	4-door wagon
Wheelbase, in.	112.2

Lexus LX 450

	4-door wagon
Overall length, in.	189.8
Overall width, in.	76.0
Overall height, in.	73.6
Curb weight, lbs.	4834
Cargo vol., cu. ft.	90.9
Fuel capacity, gals.	25.1
Seating capacity	7

Engines

	dohc I-6
Size, liters/cu. in.	4.5/275
Horsepower @ rpm	212 @ 4600
Torque (lbs./ft.) @ rpm	275 @ 3200

EPA city/highway mpg

4-speed OD automatic	13/15

Built in Japan.

PRICES

Toyota Land Cruiser	Retail Price	Dealer Invoice	Fair Price
4-door 4WD wagon	$41068	$35319	—
Destination charge	420	420	420

Fair price not available at time of publication. Prices are for vehicles distributed by Toyota Motor Sales, U.S.A., Inc. The dealer invoice, fair price, and destination charge may be higher in areas served by independent distributors.

Prices are accurate at time of publication; subject to manufacturer's change.

TOYOTA

Standard Equipment:

4.5-liter DOHC 6-cylinder engine, 4-speed automatic transmission, permanent 4-wheel drive, anti-lock 4-wheel disc brakes, driver- and passenger-side air bags, air conditioning, power steering, cruise control, cloth reclining front bucket seats, folding rear seat, front storage console, middle-seat armrests, power windows and door locks, power mirrors, tilt steering column, tinted glass, tachometer, voltmeter, oil-pressure and coolant-temperature gauges, trip odometer, AM/FM/cassette, power antenna, digital clock with stopwatch and alarm, remote fuel-door release, rear heater, rear defogger, variable intermittent wipers, rear intermittent wiper/washer, automatic headlamps, front and rear tow hooks, passenger-side illuminated visor mirror, skid plates for fuel tank and transfer case, rear step bumper, trailer wiring harness, 275/70R16 tires.

Optional Equipment:

	Retail Price	Dealer Invoice	Fair Price
Premium cassette w/CD player	$945	$709	—
Includes equalizer.			
Leather Trim Pkg.	4280	3455	—
Leather upholstery, power seats, leather-wrapped steering wheel and transfer-case knob, leather-covered center console, Third Seat Pkg.			
Differential locks	825	681	—
Locking front and rear differentials.			
Power moonroof	1185	948	—
Third Seat Pkg.	1515	1212	—
Includes split folding rear third seat, rear 3-point seat belts, cloth headrests, child-safety hatch lock, privacy glass, rear assist grip, sliding rear quarter windows. NA Leather Trim Pkg.			
Alloy wheels	525	420	—
2-tone paint	285	228	—
Black paint	NC	NC	NC

Lesus LX 450	Retail Price	Dealer Invoice	Fair Price
4-door wagon	$48450	$41595	—
Destination charge	495	495	495

Fair price not available at time of publication.

Standard Equipment:

4.5-liter DOHC 6-cylinder engine, 4-speed automatic transmission, full-time 4-wheel drive, anti-lock 4-wheel disc brakes, automatic climate control, driver- and passenger-side air bags, variable-assist power steering, cruise control, leather upholstery, power front bucket seats with driver-side lumbar support, split folding middle bench seat, retractable rear seats, rear folding armrests, front storage console with cupholders, tilt steering wheel, leather-wrapped steering wheel and shifter, Lexus/Pioneer AM/FM/cassette with seven speakers, power antenna, front green-tinted glass, rear privacy glass, sliding rear-quarter windows, remote outside mirrors, power windows and door locks, rear defogger, theft-deterrent system, tachometer, voltmeter, coolant-temperature and oil-pressure gauge, digital clock, illuminated visor mirrors, map lights, simulated wood interior trim, variable intermittent wipers, automatic headlamps, rear heat ducts, remote fuel-door release, first-aid and tool kits, 275/70HR16 tires, full-size spare tire, alloy wheels.

Optional Equipment:	Retail Price	Dealer Invoice	Fair Price
Differential locks	$900	$720	—
Power moonroof	1300	1040	—
6-disc CD changer	1050	840	—

TOYOTA PASEO

Toyota Paseo

Specifications	2-door notchback	2-door conv.
Wheelbase, in.	93.7	93.7
Overall length, in.	163.6	163.6
Overall width, in.	65.4	65.4
Overall height, in.	51.0	51.0
Curb weight, lbs.	2025	2160
Cargo vol., cu. ft.	7.5	6.6
Fuel capacity, gals.	11.9	11.9

Prices are accurate at time of publication; subject to manufacturer's change.

TOYOTA

	2-door notchback	2-door conv.
Seating capacity	4	4

Engines

	dohc I-4
Size, liters/cu. in.	1.5/90
Horsepower @ rpm	93 @ 5400
Torque (lbs./ft.) @ rpm	100 @ 4400

EPA city/highway mpg

5-speed OD manual	31/37
4-speed OD automatic	27/32

Built in Japan.

PRICES

Toyota Paseo	Retail Price	Dealer Invoice	Fair Price
2-door notchback, 5-speed	$13208	$11834	$12134
2-door notchback, automatic	14008	12551	12851
2-door convertible, 5-speed	16728	15390	15990
2-door convertible, automatic	17528	16107	16707
Destination charge	420	420	420

Prices are for vehicles distributed by Toyota Motor Sales, U.S.A., Inc. The dealer invoice, fair price, and destination charge may be higher in areas served by independent distributors.

Standard Equipment:

1.5-liter DOHC 4-cylinder engine, 5-speed manual or 4-speed automatic transmission, power steering, driver- and passenger-side air bags, manual folding top w/glass rear window (convertible), cloth reclining bucket seats, folding rear seat, cupholders, tinted glass, tachometer, coolant temperature gauge, trip odometer, AM/FM radio, digital clock, intermittent wipers, remote outside mirrors, visor mirrors, rear defogger, remote trunk and fuel-door releases, 185/60R14 tires, wheel covers.

Optional Equipment:

Anti-lock brakes	550	473	506
NA with cruise control.			
Air conditioning	925	740	851
Cruise control	290	232	267
NA with anti-lock brakes.			

	Retail Price	Dealer Invoice	Fair Price
Pop-up glass moonroof, notchback	$410	$328	$377
Includes sunshade and storage pouch.			
Power Pkg.	525	420	483
Power windows and door locks.			
Cassette player with four speakers	225	169	207
All Weather Guard Pkg.	70	59	64
Heavy-duty battery, rear defogger, and heater.			
Alloy wheels	415	332	382
Poly-cast wheels	115	92	106
Rear spoiler, notchback	415	332	382

TOYOTA PREVIA

Toyota Previa LE

Specifications

	3-door van
Wheelbase, in.	112.8
Overall length, in.	187.0
Overall width, in.	70.8
Overall height, in.	70.1
Curb weight, lbs.	3755
Cargo vol., cu. ft.	157.8
Fuel capacity, gals.	19.8
Seating capacity	7

Prices are accurate at time of publication; subject to manufacturer's change.

TOYOTA

Engines

	Supercharged dohc I-4
Size, liters/cu. in.	2.4/149
Horsepower @ rpm	161 @ 5000
Torque (lbs./ft.) @ rpm	201 @ 3600

EPA city/highway mpg

4-speed OD automatic	18/22

Built in Japan.

PRICES

Toyota Previa	Retail Price	Dealer Invoice	Fair Price
DX S/C 2WD	$24808	$21847	$22547
LE S/C 2WD	29438	25772	26472
DX S/C All-Trac	28418	24879	25579
LE S/C All-Trac	32838	28749	29449
Destination charge	420	420	420

Prices are for vehicles distributed by Toyota Motor Sales, U.S.A., Inc. The dealer invoice, fair price, and destination charge may be higher in areas served by independent distributors.

Standard Equipment:

DX: 2.4-liter supercharged 4-cylinder engine, 4-speed automatic transmission, driver- and passenger-side air bags, power steering, cloth reclining front bucket seats w/folding armrests, console with storage, 2-passenger second-row seat, 3-passenger split-folding third-row seat, cupholders, tilt steering wheel, tinted glass, digital clock, AM/FM radio, rear defogger, passenger-side visor mirror, variable intermittent wipers, rear intermittent wiper/washer, automatic headlamps, dual outside mirrors, 215/65R15 all-season tires, wheel covers, full-size spare tire. **LE** adds: dual air conditioners, 4-wheel disc brakes, cruise control, upgraded upholstery and interior trim, power windows and door locks, power mirrors, cassette player, illuminated visor mirrors. **All-Trac** adds: permanently engaged 4-wheel drive.

Optional Equipment:

Anti-lock brakes, DX	745	634	671
LE	590	507	531
DX includes 4-wheel disc brakes. DX requires Value Pkg. 1.			
Dual air conditioners, DX	1735	1388	1562
Value Pkg. 1, DX	1765	1589	1633

	Retail Price	Dealer Invoice	Fair Price
LE	$315	$284	$291

DX includes air conditioning, cruise control, Power Pkg., cassette player, privacy glass. LE includes anti-lock brakes, privacy glass. NA Security Pkg.

Value Pkg. 2, LE	635	572	587

Pkg. 1 plus anti-lock brakes, captain's chairs, privacy glass.

Value Pkg. 3, LE	1165	1049	1078

Pkg. 1 plus leather captain's chairs.

Power Pkg., DX	775	620	698

Power windows, door locks, and mirrors.

Privacy glass	425	340	383
Cruise control, DX	305	244	275
Cassette player, DX	225	169	203
Premium cassette player, LE	280	210	252

Includes seven speakers. Requires Value Pkg. 1, 2, or 3.

Premium cassette and CD players, LE	1265	949	1139

Includes nine speakers and programmable equalizer. Requires Value Pkg. 1, 2, or 3.

Dual moonroofs, LE 2WD	1610	1288	1449

Includes sunshade and rear spoiler.

Captain's chairs with armrests, LE	870	696	783

NA w/Value Pkg. 1.

Leather Trim Package, LE	1900	1520	1710

Includes captain's chairs. NA Value Pkgs.

Security Pkg., DX	995	796	896
LE	220	176	198

Theft-deterrent system. DX also includes Power Pkg. NA Value Pkg 1 (DX).

Alloy wheels, LE	435	348	392

TOYOTA RAV4

Specifications

	2-door wagon	4-door wagon
Wheelbase, in.	86.6	94.9
Overall length, in.	147.2	163.4
Overall width, in.	66.7	66.7
Overall height, in.	65.2	65.4
Curb weight, lbs.	2469	2612
Cargo vol., cu. ft.	34.7	57.9

Prices are accurate at time of publication; subject to manufacturer's change.

TOYOTA

Toyota RAV4 4-door

	2-door wagon	4-door wagon
Fuel capacity, gals.	15.3	15.3
Seating capacity	4	4

Engines

	dohc I-4
Size, liters/cu. in.	2.0/122
Horsepower @ rpm	120 @ 5400
Torque (lbs./ft.) @ rpm	125 @ 4600

EPA city/highway mpg
5-speed OD manual	22/26
4-speed OD automatic	22/26

Built in Japan.

PRICES

Toyota RAV4	Retail Price	Dealer Invoice	Fair Price
2WD 2-door wagon, 5-speed	$15118	$13779	—
2WD 2-door wagon, automatic	16168	14738	—
2WD 4-door wagon, 5-speed	15818	14417	—
2WD 4-door wagon, automatic	16868	15375	—
4WD 2-door wagon, 5-speed	16518	14801	—
4WD 4-door wagon, 5-speed	17218	15428	—
4WD 4-door wagon, automatic	18268	16368	—
Destination charge	420	420	420

Fair price not available at time of publication. Prices are for vehicles distributed by Toyota Motor Sales, U.S.A., Inc. The dealer invoice, fair price, and destination charge may be higher in areas served by independent distributors.

Standard Equipment:

2.0-liter DOHC 4-cylinder engine, 5-speed manual transmission or 4-speed automatic transmission, driver- and passenger-side air bags, power steering, reclining cloth front bucket seats, split folding and reclining rear seat, front storage console, cupholders, dual outside mirrors, tachometer, trip odometer, coolant-temperature gauge, digital clock, rear defogger, intermittent front and rear wipers, 215/70R16 tires. **4WD models** add: permanent 4WD.

Optional Equipment:	Retail Price	Dealer Invoice	Fair Price
Anti-lock brakes	$590	$507	—
Air conditioning	985	788	—
Limited slip differential, 4WD	375	309	—
Upgrade Pkg., 2-door	870	705	—
4-door	1050	849	—
Power windows, door locks, and mirrors, tilt steering wheel, front-speaker upgrade. Requires AM/FM radio or cassette player.			
All Weather Guard Pkg.	70	59	—
Heavy-duty battery, heavy-duty rear heater, heavy-duty starter motor, large window-wiper reservoir.			
L Pkg., 2-door	1575	1418	—
4-door	2620	2358	—
Air conditioning, AM/FM radio, alloy wheels, spare tire cover, tilt steering wheel, "L" striping and badging, floor and cargo mats. 4-door adds cassette player, power windows, door locks, and mirrors, cruise control. Note: available in black or silver paint only. NA 4WD 2-door wagon with 5-speed.			
Cruise control	290	232	—
Tilt steering wheel	170	145	—
Twin removable moonroofs, 2-door	600	480	—
Power moonroof, 4-door	915	732	—
AM/FM radio	190	143	—
AM/FM/cassette player	415	311	—
Alloy wheels	685	548	—

TOYOTA TERCEL

Specifications	2-door notchback	4-door notchback
Wheelbase, in.	93.7	93.7

Prices are accurate at time of publication; subject to manufacturer's change.

Toyota Tercel CE 2-door

	2-door notchback	4-door notchback
Overall length, in.	161.8	161.8
Overall width, in.	64.8	64.8
Overall height, in.	53.2	53.2
Curb weight, lbs.	2010	2035
Cargo vol., cu. ft.	9.3	9.3
Fuel capacity, gals.	11.9	11.9
Seating capacity	5	5

Engines

	dohc I-4
Size, liters/cu. in.	1.5/89
Horsepower @ rpm	93 @ 5400
Torque (lbs./ft.) @ rpm	100 @ 4400

EPA city/highway mpg

5-speed OD manual	32/39
3-speed automatic	29/34
4-speed OD automatic	30/37

Built in Japan.

PRICES

Toyota Tercel	Retail Price	Dealer Invoice	Fair Price
CE 2-door notchback, 5-speed	$10648	$10033	$10333
CE 2-door notchback, automatic	11148	10503	10803
Limited Edition 2-door notchback 5-speed	10648	10033	—
Limited Edition 2-door notchback automatic	11148	10503	—

Toyota Tercel CE 4-door

	Retail Price	Dealer Invoice	Fair Price
CE 4-door notchback, 5-speed	$12108	$11222	$11522
CE 4-door notchback, automatic	12818	11881	12181
Destination charge	420	420	420

Fair price for Limited Edition not available at time of publication. Prices are for vehicles distributed by Toyota Motor Sales, U.S.A., Inc. The dealer invoice, fair price, and destination charge may be higher in areas served by independent distributors.

Standard Equipment:

1.5-liter DOHC 4-cylinder engine, 5-speed manual transmission or 3-speed automatic transmission (2-door) or 4-speed automatic transmission (4-door), driver- and passenger-side air bags, cloth upholstery, reclining front bucket seats, front storage console, cupholders, trip odometer, dual outside mirrors, 175/65R14 tires, wheel covers.

Optional Equipment:

Anti-lock brakes	550	473	495
Air conditioning	925	740	833
Rear defogger	185	148	167
Power steering	270	231	243
Power Pkg.,			
4-door	640	512	576
2-door	525	420	473
Power windows and door locks.			
Convenience Pkg.	365	293	329

    Intermittent wipers, digital clock, remote outside mirrors, 60/40 split folding rear seat, remote fuel-door and decklid releases.

TOYOTA

	Retail Price	Dealer Invoice	Fair Price
Value Equipment Pkg. 1, CE........................	$857	$771	—
Air conditioning, power steering, floormats.			
Value Equipment Pkg. 2, CE 2-door	1287	1158	—
4-door..	1357	1221	—
Air conditioning, power steering, remote trunk/fuel release, color-keyed bumpers, AM/FM radio with four speakers, 60/40 split folding rear seats, digital clock, intermittent wipers, dual manual remote outside mirrors (4-door), bodyside molding, floormats.			
Hawk Value Pkg. Limited Edition.................	1711	1540	—
Air conditioning, power steering, AM/FM radio with four speakers, 60/40 split folding rear seat, digital clock, intermittent wipers, bodyside molding, P185/60R14 tires, floormats, color-keyed bumpers, color-keyed spoiler.			
AM/FM radio with two speakers	245	184	221
AM/FM radio with four speakers	390	293	351
AM/FM/cassette with four speakers	615	461	554
All Weather Guard Pkg.	255	215	230
Heavy-duty battery, heater, starter, and rear defogger.			
Color-keyed bumpers	95	76	86
Bodyside moldings	50	40	45
Tire upgrade	90	72	81

TOYOTA 4RUNNER

Toyota 4Runner Limited

Specifications

	4-door wagon
Wheelbase, in.	105.3
Overall length, in.	178.7

	4-door wagon
Overall width, in.	66.5
Overall height, in.	67.5
Curb weight, lbs.	3440
Cargo vol., cu. ft.	79.7
Fuel capacity, gals.	18.5
Seating capacity	5

Engines

	dohc I-4	dohc V-6
Size, liters/cu. in.	2.7/164	3.4/207
Horsepower @ rpm	150 @ 4800	183 @ 4800
Torque (lbs./ft.) @ rpm	177 @ 4000	217 @ 3600
EPA city/highway mpg		
5-speed OD manual	16/21	16/19
4-speed OD automatic	18/22	16/19

Built in Japan.

PRICES

Toyota 4Runner	Retail Price	Dealer Invoice	Fair Price
Base 2WD 4-door wagon, 5-speed	$19888	$17412	—
Base 2WD 4-door wagon, automatic	20788	18199	—
Base 4WD 4-door wagon, 5-speed	21988	19249	—
Base 4WD 4-door wagon, automatic	22888	20038	—
SR5 2WD 4-door wagon, automatic	24558	21499	—
Limited 2WD 4-door wagon, automatic	31418	27506	—
SR5 4WD 4-door wagon, 5-speed	25678	22480	—
SR5 4WD 4-door wagon, automatic	26578	23267	—
Limited 4WD 4-door wagon, automatic	33738	29536	—
Destination charge	420	420	420

Fair price not available at time of publication. Prices are for vehicles distributed by Toyota Motor Sales, U.S.A., Inc. The dealer invoice, fair price, and destination charge may be higher in areas served by independent distributors.

Standard Equipment:

Base: 2.7-liter DOHC 4-cylinder engine, 5-speed manual or 4-speed automatic transmission, 4WDemand part-time 4WD (4WD models), power steering, driver- and passenger-side air bags, cloth bucket

TOYOTA

seats, 50/50 split folding rear seat, front and rear cupholders, tachometer, voltmeter, oil-pressure gauge, trip odometer, AM/FM radio with four speakers, power tailgate window, tinted glass, intermittent front and rear wipers, passenger-side visor mirror, remote fuel-door release, mud guards, 225/75R15 tires. **SR5** adds: 3.4-liter DOHC V-6 engine, anti-lock brakes, tilt steering wheel, power door locks and mirrors, digital clock, cassette player, spring rear antenna, rear defogger, rear cupholders, variable intermittent wipers, map and courtesy lights, privacy glass, chrome bumpers and grille. **Limited** adds: 4-speed automatic transmission, One-Touch Hi-4 4WD (4WD), remote 4-wheel drive selector (4WD), air conditioning, cruise control, power front sport seats, leather upholstery, premium cassette player with six speakers, power antenna, leather-wrapped steering wheel and shift knob, power windows, wood interior trim, tonneau cover, All Weather Guard Pkg., bodyside cladding, fender flares, running boards, floormats, 265/70R16 tires, alloy wheels.

Optional Equipment:

	Retail Price	Dealer Invoice	Fair Price
Anti-lock brakes, base	$590	$507	—
Air conditioning, base, SR5	985	788	—
Locking rear differential, base 4WD, SR5 4WD w/5-speed, Limited 4WD	325	268	—

Base requires styled steel wheels or alloy wheels w/31-inch tires (265/70R16 tires). 4WD SR5 w/5-speed requires alloy wheels w/31-inch tires, Sports Pkg., or Group 1.

	Retail Price	Dealer Invoice	Fair Price
Alloy wheels w/locking rear differential, SR5 4WD w/automatic	1355	1092	—
Preferred Equipment Group 1, SR5	2750	2190	—

Air conditioning, power windows, premium cassette player with six speakers, power antenna, alloy wheels with 31-inch tires (265/70R16 tires).

	Retail Price	Dealer Invoice	Fair Price
Preferred Equipment Group 2, SR5	2135	1698	—

Group 1 without 31-inch tires.

	Retail Price	Dealer Invoice	Fair Price
Upgrade Pkg., base	2500	1974	—

Air conditioner, cruise control, power windows and door locks, power mirrors, deluxe cassette, power antenna, floormats.

	Retail Price	Dealer Invoice	Fair Price
Sports Pkg., SR5	1760	1422	—

Sports Seat Pkg., leather-wrapped steering wheel, leather-wrapped shifter (5-speed), fender flares, P265/70R16 tires, alloy wheels.

	Retail Price	Dealer Invoice	Fair Price
Sports Pkg. w/locking rear differential, 4WD SR5 w/automatic	2085	1690	—

	Retail Price	Dealer Invoice	Fair Price
Convenience Pkg., base	$705	$577	—

Tilt steering wheel, variable intermittent wipers, digital clock, intermittent rear wiper/washer, rear defogger, map light.

Cruise control, base, SR5	290	232	—
Power Pkg. #1, base	435	348	—

Power door locks, power mirrors, additional lighting.

Power Pkg #2, base	920	736	—
SR5	540	432	—

Power windows and door locks, power mirrors, power antenna. SR5 requires premium cassette player or cassette/CD player.

Sports Seat Pkg, SR5	685	548	—

Cloth sport seats, cruise control, upgraded door trim, leather-wrapped steering wheel, leather-wrapped shift knob (4WD SR5 w/5-speed).

Leather Trim Pkg., SR5	1535	1228	—

Leather sports seats, leather door trim, leather-wrapped steering wheel, leather-wrapped shift knob (4WD SR5 w/5-speed), cruise control.

All Weather Guard Pkg.	70	59	—

Heavy-duty battery, heavy-duty wiper motor and starter motor, large window-wiper reservoir. Base requires rear heater, and rear wiper/defogger or Convenience Pkg. 2WD SR5 and 2WD Limited require rear heater.

Rear wiper/defogger, base	365	292	—
Tilt steering column, base	235	201	—

Includes variable intermittent wipers.

Rear heater	165	132	—

Includes rear storage console w/cupholders.

Privacy glass, base	295	236	—
Power sunroof, SR5, Limited	915	732	—
Tonneau cover, base, SR5	85	68	—
Premium cassette player, SR5	195	146	—

Includes six speakers. Requires Power Pkg. #2.

Deluxe cassette player, base	225	169	—

Includes four speakers.

Cassette/CD player, SR5	1140	855	—
Limited	945	709	—

Includes six speakers. Requires Power Pkg. #2.

Styled steel wheels, base	600	480	—

Includes 265/70R16 tires. 2WD requires anti-lock brakes.

Alloy wheels w/31-inch tires	1030	824	—

Includes 265/70R16 tires. Base 2WD requires anti-lock brakes.

Alloy wheels, base, SR5	415	332	—

Prices are accurate at time of publication; subject to manufacturer's change.

	Retail Price	Dealer Invoice	Fair Price
Metallic paint	NC	NC	NC

VOLKSWAGEN CABRIO

Volkswagen Cabrio

Specifications

	2-door conv.
Wheelbase, in.	97.2
Overall length, in.	160.4
Overall width, in.	66.7
Overall height, in.	56.0
Curb weight, lbs.	2701
Cargo vol., cu. ft.	7.8
Fuel capacity, gals.	14.5
Seating capacity	4

Engines

	ohc I-4
Size, liters/cu. in.	2.0/121
Horsepower @ rpm	115 @ 5400
Torque (lbs./ft.) @ rpm	122 @ 3200

EPA city/highway mpg

5-speed OD manual	24/31
4-speed OD automatic	22/29

Built in Germany.

PRICES

Volkswagen Cabrio	Retail Price	Dealer Invoice	Fair Price
Base 2-door convertible	$17925	$16244	—
Highline 2-door convertible	21675	19688	—
Destination charge	500	500	500

Fair price not available at time of publication.

Standard Equipment:

Base: 2.0-liter 4-cylinder engine, 5-speed manual transmission, anti-lock brakes, driver- and passenger-side air bags, power steering, manual folding top, cloth reclining front sport seats with driver-side height adjustment, folding rear seat, console, cupholders, power door locks, tinted glass, tilt steering column, digital clock, trip odometer, tachometer, coolant-temperature gauge, service indicator, front door storage pockets, AM/FM/cassette, rear defogger, theft-deterrent system, variable intermittent wipers, daytime running lights, integral roll bar, 195/60HR14 tires, wheel covers. **Highline** adds: air conditioning, cruise control, upgraded cloth top, leather upholstery, power windows, heated power mirrors, illuminated visor mirrors, fog lights, alloy wheels.

Optional Equipment:

4-speed automatic transmission	875	856	—
Air conditioning, base	860	750	—
Cold Weather Pkg.	250	218	—
Heated front seats and windshield washer nozzles.			
Convenience Group, base	625	546	—
Cruise control, power windows, heated power mirrors.			
6-disc CD changer	495	412	—
Metallic paint	175	153	—

VOLKSWAGEN JETTA/GOLF

Specifications	Golf 2-door hatchback	Golf 4-door hatchback	Jetta 4-door notchback
Wheelbase, in.	97.4	97.4	97.4
Overall length, in.	160.5	160.5	173.4
Overall width, in.	66.7	66.7	66.7
Overall height, in.	56.2	56.2	56.1

Prices are accurate at time of publication; subject to manufacturer's change.

VOLKSWAGEN

Volkswagen Golf GTI VR6

	Golf 2-door hatchback	Golf 4-door hatchback	Jetta 4-door notchback
Curb weight, lbs.	2511	2577	2647
Cargo vol., cu. ft.	17.5	16.9	15.0
Fuel capacity, gals.	14.5	14.5	14.5
Seating capacity	5	5	5

Engines	ohc I-4	ohc V-6	Turbodiesel ohc I-4
Sizes, liters/cu. in.	2.0/121	2.8/170	1.9/116
Horsepower @ rpm	115 @ 5400	172 @ 5400	90 @ 3750
Torque (lbs./ft.) @ rpm	122 @ 3200	173 @ 4200	149 @ 1900
EPA city/highway mpg			
5-speed OD manual	24/31	19/25	40/49
4-speed OD automatic	22/29	18/24	

Built in Mexico.

PRICES

Volkswagen Golf/Jetta	Retail Price	Dealer Invoice	Fair Price
Golf GL 4-door hatchback	$13470	$12432	$12932
Golf K2 4-door hatchback	14275	13266	13561
GTI 2-door hatchback	16320	15032	15532
GTI VR6 2-door hatchback	19710	18198	18698
Jetta GL 4-door notchback	14570	13219	13719
Jetta GT 4-door notchback	14965	13628	14128
Jetta TDI 4-door notchback	15745	14499	—
Jetta GLS 4-door notchback	16920	15318	15818

Volkswagen Jetta GL

	Retail Price	Dealer Invoice	Fair Price
Jetta GLX 4-door notchback	$20555	$18999	$19499
Destination charge	500	500	500

Jetta TDI prices not available at time of publication.

Standard Equipment:

Golf GL and Jetta GL: 2.0-liter 4-cylinder engine, 5-speed manual transmission, driver- and passenger-side air bags, power steering, cloth reclining bucket seats, driver-seat height adjustment, 60/40 split folding rear seat, front storage console, cupholders, tilt steering wheel (Jetta), power door locks, manual outside mirrors, tachometer, remote hatch and fuel-door releases, variable intermittent wipers, rear defogger, rear wiper/washer (Golf), theft-deterrent system, visor mirrors, daytime running lights, rear spoiler (Golf), cargo cover, trunk light, 185/60HR14 tires, wheel covers. **Golf K2** adds to Golf GL: heated front seats, heated power outside mirrors, AM/FM/cassette player, sport instrument gauges, heated windshield washer nozzles, floormats, roof-mounted whip antenna, roof rack, fog lamps, 195/60HR14 tires, Siesta-style wheel covers, K2 skis or snow board. **GTI** adds to Golf GL: anti-lock 4-wheel disc brakes, air conditioning, AM/FM/cassette, cloth sport seats, power sunroof, dark-tinted tail-light lenses, reading light, 195/60HR14 tires, 5-spoke alloy wheels. **GTI VR6** adds: 2.8-liter V-6 engine, close-ratio 5-speed manual transmission, sport suspension, traction control, cruise control, power windows and mirrors, tilt steering wheel, leather-wrapped steering wheel, trip computer, 205/50HR15 tires, Pinanfarina-style alloy wheels. **Jetta GT** adds to Jetta GL: cloth sport seats, dark-tinted tail-light lenses, rear spoiler, fog lamps, alloy wheels. **Jetta TDI** adds Jetta GL: 1.9-liter turbodiesel engine, cruise control, 195/60HR14 tires. **Jetta GLS** adds to Jetta GL: air conditioning, cruise control, AM/FM/cassette, power windows, heated power mirrors, tilt steering wheel. **Jetta GLX** adds: 2.8-liter V-6 engine, close-ratio 5-speed manual transmission, anti-lock 4-wheel disc brakes, sport suspension, traction control, cloth sport seats, power sunroof, leather-wrapped steering wheel, Bose sound system, trip computer, reading lights, rear spoiler, fog lamps, 205/50HR15 tires, Bugatti-style alloy wheels.

Optional Equipment:

	Retail Price	Dealer Invoice	Fair Price
4-speed automatic transmission	$875	$856	$866
NA TDI or GTI VR6.			
Cold Weather Pkg., GLS, GLX	250	218	225
Heated front seats and windshield washer nozzles.			
Air conditioning, GL, GT	860	750	817
Leather upholstery, GTI VR6	550	480	495
Jetta GLX	800	698	720
Anti-lock brakes, GL, GT, GLS	775	727	751
AM/FM/cassette, GL, GT	485	423	437
Includes eight speakers.			
Bose sound system, GLS	375	313	338
6-disc CD changer	495	412	446
Cruise control, Jetta GL, GT	225	197	203
Power sunroof, GL, GT, GLS	590	516	531
Clearcoat metallic paint	175	153	158

VOLKSWAGEN PASSAT

Volkswagen Passat GLX

Specifications

	4-door notchback	4-door wagon
Wheelbase, in.	103.3	103.3

Volkswagen Passat GLX wagon

	4-door notchback	4-door wagon
Overall length, in.	180.0	179.9
Overall width, in.	67.5	67.5
Overall height, in.	56.4	58.7
Curb weight, lbs.	3140	3197
Cargo vol., cu. ft.	14.4	68.9
Fuel capacity, gals.	18.5	18.5
Seating capacity	5	5

Engines

	ohc V-6	Turbodiesel ohc I-4
Size, liters/cu. in.	2.8/170	1.9/116
Horsepower @ rpm	172 @ 5800	90 @ 3750
Torque (lbs./ft.) @ rpm	177 @ 4200	149 @ 1900

EPA city/highway mpg

5-speed OD manual	19/26	38/47
4-speed OD automatic	18/25	

Built in Germany.

PRICES

Volkswagen Passat	Retail Price	Dealer Invoice	Fair Price
TDI 4-door notchback	$19430	$17498	—
TDI 4-door wagon	19860	17882	—
GLX 4-door notchback	21890	19694	—
GLX 4-door wagon	22320	20078	—
Destination charge	475	475	475

Fair price not available at time of publication.

Prices are accurate at time of publication; subject to manufacturer's change.

Standard Equipment:

TDI: 1.9-liter turbodiesel engine, 5-speed manual transmission, 4-wheel disc brakes, driver- and passenger-side air bags, air conditioning, power steering, cruise control, cloth reclining front bucket seats w/adjustable height, thigh, and lumbar supports, 60/40 folding rear seatback, rear armrest, front storage console, tilt steering column, power windows and door locks, heated power mirrors, lights, tachometer, coolant-temperature gauge, digital clock, tinted glass, AM/FM/cassette w/anti-theft, rear defogger, theft-deterrent system, remote fuel-door and decklid releases, variable-speed intermittent wipers, reading lights, interior air filter, illuminated visor mirrors, daytime running lamps, rear spoiler, 195/60HR14 tires, wheel covers. **GLX** adds: 2.8-liter V-6 engine, anti-lock brakes, traction control, trip odometer, trip computer, leather-wrapped steering wheel, leather-wrapped shifter and parking-brake handle, fog lights, 215/50HR15 tires, alloy wheels. **Wagon** deletes power decklid release, rear spoiler, and adds: rear wiper/washer, remote tailgate release, cargo cover, black roof rails.

Optional Equipment:	Retail Price	Dealer Invoice	Fair Price
4-speed automatic transmission, GLX	$800	$777	—
Anti-lock brakes, TDI	775	727	—
Leather upholstery, GLX	875	764	—
6-disc CD changer, notchbacks	495	412	—
Power sunroof	855	746	—
All Weather Package, GLX	325	284	—

Includes heated front seats and windshield washer nozzles.

VOLVO 850

Specifications	4-door notchback	4-door wagon
Wheelbase, in.	104.9	104.9
Overall length, in.	183.5	185.4
Overall width, in.	69.3	69.3
Overall height, in.	55.7	56.9
Curb weight, lbs.	3232	3342
Cargo vol., cu. ft.	14.7	67.0
Fuel capacity, gals.	19.3	19.3
Seating capacity	5	5

Engines	dohc I-5	Turbo dohc I-5	Turbo dohc I-5	Turbo dohc I-5
Size, liters/cu. in.	2.4/149	2.4/149	2.3/141	2.3/141

Volvo 850 GLT 4-door

	dohc I-5	Turbo dohc I-5	Turbo dohc I-5	Turbo dohc I-5
Horsepower @ rpm	168 @ 6200	190 @ 5200	222 @ 5200	240 @ 5600
Torque (lbs/ft) @ rpm	162 @ 4700	191 @ 1800	221 @ 2100	221 @ 2100
EPA city/highway mpg				
5-speed OD manual	20/29			
4-speed OD automatic	20/29	20/27	19/26	19/26

Built in Belgium and Canada.

PRICES

Volvo 850	Retail Price	Dealer Invoice	Fair Price
O 4-door notchback, 5-speed	$26710	$24510	—
A 4-door notchback, automatic	27685	25485	—
O 4-door wagon, 5-speed	28010	25810	—
A 4-door wagon, automatic	28985	26785	—
GTO 4-door notchback, 5-speed	28040	25740	—
GTA 4-door notchback, automatic	29015	26715	—
GTO 4-door wagon, 5-speed	29340	27040	—
GTA 4-door wagon, automatic	30315	28015	—
GTOS 4-door notchback, 5-speed	29240	26940	—
GTAS 4-door notchback, automatic	30215	27915	—
GTOS 4-door wagon, 5-speed	30540	28240	—
GTAS 4-door wagon, automatic	31515	29215	—
GLT 4-door notchback, automatic	31835	29435	—
GLT 4-door wagon, automatic	33135	30735	—
T5 4-door notchback, automatic	34500	31550	—
T5 4-door wagon, automatic	35800	32850	—

Prices are accurate at time of publication; subject to manufacturer's change.

VOLVO

Volvo 850 GLT wagon

	Retail Price	Dealer Invoice	Fair Price
R 4-door notchback, automatic	$38685	$34985	—
R 4-door wagon, automatic	40135	36435	—
Destination charge	495	495	495

Fair price not available at time of publication.

Standard Equipment:

O/A: 2.4-liter DOHC 5-cylinder engine (168-horsepower), 5-speed manual or 4-speed automatic transmission, front and side air bags, anti-lock 4-wheel disc brakes, air conditioning w/dual climate control, variable-assist power steering, cruise control, cloth upholstery, reclining front bucket seats, 8-way manually adjustable driver seat, fully folding passenger seat, 60/40 split folding rear seat, rear-seat trunk pass-through (notchback), child booster seat (wagon), front armrest w/cupholder, tilt/telescoping steering column, power windows and door locks, heated power mirrors, tinted glass, coolant-temperature gauge, trip odometer, tachometer, digital clock, 6-speaker AM/FM/cassette w/anti-theft, power antenna (notchback), integrated window antenna (wagon), rear defogger, intermittent wipers, illuminated visor mirrors, front and rear reading lights, daytime running lights, rear fog light, front mud guards, floormats, tool kit, 195/60VR15 tires, wheel covers. **GTO/GTA** adds: 8-way power driver seat w/memory feature, remote keyless entry, theft-deterrent system, 6-spoke alloy wheels. **GTOS/GTAS** adds: power sunroof. **GLT** adds: 2.4-liter DOHC turbocharged 5-cylinder engine (190-horsepower), 4-speed automatic transmission, automatic climate control, velour upholstery, Premium Sound System w/AM/FM/cassette, 6-spoke alloy wheels. **T5** adds: 2.3-liter DOHC turbocharged 5-cylinder engine (222-horsepower), power passenger seat w/memory feature, leather-wrapped steering wheel, trip computer, 8-speaker cassette/CD player, 205/50ZR16 tires, 5-spoke alloy wheels. **R** deletes child booster seat (wagon) and adds: 2.3-liter DOHC turbocharged 5-cylinder engine (240-horsepower), TRACS traction-control system, automatic load leveling (wagon), sport suspension, leather upholstery, heated front seats, outside-temperature indicator, sound-system amplifier, headlamp wiper/washer, wood interior trim, front fog lights, rear spoiler (notchback), cargo net (wagon), 205/45ZR17 Pirelli tires (notchback), full-size spare tire (notchback), 195/65R15 tires (wagon), 7-spoke alloy wheels (notchback).

Optional Equipment:

	Retail Price	Dealer Invoice	Fair Price
Sport Pkg., notchbacks (std. R)	$595	$475	—
Fog lights, rear spoiler.			
Touring Pkg., O/A, GTO/GTA, GTOS/GTAS, GLT	395	315	—
Trip computer, leather-wrapped steering wheel.			
Grand Touring Pkg., O/A	1980	1580	—
GTO/GTA, GTOS/GTAS, GLT	1485	1185	—
Power passenger seat, CD player, wood interior trim.			
Cold Weather Pkg. (std. R)	485	385	—
Heated front seats, headlamp wiper/washer, outside-temperature indicator.			
TRACS traction-control system and Cold Weather Pkg. (std. R)	810	645	—
Automatic load leveling, wagons (std. R wagon)	495	395	—
CD player, base, O/A, GTO/GTA, GTOS/GTAS, GLT	485	385	—
Leather upholstery (std. R)	1195	955	—
Velour upholstery, O/A, GTO/GTA, GTOS/GTAS	200	160	—
8-way power driver seat w/memory feature, O/A	495	395	—
Power passenger seat (std. R)	495	395	—
Decklid spoiler, notchbacks (std. R notchback)	385	305	—
Sport suspension, notchbacks (std. R notchback)	175	140	—
Wood interior trim (std. R)	810	645	—
6-spoke alloy wheels, O/A	400	320	—
Includes 195/60R15 all-season tires.			

Prices are accurate at time of publication; subject to manufacturer's change.

VOLVO 960

Volvo 960 4-door

Specifications

	4-door notchback	4-door wagon
Wheelbase, in.	109.1	109.1
Overall length, in.	191.8	191.4
Overall width, in.	68.9	68.9
Overall height, in.	56.6	57.6
Curb weight, lbs.	3461	3547
Cargo vol., cu. ft.	16.6	74.9
Fuel capacity, gals.	19.8	19.8
Seating capacity	5	5

Engines

	dohc I-6
Size, liters/cu. in.	2.9/178
Horsepower @ rpm	181 @ 5200
Torque (lbs./ft.) @ rpm	199 @ 4100

EPA city/highway mpg

4-speed OD automatic	18/26

Built in Sweden and Canada.

PRICES

Volvo 960	Retail Price	Dealer Invoice	Fair Price
960 4-door notchback	$34300	$31600	—
960 4-door wagon	35850	33150	—

Volvo 960 wagon

	Retail Price	Dealer Invoice	Fair Price
Destination charge	$495	$495	$495

Fair price not available at time of publication.

Standard Equipment:

2.9-liter DOHC 6-cylinder engine, 4-speed automatic transmission, anti-lock 4-wheel disc brakes, automatic locking differential, power steering, front and side front air bags, automatic climate control, cruise control, leather upholstery, reclining front bucket seats w/lumbar adjuster, 8-way power front seats w/memory feature, rear-seat trunk pass through (notchback), 60/40 split folding rear seat (wagon), integrated child booster seat (wagon), power sunroof, power windows and door locks, heated power mirrors, leather-wrapped tilt steering wheel, tinted glass, AM/FM/cassette w/amplifier and anti-theft, power antenna (notchback), integrated antenna (wagon), remote keyless entry, remote trunk/hatch release, theft-deterrent system, wood interior trim, illuminated visor mirrors, front and rear reading lights, headlight wiper/washers, front and fog lamps, daytime running lights, luggage rack (wagon), tool kit, floormats, 195/65HR15 tires (wagon), 205/55VR16 tires (notchback), alloy wheels.

Optional Equipment:

Cassette/CD player	485	385	—
Cold Weather Pkg.	645	415	—
Heated front seats, locking differential, outside temperature indicator.			
Automatic load-leveling suspension,			
wagon	495	320	—

Prices are accurate at time of publication; subject to manufacturer's change.

1998 VOLVO S70/V70

1998 Volvo S70

Specifications

	4-door notchback	4-door wagon
Wheelbase, in.	104.9	104.9
Overall length, in.	185.9	185.9
Overall width, in.	69.3	69.3
Overall height, in.	55.2	56.2
Curb weight, lbs.	3152	3259
Cargo vol., cu. ft.	15.1	77.2
Fuel capacity, gals.	18.5	18.5
Seating capacity	5	5

Engines

	dohc I-5	Turbo dohc I-5	Turbo dohc I-5
Size, liters/cu. in.	2.4/149	2.4/149	2.3/141
Horsepower @ rpm	168 @ 6100	190 @ 5200	236 @ 5100
Torque (lbs/ft) @ rpm	162 @ 4700	199 @ 1800	243 @ 2100

EPA city/highway mpg

5-speed OD manual	20/29	20/29	NA
4-speed OD automatic	20/29	19/26	

Built in Sweden, Belgium, and Canada.

PRICES

Volvo S70/V70	Retail Price	Dealer Invoice	Fair Price
S70 4-door notchback, 5-speed	$26985	—	—

CONSUMER GUIDE®

1998 Volvo V70

	Retail Price	Dealer Invoice	Fair Price
S70 4-door notchback, automatic	$27960	—	—
S70 4-door notchback w/sunroof, 5-speed	29540	—	—
S70 4-door notchback w/sunroof, automatic ..	30515	—	—
V70 4-door wagon, 5-speed	28285	—	—
V70 4-door wagon, automatic	29260	—	—
V70 4-door wagon w/sunroof, 5-speed	30840	—	—
V70 4-door wagon w/sunroof, automatic ...	31815	—	—
S70 GLT 4-door notchback, automatic	32440	—	—
V70 GLT 4-door wagon, automatic	33740	—	—
S70 T5 4-door notchback, 5-speed	34010	—	—
S70 T5 4-door notchback, automatic	34985	—	—
V70 T5 4-door wagon, 5-speed	35310	—	—
V70 T5 4-door wagon, automatic	36285	—	—
Destination charge	575	575	575

Dealer invoice and fair price not available at time of publication.

Standard Equipment:

2.4-liter DOHC 5-cylinder engine, 5-speed manual or 4-speed automatic transmission, front and side air bags, anti-lock 4-wheel disc brakes, air conditioning w/dual climate control, variable-assist power steering, cruise control, velour upholstery, reclining front bucket seats, 8-way manually adjustable driver seat, fully folding passenger seat, 60/40 split folding rear seat, rear-seat trunk pass-through (notchback), front armrest w/cup holder, tilt/telescoping steering column, power windows and door locks, remote keyless entry, theft-deterrent system, remote decklid/tailgate release, heated power mirrors, tinted glass, coolant temperature gauge, trip odometer, tachometer, digital clock, outside temperature indicator, 6-speaker AM/FM/cassette w/anti-theft,

Prices are accurate at time of publication; subject to manufacturer's change.

VOLVO

power antenna (notchback), integrated window antenna (wagon), rear defogger, intermittent wipers, illuminated visor mirrors, front and rear reading lights, daytime running lights, rear fog light, front mud guards, floormats, tool kit, 195/60VR15 tires, wheel covers. **Sunroof** models add: power glass sunroof, six-spoke alloy wheels. **GLT** adds: 2.4-liter DOHC turbocharged 5-cylinder engine, 4-speed automatic transmission, automatic climate control, 8-way power driver's seat w/memory feature, premium AM/FM/cassette. **T5** adds: 2.3-liter DOHC turbocharged 5-cylinder engine, 8-way power passenger seat w/memory feature, leather-wrapped steering wheel, trip computer, 205/50ZR16 tires, 5-spoke alloy wheels.

Optional Equipment:	Retail Price	Dealer Invoice	Fair Price
Touring Pkg., base, GLT	$395	—	—
Trip computer, leather wrapped steering wheel.			
Sport Pkg., notchbacks	595	—	—
Fog lights, rear spoiler.			
Grand Touring Pkg., base	1780	—	—
GLT	1285	—	—
Power driver's seat (base), power passenger seat, CD player, burled walnut interior trim.			
TRACS/Cold Weather Pkg.	785	—	—
Traction control, heated front seats, headlamp wiper/washer.			
Automatic load leveling, wagons	495	—	—
CD player	485	—	—
Leather upholstery	1195	—	—
8-way power driver seat w/memory feature, base	495	—	—
Sport suspension	175	—	—
Burled walnut interior trim, T5	575	—	—
Alloy wheels, base	450	—	—

1998 VOLVO S90/V90

Specifications	4-door notchback	4-door wagon
Wheelbase, in.	109.1	109.1
Overall length, in.	191.8	191.4
Overall width, in.	68.9	68.9
Overall height, in.	56.6	57.6
Curb weight, lbs.	3461	3547
Cargo vol., cu. ft.	16.6	74.9
Fuel capacity, gals.	20.3	20.3
Seating capacity	5	5

1998 Volvo S90

Engines

dohc I-6

Size, liters/cu. in.	2.9/178
Horsepower @ rpm	181 @ 5200
Torque (lbs./ft.) @ rpm	199 @ 4100

EPA city/highway mpg

4-speed OD automatic	18/26

Built in Sweden.

PRICES

Volvo S90/V90	Retail Price	Dealer Invoice	Fair Price
S90 4-door notchback	$34300	—	—
V90 4-door wagon	35850	—	—
Destination charge	575	575	575

Dealer invoice and fair price not available at time of publication.

Standard Equipment:

2.9-liter DOHC 6-cylinder engine, 4-speed automatic transmission, anti-lock 4-wheel disc brakes, automatic locking differential, power steering, front and side front air bags, automatic climate control, cruise control, leather upholstery, reclining front bucket seats w/lumbar adjuster, 8-way power front seats w/memory feature, rear-seat trunk pass through (notchback), 60/40 split folding rear seat (wagon), integrated child booster seat (wagon), power sunroof, power windows and door locks, heated power mirrors, leather-wrapped tilt steering wheel, tinted glass, AM/FM/cassette w/amplifi-

VOLVO

er and anti-theft, power antenna (notchback), integrated antenna (wagon), remote keyless entry, remote trunk/hatch release, theft-deterrent system, wood interior trim, illuminated visor mirrors, front and rear reading lights, headlight wiper/washers, front and fog lamps, daytime running lights, luggage rack (wagon), tool kit, floor-mats, 195/65HR15 tires (wagon), 205/55VR16 tires (notchback), alloy wheels.

Optional Equipment:

	Retail Price	Dealer Invoice	Fair Price
Cold Weather Pkg.	$645	—	—
Heated front seats, locking differential, outside temperature indicator.			
Automatic load-leveling suspension, wagon	495	—	—
CD player	485	—	—